CW00541680

Lesley A. Hall is Senior Archivist at the Wellcome Library and an honorary lecturer in History of Medicine at University College London. Her many publications include *The Facts of Life: The Creation of Sexual Knowledge in Britain, 1650–1950* (with the late Roy Porter), *Sex, Gender and Social Change in Britain Since 1880* and *Outspoken Women: An Anthology of Women's Writing on Sex, 1870–1969.* She is a Fellow of the Royal Historical Society. Her website can be found at http://www.lesleyahall.net.

'Anyone who has investigated the history of sexuality in twentieth-century Britain has inevitably come across stray references to Stella Browne, self-described socialist and extreme left feminist. Now, thanks to Lesley Hall's exhaustive search of British, European, and North American archives we have the long anticipated biography of this resolute opponent of class and sex injustices. An important study, it has been well worth the wait. Stella Browne was best known for her early, courageous defense of women's right to abortion but, as Hall skillfully demonstrates, she was also a pacifist and humanitarian, and was involved in a wide range of sex reform campaigns relating to birth control, sex education, and divorce which won the attention of such luminaries as Edward Carpenter, Bertrand and Dora Russell, C. P. Blacker, Havelock Ellis, Rebecca West, Marie Stopes, and Margaret Sanger. Thanks to Hall's sensitive sleuthing we learn how in the inter-war years Browne helped link up many different networks of individuals involved in various reform movements. The study evocatively fleshes out our knowledge of a past progressive world and though absolutely crammed with information, is a pleasure to read, leavened as it is by Halls' dry wit.

Hall brilliantly meets the difficult challenge of writing the biography of an activist rather than a major theorist; someone whose key ideas did not change all that much in forty years, who produced no major book, but churned out essays, edited books and pamphlets, produced countless speeches and letters to the editor, and was constantly engaged in committee meetings, petitioning, and political lobbying. Through a close and sympathetic analysis of Browne's hectic life, Hall has produced an innovative and enthralling history of the struggle for sex reform in the first half of the twentieth century as seen from the trenches. But she not only analyses Browne's public presentations; having unearthed evidence of a number of her love affairs, Hall suggests how the public declarations on sexual issues of this complex and fascinating figure also reflected her personal experiences. The result is that Hall has crafted both an insightful history of the early twentieth-century fight for female reproductive choice and a moving portrait of the movement's most indefatigable and high-spirited campaigner.' – **Angus McLaren**

'A rigorous work of scholarship and an astute evocative account of an inspiring fighter for birth control, abortion and sexual freedom. This is an historically illuminating and exceedingly relevant book.' – **Sheila Rowbotham**

The Life and Times of Stella Browne

Feminist and Free Spirit

Lesley A. Hall

This book is dedicated to the memory of my mother,
Marjorie Elise Hall, née Priestley (1925–93).
Although in many respects a woman very unlike Stella Browne,
I think she would have appreciated her endeavours.

Published in 2011 by I.B.Tauris & Co Ltd
6 Salem Road, London W2 4BU
175 Fifth Avenue, New York NY 10010
www.ibtauris.com

Distributed in the United States and Canada
Exclusively by Palgrave Macmillan
175 Fifth Avenue, New York NY 10010

ISBN: 978 1 84885 583 0

A full CIP record for this book is available from the British Library
A full CIP record is available from the Library of Congress

Library of Congress Catalog Card Number: available

Printed and bound in Great Britain by
CPI Antony Rowe, Chippenham, Wiltshire

Contents

Acknowledgements

This work owes a particular debt to the late Roy Porter, who asked me the crystallising question 'Who was Stella Browne?' at a post-Wellcome symposium dinner just after my return from delving into the archives of the British Society for the Study of Sex Psychology.

Throughout my engagement in the task of writing this biography, I have been employed as an archivist at the Wellcome Library, formerly the Wellcome Institute for the History of Medicine. This has been an excellent and supportive base for my endeavours, with a number of archival collections of central importance to any study of Stella Browne, as well as being a first-class research library. I am thus grateful to all the colleagues who over the years have facilitated my researches. I am also grateful to my employers, the Wellcome Trust, for providing several periods of research leave and also financial support for my research trip to Washington, Princeton, Austin and Houston in the autumn of 1995 to glean information from materials in US repositories.

I am also grateful to the British Academy, which provided me with a small travel grant to enable me to visit repositories in Boston, Cambridge and New York; the Sophia Smith Collection at Smith College; the collections in the Beinecke Library, Yale University; the manuscript collections at McMaster University Hamilton, Ontario; and to pursue sources in Halifax, Nova Scotia, in the spring of 1996. I should also record my gratitude to the Harry Ransom Center at the University of Texas for the award of the research fellowship which enabled me to make my first trip to consult the archives of the British Society for the Study of Sex Psychology and related collections among their holdings, which led to me to this project.

Many individuals and institutions have been extraordinarily helpful in facilitating my research into Stella Browne's extremely scattered legacy.

I owe a very particular debt to John Dodwell for providing me with family information and the Dodwell family tree, for which I am exceedingly grateful. Sheila Rowbotham's work in first bringing Stella Browne to wider notice was, of course, an inspiration, and she also very kindly provided me with some of her own research materials, including what she had discovered about Edward Carpenter's interactions with Stella while writing her biography of him. Christine Holden and I discussed Stella Browne before I had even thought of embarking on a biography, and she provided me with some valuable leads.

I am also very grateful to the following individuals: Leslie Minchin and Celia Fremlin, for talking to me about the Progressive League and very kindly giving me various rare documents of the Federation of Progressive Societies and Individuals; Dorothy Forsyth for access to the Progressive League scrap-books and permission to cite material from the Progressive League archives now at the London School of Economics; Dr Janet Shepherd for letting me look at the FPSI records she had inherited from her father before she gave them to the London School of Economics; the Archivist at St Felix School and Bernard Keeling for sharing his unpublished work on the school; the Headmistress, Haberdashers' Monmouth School for Girls; the Headmistress, Redlands High School for Girls; Professor Christopher Elrington of the *Victoria County History*; Annabel Kitson for her helpful comments on Stella as an astrologer; Timothy D'Arch Smith for providing me with useful background material on early twentieth-century occultism and Montague Summers; Marion Shaw; Jenny Calder; Andy Croft; Fred Hunter; Hermione Lee. Anke Sandleben translated Stella's article in *Die Neue Generation* on novels of feminine inversion, and Ralf Dose very kindly provided translations of the German passages in Stella's letters to Max Hodann. Bruno Wanrooij clarified certain Papal rulings.

This work would not have been possible without the assistance of archivists and librarians in a range of institutions in the UK, Europe, North America and Australia, both remotely and in the course of visits: the Fawcett Library (now The Women's Library), especially the then Librarian, David Doughan; Morley College Library; Anne Summers at the Department of Manuscripts, British Library, who drew my attention to Stella Browne's letters to Havelock Ellis; the Archivist at Somerville College; Manuscript Collections, Liverpool University; London School of Economics; Sheffield City Archives; Labour Movement Archives, Manchester; Hull University Library and Hull City Archives; Leonore Symons at the Institute of Electrical Engineers; South Wales Miners' Library, University of Swansea; Archives of British Publishing and Printing at the University of Reading; the Theosophical Society; Liverpool Record Office; The Labour Archive

Stockholm; the International Institute for Social History, Amsterdam; Fisher Library, University of Sydney; The Margaret Sanger Papers Project; Library of Congress, Washington; National Library of Medicine, Bethesda; Princeton University Library; Harry Ransom Humanities Research Center, University of Texas at Austin; the Rare Books and Manuscripts Library, University of Illinois at Urbana-Champaign; Fondren Library, Rice University, Houston; Boston Medical Library in the Francis A. Countway Library of Medicine, Boston; Arthur and Elizabeth Schlesinger Library on the History of Women in America, Cambridge MA; the Howard Gotlieb Archival Research Center, Boston University; the Sophia Smith Collection, Smith College, Northampton MA; Beinecke Library, Yale University; New York Academy of Medicine Library; New York Public Library; Archives and Research Collections, McMaster University, Hamilton, Ontario; the Public Archives of Nova Scotia and the Probate District of the County of Halifax, Nova Scotia; Maritime Command Museum, Halifax.

A number of institutions were very helpful in chasing up what turned out to be dead ends, and thus saving me from unnecessary journeys: the Peace Archive, Swarthmore College; Cumbria Record Office; the Manuscripts Section and the Mass Observation Archive at the University of Sussex; the Emanuel Miller Centre for Families and Children; Special Collections and Manuscripts, University of Iowa Libraries; Special Collections, Colby College Maine; the Mitchell Library, Glasgow; the Brotherton Collection, University of Leeds; Special Collections, University of Tulsa; the Library, Street, Somerset; Trinity College Library Cambridge; the Churchill Archives Centre, Cambridge; the Archivist, Girton College, Cambridge; Bromsgrove Library; Special Collections, Fisk University Library; National Archives of Canada; the National Secular Society; Kinsey Archives, the Kinsey Institute; Temple University Library; Special Collections, Washington University Libraries, St Louis.

An invaluable resource for estimating the present purchasing power of monetary sums has been the MeasuringWorth website: http://www.measuringworth.com/index.html: all calculations have been based on the retail price index figures as at 2007, currently the latest date for which figures are available.

I have discussed Stella Browne and her milieu with many individuals over the years during which I have been working on her, and am grateful for their insights and suggestions and allowing me to clarify my own ideas in conversation (especially Heather Creaton and Dorothy Porter during the early stages). The following people also very kindly read and commented on all or part of earlier drafts of this book: Lucy Bland, Alison Bashford, Barbara Brookes, Karen Hunt, Angus McLaren, Sybil Oldfield, Alison Oram, and the late Richard Soloway. Any remaining defects are my own responsibility.

Some of the material herein has previously appeared in a rather different form in the following articles and chapters: '"I have never met the normal woman": Stella Browne and the politics of womanhood', *Women's History Review*, 6, 1997; 'Feminist reconfigurations of heterosexuality in the 1920s', in *Sexology and Culture: Labelling Bodies and Desires*, edited by Lucy Bland and Laura Doan, Polity Press, 1998; '"What a lot there is still to do': Stella Browne (1880–1955) carrying the struggle ever onward', in *A Suffrage Reader: Charting Directions in British Suffrage History, 1850–1950*, edited by Claire Eustance, Joan Ryan, and Laura Ugolini, Leicester University Press, A Cassell Imprint, 2000; '"Not a domestic utensil, but a woman and a citizen": Stella Browne on women, health and society' in *Regenerating England: Science, Medicine and Culture in Inter-war Britain*, edited by Chris Lawrence and Anna Mayer, Rodopi; 'The Next Generation: Stella Browne, the New Woman as Freewoman', in *The New Woman in Fiction and in Fact: Fin-de-Siècle Feminisms*, edited by Angelique Richardson and Chris Willis, Palgrave, 2001; '"In great haste": the personal and the political in the letters of F. W. Stella Browne (1880–1955), feminist socialist sex radical', in *The Age of Letter Writing: Gender and Politics 1750–2000*, edited by Caroline Bland and Maire Cross, Ashgate (2004); '"A masculine mythology suppressing and distorting all the facts": British women contesting the concept of the male-as-norm, 1870–1930', in *Histories of the Normal and the Abnormal: Social and Cultural Histories of Norms and Normativities*, edited by Waltraud Ernst, Routledge, 2006; 'Arrows of desire: British sex utopians and the politics of health', in *Medicine, Madness and Social History: Essays in Memory of Roy Porter*, edited by Roberta Bivins and John Pickstone, Palgrave Macmillan, 2007; 'Stella Browne and the German Radical Sex Reform Tradition', in *Sisters of Subversion: Histories of Women, Tales of Gender: A Festschrift*, edited by Willem de Blécourt, AMB Amsterdam, 2008.

Ray McNamee's companionship has continued to sustain me throughout the years I was working on this biography, and he also undertook on my behalf some 'above and beyond the call of duty' early and essential research into vital records and wills.

Abbreviations and Acronyms

ALRA	Abortion Law Reform Association
BMA	British Medical Association
BSS	British Sexological Society
BSSSP	British Society for the Study of Sex Psychology
CPGB	Communist Party of Great Britain
DORA 40D	Regulation under the Defence of the Realm Act regarding communication of venereal diseases to members of the Services
FPSI	Federation of Progressive Societies and Individuals
NBCA	National Birth Control Association
NCW	National Council of Women
SPSL	Society for the Protection of Science and Learning
VCH	*Victoria County History*
WIL	Women's International League of Peace and Freedom
WLSR	World League for Sexual Reform
WSPU	Women's Social and Political Union

Introduction: 'The Knowledge in My Own Person'

On 17 November 1937, an unmarried woman of 57 made the following admission of something seldom mentioned in public to the British government Interdepartmental (Birkett) Committee on Abortion:

> I have ... I say this as a matter of public duty – the knowledge in my own person that, if abortion were necessarily fatal or injurious, I should not now be here before you.[1]

This apparently respectable, educated, unmarried, middle-aged woman had undergone 'an illegal operation', implicitly, as a result of sexual activity out of wedlock. Her name was Frances Worsley Stella Browne.

Stella Browne did not fit any stereotypes of what a passionate advocate of abortion law reform or a woman who had had an abortion might look like. A contemporary newspaper photograph reveals a concerned, careworn figure.[2] She was 'rather untidy, careless about her looks and appearance',[3] wearing 'aggressively unfashionable clothes',[4] with 'wisps of hair floating from her untidy coiffure'.[5]

Her personal memorandum to the Committee distinguished her views, which many considered 'very heretical',[6] from those of the recently formed Abortion Law Reform Association (ALRA), of which she was a founder. ALRA's evidence focused on the suffering of working-class women burdened with perpetual pregnancies, framed from the perspective of humane middle-class left-wing observers proposing the radical solution of legalisation of safe surgical abortion (and improved birth control provision).[7] Stella, however, advanced the argument that the individual woman had an 'absolute right to decide whether or not she will bear a child or children'.[8]

This episode was the culmination of nearly three decades' campaigning, for much of that period a single-handed struggle. Janet Chance's chronology of the struggle to amend British laws on abortion reads, between 1861 (the Offences Against the Person Act) and the early 1930s, 'STELLA CAMPAIGNS ALONE'.[9] During a period when even birth control was contentious, with advocates almost unanimously positing it as a beneficent alternative to the epidemic prevalence of illegal abortion, Stella Browne publicly and loudly argued for safe legal abortion as not only essential to any meaningful birth control programme, but also as a woman's right on the grounds of bodily autonomy.

As a result, she was regarded by many colleagues in the campaign for women's rights to control their own fertility as embarrassing, eccentric, or even mad. Dora Russell, although a leading birth control activist during the 1920s and one of the founders of the Workers' Birth Control Group, feared mentioning abortion would damage the campaign for birth control advice in publicly funded maternal welfare centres.[10] ALRA colleagues later described her as 'eccentric, somewhat weird in appearance'.[11] Dr Carlos Paton Blacker of the Eugenics Society, a powerful supporter of the birth control movement, considered her 'a very difficult type and moderately mad'.[12]

Stella Browne's fleeting appearances in histories of the birth control and abortion law reform movements, and in debates on sexuality within the suffrage movement, tend to give a one-dimensional perspective on a complex and fascinating woman. The simplistic reading of her life might be that she moved from her pre-Great War interest in wide questions of sexual reform, to a single-issue activist fixation. This was far from the case. The number and vigour of her public pronouncements of abortion were surely due to the fact that she perceived herself as the only person speaking out on a subject she considered was being left out of the debates on birth control. Her writings, and reports of the lectures she was giving to diverse audiences during the interwar years, indicate her to have been more than a single-issue fanatic, an identity she rejected, responding to one invitation to speak that she did 'not wish to be too closely tied to the one subject of birth control, however great its importance.'[13]

The campaign for women's control over their own reproduction was, for Stella Browne, one facet in a much broader vision of the better society. She was actuated by a blend of very radical feminism, socialism, and commitment to the rights of the individual, which she perceived as synergistic rather than competing values. She contradicts many beliefs and assumptions; for example, her interwar activities must lead us to reconsider claims that feminism was either dead or split into warring 'New' and 'Old' feminist camps. She demonstrates that other intellectual systems sometimes considered as embattled opposites were not necessarily so: for her, 'the new psychology' – in which she included Freud, although she did not consider him its only exemplar – and discoveries about the endocrine glands both contributed to a greater understanding of the puzzles of sex. She seems to have been capable of being a committed Communist, with, presumably, a belief in Marxist dialectical materialism, and also an adherent of astrology (and possibly a believer in reincarnation), who contributed to debates in astrological journals, prepared horoscopes for her friends, and used zodiacal categories to describe herself and associates.

She advanced ideas presaging those of the so-called 'second wave' of the feminist movement. Women's Liberation, as it was known, arising at the end of the 1960s, called not merely for the traditional feminist aims, but also for the liberation of female sexuality (facilitated by the advent of the contraceptive pill). Her commitment to a position of 'woman's choice' on abortion has already been mentioned. While intrigued by the potential of Freud's theories, she critiqued his phallocentric assumptions and the conservative potential of psychoanalysis in the early 1920s.[14] Around the same time, she argued that lesbians often had strong maternal instincts and should be allowed to express these.[15] Far from fearfully eschewing possible identification as a lesbian, as argued by Sheila Jeffreys,[16] by 1930 she celebrated the 'articulate, vigorous and adventurous' female bisexual 'sexual epicure'.[17] In addition, she saw masturbation as one element within the full sexual life, rather than as a dangerous and stigmatised practice.[18]

A woman of her period who did not marry yet led an 'intellectually and sexually active life',[19] she could perhaps be described as living an experimental life: her 'personal history' was 'vivid and strenuous', and marked by 'actions and decisions of her own, against considerable pressure of opposition'.[20] Her writings on female sexuality reflect her own experience in many different ways. The arguments in her best-known work on the subject, *The Sexual Variety and Variability of Women*, were supported by examples taken from her own erotic and emotional odyssey.[21] From around 1926, in her mid-forties, she was addressing women's groups on 'adjustments of middle life',[22] which she was presumably making herself. When she mentioned 'episodical homosexuality on the part of women who are normally much more attracted to men',[23] or posited the 'woman who is inherently bisexual', she was surely grappling to define her own sexual desires and identity.[24]

She was extremely well-read and well-informed, with a 'very wide range of academic knowledge'.[25] The books she reviewed regularly in the columns of *The New Generation* testify to the enormous range of her interests and enthusiasms. Her articles in this and other periodicals, and her translator's footnotes to F. Müller-Lyer's *The Family* (1931) and Max Hodann's *The*

History of Modern Morals (1936) demonstrate her grasp of current events and of contemporary scientific ideas, as well as revealing her extensive acquaintance with modern literature in Britain, Europe and North America.

Her knowledge of laws on abortion worldwide and on the state of scientific understanding about it was internationally acknowledged as outstanding. However, her attitude to her own knowledge-base was remarkably generous: in 1937, she made her materials available to David Glass of the London School of Economics for a book he was writing on the 'foreign legal position' on abortion.[26]

Her long-time friend Ashton Burall summarised her character as 'a remarkable blend of moral earnestness, crusading fervour, and a light-hearted determination to get the best out of life'. He emphasised her humour, high spirits, sense of fun and affectionate nature.[27]

Sheila Rowbotham first drew feminist historians' attention to Stella Browne, initially in *Hidden from History* (1973) and then in the short essay *A New World for Women: Stella Browne – socialist feminist* (1977). She has subsequently figured in studies of the British birth control and abortion law reform movements, and in accounts of the debates on female sexuality in the pages of *The Freewoman* journal in 1912 and beyond, during the years immediately before, during, and after the First World War. Yet, she often appears a marginal or hazy figure – a footnote in biographies of associates such as Havelock Ellis, Margaret Sanger and Rebecca West. But she was an extraordinarily fascinating figure, expressing radical and sophisticated ideas about women, sex, and social and political change.

Piecing together her life and opinions is a difficult task. Her own papers do not survive. However, several hundred letters from her can be located among the papers of friends and associates, and in the archives of organisations in which she was active, scattered through a number of repositories in Britain, Europe, and North America. There are discernable lacunae. Only a single letter to the socialist sex reformer Edward Carpenter can be found. Her close colleagues in the birth control movement, Dorothy Jewson and Cicely Hamilton, did not leave any papers, although there is evidence of correspondence between both women and Stella.[28] Her decades-long correspondence with Ashton Burall has not been traced. In other cases, personal contact probably obviated the need for writing. Some of her activities are only known through passing allusions in her own letters, or fleeting mentions by acquaintances: her relatively late conversion to a complete pacifist stance during the First World War (1916) and subsequent involvement with the No-Conscription Fellowship are the subject of a half-sentence in a letter from her friend, the male suffragist, socialist, humanitarian and pacifist E. Bertram Lloyd, to Edward Carpenter.[29]

Her published writings are similarly scattered. The full extent of these is unlikely ever to be known: a handful of anonymous reviews in literary periodicals are identifiable only because she mentioned them to Havelock Ellis.[30] Many of her articles, reviews, and translations appeared in obscure and hard-to-find journals. Although she 'occasionally dream[ed]' of writing a book,[31] this never came to fruition, her most extended work being the 1935 essay on 'The Right to Abortion' published as part of a symposium on the subject. Yet, her vigorous and vivid writing was praised by Havelock Ellis and Bertrand Russell.[32] Her competence in rendering their texts into English was much appreciated by the Dutch gynaecologist Theodor van de Velde and the German radical sexologist Max Hodann. Her translations of French and German poetry are sensitive and effective, and her own poems not without merit.

She considered herself 'essentially better as a writer than a speaker',[33] but her capacities as a public speaker, one of the most evanescent of arts, were attested by repeated invitations to address a wide variety of bodies. Contemporaries deemed her 'a first-rate speaker';[34] 'impressive, direct, emphatic, totally unembarrassed, with a fine vocabulary and a speaking voice of unusual range and power – a deeper rather musical alto'.[35] The editor of *Plan*, the journal of the Progressive League, had 'vivid recollections' of her talk on 'Jealousy'.[36] A colleague's recollection of 'a voice like a foghorn'[37] may reflect a coarsening of the voice with age and over-exercise, or simply prejudice against a woman who had no hesitation in speaking up and making her voice heard.

Information is frustratingly scanty or completely lacking on a number of aspects of her life. How she managed to earn a living is one of them. She was reportedly 'a vehement worker' but found routine 'difficult and distasteful', even though she managed 'heavy routine work conspicuously well'.[38] After she left her position as Librarian at Morley College in 1912, there were various writing and translation jobs, stints in more regular employment, but a general sense of a life on the economic margins very close to, and sometimes becoming, actual poverty (which may well account for her lack of stylishness). Her state of penury was not helped by her determination to assist causes in which she was passionately involved, either with time or such money as she could afford.[39]

The poverty may have been both cause and effect of what seems to have been a fairly continuous state of poor health, even though she claimed that after 'a delicate childhood and difficult adolescence' her health had steadily improved.[40] Although said to have suffered from a 'weak'[41] or 'strained' heart,[42] it seems unlikely that anyone with a serious heart-complaint would have survived to the age of 75 and been capable of so active a life.[43] She seems to have succumbed to, but recovered from, the lethal strain of 'Spanish flu' in 1918–19,[44] although there were continuing after-effects.[45] She suffered from a range of other ailments, including recurrent hay-fever every summer.[46]

In spite of the poverty, the ill-health and the unfashionable clothes, she had a number of lovers, both long-term and occasional, whose identities can, unfortunately, only be guessed. She told Havelock Ellis that 'a woman – at all counts an exceptional woman – should not attach her love to one man only. Then she will escape much suffering'.[47] That her lovers included women as well as men seems plausible.

Some periods of her life can be reconstructed in far greater detail than others. The years following her appearance on the scene of public debate with her letters to *The Freewoman* are particularly fully documented. She was reviewing in several journals and having letters published in others, several sequences of correspondence survive; at the same time, she produced several articles exploring and shaping the ideas which her experiences and encounters had generated. Thus, an important phase in her development can be described in a fair degree of depth, and a wide range of activities and interests is apparent, whereas for some years during the 1920s and 1930s the *New Generation* is the main source, focusing on her work for the birth control campaign. The more copious information on the earlier period, however, clearly sets in its context what is sometimes interpreted as narrow single-issue activism.

While Stella Browne is fascinating in her own right, she is also of interest to the historian as an example of the possibilities of women's lives in the early twentieth century. Although a particularly radical woman living a life many doubtless considered extreme, it cannot be supposed that in the various aspects of her life she was unique. She is a prism through which we can examine numerous issues of the early twentieth century, shedding light into many obscure corners.

Notes

1. Inter-Departmental Committee on Abortion A.C. Paper no. 51: 'Evidence of: Miss F.W. Stella Browne', Wednesday, 17 November 1937: The National Archives, MH71/23.
2. '"It is not selfishness or luxury that stops our people from having children but the fear of poverty and war". By Stella Browne (Vice-Chairman of the Abortion Law

Reform Association), Questioned for the *Sunday Mercury* by Ormsby Lennon', *Sunday Mercury and Sunday News* (Birmingham), 31 July 1938, p. 8.

3. Keith Hindell and Madeleine Simms, *Abortion Law Reformed* (London: Peter Owen, 1971), p. 59.
4. Hindell and Simms, *Abortion Law Reformed*, p. 59.
5. Dora Russell, *The Tamarisk Tree, Volume I* (London: Virago Press, 1975), p. 174.
6. 'Evidence of: Miss F.W. Stella Browne', MH71/23.
7. Inter-Departmental Committee on Abortion A.C. Paper no. 13: Memorandum for Presentation to the Inter-Departmental Committee on Abortion from the Abortion Law Reform Association: TNA, MH71/21.
8. Alice Jenkins, 'Obituary: Miss F.W. Stella Browne', *The Eugenics Review*, XLVII (n.s. XXVIII), 1955/56, pp. 78–9.
9. Janet Chance's scrapbook, Abortion Law Reform Association Archives, Wellcome Library, SA/ALR/B.2.
10. Manuscript of *The Tamarisk Tree, Volume 1*, p. 449, Dora Russell papers in the International Institute for Social History, Amsterdam, file 180. This version reads rather more kindly than the passage actually published.
11. Hindell and Simms, *Abortion Law Reformed*, p. 59.
12. C.P. Blacker to J.R. Baker, 17 April 1935, Eugenics Society Archives, Wellcome Library, SA/EUG/C.10.
13. Stella Browne to Mr Basil Lonsdale Deighton, 30 June 1921, 'BSS Misc', British Sexology Society Archives, Harry Ransom Humanities Research Center, University of Texas, Austin.
14. F.W. Stella Browne, 'Reviews: Concerning women and children', *The New Generation*, vol. 4, March 1925, p. 33–4; Review of Dr William J. Robinson's *A Doctor's Views on Life*, *Medical Critic and Guide* 25E/7 (July 1927), pp. 297–300.
15. F.W. Stella Browne, 'Studies in feminine inversion', *Journal of Sexology and Psychanalysis*, 1, 1923, pp. 51–8.
16. Sheila Jeffreys, *The Spinster and Her Enemies: Feminism and Sexuality, 1880–1950* (London: Pandora Press, 1985), pp. 115–18.
17. Stella Browne, 'Women bear witness', *The New Generation*, vol. 9, 1930, pp. 127–8.
18. F.W. Stella Browne, *The Sexual Variety and Variability among Women, and their Bearing on Social Reconstruction* (London: British Society for the Study of Sex Psychology, 1917).
19. Memorandum for Presentation to the Inter-Departmental Committee on Abortion from Miss F.W. Stella Browne, A.C. Paper no. 16, TNA: MH71/21.
20. 'The most radical British feminist and birth control advocate of today', *Medical Critic and Guide*, 25E/5, May 1927, pp. 192–4. This article is not specifically

attributed, but as the greatest part of all issues of Robinson's journal *Medical Critic and Guide* were written by himself, it seems reasonable to assume that this article was by him.

21. Stella Browne to Havelock Ellis, 28 December 1914, 25 December 1922, Ellis papers in the Department of Manuscripts, British Library, Additional Manuscript 70539 [BL Add Ms 70539]. refer to incidents described impersonally in *Sexual Variety and Variability.*
22. 'Miss Browne's meetings', *The New Generation*, vol. 10, 1931, p. 29.
23. Browne, 'Studies in feminine inversion'.
24. Browne, 'Women bear witness'.
25. A.A. Burall, 'Stella Browne (1880–1955): obituary', *Plan: the journal of the Progressive Society*, 25/7, July 1955, p. 81.
26. Minutes of the Abortion Law Reform Association Executive Committee, 29 November 1937, 20 December 1937, 28 March 1939, SA/ALR/A.1/2/1.
27. Burall, 'Stella Browne'.
28. *The New Generation*, vol. 7, March 1928, p. 32, quotes a letter from Jewson to Stella about birth control work in Norwich.
29. E. Bertram Lloyd to Edward Carpenter, 4 May 1916, Sheffield City Council: Libraries, Archives and Information: Sheffield Archives. Carpenter/Mss/368/18.
30. Browne to Ellis, 9 February 1914, BL Add Ms 70539.
31. 'The most radical British feminist'.
32. Bertrand Russell to Philip E.B. Jourdain, 5 September 1917, *Cambridge Magazine* correspondence, C.K. Ogden papers, Box 108/F10, McMaster University, Hamilton, Ontario.
33. 'The most radical British feminist'.
34. Burall, 'Stella Browne'.
35. 'The most radical British feminist'.
36. 'Editor's notes', *Plan*, vol. 13, no. 4, April 1946, p. 1.
37. Hindell and Simms, *Abortion Law Reformed*, p. 59.
38. 'The most radical British feminist'.
39. Stella Browne to Margaret Sanger, 7 September 1915, Sanger papers in the Sophia Smith Collection, Smith College; Stella Browne to S.H. Halford, 19 August 1921, 'BSS Misc', HRC; *The Communist*, 24 September, 19 November 1921; Alice Jenkins to Stella Browne, 25 March 1954, SA/ALR/B.5.
40. Memorandum ... from Miss F.W. Stella Browne, MH71/21.
41. George Ives, 'Notes and Writings', Volume LXXII, 14 May 1919: Ives papers in the Harry Ransom Humanities Research Center, University of Texas at Austin.
42. 'The most radical British feminist'.
43. I am indebted to the late Dr Ann Dally for a medical opinion on this.
44. Stella Browne to Janet Carson, 20 March 1919, 'BSS Misc', HRC.

45. Ives, 'Notes and Writings', Volume LXXII, 14 May 1919; Stella Browne to Janet Carson, 7 June 1919, 'BSS Misc', HRC.
46. Browne to Carson, passim, 'BSS Misc', HRC.
47. Browne to Ellis, 25 December 1922, BL Add Mss 70539; Havelock Ellis to Françoise Lafitte-Cyon, 21 [possibly 27] February 1921, Howard Gotlieb Archival Research Center, Boston University.

1

The Early Years, 1880–1911

Frances Worsley Stella Browne was born on 9 May 1880 in Halifax, Nova Scotia, the daughter of Anna Dulcibella Mary (Dulcie) (née Dodwell) and Daniel Marshall Browne.[1] Daniel was employed in the Canadian Department of Marine and Fisheries,[2] having resigned his post as Navigating Lieutenant in the Royal Navy on half-pay.[3] According to a much later account, he was the fifth generation of his family to be a naval officer:[4] Certainly his father, William Lindsay Browne, had also been in the Navy, reaching the rank of Master.[5] Dulcie was the eldest daughter of the Reverend George Branson Dodwell, M.A., and his wife Isabella (or Isabel) Naysmith.[6] Stella later described her as 'highly intelligent ... *much* more so in many ways than I am', and, although without 'any strong and definite religious belief', had 'the qualities which might have made a mystic under other circumstances'.[7]

Neither of Stella's parents was native to Nova Scotia or Canada. Both were part of that peripatetic 'professional and administrative class'[8] that kept the British Empire running. Daniel Browne, born in Hampshire,[9] joined the Navy as a Master's Assistant shortly before his fifteenth birthday, and had seen service on the West Indies and North Atlantic stations before arriving in Halifax.[10] On the other side of the family, 'the English Church and the teaching professions have been largely represented'.[11] Both of these aspects were present in George Dodwell, who, educated at Clare College Cambridge, had arrived in Canada in 1862 (with his wife and five children) to take up the post of Professor of Theology, Bishop's College, Lenoxville, Quebec, at a later date accepting the cure of various parishes in Ontario and finally Nova Scotia, dying as rector of Wilmot in 1891.[12]

Daniel Browne was aged nearly 37 at the time of Stella's birth. He had previously been married to Catherine Magdalene MacLean in 1867 in Toronto,[13] who died aged 35 in Halifax from 'chronic gastritis':[14] Their daughter, Maud was born in 1869.[15]

Dulcie, the eldest child, had been born in London. That she remained single until the age of 29 suggests she may have been expected to be the dutiful daughter at home, but on 23 February 1878 she was married to Daniel Browne by the Bishop of Nova Scotia.[16]

In 1882, a second daughter, Alice Lemira Sylvia (always known as Sylvia), was born.[17] A serious blow struck the small family on 3 December 1883: Daniel Marshall Browne (by that time Superintendent of Lighthouses) died 'at the post of duty on board the Dominion steamship *Princess Louise*' off Point Prim in the Bay of Fundy.[18] In a letter to her mother-in-law, Dulcie described him as 'the best & dearest husband a woman ever had'.[19]

Daniel had made a will shortly after their marriage, leaving all the 'interest, money and dividends from all my real and personal property' to be divided between his 'beloved wife', his child Isabel Maud, and any other children that might have been born by the time of his death, as long as Dulcie remained unmarried. If she remarried, or died, her share was to be equally divided among the children. The inventory of his estate indicates that this was not large. It included the family residence at 75 Inglis Street, Halifax, valued at $3,250; the household furniture and effects (including a piano), valued at $750; and two life insurance policies amounting to $950 (at the then value of the Canadian dollar against the pound sterling: this amounted to just over £1,017, approximately equivalent in purchasing power to £73,400 in 2007).[20] Daniel had spent his commutation (presumably of his Naval pension) on their (mortgaged) 'cottage', but had a small life insurance policy. Dulcie considered that 'The Dominion Government are morally bound to do something for his children' and intended 'to put their sincerest claims strongly before the House of Parliament in Ottawa'.[21]

It looks as if Dulcie sold the family home. By 1890, she was running a boarding house: Maud Browne was no longer living with them, but there were four lady lodgers in the household.[22] So, Stella was brought up in a single parent family by a mother who had to work for her family's living.

She later claimed that she had been 'delicate' as a child, but without giving any specific details. When reading that she was born in Canada, the image conjured up may be the small town rural idyll of L.M. Montgomery's *Anne of Green Gables* (1908). Halifax, however, was a thriving port and garrison town which had evolved into a bustling metropolis with all the appurtenances of modernity, although, given Stella's delicate health,[23] she may well have spent considerable periods with her grandparents at the Reverend

George's various livings 'among the apple orchards and pine trees of the Annapolis Valley'.[24]

Little is known about Stella's childhood years – she seldom harked back to this period of her life in her published writings or surviving correspondence. In 1927, she wrote to Havelock Ellis about 'I… who have the heavy salt North Atlantic soaked through & through my blood and marrow',[25] but seems to be attributing this to her Nordic – or 'Norse sea-rover'[26] – ancestry as much as to the environmental influence of living adjacent to the spectacular tides of the Bay of Fundy for her first twelve or so years. She intriguingly attributed Ellis's own 'pioneer' temperament to his roots in 'adventurous, sea-faring families'.[27] She does not seem to have identified herself as Canadian – this would probably be anachronistic – but, like so many members of these families scattered throughout the Empire, saw herself as essentially British.

Dulcie and her daughters appear to have left Halifax around 1892. Where they went and what they did is not definitely known, but the most plausible hypothesis is that they either went to live with Dulcie's sister Louisa Frances Siemens, who had made a good 'catch' – the Anglo-German engineer Alexander (later Sir Alexander) Siemens, when he came to Halifax in connection with setting up the submarine cable[28] – or, through his family connections, to reside in Germany.

Stella claimed to have had a 'difficult adolescence' but did not elaborate with any details.[29] Her comment that 'Many girls suffer for years… as a result of the neglect which allowed them to meet the shock of puberty unprepared, or with only a revoltingly crude, inadequate warning' may well have had roots in personal trauma.[30] She quoted with approval a remark about the 'tortures of the damned' undergone by 'a really shy adolescent'.[31] Adolescence may not have been all grim, however; her suggestion that

> day-dreaming, the production of a high degree of excitement, and sometimes of the actual climax of enjoyment, by means of vague yet delightful imaginings, is the most exquisite pleasure and deepest secret of many imaginative and sensitive girls, and may even begin before puberty[32]

may have had an autobiographical element.

She was said to have been educated on the Continent[33] and, by 1899, she was sufficiently competent in both French and German to pass the 'Women's First' for Oxford entrance.[34] In later life, she gained considerable accolades for her translations from the German, and wrote an extremely refined and correct German.[35]

The next thing definitely known about Stella Browne is that, in 1897, she entered the recently established St Felix School for Girls, Southwold, Suffolk,[36] then under the care of its founder, Margaret Isabella Gardiner, one of several remarkable headmistresses of the Victorian era.[37] St Felix's reputedly healthy coastal location may have had something to do with the choice. Among the early established traditions of the school was sea-bathing[38] – perhaps how Stella developed her fondness for swimming.[39]

The school was run upon very liberal lines, aspiring to treat the girls 'as sensible creatures', and to educate them as far as possible in a manner adjusted to their individual physical and mental powers. There was no competition for marks or prizes. Girls were encouraged to find things out for themselves in the school library and by observations outdoors, and allowed time for private reading. The intrusive rules often associated with girls' boarding schools were absent. There was also no chapel. Commitment to feminism was manifested in the naming of the school houses after women of achievement.[40]

Little beyond these basic facts about Stella Browne's schooldays in Suffolk can be retrieved. However, at some time in her life she wrote a poem which suggests that she had a deep attachment to Southwold:

> I know a town, by a low shore
> Whereon, encroaching evermore,
> The yellow weight of water beats.
> The wind walks always by that sea,
> The many tongues of memory
> Call on wide heath and winding streets.
> The long cliff crumbles; golden burns
> The gorse on the bleak common; turns
> Each flying wheel on tower mill.
> Between the clouds that stream & fly
> And sunken fields that fruitless lie,
> The throbbing sea is never still.
>
> Still may it bravely stand; its home
> Under the arch of the sky's dome,

Where the faint cloud wreaths soar and run,
Beside the old sea's battered brim,
The wind its lullaby & hymn
Its light the splendour of the sun.[41]

Stella Browne's is the first name on the St Felix Honours Board, commemorating her achievement, in 1899, of winning a History Exhibition to Somerville College, Oxford,[42] worth £20 a year (approximately equivalent in purchasing power to £1,614 in 2007) for three years. Her guardian at that time was given as Mrs Siemens of Campden Hill, London – possibly Dulcie had remained in Germany with Sylvia since, a few years later, Stella was mentioned as 'Living at home, Germany'.[43]

It was twenty years since Somerville had opened as a non-denominational residence for women studying in Oxford. It had a specific character among the Oxford women's colleges as 'free from episcopal influence, social exclusiveness, and Victorian values',[44] 'born ... of enlightened ideas, and in particular of a progressive conception of woman'.[45] Women were already able to sit the same examinations as men taking the Final Honours Schools of the University,[46] and the women's colleges had a policy of admitting only students reading for Honours, rather than a mere Pass Degree.[47]

It has been argued that Somerville produced 'no typical Somervillian', except for encouraging a broad-minded tolerance.[48] Exchanges of diverse points of view took place in the thriving debating societies of the College. The 'Somerville Parliament', in which 'high-minded debates were interspersed with comic set-pieces', took the Westminster system as its precedent, and participants took on the character of MPs.[49] In March 1901, S. Browne, the 'Member for Milford' brought forward a Bill on 'Private Member's Night', for the 'preservation of a portion of the public thoroughfare to the use of bicycles, tricycles, etc.' – a motion, after some discussion, 'relegated to the Board of Trade, to be dealt with in conjunction with the local authorities'.[50] There is no record of whether Stella Browne was a dashing lady cyclist herself. Some months later she addressed the Somerville Parliament again, in the character of 'The Hon Member for Sligo'. Speaking to a proposed Bill 'for the Regulation of Street Noises, including a scheme for the musical training of bicycle bells, flower vendors and organ grinders', she asked 'who would find the money to establish the enormous number of lunatic asylums which it would be necessary to erect for those unfortunate beings to whom the musical education was to be entrusted?'[51]

Stella seems to have found her feet in this ambiance of debate and discussion. In October 1901, she was amongst those who 'also spoke' on a rather more serious topic at the Oxford Student's Debating Society: 'That Cosmopolitanism is a higher ideal than Patriotism', at which 'the discussion was, on the whole, animated, but the majority of speeches lacked point'.[52] Around the same time, she became joint President of the Somerville 'Sharp Practice' debating society, which developed skills in extempore speaking. According to the report on the three meetings during Michaelmas Term, 1901,

> on two occasions the debates were very spirited, but on the third the House appeared to be in a somewhat refractory frame of mind. At the first meeting the motion 'that it is the duty of every woman to take an active interest in public affairs,' was rejected by a large majority, and at the second, members waxed eloquent on the merits and demerits of High School training.

At the third debate, after rejecting several motions as unsuitable, it was finally almost unanimously agreed that 'self-effacement is not an unqualified virtue'.[53]

In spite of this evidence of her participation in the culture of Somerville, Stella Browne does not seem to have looked back on her years there with any affection, alluding rather bitterly to 'three or four years of strangely irrelevant immaturity cushioned from the world, woolly with suppressions',[54] the 'snobbish, pretentious fraud of the Higher Education for Women at the older universities',[55] and claiming that Somerville was 'saturated with unreality and snobbery ... even less favourable to the development of originality and intellectual initiative among women than its analogue among men'[56] – which suggests that she did not rank the experience highly in her intellectual formation.

Whereas many young women reported the liberating experience they found there, after St Felix, Somerville may have seemed staid, conventional, and over-regulated. The low-lying river meadows and their chilly mists might also have been an unwelcome contrast to the bracing Suffolk seacoast. The domestic management was the subject of many complaints.[57] Stella claimed adverse effects from

> the long course of underfeeding at Somerville College – the food there & at Newnham is a disgrace ... the women are such sheep and so 'on sufferance' still with regard to life itself that they eat & suffer[58]

comments which resonate with the debate topic that 'self-effacement is not an unqualified virtue'.

Stella Browne received her certificate of second class Honours in Modern History at the conclusion of Trinity Term 1902. The positions available to a woman with a degree or (in the case of Oxford and Cambridge) degree equivalent remained limited. The majority went into teaching.[59] In September of that year, therefore, Stella took up a post as Assistant Mistress at Monmouth High School,[60] 'in a hurry to make myself independent', but encountered 'bad conditions as to food and overwork'.[61]

A schoolteacher's life could be very miserable, with the awfulness and stodginess of school food, domineering headmistresses, meagre and chilly accommodation. The work was hard and demanding.[62] Even a woman with a good honours degree could not anticipate a salary allowing for more than the bare necessities of life until after the First World War.[63]

In 1903, Stella Browne moved to a new job at Redlands High School, Bristol,[64] where, presumably, she had 'the accident – the bite of a rat – which led to my complete nervous breakdown', as a result of which 'I was tormented with the most acute intermittent terror of tetanus or hydrophobia, which took all the course & reason out of me for days together'.[65] This was more or less the end of her teaching career, which she later referred to as 'a brief and highly strenuous and uncongenial interlude'.[66] In 1904, she was living 'at home, Germany',[67] probably with her mother and sister. The 'recurrent spasms of maniacal terror' lasted for three years, and she later attributed them to the 'indirect psychic effects of involuntary and prolonged [sexual] abstinence',[68] after encountering Freud's theory of '*angst neurose*' in 1912.[69]

Some time during this period, while still subject to 'fits of terror' and 'broken in spirit', she met 'the man I first cared for in such an insane and unsatisfied way'.[70] His identity is unknown: she apparently gave Havelock Ellis greater detail in a communication which does not survive. This was the first appearance of any heterosexual liaison, but comments in her writings hint at the possibility of at least emotional entanglements with women, going perhaps beyond the 'real, though perfectly unconscious, spark of desire' in 'devoted admiration and friendship ... for certain girl friends'.[71] She later claimed that 'most northern women of *marked intelligence* are emotionally immature at twenty', although she added the proviso, 'of course, my experience may be exceptional'.[72] '[A]s a result of the repression of normal gratification and the segregation of the sexes', she considered that 'artificial or substitute homosexuality' was 'very widely diffused among women': unlike 'true affectionate friendship between women', this took on a 'jealous, exacting and extravagant tone'.[73] She drew attention both to the 'passionate but unconscious inversion in girls whose sex-life is just beginning' and to the 'huge, persistent, indirect pressure on women of strong passions and fine brains to find an emotional outlet with other women'.[74] These comments, and also the claim that 'the heterosexual woman of passionate but shy and sensitive nature, is often responsive to the inverted woman's advances, especially if she is erotically ignorant and inexperienced',[75] suggest that she may have been writing out of personal experience. The problem of jealousy continued to concern her, perhaps as a result of some formative individual experience.[76]

Probably during this second sojourn in Germany, Stella became aware of the German women's movement, in particular the radical wing around Helene Stöcker. The year 1904 saw the establishment of the *Bund für Mutterschutz* (Federation for the Protection of Mothers), initially a body to support the unmarried mother, which under Stöcker's leadership developed a far more wide-ranging agenda on sexual ethics. Stöcker saw herself not merely as an activist, but also as part of the developing movement aimed at subjecting sex to scientific investigation, and clearly formed a model for Stella Browne's similar aims. The German movement was more concerned with protection of motherhood than political rights. While this could clearly entail a rather conservative agenda, the strand of the movement associated with Stöcker was arguing for free love and free choice of motherhood, and also for the support of the unmarried mother without the usual moralising and punitive agenda. Birth control was also on the agenda, as an essential aid to women's free choice of maternity at the right time and with the right partner.[77] This influence on Stella Browne's developing views can be clearly seen in her earliest public statements in the correspondence columns of *The Freewoman*, and she mentioned the *Bund für Mutterschutz* as a model for activism on illegitimacy to Havelock Ellis.[78]

At some point, the family moved to London, since Stella Browne is reported to have been working as an assistant on the *Victoria County History* (VCH), based there.[79] In 1903, the VCH assembled 'a team of university women' qualified in history or classics – initially with a view to their writing up parish histories from materials supplied, but soon trained as researchers – to extract relevant information from a wide variety of materials, for the production of scholarly histories of all the counties in England.[80] Over two decades later, Stella referred to the evidence for the high level of infant mortality in the medieval era to be found in 'any available family records or parish registers', so it seems probable that she gained hands-on experience of primary research.[81] None of the published articles bears Stella's name, probably due to the limited amount of time she spent there.[82] The pay was doubtless not particularly generous.[83]

However, this brief sojourn gave her a basis of research and bibliographical skills. By January 1907, she was in a rather different post, as Librarian at Morley College, an adult education institution in South London.[84] This position had been suggested in December 1906 by the Vice-Principal, Mary Sheepshanks, as a possibility to Virginia Stephen (later Woolf), who was already teaching there.[85] How Stella got this job instead is unknown. Her Somerville education and experience with the VCH may have tipped the balance. It was generally recognised by this date that women had 'completely vindicated their right to rank as first-class librarians', in spite of persistent controversy about their 'suitability and aptitude'.[86] As with women graduates entering teaching in secondary schools, a degree was apparently regarded as sufficient qualification, and a professional diploma as unnecessary.[87]

Morley was a 'radical, innovative college' with a democratic approach: students shared in decision-making, and emphasis on the humanities was intended to counteract a narrowly utilitarian and technical approach to further education. Many well-known contemporary figures in the arts and sciences taught there, and the student body included not only a range of lower-middle and upper working-class occupations, but also unskilled workers.[88] Mary Sheepshanks, as Vice-Principal, encouraged women in a wide variety of ways. College debates featured women's interests, and guest lecturers included individuals prominent in the suffrage movement – most notably, Christabel Pankhurst herself.[89]

Working at Morley would appear to have been a politicising experience for Stella, or at least to have crystallised her ideas and opinions. She later claimed that her interest in the subject of the right to abortion had first been aroused by 'the unnatural sufferings and complications in the lives of women', which she encountered among the working (and indeed, professional) women she met there, when she learnt of 'the evils which arise from unskilled abortion'.[90] The atmosphere at Morley may well have been conducive to the discussion of issues around reproduction and its control, usually anathema within the suffrage movement. The college programme included lectures on controversial issues such as marriage and divorce law reform, and eugenics.[91] Mary Sheepshanks is known to have been hostile to large families from her own experience,[92] and was later overtly sympathetic towards birth control.[93] Stella also took a broader interest in the injustices bearing upon women, joining the militant suffrage organisation, the Women's Social and Political Union (WSPU), in 1908.[94] It must have appeared the largest, most vibrant, and most potentially effective of the suffrage societies, and had not yet rejected its alliance with the Labour movement.

On the emotional and physical side, things were improving for Stella. In 1907, she entered into a relationship with a man who remained her 'demi-semi-lover' for several years, only fully consummating the relationship in 1910, and her 'technically complete, though very intermittent and occasional' lover for many years after that. His identity is not known: she described him as 'very dominating & hot-tempered, & our only common ideals are a certain love of what appeals to us as beauty & a certain contempt for public opinion & public stupidity'. The liaison remained on an occasional basis, and she suggested that had she been his wife or '*established mistress*... I sh$^{d.}$ have quarrelled with him hopelessly very soon'.[95] However, its benefits are perhaps attested by a number of her comments in *The Sexual Variety and Variability of Women*, not merely that 'the sexual relation... vivifies a woman's brain, develops her character, and trebles her vitality', but her testimony that, '*even when sexual gratification stops short of complete intercourse*', it could lead to a noticeable decrease in 'periodic pain and weakness'. In this pamphlet, she also promoted the importance of the women being 'very gradually and skilfully initiated into the sexual relation', and the necessity of a lover with 'insight and intuition as well as virility and passion'.[96] This may well be taken as a tribute to her 'demi-semi-lover', whoever he was. He may be deduced to have been something of a sexual sophisticate. Stella remarked that 'the unruptured hymen... may co-exist with the most varied, and even perverted, sex experience', and also commented that 'The pleasure in either inflicting a certain degree of pain on the beloved one, or suffering a certain degree of pain from them, is almost inextricably a part of desire.'[97]

It was also around this time that Stella the writer began to emerge, although initially only within the professional constraints of occasional 'Library notes' in *Morley College Magazine*. She demonstrated, in her comments on books donated to or purchased by the Library, the extent of her reading and knowledge of literature.[98] Her appreciative comments on Jack London's *Call of the Wild* and *White Fang* ('vivid, savage and absorbing') look forward, perhaps, to her later involvement with the Humanitarian League and concern for the animal world.[99] Other works attest developing interests in sexual reform: anthropologist Edvard Westermarck's *Origin and Development of Moral Ideas*; Arnold Bennett's divorce novel, *Whom God Hath Joined* (given to the Library by Stella herself); and several volumes by

Havelock Ellis, including *Man and Woman*, *The Soul of Spain* and *A Study of British Genius* (the latter two volumes donated 'by the Librarian').[100]

The essay 'Elegant Extracts' – 'Among much material and mental dust the search among any miscellaneous heap of literary rubbish occasionally strikes some interesting scraps' – is unsigned, but there are touches which suggest Stella Browne's authorship. The comment on

> advice to a district visitor:
>
> – when visiting the poor, be always in your intercourse with them genial, cordial and firm.
>
> One is tempted to wonder whether 'the poor' selected for the experiment met it with equal firmness – and the dishmop or the fire-shovel.

strikes a note often found in the later Stella, as does the remark that 'It is difficult to imagine a time' when the novels of George Eliot were 'considered somewhat "advanced" or "daring" by any sane person'.[101] It was very likely stimulated by the preliminary investigation of the lesser-visited shelves, in connection with a move and new cataloguing of the collection.[102]

By 1911, Stella Browne had come to identify herself as 'a Socialist and "extreme" Left-Wing feminist'.[103] Indeed, in the 1911 census return she features as 'A Worker', whereas her mother is described as being 'of independent means'[104] (meagre though these must have been). She was still in the WSPU and, indeed, was for several years a 'self-denial card collector' (during the annual week in which members denied themselves some luxury in order to donate the money to the organisation's funds).[105] She was living with her mother and sister at 16 King's Mansions, Lawrence Street, Chelsea,[106] an area she would reside in until early in the Second World War. She had (one must assume) lost her virginity to her 'demi-semi-lover' the previous year and was already moving towards a theory of female 'polyandry'.

H.G. Wells's delineation of 'sex as a thing collectively portentous' and the need for 'the power and beauty of the love of man and woman ... [to] frame a justifiable vision of the ordered world' in *The New Machiavelli* (1911) did not go far enough for her. Writing to Wells, she argued (after remarking 'I don't think you do women as well as men'):

> I just want to suggest, that whereas most men are admitted to be polygynous, there is much less acknowledgement of the fact that *many* women, & not the least attractive and intelligent, are polyandrous ... & this fact must be faced & provided for & allowed for under sensible & humane conditions, i.e. Socialist

> conditions. Of course I mean real personal preference, not the pressure of hunger or unpaid bills! & not the indiscriminate animalism of some low types.

She advanced her developing notion that: 'All women are not born mothers, mothers par excellence', and also suggested that for a woman with 'a great deal of temperament ... a baby is not always an efficient safety valve'.[107]

At this point in her life, Stella Browne had come through her delicate childhood and difficult adolescence, and the crises of her early adulthood. Having already passed her thirtieth birthday, she was about to burst upon a wider world as a woman with a very radical message on women and sex.

Notes

1. Baptism records, St Luke's Halifax, Public Archives of Nova Scotia; Dodwell family tree.
2. Obituary, *The Dominion Annual Register and Review for the Seventeenth Year of the Canadian Union, 1883*, Toronto, 1884, p. 301.
3. *Navy List*.
4. [? William J. Robinson], 'The most radical British feminist and birth control advocate of today', *Medical Critic and Guide*, vol. 25E/5, May 1927, pp. 192–4.
5. Marriage register, St Stephen's (Bishop's Chapel), Halifax, Public Archives of Nova Scotia.
6. Dodwell family tree.
7. Stella Browne to Havelock Ellis, 9 August 1915, Havelock Ellis papers, British Library Department of Manuscripts, Additional Manuscript 70539.
8. F.W. Stella Browne, 'A few straight questions to the Eugenics Society', *The Freewoman*, 1 August 1912, p. 217.
9. Marriage register.
10. Obituary, *Dominion Annual Register*; The National Archives: Admiralty Records ADM196/22.
11. 'The most radical British feminist'.
12. Dodwell family tree; 'In memoriam' notice of Rev. George Branson Dodwell, Rector of Wilmot, *Diocesan Synod Report, 1892*, Rev. K.B. Wainwright, *Our Story of Stewiacke and Shubencadie* (privately published, manuscript annotations), Public Archives of Nova Scotia.
13. Entry in the register of St John the Evangelist, Toronto, on RootsWeb, http://homepages.rootsweb.com/~maryc/stjohnev.htm
14. Death register, Public Archives of Nova Scotia.
15. 1881 Census return for Halifax, Public Archives of Nova Scotia.
16. Dodwell family tree; marriage register.
17. Dodwell family tree.

18. 'The Point Prim disaster', *The Novascotian*, 8 December 1883.
19. Letter from Anna I.M. Browne [sic] to her mother-in-law, 3 December 1883, scanned images and transcription on http://www.lostatsea.ca/brownel.htm, Website 'Fishing – it was a way of life – and lost at sea', accessed November 2006.
20. Probate records, Public Archives of Nova Scotia.
21. Anna Browne to her mother-in-law, 3 December 1883.
22. *Halifax City Directory* 1885, 1888/9, 1889/90, 1890/1; Census returns, Public Archives of Nova Scotia.
23. Memorandum for Presentation to the Inter-Departmental Committee on Abortion from Miss F.W. Stella Browne, A.C. Paper no. 16, The National Archives, MH71/21.
24. 'The most radical British feminist'.
25. Browne to Ellis, 3 April 1927, BL Add Ms 70539.
26. 'The most radical British feminist'.
27. F.W. Stella Browne, 'Havelock Ellis: his view of women's nature and position', *Birth Control Review* (New York), vol. III, no. 2, February 1919, pp. 9–11.
28. Dodwell family tree; Obituary Notice for Alexander Siemens, *Journal of the Institution of Electrical Engineers*, vol. 66, 1928, pp. 1242–3, entry in David J. Jeremy and Christine Shaw (eds), *Dictionary of Business Biography: A Biographical Dictionary of Business Lleaders Active in Britain in the period 1860–1980, Volume V, S–Z* (London: Butterworths, 1986), pp. 155–6. Many thanks to Leonore Symons, archivist at the Institution of Electrical Engineers, for providing this information.
29. Memorandum ... from Miss F.W. Stella Browne, MH71/21.
30. F.W. Stella Browne, *Sexual Variety and Variability Among Women, and Their Bearing upon Social Reconstruction* (London: British Society for the Study of Sex Psychology, 1917), p. 9.
31. F.W. Stella Browne, 'The age of bewilderment', *The New Generation*, vol. 11, July 1932, p. 80.
32. Browne, *Sexual Variety and Variability*, p. 11.
33. K. Hindell and M. Simms, *Abortion Law Reformed* (London: Peter Owen, 1971), p. 58.
34. Somerville College register.
35. According to Ralf Dose, on the basis of passages in German in her letters of the 1940s to Max Hodann.
36. Thanks to the Archivist at St Felix School for providing this information, communicated in a letter from the Personal Assistant to the Headmistress, 11 October 1993.
37. Bernard Keeling, assisted by Nancie Pelling, *St Felix School Southwold and the Old Felicians: Pioneers in the Emancipation of Women since 1897* (Sevenoaks: Bernard Keeling, 1999), pp. 2–7. I am indebted to Mr Keeling for providing me with relevant extracts of an earlier typescript of this book.

38. Keeling, *St Felix School*, p. 9.
39. 'The most radical British feminist'.
40. Keeling, *St Felix School*, pp. 2, 14–16.
41. F.W. Stella Browne, 'A Suffolk town (Southwold)', [n.d.], Ellis papers, BL Add Ms 70539.
42. Keeling, *St Felix School*, p. 95.
43. Somerville College Register.
44. Vera Brittain, *The Women at Oxford: A Fragment of History* (London: George G. Harrap & Co. Ltd, 1960), p. 87.
45. Muriel St Clare Byrne and Catherine Hope Mansfield, *Somerville College 1897–1921* (Oxford: Oxford University Press [1922]), p. 15.
46. Byrne and Mansfield, *Somerville*, p. 65.
47. Byrne and Mansfield, *Somerville*, p. 84.
48. Byrne and Mansfield, *Somerville*, pp. 71–2.
49. Pauline Adams, *Somerville for Women: An Oxford College 1879–1993* (Oxford: Oxford University Press, 1996), pp. 135–6.
50. 'Somerville College: Parliament', *Fritillary*, no. 22, March 1901, p. 361.
51. 'Somerville Parliament', *Fritillary*, no. 24, December 1901, p. 382.
52. 'Oxford Students Debating Society'. *Fritillary*, no. 24, December 1901, p. 384.
53. 'Somerville College: report on "Sharp Practice"', *Fritillary*, no. 24, December 1901, pp. 388–9.
54. F.W. Stella Browne, 'Reviews: *Neapolitan Ice. A Novel of Oxford and Bohemia.* By Renée Haynes', *The New Generation*, vol. 7, July 1928, p. 78.
55. F.W. Stella Browne, 'Short notice of *Towards a Sane Feminism*. By Wilma Meikle', *International Journal of Ethics*, 1916/1917, vol. 27, p. 407.
56. F.W. Stella Browne, 'Women and the race', *The Socialist Review: A Quarterly Review of Modern Thought. Edited by J. Bruce Glasier*, vol. 14, no. 81, May–June 1917, pp. 151–7.
57. Brittain, *The Women at Oxford*, p. 119.
58. Browne to Ellis, 28 December 1914, BL Add Ms 70539.
59. Byrne and Mansfield, *Somerville*, pp. 84–5.
60. Somerville College Register; Letter from Headmistress, Haberdashers' Monmouth School for Girls, 4 November 1993.
61. Browne to Ellis, 28 December 1914, BL Add Ms 70539.
62. Gillian Avery, *The Best Type of Girl: A History of Girls' Independent Schools* (London: Andre Deutsch, 1991), pp. 212, 217, 231–3.
63. Byrne and Mansfield, *Somerville*, p. 85; Alison Oram, *Women Teachers and Feminist Politics 1900–39* (Manchester: Manchester University Press, 1996), pp. 104–7.
64. Somerville College Register.
65. Browne to Ellis, 28 December 1914, BL Add Ms 70539.

66. 'The most radical British feminist'.
67. Somerville College Register.
68. Browne, *Sexual Variety and Variability*, pp. 12–13.
69. Browne to Ellis, 28 December 1914, BL Add Ms 70539.
70. Browne to Ellis, 28 December 1914, BL Add Ms 70539.
71. Browne, *Sexual Variety and Variability*.
72. 'A new subscriber', 'Experience and understanding', *The Freewoman*, 21 March 1912, p. 398.
73. Browne, *Sexual Variety and Variability*, pp. 11–12.
74. F.W. Stella Browne, 'Studies in feminine inversion', *Journal of Sexology and Psychanalysis*, vol. 1, 1923, pp. 51–6.
75. Browne, *Sexual Variety and Variability*.
76. 'Editor's notes', *Plan*, vol. 13, no. 4, April 1946.
77. Amy Hackett, 'Helene Stöcker: left-wing intellectual and sex reformer', in Renate Bridenthal, Atina Grossman and Marion Kaplan, *When Biology Became Destiny: Women in Weimar and Nazi Germany* (New York: Monthly Review Press, 1984), pp. 109–30; Cornelie Usborne, *The Politics of the Body in Weimar Germany: Women's Reproductive Rights and Duties* (Ann Arbor, MI: University of Michigan Press, 1992), pp. 6–8.
78. Browne to Ellis, 9 Febrary 1914, BL Add Ms 70539; Lesley A. Hall, 'Stella Browne and the German radical sex reform tradition', in Willem de Blécourt (ed.), *Sisters of Subversion: Histories of Women, Tales of Gender: A Festschrift* (Amsterdam: AMB, 2008), pp. 152–61.
79. Somerville College Register.
80. R.B. Pugh, 'General introduction', *The Victoria History of the Counties of England* (London: University of London Institute of Historical Research, 1970), pp. 1–27.
81. F.C. Müller-Lyer, *The Family* (Translated by F.W. Stella Browne) (London: Allen & Unwin, 1931), p. 244.
82. Pugh, 'General introduction', *Victoria History*; letter from Christopher Elrington, General Editor of the *Victoria County History*, 22 September 1993.
83. 'A new subscriber', 'Experience and understanding', *The Freewoman*, 21 March 1912, p. 354.
84. Somerville College Register; 'Library Notes', *Morley College Magazine*, January 1907, pp. 59–61.
85. Lindsay Martin, 'Virginia Woolf at Morley College', *The Charleston Magazine*, winter/spring 1991, pp. 20–5.
86. Mizpah Gilbert, 'The position of women in public libraries', first published in *Library World*, vol. 18, October 1915, pp. 100–5, reprinted in Kathleen Webel and Kathleen M Heim with assistance from Dianne J. Ellsworth (eds), *The Role of Women in Librarianship, 1876–1976: The Entry, Advancement and Struggle for Equalization in One Profession* (London: Oryx Press, 1979), pp. 67–71.

87. The historiography of women in librarianship is still minimal (for an overview of some of the debates, see Webel and Heim, *The Role of Women in Librarianship*), and most of it relates to women in public libraries, most of whom would not have had degrees.
88. Sybil Oldfield, *Spinsters of this Parish* (London: Virago, 1984), pp. 65–6.
89. Oldfield, *Spinsters of this Parish*, pp. 92–3, 147–8; *Morley College Magazine*, May 1907.
90. Inter-Departmental Committee on Abortion, A.O. Paper no. 51... Evidence of: Miss F.W. Stella Browne, Wednesday, 17 November 1937, MH71/23.
91. Annual Reports of Morley College.
92. Oldfield, *Spinsters of this Parish*, pp. 3–9, 19.
93. Stella Browne to Janet Carson, 18 May 1920, 'BSS Misc', British Sexology Society Archives, Harry Ransom Humanities Research Center, University of Texas at Austin.
94. Women's Social and Political Union, *Second Annual Report 1908*, The Women's Library, London Metropolitan University.
95. Browne to Ellis, 25 December 1922, BL Add Ms 70539.
96. Browne, *Sexual Variety and Variability*, pp. 7–9.
97. Browne, *Sexual Variety and Variability*, pp. 8, 10.
98. S. Browne, 'Library Notes', *Morley College Magazine*, January 1907, p. 60; February 1907, p. 73.
99. S. Browne, 'Library Notes', *Morley College Magazine*, January 1907, p. 60, June 1907, p. 133.
100. S. Browne, 'Library Notes', *Morley College Magazine*, April 1909, February 1910, March 1910, November 1911.
101. 'Elegant Extracts', *Morley College Magazine*, March 1909, pp. 92–3.
102. S. Browne, 'Library', *Morley College Magazine*, April 1909, p. 110, September/October 1909, pp. 16–17.
103. F.W. Stella Browne to Olaf Stapledon, 7 February 1949, Stapledon papers, Special Collections, Liverpool University Library, STAP: H.VIII B 9/21.
104. 1911 Census online http://www.1911census.co.uk/ [accessed 15 January 2009].
105. Women's Social and Political Union, *Annual Reports*, 1910–1912, The Women's Library.
106. Electoral register 1911, Chelsea Local Studies Library. Dulcie was able to vote – but only in the local government elections, which had been open to women for several decades.
107. Stella Browne to H.G. Wells, (n.d. [? 1911/12]), H.G. Wells Archive, Rare Book and Special Collections Library, University of Illinois at Urbana-Champaign.

2

The Emergence of a Freewoman, 1912–14

On 19 February 1912, Stella Browne did something momentous. She wrote a letter on 'The Chastity of Continence' to the recently established, radical, subversive and shocking feminist journal *The Freewoman*, founded by former suffragette activist Dora Marsden to provide a forum for facets of the women's struggle which she believed that the suffrage movement was ignoring or neglecting. *The Freewoman* immediately gained a reputation for unblushing outspokenness on matters normally kept discreetly veiled in silence and its determination to discuss issues excluded from journals of the various suffrage societies, let alone more mainstream periodicals. Leading anti-suffragist Mrs Humphrey Ward deemed it 'the dark and dangerous side of the "Woman Movement"': others were moved to nausea or physical acts of destruction;[1] for yet others, it provided a welcome forum and a stimulus to thought and discussion.

The writer Rebecca West, who had been a leading figure in *The Freewoman* inner circles, was retrospectively disdainful of the 'utterly futile and blundering discussions' on sexual attitudes and society prior to the advent of Freud and Jung,[2] perhaps assigning them rather too much significance in facilitating the useful discussion of sexual matters. Stella Browne and others deployed the pioneering work of Havelock Ellis and continental sexologists providing new ways of talking about sex, while drawing upon a long tradition of feminist critique of sexual mores in a male-dominated society. Ellis's influence on Stella, and that of his colleague Edward Carpenter, has been commented upon (and often overstated): it has been less recognised that she was marrying these new forms of knowledge to this feminist tradition.[3] *The*

Freewoman and its readers had strong links to an earlier generation of 'New Woman' and a radical free-love tradition.[4]

Previous correspondents had questioned assumptions that celibacy was necessarily deleterious to health and Kathlyn Oliver, in particular, had given personal testimony that, as an unmarried woman of thirty, her health was excellent.[5] Stella must have known Oliver, who was associated with Morley College,[6] which possibly explains her use of the pseudonym 'A New Subscriber'. She took issue with Oliver's assumption that abstinence was an absolute good and benefit to health, arguing that there were

> many woman whose constitutions and temperament are what Professer Forel [Swiss sexologist, author of *The Sexual Question*] calls 'sexually anaesthetic,' without thereby suffering any lack of mental or motor energy, or of capacity for affection, or even the maternal instinct.

She had no problem with such women 'abstain[ing] from what affords them no pleasure', but denied that they should 'make their temperamental coldness into a rigid standard for others'. But, she contended, there was 'probably *a far greater range of variation sexually* among women than among men', and she had known 'specimens of all varieties intimately'. As a result, she could assure Oliver (and others who had made similar contentions)

> that the health, the happiness, the social usefulness and the mental capacity of many women have been seriously impaired and sometimes totally ruined by the unnatural conditions of their lives.

She agreed that 'many women have been made ill and wretched by the unrestrained indulgence of married life with ignorant or brutal husbands', but surely such abuse did not render a natural pleasure 'entirely injurious and to be deprecated?'

She alluded to the very recent development of sex 'beginning to be scientifically studied'. Making a plea for 'a spirit of mutual tolerance', she deplored Oliver's classification of the male sex among 'the lower animals'. Controversial stuff in itself: but in conclusion she went even further, in the belief that *The Freewoman* was 'the only lay publication in English' in which she could make her final point. This was that few single women entirely refrained from auto-erotic practices – 'including imaginative and psychic excitation in its various forms'. Stella repudiated conventional judgements, arguing that the 'danger to health and sanity has, on the whole, been much overrated': but argued that without recourse to these practices 'many women would find abstinence from normal sexual relations impossible'.[7]

Kathlyn Oliver's response was to surmise that '"A New Subscriber" is of the male persuasion' and, to defend her position, that 'we women are miles above and beyond men' in 'sex matters'.[8] Stella protested against the 'cruel stupidity that would enforce complete abstinence…on all, irrespective of temperament, circumstances and point of view.' She went on to argue that

> an ardent temperament does not necessarily imply indulgence in indiscriminate promiscuity. The passionate woman may be, and often is, as fastidious in her choice of a lover as her placid sister.

She repudiated any intention of insult, claiming, in the first statement of a credo that was basic to her thinking throughout her life:

> I dislike the use of the word 'normal' as applied to certain types of mind and temperament. There is more in human nature than most people will admit.[9]

Margaret Jackson has deployed terms such as 'contempt' and 'patronizing' about Stella Browne's tone in this debate,[10] an accusation which seems disingenuous, given that Oliver more or less attributed 'all laxity in sex matters' to her adversary. Oliver, indeed, indicted 'A New Subscriber' for advocating '*habitual sexual promiscuousness*' (something that Stella had explicitly dissociated herself from) and also mercenary sexual transactions.[11] Stella was 'neither choked nor crushed', but considered that the charge of advocating prostitution 'shows a deplorable mental dishonesty'. Did Miss Oliver see 'no distinction between a free gift and a bargain… generally not even a bargain between approximate equals?' She accentuated the positive: 'Would it not be better to acknowledge the infinite variety of human nature?… Let us admit our joy and gratitude for the beauty and pleasure of sex'.[12]

Both women were writing from lived experience: Oliver, indeed, was of the opinion that 'girls and women do not discuss the sex question as it affects themselves',[13] so her own experience was all she had to go on. A few years later, Oliver was to realise that her ability to subdue sexual feelings for men might have owed something to her intense feelings for women.[14] A couple of years later, she even joined the British Society for the Study of Sex Psychology, proposed by – Stella Browne.[15] It is tempting, although perhaps a little too neat, to try and identify the woman who introduced

Oliver to the idea that 'she was more closely related to the intermediate sex than I had hitherto imagined', as Stella: she was not the only 'woman rebel' who might have opened Oliver's eyes.[16] But clearly, following their heated exchange, they had reached some kind of rapprochement.

The correspondence halted after Stella's letter published on 18 April 1912, in which she concluded:

> let those women who, owing to pressure of circumstances or to cowardice, will not at least try to enjoy their elementary human rights, refrain from unmeasured public attacks on the others, who have the courage of their desires as well as their convictions.[17]

This was not, however, the end of her connection with *The Freewoman* any more than with Kathlyn Oliver.

Other things were going on in Stella's life. At the end of March, she left her position at Morley College, for obscure reasons. In her farewell letter, she insisted that her departure:

> will not by any means imply that my friendship for the College is broken off: on the contrary, I hope to keep in touch with all that goes on at Morley College and to come and see you sometimes.

She had enjoyed her work and was 'very glad ... to have learnt to know you. It has been an unfailing interest to me and in many ways a lesson'. She expressed her thanks for the 'dear little remembrance' of a 'pretty and dainty' watch, which would be 'of the greatest use to a person who is naturally dilatory'.[18] However, given that she later wrote about Mary Sheepshanks, the Vice-Principal, that 'I ... have not since 1912, been on speaking terms with her!!! I got to know her *practical methods as distinct from her theoretical principles, rather too well*',[19] there may well have been more to the story than this apparently amicable departure. Sybil Oldfield's sympathetic account of Sheepshanks suggests that she was not easy to get on with.[20]

However, Stella was inclined to have 'authority issues'. Around the same time, she became disenchanted with the suffrage movement – in particular, the Women's Social and Political Union – on the grounds of the 'towering spiritual arrogance' she perceived in the leadership,[21] and its 'dogmatic and tyrannical' bureaucracy.[22] She criticised the 'self-advertising *arrivisme* and snobbery' of 'arrant humbug[s]' within the movement, whose behaviour towards other women and men in a 'less advantageous social position' formed an 'illuminating commentary on [their] incessant protestations of feminism and democracy'.[23] As with several other activists,[24] disillusion had set in: Stella quit.[25]

For the next few years, Stella seems to have been out of permanent employment. She did some periodical reviews, and was trying to develop this and other journalistic activities. Dulcie was 'elderly and suffer[ing] terribly from acute neuralgia' and Stella was 'able to be of some help to her about the house – or rather flat!' (this may have been another reason to leave her job at Morley) where they lived 'very quietly'. Lawrence Street is a quiet, rather gloomy side-street overshadowed by large blocks of flats running down towards the river Thames, in Chelsea – in those days, a rather socially mixed area. Membership of the Divorce Law Reform Union, the Malthusian Society, and an attempt to get up 'a movement for the alteration of the laws on Illegitimacy... on the lines of the Mutter-Schutzbund' indicate that Stella did not spend all her time quietly at home with her aged parent.[26] The lack of any mention of Sylvia suggests that she may not have been part of the household at this time.

Many readers of *The Freewoman* were eager for 'more free and extensive discussion':[27] on 18 April 1912, a preliminary meeting was held in the hall at the International Suffrage Shop in the Strand. One of numerous similar establishments selling suffrage and other literature, badges, posters and other suffrage-related items, and providing informal and more formal meeting spaces, it was, uniquely, unaffiliated to any of the specific suffrage organisations. The meeting attracted an unexpectedly large audience of between eighty and ninety, but nonetheless 'much unanimity and enthusiasm prevailed'.[28] It was decided to hold fortnightly meetings, open to both sexes, in London, a subscription of five shillings in order to defray costs, and with talks followed by free discussion. Speakers addressed a range of subjects, including not only sex oppression, eugenics, the problem of celibacy, prostitution and divorce, but also domestic drudgery and its abolition. After at least one of these (anarchist Guy Aldred on 'Sex Oppression and the way out'), a smaller group continued the discussion in the Knightsbridge studio of the photographer G.C. Beresford.[29] Rebecca West famously claimed that attending these circles was 'like being in Church',[30] but Françoise Lafitte-Cyon, later Havelock Ellis's common-law wife, found them 'vital, and... carried on in a manner befitting human beings rather than hooligans'. Sitting shyly in a corner, she envied 'these people who interested me, who arrived at these meetings in small groups or two together'.[31]

'A New Subscriber' returned to the correspondence columns of *The Freewoman* on 4 July 1912 with a long letter on 'The Immorality of the Marriage Contract'. Responding to a leading article, Stella drew attention to the omission of certain 'considerations which have somewhat improved the woman's position *ethically*, though they have, on the whole, added to her hardships'. In the 'smaller, articulate, educated class', marriage was increasingly being deferred, men tended to look for wives with some private means, and families were limited, a development not altogether to be deplored. Such changes were making 'the older forms of the contract ... untenable'. At this point, Stella put in a plug for the work of the Divorce Law Reform Union, a body which she considered had 'scientific as well as humanitarian importance' through its accurate statistics and thorough investigations.[32] (A few weeks later she added that, while desiring easier facilities for divorce, she 'did not for a moment wish to imply approval of the institution of marriage'.)[33]

She extended her analysis to the 'obverse' of the picture, prostitution. Stella, channelling the spirit of Josephine Butler, leader of the nineteenth-century campaign against government regulation of prostitution, declared that 'State Regulation subtly but unmistakably debases the status of *all* women'. She suggested various remedies, including gender-equitable notification and free treatment as in Norway, while conceding

> all these are palliatives: the true remedy is the socialised State, not the organised exploitation of today, and the evolved humanity for which we hope and fight.

She alluded to recent works of sexology, offering to lend her copy of the work (in German) of Auguste Forel, the Swiss sexologist and social purity activist, and praising Havelock Ellis's works – 'in substance and style, they are incomparable' – and inquiring as to the availability of Iwan Bloch's work.[34] Ellis was the doyen of British sexual reform: he was personally shy and retiring, but his six-volume *Studies in the Psychology of Sex* (1897–1910), as well as the precursor volume *Man and Woman*, were extremely influential. The *Studies*, although hard to obtain in the UK following the prosecution for obscenity of the first volume in 1897, had significant circulation in radical and feminist circles. Iwan Bloch was another continental sexologist whose works were becoming known at this time, but, as with many works of a similar nature, were published with cautions that they were for the perusal of the medical and legal professions and serious students of the social sciences only.

In the next issue of *The Freewoman*, Stella 'came out', revealing herself as 'A New Subscriber'.[35] The reasons for her assumption of the pseudonym, and her discarding of it alike, remain mysterious. Her initial anonymity may have had to do fears that openly advocating her radical views in a scandalous periodical might have a negative impact on her employment, but why wait three months after leaving Morley before making the revelation? Perhaps her views were already becoming known through participation in the Discussion circles? She was moving into the inner circles of *The Freewoman* group: a few surviving notes to Grace Jardine, one of the editors, are informal and chatty in tone and allude to personal meetings.[36]

Stella returned to the question of prostitution, responding to Dr Wrench's praises of the Yoshiwara system of organised prostitution in Japan with hard-hitting questions about the women's legal and financial position; its effects on the prevalence of venereal disease; and the implications, if any, for the European situation. While '*not* advocating the State endowment of prostitution', she argued that 'if regulation by the State be insisted on, endowment is the barest justice'.[37] It is hard to discern any basis for Sheila Jeffreys' claim that Stella Browne 'suffered from constraint and the need for men's approval when writing about sex' (Dr Wrench was not the only man to find himself on the receiving end of one of Stella's 'Forward! Charge!'[38] attacks) or allegation that she 'did not seek to transform men or agitate against the sexual abuse of women and girls'.[39]

'Forward! Charge!' was clearly Stella Browne's motto at this time. Her swingeing attack on the Eugenics Education Society seriously undermines the arguments of those who have tried to identify her as a eugenic sympathiser or fellow-traveller.[40] In the summer of 1912, Stella engaged with the claims of the International Eugenics Congress then taking place in London to 'decide... who is to be born and who is not', from both a socialist and a feminist perspective. She conceded that she belonged to that class 'outside of which, we are assured, there is no salvation', but expressed grave doubts as to whether she was really 'a "fit" and "desirable" person... for various relatives and acquaintances have at different times emphatically pronounced me incapable of managing my affairs with ordinary prudence'. '[I]n a spirit of humility, quickened by acute personal fear', she craved enlightenment 'from the wise' foregathered at the Congress. The Eugenics Society did not take its arguments to their logical outcome:

> the positive side of selective breeding is resolutely ignored. Yet why should the procreative capacities of the really 'fit'

> man – when you have once decided who and what he is – be limited to the child-bearing capacities of *one* woman, however healthy and heroically devoted to biennial suffering?

If eugenists really had the courage of their convictions, they would have to 'face the possibility of legal selective fertile polygamy and occasional fertile polyandry as well'. Instead of applying 'indirect pressure and compulsion ... to compel able and healthy women to bear children in marriage', she exhorted them to consider 'the importance to the child that it should be loved and wanted'. For Freewomen, the issue, she stated, was clear:

> We must secure a decent chance in material environment for every child born into the world. We must see to it that the woman who is passionately and pre-eminently maternal shall not be condemned to childlessness. We must demand thorough investigation of the transmissibility of disease and stringent legislation in certain cases. But our *right to refuse maternity* is also an inalienable right. Our wills are ours, our persons are ours: nor shall all the priests and scientists in the world deprive us of the right to say 'no'.[41]

Receiving no response, a fortnight later she returned to the fray: were eugenists 'driven to ignore what they are so far unable to suppress?' She raised further questions: about 'applied' or 'artificial' reproduction, the relationship between genius and eugenic concepts of 'fitness' ('the occasional union of genius and deformity ... close connection ... between genius and insanity'). Meanwhile, 'the question of the social and material environment of the majority still remains'.[42]

The Discussion Circle remained lively: it was addressed on 4 September by Dr Charles Vickery Drysdale of the Malthusian League, the only British organisation publicly advocating contraception. In her report, Stella remarked that 'The need of giving information on these subjects, especially to women of the poorer classes, was very clearly demonstrated'.[43] Drysdale reported that

> Miss Stella Brown [sic] stated that medical men received dozens of letters from frantic girls anxious to procure abortion, and if their humanity led them to comply, they were faced with ruin and penal servitude. It ought to be brought to the notice of the General Medical Council that instruction in the means of prevention was the only method of avoiding this terrible dilemma.[44]

Shortly after this, Stella joined the Malthusian League. By early 1914, she was on its panel of speakers.[45] As did a number of other contemporaries, she distinguished the valuable work she felt that the League was doing in raising the issue of birth control from the anti-socialist and eugenicist views of C.V. Drysdale and his wife Bessie. The League's journal *The Malthusian*, and its successor *The New Generation*, would become a major forum for Stella.

The Freewoman was in difficulties: leading newsagents W.H. Smiths had imposed a ban, and the proprietor (Charles Granville) decided to remove his support, while Dora Marsden was moving away into remote realms of metaphysics: *The Freewoman* came 'to an end psychically' as external forces forced a physical halt.[46] The final issue appeared on 10 October 1912.[47]

The Discussion Circle, of which Stella had become Treasurer by a unanimous vote,[48] remained a venue for debate and mutual support and, according to Rebecca West, the winter of 1912/1913 saw 'an epidemic of kissing ... I have been kissed by Mrs Macdonald, Stella Browne, Barbara Low, Helena Kingsland Greenland, Mrs Gallichan, and a lady in deep mourning.' West considered the circle quaint, and remarked, 'Stella Browne sends me horoscopes occasionally. I am to "form a union with an American" and "not wear Chinese curios".'[49] This is the first mention of Stella's interest in astrology, a subject which seems to have been of abiding interest and which she had pursued to the extent that she was capable of drawing up a horoscope.

There was a considerable eagerness to restart the journal, which was eventually relaunched in June 1913 as *The New Freewoman*, due to energetic liaison work by Rebecca West and the organisational abilities (and capital input) of the wealthy political activist and patron of modernist literature Harriet Shaw Weaver.[50] West was anxious to beef up the literary side,[51] and steer away from the realms of sexual controversy:

> [I]n reference to our desertion of sex problems you might say that in the words of our dear late Queen, 'we will be good'. All the Stella Brownes and people are so upset.[52]

This rejection of 'sex problems' may have been realistic in view of the need to find a publisher and be acceptable to distributors. It is, therefore, all the more remarkable that West later considered that *The Freewoman*'s 'greatest service ... was through its unblushingness' and its determination to mention sex 'loudly and clearly and repeatedly'.[53] This epitomises the contribution that Stella Browne (among others) made to the journal. For her part, Stella seems to have been impressed by the younger woman (still in her teens at that period), remarking to Havelock Ellis:

> if we two meet again there is going to be some liveliness! She is a born actress of remarkable dramatic power, who has been unable to sink or forget her personality in another branch of art. Striking looking girl: *superb* eyes, like black pools: Spanish-Irish type.

From West's comments in her letters and Stella's suggestion of 'liveliness' to be anticipated from an encounter, their relationship appears somewhat turbulent: they were both combative characters who thrived on controversy.

Harriet Shaw Weaver took a leading part in trying to establish the new publishing enterprise on a sound financial footing.[54] Stella contributed three shillings and sixpence towards the Thousand Club in April 1913 and 'Hopes to pay more later, and is trying to get members'.[55] A New Freewoman Ltd company was set up,[56] and Stella was named as a shareholder, in a rather curious fashion. The fashionable London photographer George C. Beresford was a great supporter of *The Freewoman*.[57] He was anxious to ensure its continuation, although not at the expense of good business practice, and did not think he could 'manage to be a director ... ought not they to be *all women*. It would look prettier'.[58] Shaw Weaver's notebook recorded this offer and added 'Mark his letters private. Will take shares in another name Miss Stella Browne. Took 18 for Miss Frances Worsley Stella Browne'.[59] According to the minutes of the New Freewoman Company, he purchased 18 shares to be held in Stella's name.[60]

How are we to interpret this gesture? Whose idea was it that his shares should be held in Stella's name? If the choice was his, why did he select her, out of the committed and devoted female supporters of the project? This tantalising bit of evidence causes one to speculate whether Beresford was Mr 'Demi-semi-lover' (by this date enjoying full penetrative rights).

Beresford (1864–1938) was an intriguing character. Educated at Westward Ho! in Devon with Rudyard Kipling, he was the original for 'M'Turk' in *Stalky and Co.*[61] An obituary paid tribute to 'a brain with an edge like that of a good razor' concealed by a 'nonchalant manner' and 'seemingly [sic] appearance of indifference'.[62] He abandoned an intended career in the Government of India Public Works Department,[63] and became a fashionable photographer in Knightsbridge and dealer in antiques.[64] His political sympathies were along very different lines to those of Kipling: he was, if not explicitly a male suffragist, a supporter of feminist causes, and a member of the Fabian Society.[65] He had also dabbled, as so many of the day had done, in theosophy.[66] While Stella was never a member of the Theosophical Society, she was certainly familiar with such associated ideas as reincarnation and psychic abilities.

Might they have been lovers? Beresford did have demonstrable heterosexual credentials, unlike many of the men in Stella's circles, maintaining a menage in Brighton (well away from his London circles) with Jessica Wilson, with whom he had two sons.[67] He certainly sounds like the kind of knowledgeable sophisticate who could have been her initiator. She remarked that the 'common ideals' between herself and her long-term lover were 'a certain love of what appeals to us as beauty & a certain contempt for public opinion & public stupidity',[68] two qualities characteristic of Beresford. But her discretion in alluding to her partners was matched by his: his papers at Sussex University shed no light on his personal life.[69]

Stella continued trying to establish herself as a reviewer. In December 1912, her very positive (unsigned) review of Havelock Ellis's *The Task of Social Hygiene* appeared in *The English Review*. Her enthusiasm for Ellis had already been expressed in her acquisition policies at Morley and her letters to *The Freewoman*: in this review, she referred to

> the sane and noble optimism, the wide range of knowledge and sympathy, and the lucid, forcible and distinguished style, which we have learnt to associate with the name of Havelock Ellis.

Echoing earlier statements on the Eugenics Society, she drew attention to Ellis's insistence on 'a sense of personal responsibility, rather than compulsion' and his refutation of the 'population fanatics'. The only fault she found was Ellis's underrating of the 'moral value of [the] active and articulate revolt against *tradition as well as present conditions*' embodied in the suffrage movement, but even then she found his 'analysis of the wider implications of the movement, of the claim to full expression and experience in both the broadly human and the sexual sphere ... wholly admirable'.[70]

Her reviews in the *English Review* included, besides some 'quite insignificant novels',[71] *The Truth About Woman* by C. Gasquoine Hartley (Mrs Walter Gallichan) ('fearless intellectual honesty and a deep sympathy and tolerance'),[72] Walter Heape's *Sex Antagonism* ('neither exhaustive nor unbiassed'),[73] and a joint review of Mrs Archibald Colquhoun's *The Vocation of Woman* ('courage of reactionary conventionality and an utter disregard for inconvenient facts') with Mrs H.M. Swanwick's *The Future of the Women's Movement* ('like a bracing wind after the stale atmosphere of privilege and platitude').[74] Some short reviews also appeared in *The New Statesman*: the one of which she thought most highly was of W.H. Woodward's biography of Cesare Borgia – 'After recent slovenly and pretentious essays in the whitewash and gold brocade school of "historical biography", one welcomes this careful study'. She mentioned her own belief that

> Lucrezia's regencies and diplomatic activity as Duchess of Ferrara, and the curious episode of June, 1501, when she was left in charge of affairs at the Vatican, on the one hand, and a series of mysterious tragedies, on the other hand, indicate that, far from being the colourless doll Gregorvius imagined, she was as able and as sensual as the men of her family – less violent and infinitely more lucky.[75]

The whole piece suggests considerable knowledge of the history of Renaissance Italy, as well as commitment to feminist revisionism of standard historiographical narratives. These reviews are only identifiable because she mentioned them in a letter to Havelock Ellis:[76] more probably lurk in anonymity.

Her attempts to extend her literary activities to *The New Freewoman* under Rebecca West's editorship do not seem to have been as fruitful: 'write and tell Stella Browne whether you do or don't want a critique of Galsworthy's [play] "The Fugitive". I am aweary of beating back her contributions'.[77] The rather churlish and cutting tone may be attributable to the fact that West's affair with H.G. Wells was causing her considerable emotional trauma.[78]

During 1914, Stella Browne's circles of acquaintance in the world of progressive reform continued to expand; she made two important friendships, as well as extending her own activities. On 3 February 1914, she wrote to Havelock Ellis, having 'often thought of doing so'. Unfortunately, this first letter does not survive, and neither does Ellis's reply. Her name was already familiar to him, probably through 'the old "Freewoman"', and they also had 'mutual acquaintances': perhaps in the Malthusian League or the Divorce Law Reform Union.[79] She wrote again, to let him know 'of a very mean piece of injustice & indirect persecution now being perpetrated' against the Malthusian League, a press boycott and refusal of the use of a hall in Southwark.[80]

However, she conceded that their 'work in Southwark is most encouraging & is assuming very large proportions'.[81] She was an active participant in the League's South London campaign, which was holding regular meetings in the Socialist Hall in Walworth.[82] She also began to publish signed reviews in its journal, *The Malthusian*, which allowed her substantial space for notices of significant works of the day on sexual ethics, eugenics, motherhood and related topics. She had qualified praise for Robert Michels' *Sexual Ethics: A Study of Borderland Questions*, approving of his stance in favour of family limitation, although considering that the book lacked 'the scope [and] the profound originality of the pioneers of sexual science in England and Germany'.[83] She returned to her critique of eugenics as currently understood in a review of Dr Caleb Saleeby's *The Progress of Eugenics*: she regretted his failure to include 'a complete and explicit statement of the Mendelian law' (which was only gradually making its impact felt in discussions on heredity), in spite of a 'trenchant analysis' of the 'highly complex nature of... hereditary traits, apart altogether from nurture and environment, which the "Neo-Darwinian" eugenists persistently ignore'. She made a swingeing attack on 'prominent amateur eugenists', with their 'glorification of war and industrialism, their class hatred and race hatred... their unspeakable view of women as automatic childbearing machines'.[84]

She thoroughly trounced the unfortunate Professor Hugo Munsterberg for his *Psychology and Social Sanity* (a collection of ten essays), which 'never once removes the academic blinkers, or doubts that the patriarchal standard of ethical and social values holds today'. His essay on 'Sex education' was 'a plea for the terrorism of ignorance which has crippled the lives of most women and many men', and he 'brushes aside the invaluable work of Freud, Moll, and other distinguished students of human nature, with contemptuous assurance and a few platitudes'. How unlike, she implied, Patrick Geddes and J. Arthur Thomson's *Sex* (Home University Library): 'full of sound information and illuminating discussion'; 'their tone is very judicious and open-minded'. They also 'repudiate the ultra-biological point of view of such scientists as Mr Heape', spoke in favour of women spacing out childbirths, and also of the enfranchisement of women.[85]

Her independence of mind was demonstrated in a review of *The Renaissance of Motherhood* by Swedish maternalist feminist Ellen Key, an internationally respected figure among feminists and progressives. While Stella found 'wise, sane, and subtle observations' in a book which she considered deplorably translated, she also perceived 'a reactionary timidity and failure to allow for those infinite shades of human variety... on whose recognition social evolution largely depends.' Without ever using the word 'sentimentality' for Key's 'worship of a free and beautiful maternity', this is definitely implied, and Stella dissented from Key's suggestion that sexual experience could only be justified by 'a *great* and lifelong love'.[86]

Stella was also participating in a rather different forum: in March 1914, a letter from her on some relatively abstruse astrological points was published in *Modern Astrology* (edited by Alan Leo, 'father of modern astrology'),[87] under the heading 'Personal Appearance: The Quincunx Aspect'. She asked the editor whether, in his opinion, 'the influence of the Ascendant on the *personal appearance*, as distinct from the *actual constitution* of the subject, has been greatly exaggerated'. In her experience:

> Again and again I have found that signs accentuated by many planets have a determining influence on the features, colouring, and expression as well as the aspects to the Ascendant degree.

She then went on to query whether the quincunx aspect (when two planets are plus or minus one hundred and fifty degrees apart in the chart) was not 'underrated, both as to its force and the adverse nature of its influence?'[88] This is the only contribution of Stella's in an astrological forum that has been traced, although her drawing up of horoscopes for members of her circle continued. As with her contributions elsewhere, she was querying received wisdom, and valuing complexity over adherence to fixed formulae.

In late September 1914, Stella became a member of the British Society for the Study of Sex Psychology. Informally founded a year previously, at a meeting at the Hotel Cecil of an all-male group predominantly interested in homosexual law reform, from an early stage it was interested in recruiting women. It was a meeting ground for a number of different groups of sexually questioning or progressive individuals, many of whom would already have been known to Stella.[89]

In December that year, Stella made another important friendship. Margaret Sanger, the radical American feminist and birth control advocate, had fled to Europe from the USA to avoid prosecution for her determined dissemination of contraceptive information. On 10 December 1914, she called at the Malthusian League to see Dr Drysdale and was welcomed 'with open arms and excitement' not only by the Drysdales, but also by a group of other Malthusians including Stella Browne – 'an ardent Feminist ... with faintly florid face ... and indefatigable vivacity'. Sanger found it 'one of the most delightful and encouraging' afternoons of her life and she developed 'a close kinship' with this group, in which 'laughter knit and welded the bonds of comradeship'.[90] Through the 'friendship of that intrepid rebel Feminist',[91] Stella, Sanger was introduced to Havelock Ellis, with whom she soon developed a passionate (although on neither side exclusive) relationship.[92] Stella sought to give Sanger's case publicity through *The New Statesman*, although 'generally *very* good about economic women's questions', it was ' *very* anti-Malthusians'.

She was 'very much honoured' when Ellis suggested that her '"case" might be helpful and worth recording', and promised to write it out more fully. She commented that, 'It will be difficult to write without bringing in various other circumstances of a quite non-sexual kind which nevertheless very much affected my sex life', instancing the underfeeding at Somerville and the bad conditions in her first job. She wondered whether it would be possible to

> give all those details which are nevertheless, in a way, important: for one thing they might give a clue to identity and that I fear I am not in a position to do. But I will write as fully as I can.[93]

Infuriatingly, neither the longer version promised nor 'the short account I have already given you' lest 'Zeppelin's, Taubes, motor-buses or other agencies remove me from life in the interim' survives among the Ellis papers (and no case remotely resembling even a carefully anonymised Stella can be tracked among those he published).[94]

She enquired whether Ellis was currently revising various volumes of the *Studies in the Psychology of Sex*, as she was building up her own set of these 'by degrees' and wanted to ensure that she had the most up-to-date editions. She was about to review his *Impressions and Comments* in the 'struggling quarterly' *The International Journal of Ethics*. Alluding indirectly to the war then in progress as 'this time of grief & tragedy and general dislocation', she thanked him for his (unspecified) 'personal kindness to myself'.[95]

Thus, within a couple of years of her first pseudonymous letter to *The Freewoman*, Stella Browne had become an increasingly well-known and well-connected member of London-based progressive circles, and was building up a modest, if not exactly wildly successful, career on the fringes of the literary world.

Notes

1. Les Garner, *A Brave and Beautiful Spirit: Dora Marsden 1882–1960* (Aldershot: Avebury, 1991), p. 60.
2. Rebecca West, 'The Freewoman' first published 16 July 1926 in *Time and Tide*, reprinted in Dale Spender, *Time and Tide Wait for No Man* (London: Pandora, 1984), pp. 63–8.
3. Lesley A. Hall, ' 'Hauling down the double standard: feminism, social purity, and sexual science in late nineteenth century Britain', *Gender and History*, vol. 16, no. 1, April 2004, pp. 36–56.

4. Lesley A. Hall, 'The next generation: Stella Browne, the new woman as freewoman', in Angelique Richardson and Chris Willis (eds), *The New Woman in Fiction and in Fact: Fin-de-Siècle Feminisms* (London: Palgrave, 2001), pp. 224–38.
5. Kathlyn Oliver, 'Asceticism and passion', *The Freewoman*, 15 February 1912, p. 252.
6. *Morley College Magazine*, 1911–1912, *passim*.
7. 'A new subscriber', 'The chastity of continence?', *The Freewoman*, 22 February 1912, p. 270.
8. Kathlyn Oliver, 'Chastity and normality', *The Freewoman*, 29 February 1912, p. 290.
9. 'A new subscriber', 'Who are the "normal"?', *The Freewoman*, 7 March 1912, pp. 312–13.
10. Margaret Jackson, *The Real Facts of Life: Feminism and the Politics of Sexuality, c. 1850–1940* (London: Taylor & Francis, 1994), pp. 91–5.
11. Kathlyn Oliver, 'On the loose principle', *The Freewoman*, 4 April 1912, pp. 398–9.
12. 'A new subscriber', 'Wanted – the grounds for differentiation', *The Freewoman*, 18 April 1912, pp. 436–7.
13. Oliver, 'Chastity and normality'.
14. K. Oliver to Edward Carpenter, 25 October 1915, Sheffield City Council Library Archives and Information: Sheffield Archives Carpenter/Mss/386/262; The 'little pacificist and socialist paper' in which she advertised for another 'lonely woman rebel' to correspond with has not been identified: it was not Margaret Sanger's *Woman Rebel*, 1914.
15. Executive Committee Minutes, 41st Meeting, 12 September 1917, British Sexology Society, Harry Ransom Humanities Research Center, University of Texas at Austin [HRC].
16. Carpenter/Mss/386/262.
17. 'A new subscriber', 'Wanted – the grounds for differentiation'.
18. F.W. Stella Browne, 'Letter (To my friends at Morley College)', *Morley College Magazine*, April 1912, p. 123.
19. Stella Browne to Janet Carson, 22 May 1920, 'BSS Misc', HRC.
20. Sybil Oldfield, *Spinsters of this Parish* (London: Virago, 1984), pp. 96–7.
21. F.W. Stella Browne, 'Studies in feminine inversion', *Journal of Sexology and Psychoanalysis*, vol. 1, 1923, pp. 51–8.
22. F.W. Stella Browne, 'Some problems of sex', *International Journal of Ethics*, vol. 27, 1916–17, pp. 464–71.
23. F.W. Stella Browne, 'Women in industry' [letter], *The New Age*, 22 July 1915, p. 293.
24. Teresa Billington-Greig, 'The militant suffrage movement: emancipation in a hurry' (first published 1911), in C. McPhee and A. Fitzgerald, *The Non-Violent Militant: Selected Writings of Teresa Billington-Greig* (London: Routledge & Kegan Paul, 1987), pp. 141–2; Edith How-Martyn to Margaret Sanger, 19 and 27 July 1915, Margaret Sanger papers in Library of Congress Washington, DC, Volume 21.

25. Women's Social and Political Union Annual Reports, 1912–1914, The Women's Library, London Metropolitan University.
26. Stella Browne to Havelock Ellis, 9 February 1914, Ellis papers in the British Library Department of Manuscripts, Additional Manuscript 70539 (BL Add Ms 70539).
27. 'A discussion circle', *The Freewoman*, 28 March 1912, p. 373.
28. John Mercer, 'Shopping for suffrage: the campaign shops of the Women's Social and Political Union', *Women's History Review*, vol. 18, no. 2, April 2009, pp. 293–309; and see also relevant entries in Elizabeth Crawford, *The Women's Suffrage Movement : A Reference Guide 1866–1928* (London: UCL Press, 1999); 'The discussion circle', *The Freewoman*, 2 May 1912, p. 464.
29. Garner, *A Brave and Beautiful Spirit,* pp. 73–4.
30. Quoted in Jane Lidderdale and Mary Nicholson, *Dear Miss Weaver: Harriet Shaw Weaver 1876–1961* (London: Faber & Faber, 1970), p. 49, and Garner, *A Brave and Beautiful Spirit*, p. 75.
31. Françoise Delisle, *Françoise: In Love with Love* (London: Delisle, 1962), pp. 201–2.
32. 'A new subscriber', 'The immorality of the marriage contract', *The Freewoman*, 4 July 1912, pp. 135–6.
33. F.D. [sic] Stella Browne, 'Divorce and the marriage contract', *The Freewoman*, 25 July 1912, p. 197.
34. 'A new subscriber', 'The immorality of the marriage contract'.
35. 'A new subscriber', 'A nom de plume', *The Freewoman*, 11 July 1912, p. 158.
36. Stella Browne to Grace Jardine, 20 and 25 July 1912, 2 August 1912, *Freewoman* files, Dora Marsden Papers, Manuscripts Division, Department of Rare Books and Special Collections, Princeton University Library [DM], CO283 2/27.
37. F.W. Stella Browne, 'Concerning the Yoshiwara', *The Freewoman*, 18 July 1912, p. 176.
38. Browne, 'Divorce and the marriage contract'.
39. Sheila Jeffreys, *The Spinster and Her Enemies: Feminism and Sexuality 1880–1930* (London: Pandora Press, 1985), p. 159.
40. Sheila Rowbotham, *A New World for Women: Stella Browne, Socialist Feminist* (London: Pluto Press, 1977), p.19; Jane Lewis, *Women in England 1870–1950* (Brighton: Wheatsheaf Books, 1984), p. 105; Greta Jones, 'Women and eugenics in Britain: the case of Mary Scharlieb, Elizabeth Sloan Chesser, and Stella Browne', *Annals of Science*, vol. 52, 1995, pp. 481–502.
41. F.W. Stella Browne, 'A few straight questions to the Eugenics Society', *The Freewoman*, 1 August 1912, pp. 217–8.
42. F.W. Stella Browne, 'More questions', *The Freewoman*, 15 August 1912, p. 258.
43. F.W.S. Browne, '"The Freewoman" discussion circle', *The Freewoman*, 12 September 1912, p. 327.

44. *The Malthusian*, vol. 36, 15 September 1912.
45. 'Malthusian League South London Campaign', *The Malthusian*, vol. 38, 15 March 1914, p. 22.
46. West, '*The Freewoman*'.
47. Garner, '*A Brave and Beautiful Spirit*', p. 86.
48. '"The Freewoman" discussion circle', *The Freewoman*, 26 September 1912, p. 371.
49. Rebecca West to Dora Marsden [winter, 1912/13], DM, CO283, Box 1/26.
50. Garner, '*A Brave and Beautiful Spirit*', pp. 90–1.
51. Lidderdale and Nicholson, *Dear Miss Weaver*, p. 56.
52. Postcard from Rebecca West to Dora Marsden, 21 February 1913, DM, CO283, Box 1/26.
53. West, '*The Freewoman*'.
54. Lidderdale and Nicholson, *Dear Miss Weaver*, pp. 56–9.
55. 'New Freewoman/Egoist Notebook', *New Freewoman/Egoist* papers, Harriet Shaw Weaver papers, British Library Additional Manuscripts 57357.
56. Lidderdale and Nicholson, *Dear Miss Weaver*, pp. 60–1.
57. G.C. Beresford to Rona Robinson, 1 June 1912 (2 letters), DM, CO 283, Box 2/26.
58. G.C. Beresford to Dora Marsden, 2 November 1912; to Grace Jardine, 13 December 1912, DM, CO 283, Box 2/26.
59. 'New Freewoman/Egoist Notebook', BL Add Ms 57357.
60. Minute book of the New Freewoman Ltd, 10 July 1913, BL Add Ms 57358.
61. Martin Seymour-Smith, *Rudyard Kipling* (London: Macdonald Queen Anne Press, 1989), pp. 32–3, 38.
62. Obituary, *The Kipling Journal*, vol. 45, March 1938, pp. 27–8.
63. 'History of Services, Bombay', India Office Records, 1889, 1893, British Library India Office and Oriental Collections, V/12/292, 294. Many thanks to Angeli Vaid for looking this up for me.
64. Obituary, *The Kipling Journal*.
65. Letter from Kipling to Dunsterville cited in Lord Birkenhead, *Rudyard Kipling* (London: Weidenfeld & Nicholson Ltd, 1978), p. 195.
66. Theosophical Society Membership Register: he became a member of the Society on 6 March 1890, but 'lapsed' at some later date not given. Many thanks to the Theosophical Society for giving me access to their records.
67. Last Will and Testament of George Charles Beresford, 1917, with codicils of 1924 and 1935, does not specify their paternity: the surviving grandson, Nick Wilson, gave some papers of Beresford's to Sussex University.
68. Browne to Ellis, 25 December 1922, BL Add Ms 70539.
69. I am indebted to Andrew Lycett for putting me in touch with Nick Wilson, Beresford's grandson, who supplied this information.
70. *The English Review*, vol. 13, 1912, p. 157.

71. Browne to Ellis, 9 February 1914, BL Add Ms 70539.
72. *The English Review*, vol. 14, 1913, p. 502–3.
73. *The English Review*, vol. 14, 1913, p. 665.
74. *The English Review*, vol. 16, 1914, p. 297.
75. *The New Statesman*, 20 December 1913, pp. 348–9.
76. Browne to Ellis, 9 February 1914, BL Add Ms 70539.
77. West to Marsden, 25 September 1913, DM, CO 283, Box 1/26.
78. Carl Rollyson, *Rebecca West: A Saga of the Century* (London: Hodder & Stoughton, 1995), pp. 26–31.
79. Browne to Ellis, 9 February 1914, BL Add Ms 70539.
80. Browne to Ellis, 19 February 1914, BL Add Ms 70539.
81. Browne to Ellis, 19 February 1914, BL Add Ms 70539.
82. *The Malthusian*, vol. 38, 15 March 1914, p. 22.
83. F.W.S. Browne, 'Review. *Sexual Ethics: a Study of Borderland Questions*. By Robert Michels', *The Malthusian*, vol. 38, 15 May 1914, pp. 37–8.
84. F.W.S. Browne, 'Review. *The Progress of Eugenics*. By C.W. Saleeby, MD', *The Malthusian*, vol. 38, 15 July 1914, p. 51.
85. F.W.S. Browne, 'Reviews. *Psychology and Social Sanity*. By Prof. Hugo Münsterberg ... *Sex*. By Prof. Patrick Geddes and Prof. J. Arthur Thomson', *The Malthusian*, vol. 38, 15 August 1914, p. 63.
86. F.W.S. Browne, 'Review. *The Renaissance of Motherhood*. By Ellen Key. Translated from the Swedish by Anna E.B. Freis', *The Malthusian*, vol. 38, 15 September 1914, pp. 70–1.
87. Patrick Curry, *A Confusion of Prophets: Victorian and Edwardian Astrology* (London: Collins & Brown, A Juliet Gardiner Book, 1992), pp. 122–59.
88. F.W. Stella Browne, 'Letter to the editor. Personal appearance: The quincunx aspect', *Modern Astrology*, vol. 25, March 1914, p. 144.
89. Lesley A. Hall, '"Disinterested enthusiasm for sexual misconduct": the British Society for the Study of Sex Psychology, 1913–1947', *Journal of Contemporary History*, vol. 30, 1995, pp. 665–86.
90. Early diaries of Margaret Sanger, Volume 1, Sanger papers, Library of Congress, Washington, DC; Margaret Sanger, *An Autobiography* (London: Victor Gollancz Ltd, 1939), pp. 126–7.
91. Margaret Sanger, *My Fight for Birth Control* (London: Faber & Faber Ltd, 1932), p. 98.
92. Phyllis Grosskurth, *Havelock Ellis: A Biography* (London: Allen Lane, 1980), pp. 242–58.
93. Browne to Ellis, 28 December 1914, BL Add Ms 70539.
94. A locked chest of personal papers was destroyed after his death by his sisters at his request: Grosskurth, *Havelock Ellis*, pp. 446–7.
95. Grosskurth, *Havelock Ellis*, p. 446.

3

Friends, War, Pacifism and Revolution

At first, Stella appears almost to have ignored the European war in progress and to have continued to focus her energies on the causes in which she was already active, although the departure of men for the front may have opened up certain employment opportunities to her.

A significant figure in her life at this time (who perhaps influenced her eventual greater engagement with the war situation) was Bertram Lloyd, although the exact details of their relationship remain a little hazy. Lloyd, although he earned his living toiling in the family insurance business, was 'much involved with various social reform movements',[1] including socialism, feminism, pacifism and the humanitarian movement, a phenomenon which united concern about cruelty towards humans (capital and corporal punishment, sweated trades, and so on) rather than as well as, towards animals.[2] He was a friend of Edward Carpenter, that pivotal figure in this particular configuration of reforming interests, pioneer advocate for homosexuals' right to live and love free from stigma, and a founder of the British Society for the Study of Sex Psychology (BSSSP), which may give some clue to his sexual orientation (and he did contribute an article on inversion to *The Freewoman*). He and Stella were close during and just after the war years, working together in several organisations and on a number of projects. It is tempting to wonder whether she was thinking of him when she wrote to Ellis that it was

> extraordinarily difficult to make one of the mental comrade friendships which are so delightful between modern men and women (& no doubt largely *subconsciously* sexual) into a big love affair, because the very nervous sensitiveness & sympathy

> which make such a man an understanding friend, tend to deprive him – unless in cases of exceptional all round vitality – of the aggressive warm lifequickening ardor and dash and aggressiveness that are so intoxicating in a lover.

A passionate love affair of 1915 from which she was 'completely cured' involved 'a delightful person aesthetically and mentally, but physically quite undersexed, nervous & hypochondriacal'. Possibly Lloyd? Carpenter, however, called Lloyd 'Wolf', which suggests other dimensions to his personality.[3]

Early in the New Year of 1915, she made another friendship, which was to prove life-long, when she met the youthful Ashton Burall at Lloyd's Hampstead flat, following a meeting of the British Society for the Study of Sex Psychology. She 'outraged' the idealistic young Burall by 'chafing my beloved Lloyd about his having to go home before the BSSSP meeting in order to change into sandals' (the hallmark of the Carpenterian simple-lifer). Burall described her as a 'youngish ['about 35'], plump, high-spirited woman with ginger hair', who was 'very much under the thumb of her parents, but inclined to break loose' (although she was living with her mother and sister, there is little sense from other sources that Stella was under anyone's thumb). According to him, she was working in the editorial office of *The Lancet* (one of the leading medical journals of the day). In spite of this somewhat adverse initial impression, Burall saw a good deal of her in the year and a half before he was imprisoned for resisting conscription, and they became close and long-enduring friends.[4]

If Stella was working at *The Lancet*, this makes her activities of the next year or so even more impressive. She was publishing signed reviews in *The Malthusian* and the *International Journal of Ethics*; bombarding a range of periodicals with letters to generate support for Sanger and on a range of other issues including war babies, women in industry, and the continuing antics of the Eugenics Education Society; contributing 'short and popular' articles on venereal diseases to the 'funny little half-American' magazine *Beauty and Health*;[5] and also managing to write the first version of the important statement of her position, 'The Sexual Variety and Variability of Women and their bearing on social reconstruction', for presentation as a talk to the BSSSP in the autumn.[6] All the while, she was 'much worried and jagged by her uncongenial family' (Ellis considered it 'a pity she cannot afford to go away and be independent'),[7] and found herself 'tied up [in] domesticity'[8] with her 'tiresome' sister,[9] as well as the problems of her mother's 'long and trying illness'.[10] She was also giving 'as many afternoons a week... as I can' to working for the Divorce Law Reform Union.[11]

Early in 1915, she made what was probably her first published statement on the desirability of abortion law reform, in a long letter to *The Malthusian*, provoked by a paper on 'Criminal Abortion and Abortifacients' presented to the Society of Medical Officers of Health – whom she considered to be living in an 'androcentric world'. While arguing for the wider dissemination of contraceptive information and reform of the 'Bastardy' laws, Stella also 'venture[d] to plead for the abolition of the present savage penalties on the performance of "illegal operations"'. Existing contraceptive methods were unreliable; the laws were a 'forcing house of blackmail'; the prejudice against abortion was based on religious and superstitious, rather than medical, grounds; and 'we cannot recognise as final, any laws on these subjects, so long as women have not full opportunities of expressing their wishes'. She argued that those who studied '*women as they are*, – as distinct from the "Woman" of traditional masculine sentiment' knew that 'a large number of women are not specially and preeminently maternal', and when 'not terrorised into subjection by ignorance, they refuse to undertake a responsibility for which they are naturally unfit'. To conclude, she suggested that 'A really adequate civilised morality will support their decision, while it honours and protects maternity'.[12]

She had alluded to women desperate to terminate pregnancy in 1912, but as an argument for wider knowledge of birth control.[13] Why had she moved on to outright advocacy of the right to abortion? In her written evidence to the Birkett Committee in 1937, one anonymised example is almost certainly her own case.[14] She mentioned three early abortions. By 1915, it seems likely that she had personal experience of the unreliability of contraceptives, and of the relative safety of properly conducted abortion, as a basis from which to advance this radical recommendation. By late 1916, she was assuring Adelyne More, the pseudonym under which C.K. Ogden wrote *Fecundity versus Civilisation*, that 'There is no *real* medical reason against them, if performed with decent care, & *sufficiently early*'.[15]

In spite of her swingeing vigour in advancing radically subversive viewpoints, she was finding life rather full of petty irritations and was '"fed up" with domesticity and disappointments'.[16] She had first-hand knowledge of '[T]he waste of women's time, energy and very life entailed by present domestic construction': in a 'very varied circle of acquaintances', she had never, 'even in the most finely-equipped and organised household ... found a convenient and well-planned kitchen sink; while as for shelf and cupboard room –'.[17] The 'unspeakable 53 stairs' to the flat in King's Mansions, and its uncertain warm water supply,[18] doubtless lay behind her invocation of the 'heart-breaking, back-breaking stairs that women climb with water and coals, and climb again and again.'[19] She was thwarted about a rendezvous in person with Ellis: 'it would have been so nice to have discussed all sorts of things & walked on the cliffs at Seaford with you'. She considered that she 'must get away for a bit: haven't been out of town since 1912 except for a weekend':[20] However, they did manage to meet for tea shortly after this.[21]

A comment in a letter to Margaret Sanger as to whether 'Paris is still the utterly abnormal place it was of late'[22] might conceivably indicate that she had actually travelled there: but more likely she had had reports of its condition. Although she may not have managed to get out of London for an extended period, Stella did enjoy 'tremendously' a pleasant walk recommended to her by Ellis in the Chilterns, from Beaconsfield to Gerrards Cross through woods and fields: 'the air was so good, & the sun not too oppressively hot' and 'the white fruit trees ... & the young larches and beeches at their loveliest, like green froth, translucent to the sun': 'a delightful afternoon' from which she gained benefit.[23]

The war gradually impinged more noticeably on Stella's life. Initially she dissented from 'the ultra-Pacifist point of view'. Had Bertrand Russell, she wondered, 'ever realised the nature & point of view of the Prussian Leutnant and non-com?' She did not dissociate herself from the 'bitterness here against Germany', commenting that 'the ill-treatment of the war prisoners is such a dastardly breach of their own military code'.[24] Her antipathy seems rather surprising, given her own years in Germany and sympathy for German culture – perhaps the identification of German militarism as 'Prussian' is the clue. Sir Alexander Siemens, 'the old uncle by marriage whom I like & much respect',[25] had been born in Hanover, later annexed by Prussia. She did argue for 'the joint responsibility of the big German industrial and commercial interests for the war',[26] even if she had not come round to the full logic of a socialist and internationalist perspective on the war. She even expressed a moderate degree of patriotism: 'how proud I was of the plucky way our people in London behaved' during a bombing raid: 'we are as a nation *very* easy to fool but *very* hard to terrorise, as apparently Wilhelm & Co haven't learnt yet.'[27] She thus falls into the category Martin Ceadel defined as 'pacificist', believing that war could only be abolished 'by improving the structure either of the international system or of its constituent states', thus war might be needed to protect these reforms until this had been universally achieved.[28]

She did not indulge in the cruder excesses of anti-German feeling, and deplored the fact that 'many people consider it patriotic to depreciate even German science and German music'. Several German achievements still merited her praise: their 'applied science in agriculture and industry ... town planning and municipal government', their theatre ('a serious and competent artistic factor') and 'the far-seeing protection and care for the unmarried mother and her child', unlike the 'stupid, niggardly barbarity of the English "Bastardy" laws'.[29] In particular, she considered worth honouring 'what German science has done for humanity in the biology and psychology of sex', a subject 'avoided ... as a thing unclean' in Britain except by the exceptional figures of Ellis, Carpenter, and Geddes and Thomson. Indeed, 'long before the war provoked a natural revulsion against all things German', there had been a shameful 'mean vulgarity of mind' which 'threw mud at German research about sex' and dismissed Freud's psychoanalysis.[30] (Stella was among the rather select group in Britain who had actually read any Freud at this date.)[31]

On the family front, Stella was having a frustrating time. Although her mother and sister were, by her own admission 'highly intelligent women, *much* more so in many ways than I am', and neither had 'any strong and definite religious belief', they manifested 'an extraordinary point of view' concerning the wartime marriage of one of her Canadian cousins, engaged to a man who had come over to England with the Canadian forces.

> She made up her mind not to wait, and came over 'on her own', was met by him at L[iver]pool ... [M]y people – & of course my aunt – have been 'impayable' about it. 'Why wasn't she met at Liverpool?' 'Why didn't she stay at Liverpool with her relatives?' 'Why wasn't she met in London'? & so on & so forth, & they are 'ashamed of her', forsooth! These conventionalists who have hardly had the courage of one of their negations. It makes me sick.

This led her on to reflect

> How sure and doubly sure it makes me – not that I have ever doubted it! – that I have chosen the better part: at least neither my *man* nor the other jolly men (you will understand the distinction) have been paraded before my relatives to be criticised & jeered at & regarded as in some special sense *their* appurtenance. I really think that to have my relatives fussing round & daring to 'approve' and 'consent' would 'put off' anybody.

Her irritation over this incident may have been exacerbated by her annual bout of hayfever, 'which always leaves me rather pulled down and exhausted'.[32]

She took a fairly cynical view about her relatives in general:

> [S]o many ... if they had been members of the exploited classes wd. certainly have been unemployable, mentally deficient, or in the case of at least one girl – not from any strong passions but sheer vanity & fecklessness – in the very 'lowest depth'. But as it is, they are artificially protected & bolstered up, & may reproduce their type.[33]

As this passage of personal anecdote might indicate, Stella had not abandoned her antagonism to the Eugenics Education Society,[34] expressed in full 'Forward, Charge!' mode in letters to *The New Age* and *The Clarion*.[35]

Several passing comments around this time suggest something about Stella's views concerning the spiritual side of life. She showed considerable respect for spiritual experience and, in particular, an appreciation of the 'gift of mystic ecstasy', although there were a relatively 'small number of people who have its potentiality'.[36] One of the people she thought might have had this capability in suitable circumstances was her mother, Dulcie.[37] While admitting things 'lovely and precious in Christian doctrine', she remarked on 'the inadequacy of the great Galilean mystic's original teaching as a system of social ethics', even when not abused by the incongruous 'mumbling [of] the Sermon on the Mount' by a Church conniving at the white slave traffic.[38] As did many others at the time, she looked towards the East, claiming that 'if Western civilisation is ever to attain any real mastery of life (apart from its material framework), we must learn much experimental psychology from the East'. However, unlike many who became interested in theosophy, she did not take a negative view of sex (indeed, her comment about the 'power of prolonging an emotion' being the secret of 'Eastern pleasure' suggests some familiarity with Indian erotic as well as religious texts), and she saw contraception as not necessarily opposed to, but in harmony with, spiritual ideals which, 'no longer petrified into obsolete institutions', might become more spontaneous in their expression.[39] She did not find a belief in life after death 'incompatible with support of Neo-Malthusian principles': in fact, 'the "selective and limited" birth-rate represents the sifting and ennobling of life in successive incarnations.'[40]

Ronald Hutton has drawn attention to the very pervasive 'struggle to adapt or reject Christianity, by mixing in or substituting concepts associated with ancient paganism' in early twentieth-century Britain and the eclectic roots from which alternatives to conventional Christianity were drawn. Stella Browne certainly seems to fit into this trend. Although there are no indications of formal ties to any specific groups, many individuals were independently devising their own new forms of spirituality. These were not necessarily incompatible with Stella's social and political commitments. Bradford Verter has pointed out that 'Many occult writers... took pains to emphasize the compatibility of rational empiricism and mystical spirituality'.[41] Occultism flourished in bohemian circles where political radicalism and the artistic avant-garde overlapped and cross-fertilised, and 'was not a unified, hermetic enterprise, but an open classification borne on the shifting tides of intellectual currents', with an 'effect of atmospheric presence' rather than direct influence.[42] Since many of the more organised manifestations had a decidedly esoteric slant and elitist attitude,[43] Stella may not have found these congenial.

Margaret Sanger became involved in Rosicrucianism around this time, but there is no record of them discussing it. Neither is there any evidence that they exchanged opinions or beliefs concerning Sanger's attempts to contact her dead daughter Peggy through spiritualist seances.[44] This is a little odd, as Stella had a number of friends upon whose psychic abilities she commented. Margaret Lumley Brown, 'probably the finest medium and psychic of this century' and later an associate of the occultist Dion Fortune in the Society of Inner Light,[45] was a close friend.[46] Another friend whose 'very considerable psychic gift' Stella noted was Havelock Ellis's wife, Edith.[47]

Stella's relationship with Sanger was that of two rebel women and campaigners for contraception, in which she was the ardent supporter of Sanger's brave stand. She shot off letters to bring Sanger's situation to the attention of the British public to various periodicals – *The Clarion*, *The Egoist*[48] – (and alluded to the case in a letter to *The New Age*),[49] although *The New Statesman* refused to publish her letter, 'the shifty skulking cowards':[50] she published her stinging riposte to the editor in *The Malthusian*.[51] And this was only the tip of the iceberg, although 'the capitalist Press in this country has, of course, suppressed all mention of the cases'.[52] She wrote to Ellis that she was finding it '*absolutely impossible* to do practically all the Press *letters* – as distinct from *articles*' and wondered why others who had been interested in Sanger and her work did not take a hand, especially when 'Their well-known names would carry *ten* times the weight of mine, and *they* are *not* in the blackbooks of the Suffragists and Fabians.'[53] She also promoted the petition being got up by Marie Stopes (at that date best known as a pioneering woman scientist) to be sent to President Wilson of the USA asking for a pardon for Sanger, but was 'rather sick' about it. While the nine signatures obtained 'were unexceptionable, splendid every one of them, the number could easily have been *doubled*' and it had surely been 'a great mistake not to ask HE [Havelock Ellis]', and other distinguished sympathisers. Between her domestic responsibilities and the increased postage rates, Stella feared that she herself could not undertake the getting up of a supplementary petition, and anyway, '*her* famous name would have carried such with *such a lot more people*.'[54]

It was not just Sanger's cause to which Stella was devoted. Her feelings for the other woman were profound: it had been 'one of the *biggest* and one of the *dearest* things' in her life to have met and known Sanger, and she refused to believe 'that I shall never see you again'. In her letters, she expressed her anxieties for Sanger's health and passed on the good wishes of mutual acquaintances.[55] At the news of the death of Sanger's young daughter, Stella wrote at once to express her deepest sympathy, and a few days later to pass on that of associates in London.[56]

In spite of her admiration for the 'plucky' behaviour of the populace faced by bombing raids,[57] during 1915 Stella was becoming disillusioned about the war. Her comments on government policy and attitudes in general grew increasingly scathing, as she perceived 'movements towards social justice and freedom ... discouraged by many former supporters on the plea of the urgency of war'.[58] In July 1915, she condemned 'the movement to break the trade unions and exploit docile, unorganised and ignorant women in the name of patriotism'.[59] Her concern over 'the general assault on our liberties, which is being pressed in the name of a War of Liberation', grew.[60]

Her 'Reflections of a (Female) Briton', written just after Christmas 1915, testified to developing rejection of the society at war around her. She alluded to 'the usual bunkum about the birth-rate ... as though human beings entered life fully grown and armed for battle' instead of requiring 'years of care and nourishing food and wholesome exercise of body and mind'. How, she enquired 'does our national expenditure on health and education compare with that very state our militarists now propose to imitate in its most Prussian barbarism, "conception by compulsion" '? When would Professor Strönig's 'great discovery' of 'twilight slumber ... during labour and childbirth[,] be as much at the disposal of British mothers as skilled care and anaesthetics at the service of our wounded soldiers'? If, she argued, 'we are to import German social ethics, let us at least have a little German knowledge and efficiency, as well!': she mentioned recent examples of wasteful military inefficiency. She thought 'regrettable and disastrous ... the attitude of crawling apology for being women, or, in fact, for existing at all, which some women think it patriotic to assume during this war'. On the contrary,

'The apology is owed by that half of humanity which has all the direct political power – such as it is – and most the wealth, for this climax of their management of national and international affairs.' '[U]nwilling pregnancy, an unwanted birth, are crimes as deep as murder, and vastly more complex in their effects', and 'No service [could] be more valuable than the fight against this ... poisoning of lives at their source'.[61]

In May 1916, Lloyd wrote to Carpenter, 'Stella Browne has now chucked "patriotism" and become a believer in freedom and pacifism (she's actually joined the N[o] C[onscription] F[ellowship])'.[62] She informed the publisher Stanley Unwin that she had been 'Anti-Conscripting as much as possible lately.'[63] In 1916, the internationalists within the British Socialist Party overthrew the old pro-War Executive and denounced the war as imperialist and reactionary.[64] However, the introduction of conscription early in 1916[65] was probably the trigger: 'One had to be for it or against it.'[66] Stella was, when it came to the choice, against.

Another contributory factor in moving her from increasing cynicism about the British government to anti-war activism was the brutal suppression of the Dublin Uprising of Easter 1916: 'the atrocities in Dublin! "Defence of Small Nations"!'[67] To Margaret Sanger she wrote:

> Oh how heartrending this Irish affair is; it *may* lead to some very necessary changes. I think all decent people over here are very much upset about it, especially the merciless militaristic executions that followed the suppression of the rising: Connolly, Pearce and Macdonagh were men of the highest integrity and courage and of great gifts and Sheehy Skeffington had persistently opposed *all* force as well. Yet he – and they – are simply shot. I will say all enlightened opinion here in England protested *unanimously*. It is an unspeakable commentary on the 'defence of small nations against wicked Prussia'.

Immediately after this, however, she expressed an apparent sudden switch of emotion in her response to the news of the Battle of Jutland:

> But oh Margaret! the news of the North Sea Battle makes me feel very British again. That cruiser squadron which fought the *whole* German High Sea Fleet for *seven* hours, till Jellicoe's main squadron came along, and the Germans bolted for Kiel!

But then added, returning to her tone of antipathy towards the war, 'but all the men dead and on both sides: and for what? Junker tyranny over there and [Lord] Northcliffe [militaristic press baron] dictatorship here'.[68]

The No-Conscription Fellowship was the largest and most comprehensive of the organisations resisting the war and defending conscientious objection, with strong socialist roots,[69] 'carrying on a challenging campaign for pacifism no less vigorous than its stand for liberty',[70] without any religious basis.[71] It carried on ceaseless propaganda activities through articles, leaflets and pamphlets, and its journal *Tribunal*. It provided information and support to conscientious objectors, arranged visitation of prisoners, harried the government by deputations to ministers, and gained concessions through informal consultations with government departments. There were also large public meetings. All of these involved myriad tasks that sound very much as though they could have deployed Stella's clerical and indexing skills.[72]

It is likely that her contributions included joining the 'corps of volunteer translators' which, under the editorship of Mrs C.R. Buxton, produced the 'Foreign Press Survey' for C.K. Ogden's *Cambridge Magazine*.[73] She was also involved with the rather shadowy League of Peace and Freedom (not the better-known Women's League of Peace and Freedom), a body with a substantial overlap of membership with the Humanitarian League, concerned with the larger philosophical questions raised by pacifism rather than immediate practical activity.[74] Some fifteen years later, Stella commented 'What a mixed bunch we were! and how alone!', and recalled: 'it was unpopular and unprofitable *then*, to "say exactly what every best-seller war book began to say in 1929"!'[75]

Stella's involvement with two bodies taking very different approaches to the problem of war is an illuminating example of her commitment to both activism and to theorising, as seen in her simultaneous membership in campaigning bodies such as the Malthusian League and the Divorce Law Reform Union, and the 'talking shop' of the BSSSP. This union of action and thought was also manifested in, for example, her letters and reviews in *The Malthusian*, which placed the apparently narrowly focused fight for birth control within a much broader context.

Stella was also trying to extend her remunerative undertakings, by looking for work as a publisher's reader (and possibly translator). Grant Richards did not 'think there is at the moment any chance of my requiring any such assistance' but would keep her letter on file.[76] Her approach to Allen & Unwin, however, seems to have been more propitious: she declared that she would 'feel much honoured to work for a house which has shown such breadth of view and independence' (it was one of the few publishing houses prepared to produce pacifist literature). For testimonials, she referred them to Sydney Waterlow of the *International Journal of Ethics* (this was one more point at which she was, indeed, a very few degrees of separation from Virginia Woolf, whom Waterlow had courted prior to her marriage to Leonard Woolf), and to Edward Carpenter.[77] Stanley Unwin gave her an appointment,[78] and took 'the trouble ... to make suggestions and recommendations', resulting in 'some paid work which will very probably lead to more'.[79]

Possibly her friendship with Edward Carpenter[80] gained her this helpful response. How and when she met Carpenter and became friends with him remains unknown, but they were active in several of the same circles and had other mutual acquaintances besides Lloyd. According to his diaries he was in the audience for her paper at the BSSSP, 'Sex variation in women', in October 1915 (published as *The Sexual Variety and Variability of Women* in 1917), and they had occasional meetings over the next few years.[81] The Home Office's 'sudden attack' on Carpenter's homophile essay, *The Intermediate Sex*, in 1916 infuriated her – 'after seven years!', she fulminated, 'Is it feared that it might endanger the innocence and virtue of the British barrack-rooms?' Carpenter forbade her 'Forward! Charge!' response of writing to *The New Age* about the issue, since 'they wanted to find out who instigated it'.[82]

Pacifist commitments and subsistence-earning did not consume all her time. She was still promoting Margaret Sanger's cause.[83] In February 1916, she was elected to the Executive Committee of the BSSSP, and was expanding and revising the paper she had given to the Society for publication as one of their pamphlets.[84] Her active support for the Divorce Law Reform Union continued, although she considered it was 'in a very critical position', like 'various admirable movements', because of the difficulties caused by the war.[85] She solicited signatures for a petition for the reform of the divorce law.[86] She was also involved in a counter-movement against the 'proposed reintroduction of the C. D. [Contagious Diseases] Acts [the cause célèbre of Victorian feminism], under the *name* of "compulsory notification" '.[87]

Although she complained to Sanger in April 1916 of being 'still frightfully seedy and run down' (yet hoping to 'pull up soon'),[88] this does not seem to have much affected her level of activity. She still had some degree of personal life, and expended both time and energy for the benefit of her increasing circle of friends. She tried to help her psychic friend Margaret Lumley Brown get her poems published, recommending that she sent them to Stanley Unwin and writing to him to commend their 'unusual mastery of form ... clear-cut vivid pictorial quality and a good deal of individual feeling'[89] – although it does not appear that Unwin actually published them.[90] Suggesting how Unwin might obtain some of Carpenter's early pamphlets, she extended a simultaneous favour to the Hendersons, the radical booksellers who ran 'The Bomb Shop' in Charing Cross Road, by advising them as a potential source.[91] She was constantly recommending one friend to another, and conveying kind messages between them, while drawing their attention to nice things said about them in print; for example, a mention of Sanger's work in freethinker Joseph MacCabe's *The Tyranny of Shams*.[92] Laurence Housman, the playwright, male feminist and pacifist, came in for a good deal of recommendation to various members of her circle: she sent a pamphlet of his to Unwin,[93] and assured Sanger that they would like one another[94] – after they had met, conveying his regrets at not seeing more of her while in the USA. Another prospective mutual friend of whose impending trip to North America Stella alerted Sanger was the health educator Norah March – 'you'll be glad to see her and she you'.[95] And she was continuing to make new contacts: 'I am hoping shortly to meet Miss Lind-af-Hageby, the great Swedish feminist and humanitarian. She has been in France, doing something to relieve the hideous mass of human and animal suffering': even before their meeting Stella was weaving her into the web, assuring Sanger 'You must meet her someday'.[96]

A recently made but significant relationship, shortly to be terminated by death, was that with Edith Lees Ellis. Although they had both been involved with *The Freewoman* and its Discussion Circle, Stella only 'first met her a few months before her death', it is not clear how:[97] Carpenter may have been the intermediary. The friendship was news to Havelock Ellis, who wrote to Margaret Sanger that 'She [i.e. Edith] and Stella Browne have become great friends, which I am pleased at.'[98]

In spite of Edith's enfeebled state of health, and 'all the untoward circumstances under which we met' (either the war, or the contemporaneous upheaval in the Ellises' marriage), she 'was one of the most remarkable people I have ever met'. What Stella described as Edith Ellis's good qualities is revelatory about her own values. She praised her 'three great gifts' of '[c]ourage, moral and physical, honesty and impulsive generosity', noting that the first, had 'owing to the peculiarities of a sensitive nervous heredity ... only been achieved heroically.' Although lacking the 'exceptional energy and power of hard work' which had characterised her prime, nonetheless, Stella summed her up sympathetically:

> She was, at one and the same time, intensely emotional and intensely practical. She had a feminine sense of 'atmosphere'; if it were congenial, interested and appreciative she expanded with the delightful naivete of a child: if it were hostile she faced

> it with reckless daring and aggressiveness which invited further attack. She would take infinite trouble over 'little' things: a meal or a gift to a friend, an original piece of design or color in bowl or chair or curtain; she understood and loved animals and could make plants grow where other people gathered only stones. She had a very considerable psychic gift, though that in her latter years became blurred and disintegrated. And she never feared physical hardship, effort or danger.

The picture is not an anodyne obituary, however:

> she was very full-blooded, she loved and hated without squeamishness or fear; she could be impulsively cruel as well as lavish with tenderness, sympathy and help. She 'warmed both hands before the fire of life', as in more primitive incarnations she might have called on the flames to avenge or punish, or faced them unflinchingly for a belief or a beloved.[99]

Given the rather negative picture of Edith Ellis in her final months which emerges from biographies of Havelock Ellis and his associates, this is a reminder that even in her desperate straits she was able to charm, captivate, and impress.

But Edith, nevertheless, created problems for those who cared about her. In September 1916, Stella dashed off an anxious letter to Edward Carpenter, having found her 'gasping and helpless with a very severe heart attack'. Her affairs were 'hopelessly involved' and she was 'almost destitute of ready cash'. With Edith's companion and friend, Miss Sylvia Bowen, Stella determined that Edith's friends 'should be informed of her state of health.' Unfortunately, things were at a state of critical impasse between Edith and Havelock Ellis: she had demanded a judicial separation, although this did little but reflect the always semi-detached nature of their union. As Stella herself and Miss Bowen were '*hardly* able to meet our own most necessary expenses', this was clearly an appeal to Carpenter to assist financially.[100] He did, indeed, furnish 'help which proved to be very welcome'.[101] Stella continued to keep Carpenter informed of the situation up to Edith's death.[102]

Stella's warm appreciation of Edith Ellis is more remarkable given Edith's resentment of Havelock Ellis's involvement with Margaret Sanger, while Sanger considered Edith 'jealous and demanding'.[103] But Stella seems successfully to have compartmentalised the two friendships. In the case of Sanger, it is possible to wonder if it was rather more than that. Her letters to Sanger are full of endearments and expressions of passionate devotion: 'It has been one of the *biggest* and one of the *dearest* things in my life to have met and known you';[104] 'It has been a great source of joy and strength to me my dear to think of our friendship and of your splendid stand in all these weary months.'[105] She addressed her as 'Margaret dearest' and signed off 'your loving Stella', which does not sound like merely comradeship, and the letters are full of phrases such as 'I simply won't believe that I shall never see you again';[106] 'I am charmed with the photo, and would much rather have that than any other present';[107] 'your dear photograph... cheers me when I am downhearted';[108] 'How I wish I could have a real long talk with you.'[109]

Sheila Jeffreys and other historians have claimed that women's emotional relationships in the early twentieth century became adversely affected by fears of being identified as lesbian, as a result of the spread of sexology. Margaret Sanger and Stella Browne, as close friends of Havelock Ellis – and, in Stella's case, also of Edward Carpenter and Edith, herself a lesbian – were more likely than most women of their day to have been aware of lesbianism and what sexologists were saying about it. Stella's letters to Sanger severely undercut Jeffreys' contention that she 'exhibited great anxiety about lesbianism' and was 'forced to redefine or reject' passionate friendships with women. Far from repudiating strong feelings towards other women,[110] quite the reverse, she clearly had no qualms about expressing her emotional feelings towards Sanger, or quite offhand referring appreciatively to Rebecca West's attractions in the letter describing her to Ellis.[111]

Around this time Stella was continuing her 'intermittent and occasional' relationship with her (erstwhile) 'demi-semi' (but by this date fully penetrative) lover, and 'passionately in love' with another man as well. There were also one or two 'very slight occasional & mainly physical episodes' with other men (unidentified).[112] It is arguable that she defined herself, at this point in her life, as heterosexual (if polyandrous), with some 'episodical homosexuality'.[113] Reviewing the revised edition of Ellis's *Sexual Inversion*, she took issue with his statement that 'in bisexual persons, the inverted impulse predominates over the heterosexual' in spite of 'observed instances to the contrary'.[114]

She also saw no harm in 'a certain amount of self-excitement, and solitary enjoyment' ('inevitable in any strongly developed sexual life').[115] It was almost certainly she who at a meeting of the BSSSP caused 'a virtuous lady [to] nearly give up the ghost – and leave the meeting before its close – because one of our members defended female masturbation, and, I think, also abortion',[116] probably during the discussion of N. Teulon Porter's 'Masturbation: A Theory', presented on 24 October.[117]

In the midst of all this hectic activity, Stella found time and energy to produce a number of more extended articles on subjects of interest to her. Some of these were written for

> two funny little half American papers, on the care of the health & allied matters. When one has recovered from their (unnecessary) advertisements & general get up, one finds quite a lot of sense buried in them. At least they do print my stuff & so far without excisions.[118]

One was the British edition of Bernarr McFadden's *Beauty and Health* and the other has not been identified.

Her July 1916 article in *Beauty and Health*, on 'The Venereal Diseases Peril in Daily Life', was one of many generated by the Report of the Royal Commission on Venereal Diseases. It was atypically conventional in stressing the common contemporary theme of innocent, non-sexual transmission, through various common practices which sound generally unhygienic, if unlikely to convey VD. But she concluded with the need for knowledge, legislation and proper treatment facilities.[119]

Beauty and Health published the first of her two articles on 'The Wastage of the Future' in November 1916. Drawing on damning official statistics, Stella suggested that it might be sensible to 'press for the representation of women' when promoting housing reform.

> Every house in our present state of material civilisation ought to have air, light (both natural and artificial), storage for food and fuel, necessary sanitation and a constant supply of hot water.

She alluded to 'cramped, evil-smelling rooms', the 'foul sleeping arrangements', and her comments on the defects of domestic arrangements have already been mentioned. She additionally advocated better facilities for physical recreation, and recommended a few minutes' regular bodily exercise morning and evening as 'the most wonderful tonic', with particular attention to breathing ('most people don't know *how* to breathe'). Another demand was 'far more lavish provision of swimming baths'.[120] In her second article, Stella made a specific case for birth control, in the context of 'a new civilisation', in which woman had

> [t]he vote, the freedom to exercise her faculties, the right to earn, the right to civic responsibility and authority ... the right to choose or to refuse motherhood freely; and the right to choose freely the father or fathers of her children.[121]

In January 1917, the same journal published her reports of the arrest of Sanger, her sister and an assistant at the Brownsville Birth Control Clinic in Brooklyn,[122] apparently her final appearance in this particular forum. A few months later, she was undergoing 'anxieties of the *most wearing* description', about, among other things, employment;[123] possibly commissions from *Beauty and Health* drying up was one factor.

During this period, Stella also produced four substantial articles laying out the thinking on sexual and social issues which underlay her involvement in such a wide range of activist campaigns. These were the pamphlet version of the talk she had given to the BSSSP, *The Sexual Variety and Variability of Women and their bearing on social reconstruction*;[124] 'Some Problems of Sex', in the *International Journal of Ethics*;[125] 'Woman and the Race' in *The Socialist Review*;[126] and 'Women and Birth-Control', in *Population and Birth-Control: A Symposium*, edited by Stella's fellow socialists, Eden and Cedar Paul.[127] They all emphasised the very incomplete nature of knowledge on these topics: 'We do not yet *know* much about the relative sex natures of men and women'[128]

All were powerfully informed by her feminism, and her belief that major social and political changes were necessary. All advanced her conviction that the conventional view of female sexuality was simplistic and wrong, based on the 'division of women into two arbitrary classes, corresponding to no psychological or ethical individual differences: (a) The prospective or actual private sex property of one man. (b) The public sex property of all and sundry.'[129] Her denial of a universal maternal instinct, and advocacy of female reproductive choice (for motherhood as well as against it – in particular, in circumstances in which contemporary society tabooed or stigmatised childbearing) were persistent themes. Women, she contended, were far more various and complex than the convenient assumptions of a patriarchal society and 'sexual institutions founded on the needs and preferences of a primitive type of man',[130] were prepared to allow: 'Prostitution and polygamy have never been the expression of *women's* needs any more than enforced celibacy and cast iron monogamy'.[131] She conceded biological and physical differences between women:

> There are women who are natural nuns – a small percentage, perhaps. There is the predominantly maternal type. There are women to whom a man, or more than one man, mean more than any child.[132]

The main tenor of her argument was that social and economic conditions had adversely influenced the development of women's sexuality: a belief in the forces of social construction which she also applied to men, pointing out that men had 'an inherited tradition – irrespective of individual disposition – of emphatic sexual swagger'.[133] She emphasised the extent to which 'Most people are apt to under-rate the real strength of desire, and at the same time, to exaggerate its indiscriminate facility'[134] – for her, discrimination, selection and individual choice were the concomitants of the free love agenda of variety and experiment that she proposed.

There were other recurrent themes. There was the regret at the 'ascetic superstitions' lingering among 'most of the official spokeswomen of the suffrage movement'.[135] Sexual anaesthesia in women was, she suggested, not merely due to repression and inculcated ignorance, but to 'lack of skill, control and sympathy on the husband's part',[136] given the 'masculine mythology suppressing and distorting all the facts of women's sexual and maternal emotions',[137] 'the outrage on decency and freedom alike involved in the ideas of "conjugal rights"', and 'the mechanical facility of the sexual process in men' fostered by prostitution.[138] Existing laws on divorce, marriage, and illegitimacy were attacked, and active participation in campaigns to reform them solicited.

These articles laid down beliefs from which Stella never diverged, even if the specificities of her campaigns changed over time as the laws themselves (gradually) changed. She looked forward to 'the finer social order' when 'revolutionary changes in all departments' would lead to 'the development of hitherto isolated human harmonies, of intense and vivid variations of faculty and type'.[139]

For her, as for so many contemporaries, this finer state of society seemed to have been heralded by the red dawn in the East: 'the glorious news from Russia is heartening' – although she also 'fear[ed] counter-revolution'.[140] There is regrettably no way of ascertaining whether she was at the Albert Hall on 31 March to 'congratulate the Russian People on the Revolution'.[141] However, the immediate impact on Stella's life appears to have been remote, although she kept up with the news, mourning 'the hideous ironies of war' whereby the first ship of returning Russian exiles was sunk by a U-boat with the loss of many lives.[142]

Although 'having a very thin time – home worries, etc' as well as anxieties over friends and employment, she persevered with her causes. She was still reviewing for and writing letters to *The Malthusian*: when H.G. Wells attacked the Drysdales, she was 'disgust[ed] at [his] arrogant rudeness'.[143] She continued to review in the *International Journal of Ethics*,[144] and managed to give notices to volumes by various friends and acquaintances, including Ellis, Carpenter, Norah March, and E.S.P. ('Ted') Haynes.

Haynes was a fixture in progressive circles, a solicitor who, besides undertaking legal work for members of the progressive vanguard, was also dedicated to reforming the laws on censorship, divorce and other matters of morality. According to Ellis, he was a relation of Stella's,[145] although she never wrote of him as more a 'very old friend...I know his family since my schooldays'.[146] She also never wrote of him in the tone taken by several female contemporaries, who found him something of a pest.[147] Stella tended to refer to 'the Hayneses', incorporating mentions of Ted's wife Ria.[148]

Besides reviewing serious tomes on aspects of social reform, Stella also found time to join 'literary epicures' in relishing the 'rarer and more pungent flavours' of the 'sympathetic and discriminative presentation of animal individualities' in Colette's *La Paix chez les Bêtes*. In spite of her 'innate repugnance', she found Colette's 'vivid phrases' about 'the great bird-catching spider of tropical America' rendered it 'less terribly and incomprehensibly remote'. Commenting that 'persons with *any* feeling for animals... may be divided into two classes, dog-lovers and cat-lovers', Stella appears to have fallen into the latter category – 'that most royal and beautiful race, in whom grace, mystery, savagery and subtle imperious pleasure seem incarnated, and to whom their devotees must give understanding and deference'.[149]

In September of the same year, Ellis reported to Sanger that Stella was 'more cheerful and contented just now as she has some work to do',[150] perhaps the 'little private teaching... only a temporary job' she had already mentioned to Sanger.[151] Or Ellis may have been alluding to the enterprise he described more fully some weeks later: 'Stella B. has gone (on trial) to conduct a co-educational school in Essex... I expect she has her hands full'.[152]

Stella was certainly still in London during September 1917, 'very indignant' at the attack made on Bertrand Russell during the riot at the pacifist meeting at Southgate Brotherhood Church.[153] She sent him some 'notes of evidence' through their mutual acquaintance, Philip Jourdain of the *International Journal of Ethics*.[154] Russell had quite by chance been reading one of her articles, which he thought 'excellent', but found at least one of her statements inaccurate.[155] She delivered a further note to Russell personally by hand ('as all your correspondence is opened in the post'), expressing her admiration for his stand on the war (a change from her earlier opinions), and his writings on political and social questions – although she regretted that 'your great mathematical work I am... unable to understand'. She enclosed a copy of *Sexual Variety and Variability*, as she understood that he had 'an aversion to cant, humbug, & cruelty in all departments of life'.[156]

Russell wrote her a 'kind & interesting note' in reply, indicating that he was, on the whole, in agreement with her views. In response, she remarked:

> Certainly a great deal of the newer manifestations of sexual liberty are very far from encouraging or attractive, but I think this is partly due to the hateful war atmosphere & conditions, & to other quite adventitious things – e.g. the ignorance & dependence of many women – which have no necessary connection with sexual liberty in itself. One cannot expect people to develop *real* responsibility, or refinement & discrimination of feeling, in one generation, especially with prostitution so firmly rooted in our social order, as it is & has been.

She conceded that she did not '*know* positively' that his mail was being opened 'but after what has happened to Mr. E. D. Morel (& also the general treatment of Pacifists, & you personally) – I shd. be *much surprised* if it were not!'[157]

By late October, she was based at 'Federation House' in Epping Forest, Essex. This was a joint undertaking with a number of other socialists, including Eden and Cedar Paul, a married couple (he a doctor, she a singer) who had translated and edited numerous works on sexology and birth control, and Nurse Maud Hebbes, who had worked with Sylvia Pankhurst in the East End, and subsequently at Marie Stopes's Holloway clinic providing birth control to poor mothers. Muriel Matters, the leading English exponent of Italian educational theorist Marie Montessori's theories was on the committee and training two further teachers in the Montessori methods. The aim of the enterprise was to

> combine a healthy & beautiful Home free from petty patronage & institutionalism, with a School on the most modern lines, for destitute & deserted children. We want to give them an education combining development of individual faculty and initiative, with mutual help and co-operation.

Unsurprisingly, the institution was to be 'vegetarian, non-sectarian, & co-educational'.[158] A few months previously she had described Cedar Paul to Sanger as 'an interesting personality rather – hard, but capable and independent, & a very keen worker',[159] but otherwise her personal views on her comrades in this enterprise are not known.

Federation House was 'ideally situated' for the purposes intended – readily accessible from London in the 'pretty scenery & wholesome air of

Epping Forest'. The beautiful and spacious garden had fallen into disrepair through neglect, and the orchard included 'specimens of every British fruit tree'. 'With proper care, & large outlay' the property could keep them supplied with fruit and vegetables. Once in full working order, they could take up to forty children. Stella was listed as 'Superintendent' as well as a Committee member.[160] Ellis did not view the project – or, at least, Stella's involvement in it – with much optimism: 'I cannot say that I think she has quite the right kind of nervous system for that particular sort of work, and I fully expect soon to hear that she has got into hot water with somebody or other'.[161] He complained of 'No news for ever so long from Stella Browne who is doubtless finding her hands more than full with the co-education school',[162] and reassured Sanger that Stella would 'probably be too busy to write at present, not a word from her yet.'[163]

Notes

1. Ashton Burall, 'Obituary: Stella Browne (1880–1955)', *Plan*, 25/7, July 1955, p. 81.
2. Dan Weinbren, '"Against all cruelty". The Humanitarian League 1891–1919', *History Workshop Journal*, vol. 38, 1994, pp. 86–105.
3. Stella Browne to Havelock Ellis, 25 December 1922, Ellis papers in the Department of Manuscripts, British Library, Additional Manuscript 70539 (BL Add Ms 70539); Sheila Rowbotham, *Edward Carpenter: A Life of Liberty and Love* (London: Verso, 2008), pp. 332–3.
4. Burall, 'Obituary'.
5. Stella Browne to Philip Jourdain, 24 October 1915, *Cambridge Magazine* correspondence, C.K. Ogden papers: Archives and Research Collections, McMaster University, Hamilton, Ontario [CKO].
6. Minutes of the 3rd Quarterly Meeting of the BSSSP, 14 October 1915, 'BSS Misc', British Sexology Society Archives in the Harry Ransom Research Center, University of Texas at Austin [HRC].
7. Havelock Ellis to Margaret Sanger, 6 September 1916, Sanger papers in Library of Congress, Washington, DC [LC], Volume 3.
8. Stella Browne to Margaret Sanger, 12 November 1915, LC, Volume 10.
9. Browne to Sanger, 7 September 1915, Sanger papers in the Sophia Smith collection, Smith College [SSC].
10. Browne to Sanger, 5 December 1915, LC.
11. Browne to Sanger, 7 September 1915, SSC.
12. F.W. S. Browne, '"Baby-killers," and others', *The Malthusian*, vol. 39, March 1915, pp. 21–2.
13. *The Malthusian*, vol. 36, 15 September 1912.

14. Interdepartmental Committee on Abortion A.C. Paper 16, Memorandum ... from Miss F.W. Stella Browne, The National Archives, MH71/21.
15. F.W. Stella Browne to 'Miss Adelyne More', 15 October 1916, CKO.
16. Browne to Ellis 14 April 1915, BL Add Ms 70539.
17. F.W. Stella Browne, 'The wastage of the future', *Beauty and Health*, November 1916, pp. 144–6.
18. Browne to Ellis, 26 April 1936, BL Add Ms 70539.
19. Browne, 'The wastage of the future'.
20. Browne to Ellis 14 April 1915, BL Add Ms 70539.
21. Ellis to Sanger, 28 April 1915, LC, Volume 3.
22. Browne to Sanger, 7 September 1915, SSC.
23. Browne to Ellis, 3 May 1915, BL Add Ms 70539.
24. Browne to Ellis, 3 May 1915, BL Add Ms 70539.
25. Browne to Ellis, 29 August 1915, BL Add Ms 70539.
26. F.W. Stella Browne, 'Short notice of *The Healing of Nations: and the Hidden Sources of their Strife*. By Edward Carpenter', *International Journal of Ethics*, 1915/1916, vol. 26, p. 143.
27. Browne to Sanger, 12 November 1915, LC, Volume 10.
28. Martin Ceadel, *Semi-Detached Idealists: The British Peace Movement and International Relations, 1854–1945* (Oxford: Oxford University Press, 2000), p. 7.
29. F.W. Stella Browne, 'Review of *German Culture: The Contribution of the Germans to Knowledge, Literature, Art and Life*', Edited by Prof. W.P. Paterson, *International Journal of Ethics*, 1915/1916, vol. 26, pp. 133–4.
30. F.W. Stella Browne, 'Review of *Man and Woman: A Study of Human Secondary Sexual Characteristics*. By Havelock Ellis', *The Malthusian*, vol. 39, April 1915, pp. 31–2.
31. Dean Rapp, 'The early discovery of Freud by the British general public', *Social History of Medicine,* vol. 3, 1990, pp. 217–43.
32. Browne to Ellis, 29 August 1915, BL Add Ms 70539.
33. Browne to Ellis, 3 September 1915, BL Add Ms 70539.
34. F.W. Stella Browne, Letter, 'Malthusianism', *The New Age*, 2 September 1915, p. 439.
35. F.W. Stella Browne, Letter, 'Eugenists versus facts', *The Clarion*, 3 September 1915, p. 5.
36. F.W. Stella Browne, 'Review of *An Essay on the Civilisations of India, China and Japan* ... By G. Lowes Dickinson', *International Journal of Ethics*, 1914/1915, vol. 25, pp. 424–6.
37. Browne to Ellis, 29 August 1915, BL Add Ms 70539.
38. F.W. Stella Browne, 'Review of *Impression and Comments*, By Havelock Ellis', *International Journal of Ethics*, 1915/1916, vol. 26, pp. 135–6. She made similar

points in a review of *The Future of Democracy*, by H.M. Hyndman, *International Journal of Ethics*, 1915/1916, vol. 26, pp. 432–4.

39. Browne, 'Review of *An Essay on the Civilisations of India, China and Japan* ...'.
40. F.W. Stella Browne, 'To the editor of *The Malthusian*', *The Malthusian*, vol. 39, April 1915, pp. 29–30.
41. Bradford Verter, 'Dark star rising: the emergence of modern occultism, 1800–1950', Dissertation, Princeton University, 1997 (Dept of Religion), p. 208. I am extremely grateful to Timothy D'Arch Smith for letting me know about this thesis and making a copy available to me.
42. Verter, 'Dark star rising', pp. 216, 334; Gary Lachman, *Politics and the Occult: The Left, the Right, and the Radically Unseen* (London: Quest Books, 2008) makes similar points.
43. For example, the Guild of Woodcraft Chivalry, Ronald Hutton, *The Triumph of the Moon: A History of Modern Pagan Witchcraft* (Oxford: Oxford University Press, 2000), pp. 165–9.
44. Ellen Chesler, *Woman of Valor: Margaret Sanger and the American Birth Control Movement* (New York: Simon & Schuster, 1992), pp. 135–6.
45. Charles Fielding, *The Story of Dion Fortune. As told to Charles Fielding and Carr Collins* (Loughborough: Thoth Publications, 1998), pp. 141–4.
46. Stella Browne to Janet Carson, 11 January 1920, BSS 'Misc', HRC.
47. F.W. Stella Browne, 'Edith Ellis: a memory', in Joseph Ishill (ed.), *Stories and Essays by Mrs Havelock Ellis* (New Jersey: published privately by the Free Spirit Press, 1924), pp. ix–xi.
48. F.W. Stella Browne, Letter 'The case of Mrs Sanger', *The Egoist*, 1 July 1915, p. 115; Letter, 'Malthusianism in the USA', *The Clarion*, 9 July 1915, p. 5; Letter, 'Free speech and the birth rate', *The Clarion*, 15 October 1915, p. 4.
49. F. D. [sic] Stella Browne, letter on Malthusianism, *The New Age*, 23 September 1915, p. 510.
50. Browne to Sanger, 2 December 1915, SSC.
51. F.W. Stella Browne, '[Copy] To the editor of the "New Statesman"', *The Malthusian*, vol. 38, November 1915, p. 92.
52. Browne, 'Free speech and the birth rate'.
53. Browne to Ellis, 13 October 1915, BL Add Ms 60539.
54. Browne to Sanger, 12 November 1915, LC, Volume 10.
55. Browne to Sanger, 7 September 1915, SSC.
56. Browne to Sanger, 2 December 1915, SSC; 5 December 1915, LC, Volume 10.
57. Browne to Sanger, 12 November 1915, LC, Volume 10.
58. F.W. Stella Browne, Letter 'Some things that matter', *The Clarion*, 13 August 1915, p. 5.
59. F.W. Stella Browne, Letter 'Women in industry', *The New Age*, 22 July 1915, p. 293.

60. Browne, 'Review of *The Future of Democracy ...*'. pp. 432–4.
61. F.W. Stella Browne, Letter 'Reflections of a (female) Briton', *The Malthusian*, vol. 40, January 1916, pp. 10–11.
62. E.B. Lloyd to Edward Carpenter, 4 May 1916, Sheffield City Council, Libraries Archives and Information, Carpenter/Mss/368/18.
63. Stella Browne to Stanley Unwin, 13 May 1916, Archives of George Allen & Unwin, Publishing Archive, University of Reading [GAU].
64. James Klugmann, *History of the Communist Party of Great Britain: Volume 1: Formation and Early Years, 1919–1924* (London: Laurence & Wishart, 1969), p. 16.
65. John W. Graham, *Conscription and Conscience: A History 1916–1919* (London: George Allen & Unwin, 1922), pp. 52–62.
66. Constance Malleson, *After Ten Years: A Personal Record* (London: Jonathan Cape, 1931), pp. 98–9.
67. Browne to Unwin, 13 May 1916, GAU.
68. Browne to Sanger, 5 June 1916, LC, Volume 10.
69. Ceadel, *Semi-Detached Idealists*, p. 198.
70. Malleson, *After Ten Years*, p. 100.
71. Graham, *Conscription and Conscience*, pp. 171–3; Paul Laity, *The British Peace Movement 1870–1914* (Oxford University Press, 2001), p. 232.
72. Graham, *Conscription and Conscience*, pp. 185–92; Malleson, *After Ten Years*, p. 101–2.
73. W. Terrence Gordon, *C.K. Ogden: A Bio-Bibliographical Study* (Metuchen, NJ and London: Scarecrow Press, 1990), pp. 16–17.
74. League of Peace and Freedom, *Towards Ultimate Harmony – Report of a Conference on the Pacifist Philosophy of Life,* Caxton Hall, 8–9 July 1915; Ceadel, *Semi-Detached Idealists*, p. 218.
75. F.W.S.B., 'Reviews: An authentic person', *The New Generation*, vol. 10, August 1931, pp. 94–5.
76. Grant Richards to Miss Stella Browne, 14 January 1916, carbon copy in Letterbook Volume 23, 1915–1916, Archives of Grant Richards Ltd in University of Illinois Library, Chicago (Chadwyck Healey *British Publishers' Archives on Microfilm*).
77. Stella Browne to Messrs Allen & Unwin, Publishers, 16th March 1916, GAU.
78. Browne to Unwin, 18 March 1916, GAU.
79. Browne to Unwin, 20 August 1916, GAU.
80. Browne to Messrs Allen & Unwin, 16 March 1916, GAU.
81. Entries for 14 October 1915, 1 August 1916, 2 February 1917, 5 January, 10 April and 22 September 1918, Carpenter/Mss/259, 260, 261, 263.
82. Browne to Ellis, 1 February 1916. BL Add Ms 70539.
83. F.W. Stella Browne, Letter 'The triumph of Margaret Sanger', *The Egoist*, 1 March 1916, p. 47.

84. Minutes of 27th meeting of the Executive Committee, 28 January 1916, 'B.S.S. Misc', HRC; Browne to Ellis, 1 February 1916, BL Add Ms 70539.
85. Browne to Ellis, (n.d. [? 1916]), BL Add Ms 70539.
86. Browne to Unwin, 2 November and 6 November 1916, GAU.
87. Browne to Unwin, 2 November 1916, GAU.
88. Browne to Sanger, 6 April 1916, LC, Volume 17.
89. Browne to Unwin, 20 August 1916, GAU.
90. 'Irene Hay' (Lumley Brown's nom-de-plume), *The Litany of the Sun and other poems* (London: Erskine Macdonald, 1918).
91. Browne to Unwin, 2 October 1916, GAU; Gordon, *C.K. Ogden: A Bio-Bibliographical Study*, p.20.
92. Browne to Sanger, 6 April 1916, LC, Volume 10.
93. Browne to Unwin, 2 October 1916, GAU.
94. Browne to Sanger, 6 April 1916, LC, Volume 10.
95. Browne to Sanger, 5 June 1916, LC, Volume 21.
96. Browne to Sanger, 8 June 1916, SSC.
97. Browne 'Edith Ellis: a memory'.
98. Ellis to Sanger, 31 May 1916, LC, Volume 3.
99. Browne 'Edith Ellis: a memory'.
100. Stella Browne to Edward Carpenter, 7 September 1916, Carpenter/Mss/358/19 (I am much indebted to the Archivist at Sheffield for providing me with a transcript of this letter). For the background to this situation see Phyllis Grosskurth, *Havelock Ellis: A Biography* (London: Allen Lane, 1980), pp. 263–72.
101. Havelock Ellis to Edward Carpenter, 11 September 1916, Carpenter/Mss/357/25.
102. Edward Carpenter to Havelock Ellis 14 September 1916, Carpenter/Ellis correspondence in Harry Ransom Humanities Research Centre, University of Texas at Austin.
103. Grosskurth, *Havelock Ellis*, pp. 247–57.
104. Browne to Sanger, 7 September 1915, SSC.
105. Browne to Sanger, 9 April 1915, SSC.
106. Browne to Sanger, 7 September 1915, SSC.
107. Browne to Sanger, 6 April 1916, LC, Volume 10.
108. Browne to Sanger, 5 June 1916, LC, Volume 21.
109. Browne to Sanger, 9 April 1915, SSC.
110. Sheila Jeffreys, *The Spinster and Her Enemies: Feminism and Sexuality 1880–1930* (London: Pandora Press, 1985), p. 115.
111. Browne to Ellis, (n.d. [? 1916]), BL Add Ms 70539.
112. Browne to Ellis, 25 December 1922, BL Add Ms 70539.
113. F.W. Stella Browne, 'Studies in feminine inversion', *Journal of Sexology and Psychanalysis*, vol. 1, 1923, pp. 51–8.

114. F.W. Stella Browne, 'Review of *Studies in the Psychology of Sex: Volume II, Sexual Inversion*, By Havelock Ellis', 3rd edn, *International Journal of Ethics*, vol. 27, 1916/17, pp. 114–15.
115. Browne, *Sexual Variety and Variability among Women, and Their Bearing upon Social Reconstruction*, British Society for the Study of Sex Psychology Publication no. 3, printed for the Society by C.P. Beaumont and Co., London, 1917, p. 10.
116. Laurence Housman to George Ives, 26 November 1931, George Ives papers in the Harry Ransom Humanities Research Center, University of Texas at Austin.
117. Minutes of 9th Quarterly Meeting, 19 April 1917; 11th Quarterly Meeting, 24 October 1917, 'B.S.S. Misc', HRC; E.B. Lloyd to Edward Carpenter, 1 November 1917, Carpenter/MSS/368/28.
118. Browne to Jourdain, 24 October 1916, CKO.
119. F.W. Stella Browne, 'A warning to women. The venereal diseases peril in daily life', *Beauty and Health*, July 1916, pp. 23–4.
120. F.W. Stella Browne, 'The wastage of the future', *Beauty and Health*, November 1916, pp. 144–6.
121. F.W. Stella Browne, 'The wastage of the future (Part II)', *Beauty and Health*, December 1916, pp. 173–5.
122. F.W. Stella Browne, 'The work of Margaret Sanger. Birth control in America', *Beauty and Health*, January 1917, pp. 25–7.
123. Browne to Sanger, 9 April 1917, SSC.
124. Browne, *Sexual Variety and Variability*.
125. F.W. Stella Browne, 'Some problems of sex', *International Journal of Ethics*, vol. 27, 1916/17, pp. 464–71.
126. F.W. Stella Browne, 'Women and the race', *The Socialist Review: A Quarterly review of Modern Thought edited by J. Bruce Glasier*, vol. 14 no. 81, May–June 1917, pp. 151–7.
127. F.W. Stella Browne, 'Women and birth-control' in Eden and Cedar Paul (eds), *Population and Birth-Control: A Symposium* (New York: Critic and Guide Company, 1917), pp. 247–57.
128. Browne, 'Some problems of sex'.
129. Browne, *Sexual Variety and Variability*, p. 4.
130. Browne, 'Women and birth-control'.
131. Browne, 'Some problems of sex'.
132. Browne. 'Women and the race'.
133. Browne, 'Some problems of sex'.
134. Browne, *Sexual Variety and Variability*, p. 6.
135. Browne. 'Women and the race'.
136. Browne. 'Women and the race'.

137. Browne, 'Women and birth-control'.
138. Browne, *Sexual Variety and Variability*, pp. 8–9.
139. Browne, 'Women and birth-control'.
140. Browne to Sanger, 9 April 1917, SSC.
141. Malleson, *After Ten Years*, p. 112.
142. Browne to Sanger, 28 May 1917, SSC.
143. F.W. Stella Browne, Letter '"Malthusianism versus Socialism"', *The Malthusian*, vol. 41, July 1917, p. 55.
144. *International Journal of Ethics*, vol. 27, 1916–1917, pp. 112–13.
145. Havelock Ellis to Françoise Lafitte-Cyon, 8 January 1919, Howard Gotlieb Archival Research Center, Boston University.
146. Browne to Carson, 14 July 1920, 'BSS Misc', HRC.
147. Elsa Lanchester, *Elsa Lanchester Herself* (New York: St Martin's Press, 1983), p. 67; Victoria Glendinning, *Rebecca West: A Life* (London: Weidenfeld & Nicolson, 1987), p. 61; Douglas Goldring to Jane Burr, 12 July 1949, Jane Burr papers in the Sophia Smith Collection, Smith College, Box 20.
148. Browne to Sanger, 28 May 1917, SSC.
149. F.W. Stella Browne, 'Review of *La Paix chez les Bêtes*, Par Colette', *The Humanitarian*, vol. 1/174, June 1917, pp. 38–9.
150. Ellis to Sanger, 1 September 1917, LC, Volume 3.
151. Browne to Sanger, 28 May 1917, SSC.
152. Ellis to Sanger, 28 October 1917, LC, Volume 3.
153. Philip Jourdain to Bertrand Russell, 4 September 1917, Russell Archives, Mills Memorial Library, McMaster University, Hamilton, Ontario [RA], VI/1 Personal Correspondence.
154. Stella Browne to Bertrand Russell, 9 September 1917, RA.
155. Bertrand Russell to Philip Jourdain, 5 September 1917, RA.
156. Browne to Russell, 9 September 1917, RA.
157. Browne to Russell, 12 September 1917, RA.
158. Browne (on headed notepaper, 'Federation House, George Lane, South Woodford, Essex') to Unwin, 12 November 1917, GAU.
159. Browne to Sanger, 28 May 1917, SSC.
160. Browne to Unwin, 12 November 1917, GAU.
161. Ellis to Sanger, 28 October 1917, LC, Volume 3.
162. Ellis to Sanger, 15 November 1917, LC, Volume 3.
163. Ellis to Sanger, 18 November 1917, LC, Volume 3.

4

Spanish Flu and Red Dawn

Federation House did not last very long – or else Stella, as predicted by Ellis, did not last long in her post there.[1] By January 1918, she was regularly attending committee meetings of the BSSSP, which would have been a substantial commute from Essex,[2] and Lloyd suggested that she should be co-opted onto the Bibliographical Committee, on which she was active for the next several years.[3]

There is also a vivid glimpse of Stella's day-to-day surroundings in Chelsea at this time:

> Certainly, some London streets, though they cannot exorcise the spring, go a long way towards nullifying it. The short stretch of greyish-drab pavement and greyish-drab houses before me, as I leave our block of flats in a day in May, has its monotony relieved by only two glimpses of foliage: in the gardens on the Embankment at one end, and through a gap, by the model dwellings, on the east side. But that flicker of foliage is at its freshest and most translucent...The sky encases the grimy monotony of the buildings like a huge limpid turquoise.

Ginger, 'a living, moving patch of rusty gold', is 'easily the handsomest living creature in L[awrence] Street', and 'Mars was certainly regnant in [his] horoscope'. His eyes are 'exactly the colour of the finest liqueur in the world – a half and half blend of green and yellow Charteuse'. While 'unable, through circumstances over which he had no control, to celebrate spring in the most time-honoured and satisfactory manner', Ginger is a handsome and fearless cat, the terror of local rats. He greets Stella with a wave of his tail, and 'with a deep croaking note, vibrant with joy, runs to me, arches his neck, drives the powerful claws of his forefeet into my old coat, and licks my fingers with a warm, *crisp* tongue'.[4] There is a rich sense of an appreciation of small pleasures in the midst of unpromising surroundings.

In March, the BSSSP committee invited Stella to give a paper on 'Some studies in feminine inversion', when a scheduled speaker dropped out. She agreed, with the proviso that no non-members should be admitted.[5] 'Female inversion' was concurrently a topic of debate and controversy. While Stella's paper preceded the actual libel trial at the Old Bailey in the famous Maud Allan 'Cult of the Clitoris' case, this *cause célèbre* arose from a February 1918 article in Noel Pemberton-Billing's patriotic scandal-sheet *The Vigilante*. This implied not merely that Allan herself (famous – or notorious – for her innovatory dance performances) was a lesbian, but also that her admirers included a coterie of high society women connected with leading politicians, constituting a danger to the safety of the realm and leading to her suing him for libel.[6] It is no wonder that Stella insisted on 'no visitors' when she spoke on a theme associated with hot gossip and titillating speculation.

The published version of her paper made no allusion to this circumstance. Far from dealing with 'vice in high society' scandals or the sexological writings on which Pemberton-Billing's defence drew, the paper, while assuming some familiarity with the concept of 'congenital inversion', emphasised that Stella's 'fragmentary data' on 'a peculiarly obscure subject' was based on 'close and careful observation, conducted, so far as I am consciously aware, without any prejudice'. She had excluded cases told her in confidence, and considered that her data 'would probably be much more illuminating had they been recorded by an observer who was herself entirely or predominantly homosexual.'

The cases she discussed were all well-known to her and 'all innate and very pronounced and deeply rooted – not episodical'. Although in several examples she was convinced that there had been 'no definite and conscious physical expression', they were all 'absolutely distinguishable from affectionate friendship' by an element of 'passion'. Stella, unlike previous writers on the subject such as Carpenter and Ellis, emphasised the femininity of the women she described. While one was an 'invert of the most pronounced physical type' (i.e. androgynous or masculine), her partner was 'strongly contrasted'. Another was of 'the typical Diana build', athletic and with a deep voice (and ability to whistle!), and one was boyish in looks but devoted to children (in a rather soppy way). But others of Stella's subjects were 'not in the least masculine': indeed, 'dainty', 'fond of children', 'entirely feminine'. Stella even drew attention to the 'marked degree' of maternal instinct which existed in some 'congenital inverts', and reported a friend's suggestion that 'in such cases in the future, the resources of developed chemistry and biology will be made use of, in artificial fertilisation'. (Unfortunately, she did not expand upon this suggestion, so it is impossible to know whether she meant some form of parthogenesis, or artificial insemination.)

Stella made a couple of passing allusions which one might well wish she had explored more thoroughly. She had

> omitted from consideration that episodical homosexuality on the part of women who are normally much more attracted to men, of which every experienced observer must know instances.

She also left out 'various instances known to me of passionate but unconscious inversion in girls whose sex-life is just beginning'. These aspects, she conceded would illuminate 'the sexual impulse of women generally'. Regretting that there was nothing in modern English literature 'comparable in authenticity or artistic merit' as a depiction of the 'female homo-sexual or bi-sexual temperament' with the poems of Renée Vivien or the novels of Colette, she found 'a good deal of subtlety' in two English novels on school life: Clemence Dane's *Regiment of Women* ('a brilliant piece of psychology'), and (Australian) Henry Handel Richardson's *The Getting of Wisdom* ('unmistakeably powerful').[7] (She developed these thoughts on literary accounts by women on female inversion into a separate article: Edward Carpenter read the manuscript in the autumn of 1918,[8] but it was not published until 1922 in the German sex reform journal *Die Neue Generation*.)[9]

This paper has been misleadingly characterised as an all-out attack on passionate female friendships, Sheila Jeffreys alleging that 'Browne was ... prescribing that these women should engage in overt sexual expression with other women' as a result of her 'horror of feminists, particularly their lack of enthusiasm for heterosexual sex, and on her fear that lack of genital sex caused women to be hostile to men'.[10] Certainly, Stella stressed 'how decisive for vigor, sanity, and serenity of body and mind, for efficiency, for happiness, for the mastery of life, and the understanding of one's fellow-creatures', physical sexual expression of passionate emotions actually was. The lack of this, '"normal" and "abnormal"' (the quotation-marks delineating her own unease with this conventional dichotomy), was, she considered, 'at the root of most of what is most trivial and unsatisfactory in women's intellectual output, as well as of their besetting vice of cruelty'.[11] Concern over female cruelty also surfaced in *Sexual variety and variability*: the case of a sudden and inexplicable 'lust of cruelty... in a woman of the most actively kind and tender heart, but highly emotional and nervous, and sexually unsatisfied'.[12] (Some personal experience?) Stella certainly argued that unconscious and repressed 'inverted impulse[s]' lay at the root of *some* women's self-righteous 'cheap, malignant cant of conventional moral indignation'.

Social conditions, as always with Stella, lay at the heart of the problem. '[T]he circumstances of women's lives and work' (given the stigmatisation of any heterosexual relationship except marriage) tended to favour 'the frigid, and next to the frigid, the inverted'. The latter, at least, had 'fuller opportunity' to satisfy 'the social and affectional side of [her] nature', while existing social arrangements, 'founded as they are on the repression and degradation of the normal erotic impulse', artificially stimulated inversion in women. There was 'a huge, persistent, indirect pressure on women of strong passions and fine brains to find an emotional outlet with other women'. Given the denigratory state of the laws on marriage and most women's unwillingness to enter prostitution, any woman who wanted to have a sexual life beyond 'auto-erotic manifestations' had to 'struggle against the whole social order ... for her most precious personal right', risking 'the most painful experiences'. Given these conditions, 'some women who *are not innately or predominantly homosexual*' nonetheless formed erotic relationships with other women.

Stella Browne was far from condemning homosexuality: she placed it on an exact plane of equality with the heterosexual impulse: 'it has a fully equal right to existence and expression, it is no worse, no lower; *but no better*'. 'Let us', she exhorted, 'recognise this force, as frankly as we recognise and reverence the love between men and women.' Given that 'every strong passion, every deep affection' had 'endless possibilities, of pain, change, loss, incompatibility, satiety, jealousy, incompleteness', why, she asked 'add wholly extraneous difficulties and burdens?'[13]

The paper was given to a select audience of thirty members, chaired by George Ives and followed by lively discussion.[14] Edward Carpenter, although unable to attend, was sufficiently interested to enquire of Ives, 'How did Stella Browne's paper go?'[15]

Also in March 1918, Stella was concerned about the notorious Regulation under the Defence of the Realm Act, DORA 40D, which made it possible to arrest and incarcerate women who communicated venereal diseases to members of the Services (but did not penalise men). It roused much protest from feminists and, indeed, formed a basis of union between groups working along very different lines.[16] She opened a discussion on the Regulation, and possible action, at the Annual General Meeting of the BSSSP that summer, but without obtaining any immediate response.[17] Her ire was further aroused by statements in the *British Medical Journal* by Dr E.B. Turner of the British Medical Association and the National Council for Combating Venereal Diseases, alleging deterioration in 'practical morality' as a result of 'Malthusian propaganda' and 'public display and advertisement of Malthusian appliances'. Dr Turner also admitted to 'recoil[ing] in horror' at the prospect of 'a general knowledge of Malthusian and anti-venereal prophylaxis among women'. It was not often, Stella commented drily, 'that we find the essential doctrine of women's subjection stated so nakedly and directly', and she declared an interest in having his 'definition of the concepts "chastity" and "morality"'. She wondered if he could be unaware of the 'widespread *morbid* (as distinct from normal) auto-erotism and sex-perversions, of insanity, of nervous breakdowns, and ... an incalculable number of cases of suicide and infanticide' resulting from the 'psychic slavery and terrorism he advocates'.[18]

She found more prepossessing the suggestions advanced by the breakaway Society for the Prevention of Venereal Diseases:

> perfectly free from the hideous barefaced sex-injustice involved in 'regulation', – though I fear for unavoidable reasons of comparative sex anatomy it must always be much easier for a man to disinfect his (external) organs than a woman hers, which are so largely internal. Still the S.P.V.D. *does* give explicit instructions to women as well as men, as to how to disinfect, and I think we should recognise this. We have no right to deny to any man, even if he *does* resort to prostitution, *protection from v.d. – which does not involve the slavery and additional degradation of women* ... my feeling about 'regulation' is as strong as anyone's, but self-disinfection *does not* involve regulation. I should intensely resent any attempt to keep the knowledge of such a possibility from me or any woman friend I was interested in, and we have no right to deny it to men either. Of course I also advocate working *from the roots*, but as we know that is a lengthy process.[19]

The subject was one about which she continued to be concerned over the decades.

Marie Stopes's recently published *Married Love* received a glowing review from Stella in the *International Journal of Ethics*. Nevertheless, her dissension from Stopes's rosy vision of monogamous erotic harmony was clear. As a critique of Stopes's elevated and feminist-inflected vision of heterosexual relations, this review forms a useful counterpart to the female inversion paper. The book, Stella began, was 'doubly important'. It was a 'brief, candid, yet idealistic account of sex processes and the physical side of marriage', containing 'much admirable advice and badly needed instruction'. It put forward 'an original theory of women's erotic periodicity' (an issue touched on in her *Sexual variety and variability* paper,[20] of which Stopes's annotated copy is now in the British Library). Furthermore, the book included 'a fine vindication of birth control', and a 'very sane and fundamental statement' on the limits to the benefits of sexual self-restraint.

Stella had two, perhaps predictable, criticisms. The book was 'quite frankly based on observation of, and addressed to, the educated, prosperous, and privileged classes.' Stopes did not even admit that 'immense industrial, social and legislative changes are necessary' in order that 'the majority of her fellow-citizens' might 'even approximately... develop and refine their erotic nature, sufficiently to follow her suggestions'. In advocating the ideal of 'a nobler and tenderer form of life-long monogamy', Stopes overlooked the sexual double standard at the root of 'present legally sanctioned patriarchal monogamy'. The feminine ignorance which caused 'a tragic amount of misery and misunderstanding' was 'inextricably connected with women's economic dependence and with the tyrannous demand for theoretical ignorance and anatomical virginity in the bride'. Thus, while Stopes did 'realise some of the deficiencies of present conditions and present model ideas', she had not gone to the 'very root of the matter'.[21]

A work on women and sexuality which Stella much appreciated around this time was an article by Havelock Ellis, probably 'The Erotic Rights of Women'. She told him that '[I] "don't know when I've read anything, even of yours, I've liked better" ... so penetrating, so interesting, so understanding, so true!'[22] In a review, she described it as 'a miniature classic ... that should be studied by all lovers and husbands', praising Ellis's 'insight and delicate sympathy', although she cavilled at his assumption that the new vision of heterosexual union he offered would not require any changes in 'the external order of our marriage system'.[23]

By the summer of 1918, Stella was again in search of remunerative work. In a letter to Stopes, she commiserated with her about the censorship of *Married Love* in the USA ('or is it *really congratulation*? For it *is* an honour to come under the Comstock ban'), and mentioned that everyone to whom she had mentioned the book was interested and '*most* women *entirely concur* in your main theory' [i.e. the periodicity of female desire], before asking a favour. An American editor had asked her to obtain an interview with the Duchess of Marlborough about her infant welfare work. Believing that Stopes had worked with the Duchess, Stella wondered if there were any chance of a personal introduction, since 'The interview would mean a good deal to me.'[24] No such interview by Stella seems to have appeared.

Stella 'at last found some work to do, with Miss McArthur, in connection with trades unions' (she informed Ellis when having tea with him on 3 August, when she also 'told [him] all her troubles [details unspecified] & seemed much cheered by doing so').[25] In this temporary post as an indexer with the National Federation of Women Workers, 'the working women's Trade Union', she first met Dorothy Jewson, the National Organiser, who became a great friend and a colleague in the struggle for birth control.[26] The work seems to have been demanding – Ellis informed Sanger that Stella 'seems tremendously busy, and only writes hurried postcards'[27] – but only lasted a few months. By January 1919, she was free to take tea again with Ellis, being 'at a loose end and looking out for a job.'[28]

Stella kept up her other activities: *The Call*, the newspaper of the British Socialist Party, published a number of reviews by her and also several of her poems. These were on relevant political themes, such as 'Scrapped: The Women Munition Workers of Britain, Before and After November 1918', which reveals her broad humanitarian sympathies towards those who, while participating in the war effort, were also victims of governmental whim:

> You have done well: To you we owe our lives
> Our soldiers' glory, and our prosperous days.
> Handmaids of Vulcan, sisters, heroes' wives!
> Our thanks shall match our praise.
>
> Well – as you see – inevitable quite,
> – ('Though very, very sad, of course, indeed!) –
> The world is ours! We've won our War for Right!
> Now, women, you can go! You've served our Need![29]

Other subjects were 'To the Allied Imperialists (Paris Conference, 1919), 'Hungary Bolsheviki', "To the Russian Soviet Socialist Republic', 'Red Russia: 7th November 1917: 7th November 1919', and 'To the White Eagle of Poland: 7th June 1920'. These are very much what might be expected and are probably fairly representative of a whole genre of poems by socialists at this period, deploying phrases such as 'red star in Eastern skies', 'spring smoulders in earth's breast 'neath frost and shower', 'oh flag of dreams unfurled', 'that proud banner, red against the snow', 'now a Promethean people struggles too'.[30] They are of sufficient merit that it would be pleasing to have more examples of Stella's own poems (rather than translations) when she was not being a mouthpiece for the spirit of the age.

Her connections with *The Call* suggest that her political allegiance was given to the British Socialist Party, the 'oldest, largest, and most important' of the British socialist groups, which affiliated to the Third International (by an overwhelming majority) in 1919.[31] Why this body appealed to Stella (rather than, for example, Sylvia Pankhurst's Workers' Socialist Federation) remains obscure. No material located elaborates on her political affiliations.

One subject that curiously failed to surface, either in her surviving correspondence or in other writings, was the grant of the suffrage to women over thirty years of age. According to the Chelsea Electoral Registers, both Stella and her sister Sylvia were entitled to vote.[32] Given her later published comments on its limited parameters and her articles about the 'flapper vote' that finally gave women the suffrage on equal terms with men, this seems strange. If nothing else, one would have expected her, given her political sympathies, to comment on the class-bias involved. Possibly, furious epistolary comments have failed to survive.

Her piece 'Havelock Ellis: His View of Women's Nature and Position' in Sanger's *Birth Control Review* indicates what this intelligent and independent-minded woman found to cherish in Ellis's work, and provides a valuable example of how contemporaries were reading him within the context of their time. Defining Ellis as a 'trebly complex genius', she praised his 'comprehension alike of women's individuality as human beings and of the destructive needs and nature of their sex'. He was equally far removed from the 'imbecile and coarse contempt of church tradition and ... the libertine who imagines that he "understands women" because he has frequently consorted with prostitutes', and was also 'sane and balanced and free from the somewhat sickly idealization of all a woman *is* and *does* ... a degraded relic of the "chivalrous" tradition'. She foregrounded his championing of 'intelligent voluntary motherhood ... a motherhood in harmony with women's intelligence'. In *Man and Woman* he gave

> an idea of the immensity and complexity of the work in investigation, annotation and comparison which still needs doing before we can forecast women's most congenial vocation and her probable place in the New Social Order.

She noted his indebtedness to 'gifted and distinguished' women friends and associates, as well as observations of 'women as citizens and workers' and 'encyclopaedic reading'. Above all, she commended his writing on 'woman the lover and beloved' and his 'knowledge of women's infinite sexual diversity'. In the latter context, she commented, intriguingly, on his

> analysis of the difference between the general tendency of many highly devoted intelligent women to mental, moral and social independence of men, and their frequently specifically sexual pleasure in submission to and suffering by the beloved man[33]

(which sounds as though she was moving towards a conception of consensual sado-masochism).

Stella was regularly attending BSSSP committee meetings,[34] and her letters to the recently appointed paid secretary, Janet Carson, illuminate her busy and active life and interests at this time, as well as her health problems (e.g. 'threatened attack of pleurisy').[35] They illustrate her activities and concerns on behalf of the Society, as she asked whether Carson had heard from individuals to whom she had promoted the Society,[36] considered ideas for possible speakers,[37] asked her to send out copies of pamphlets[38] and notices of forthcoming meetings,[39] and advised her about Society business matters such as giving adequate notice of meetings[40] and what fee they might offer to a particularly desired speaker.[41] They also mention encounters with other members, some of whom, for example the Reverend Montague Summers,[42] one would not have expected to appear in her circles. Summers was an exceedingly spooky character who claimed to be ordained as a Catholic priest, which sorted oddly with his fascination with erotica and his interests in the occult. Until 1923, he was an active member of the BSSSP, and a colleague of Stella's on the Bibliographical Committee.[43]

Carson was 'interested in the society's aims, a well-known suffrage worker, and thoroughly experienced in organization and committee work':[44] the correspondence reveals various points of common interest. They both appear to have been friends of Margaret Lumley Brown, sharing an interest in her psychic activities. They were both, from various allusions, feminists interested in pacifism and international relations. Stella endeavoured to convert Carson to her own sympathy with the contemporary regime in Russia, asking her to 'make the little Lunacharski pamphlet known as far as possible to members of your Society'[45] (Anatoly Vassilevich Lunacharski, Soviet Commissar for Education and Culture 1917–29). Slightly later, she sent

> two more which may interest you. It is frightfully hard to get facts about Russia known or appreciated here – ignorance is so great and wilful misrepresentation so malignant and powerful.[46]

A later allusion – 'if only the general European movement *has* forced Paris [i.e. the Paris Conference of 1919 to settle peace terms] to reconsider things' (concerning the communist regime in Russia)[47] – rather assumes common political sympathies. This exchange seems to have been reciprocal: Stella thanked Carson for sending her cards for various meetings.[48] They were also apparently socialising together: 'I so much enjoyed my visit!';[49] 'So many thanks for my *delightful* Sunday afternoon.'[50]

Stella's health was poor during these early months of 1919. It is not clear whether the pleurisy was an after-effect of the 'prevailing plague'[51] (the Spanish Influenza epidemic, 1918–19) but, at some point, Stella certainly succumbed to flu which, on top of 'long war strain', rendered her 'very run down' and subject to 'immense fatigue and depression',[52] with a persistent cough.[53] This very unusually meant that she had to 'cut out *heaps* of things that badly need doing and I want to do so much'.[54] Some of the fatigue may have been due to her employment in the Petrol Control Department of the Board of Trade,[55] which does not sound particularly congenial. Even so, she hoped (after a Saturday morning's work) to drag herself over to Bow Street to observe a legal case in which Eden and Cedar Paul were involved.[56] And, in spite of complaints about 'tired... head and eyes',[57] she wrote a long letter on BSSSP business to Carson. If Prince Antoine Bibesco of the Roumanian Legation had not paid his subscription, 'on reflection' she thought it might be better to wait before chasing him up – 'He is marrying Elizabeth Asquith, and I don't think we want B.S.S.P. to become a happy hunting ground for Mayfair in search of "thrills", *do we*?'[58]

As usual, she was networking between different areas of her life: following a tea-time visit, Ellis wrote to Françoise Lafitte-Cyon (his lover, later his common-law wife) that she might expect to hear from friends of Stella's about French lessons.[59] A Mr Ernest Crawford approached her as an intermediary to propose to the committee of the BSSSP the collection and tabulation of anonymous data on sex.[60] She made efforts to interest S.H. Halford, 'a keen and independent thinker on social problems',[61] and the radical Liberal reformer Colonel Wedgewood in BSSSP activities.[62] Ellis wrote to Hugh de Selincourt that he had mentioned the latter's manuscript on 'Women and Children' to Stella, who had suggested that de Selincourt might be interested in joining the BSSSP.[63] Agreeing to second the membership proposal of Adrian and Karin Stephen (Virginia Woolf's psychoanalyst brother and his wife), she admitted that she didn't know them 'personally, but I know of them, we've many mutual acquaintances'.[64] She recommended for appointment to the Executive, with comments as their suitability, the psychoanalyst Dr James Glover; the Rev. Mr Northcote, a clergyman interested in sex education; and Edward Fuller, 'well-known among pacifist and humanitarian associations and has taken a lot of trouble over the Educational Group'.[65]

Several months later, her health was still not strong: she fainted at a BSSSP committee meeting in May and was 'sent home under friendly escort',[66] and three weeks later found 'my heart is still apt to behave like the "Panther" at the starting-post': on top of that, with the advent of summer 'my hay-fever (*an annual festivity!*) has begun.'[67] Meanwhile 'the thought of Russia' (still in the early phases of establishing the Soviet state) was 'haunting' her,[68] and she was not 'in the mood for festive "Peace and Victory" celebrations, what ludious [? ludicrous] nonsense it is'.[69] However, in July 1919 she did manage a 'very much needed holiday, or rather, rest' in the country.[70]

On 22 August 1919, Stella's mother died at their home in Chelsea, of 'Ascites and Malignant Disease of the Abdomen'. The death was certified by the local woman doctor, Alice M. Benham. Sylvia, who had been present at the death, registered it.[71] Dulcie did not leave a will, but administration of her estate (£441 and 11 shillings – equivalent in purchasing power to £14,544 in 2007) was granted to Sylvia on 27 November.[72]

Her mother's terminal illness and its impact on home life may have played some part in Stella's persistent health troubles and fatigue around this time. There is, however, no mention of her mother's demise in surviving correspondence. Within just over a month of Dulcie's death, Stella was participating in the discussion of Montague Summers's paper on the Marquis de Sade at the BSSSP quarterly meeting.[73] According to Havelock Ellis, this bereavement 'seems to have made her home conditions easier for her'.[74] Some years later, Stella commented that 'no woman liked to live in another woman's house' and deprecated proposals that 'women should continue to live with their own relations'.[75] But aside from any tensions within a shared household, Dulcie's lengthy illness must have weighed on Stella both emotionally and practically. Sylvia continued to reside with her, and even to share her social life,[76] for a while.

By the end of the year, 'working in a Government office ... [took] all her time and energy'.[77] By April 1920, she was working in the Insurance Department of the Ministry of Health in Maida Hill.[78] She does not seem to have found the work congenial, referring to it as 'The House of Bondage' and to 'the beastly long hours at this place which make a tea at a reasonable hour impossible for me',[79] but stuck it out for several years. Her scathing attacks on 'the Ministry of Disease'[80] may owe something to this experience.

Even so, she was getting back on form, taking a detailed and active interest in BSSSP affairs, attending a reception at 'Mrs S's' (possibly Helena Swanwick of the Union of Democratic Control, whose publication *Foreign Affairs* met with her approval – 'how excellent ... [it] is!'),[81] admiring Margaret Lumley Brown's psychic drawings ('she did some rather remarkable ones lately with a beautiful fantastic delicacy'),[82] and writing to George Ives.[83] For some months, the Bibliographical Committee of the BSSSP had been endeavouring to open negotiations with the British Museum authorities about their 'collection of literature on sex subjects, with a view to having the catalogue 'placed at the service of serious students of the subject'.[84] By February, Carpenter and Lloyd perceived 'the beginning of a *slow and dignified* climb down', although Stella herself and Montague Summers were less sanguine.[85]

By March 1920, Stella was again in poor health – 'seedy and very wretched' – which she attributed to 'sudden warmth' in the weather.[86] In April, she was 'laid up by a touch of gastritis following on a specially severe chill', exacerbated by going out too soon after a weekend '"hors de combat" with slight food poisoning ... very trying'. As a result, she had to miss a couple of meetings and 'many private engagements', and was 'very depressed and worried about these continual chills and crippling of every activity that is human and worth while'. She was particularly put out about not attending the committee meeting. Mrs James, a journalist, had applied to join the BSSSP. To Stella, this was a '*test case*. If we give way over it, we shall have no power in future to exclude *anyone*: Bottomley or Billing [scandalmongering media figures] or the worst "Sporting Times" blackmailer-pimp type of press-man'. She was so concerned about this, that if the nomination were to be accepted, 'I shall be *very much less* inclined to interest myself in future in the Society's concerns, after all the time and energy I have given them in the past'.[87] Clearly, she was in a state of low spirits. In May, she was still suffering from enteritis, although 'benefitting by country air' in Puttenham for a few days, where she enjoyed 'glorious weather.[88] However, shortly afterwards she was hoping that Janet Carson had not been 'killed by the heatwave',[89] suggesting that the hot weather was getting to her again. A month later, she was 'enjoying another bout of enteritis on top of hayfever', her annual torment.[90]

A tantalising glimpse of the range of her social circles appears in her request to Janet Carson to send a card for the BSSSP quarterly meeting to Miss Ivy Compton-Burnett, whom Stella had met

> three or four times. She is a friend of my friend Miss Jourdain, and a sensible highly cultivated middle-aged woman who may very likely join us. She knows and admires H. Ellis's work.[91]

Compton-Burnett, who had not yet written the novels for which she became renowned, resided in Bayswater with her life's companion, Margaret Jourdain, whom Stella presumably knew through the *International Journal of Ethics*. As with so many of Stella's contacts, there is little beyond this brief mention to illuminate the details of their relationship. Stella referred to Margaret Jourdain, as 'very able woman ~~great~~ good friend of mine',[92] although a few years later commented to Ellis that the *International Journal of Ethics* had become 'more stuffy & conventional under Margaret Jourdain's technically *competent* but curiously *arid* management.'[93]

What does not figure, at least explicitly, in Stella's correspondence at this time is anything concerning the intensive activity which eventually resulted in a unified Communist Party of Great Britain. In *The Call*, she reviewed Edward Carpenter's *Pagan and Christian Creeds: Their Origin and Meaning*, mentioning approvingly his suggestion of 'incorporating the finest primitive belief and ceremonies into the great social order, which, being based on reason and justice, should give freer play to instinct and imagination', and concluded 'Do we not celebrate our Socialist faith and hope in the setting of the loveliness of May?'[94] Her review of Bertram Lloyd's anthology *The Paths of Glory* suggested that it would 'provid[e] ammunition against – Amritsarism', (in April 1919, British troops fired into a crowd of peaceful protesters in Amritsar, in the Punjab, at the order of General Dyer).[95] The volume included her translations from the French of two poems by George Bannerot, 'To the Toilers' and 'As Ye Have Sown ...'.[96] At the Annual General Meeting of the Malthusian League, she endeavoured to append to a resolution concerning world scarcity and deprecating incitements to increase the birth rate an addendum calling 'upon the government to modify its Eastern policy accordingly', referring particularly to the blockading of Russia. Nobody seconded this and it was opposed by a Mr O'Neill.[97] Her poem in *The Call*, 'To the White Eagle of Poland', expressed her concern over the struggle between White and Red Armies in Poland: 'leprous vulture, tearing at [the] heart' of a 'Promethean people',[98] while in a letter to Janet Carson she wrote '*At last* our people [not clear who 'our people' were in this context] are moving about Poland: – at *last*? I wonder if it is too late.'[99]

She may have been cheered by Margaret Sanger's visit to Britain in the late spring of 1920. The Malthusian League held a public meeting for Sanger on 12 May:[100] 'Wasn't Margaret excellent ...? I do hope it will be the beginning of a most useful and successful campaign throughout the country.' She asked Janet Carson to '*make a point* of *pushing her work with the W. I. L* [Women's International League of Peace and Freedom]'.[101]

Stella seems to have been rather overwhelmed by her work for the BSSSP. She wrote rather sharply to Janet Carson at the end of June that

> I fear you are quite mistaken about the Schroeder letter [New York publisher]! I couldn't undertake any more B.S.S.P. work at present what between the report and the recopying of the Hirschfeld letter, and I *certainly didn't* say I'd draft the letter.[102]

The controversial and eccentric Magnus Hirschfeld of Berlin was one of the leading European figures in sexual reform: in 1919, he had set up an Institute for Sexual Science and a sex-counselling clinic in Berlin. Presumably, Stella was using her capabilities in German to compose a letter to him on behalf of the Society.[103]

This was not the first hint of some strain between the two women: in April, Stella had written that 'I think it w^d. be advisable to take *very* full notes during C^tee meetings, so as to avoid mistakes.'[104] However, they still had much in common: just over a week later Stella thanked Carson for

> forwarding me the VD literature. It seemed to me very important, and I shall make it known as widely as possible.

She also asked 'Shall I see you tonight at the Albert Hall? I hope to be in the stalls – Block M,' in the clear expectation that Carson would already know what was going on there, and concluded 'With love and au revoir soon, yours affectionately.'[105]

But while 'Sylvia and I will be very pleased to lunch with you on Sunday next',[106] trouble blew up shortly afterwards. There had been some muddle about sending pamphlets to E.S.P. Haynes, 'a man of wealth influence and public spirit whom we *cannot afford* to offend'. As a result

> I have spent most of the evening after a hard office day writing a long letter to him, shielding and supporting you and the Society...I cannot undertake regularly to meet responsibilities which are not mine, either officially or morally. I think Mr

> Haynes' manner was unduly hasty… But the whole thing was most unfortunate.

And this was not all:

> Another point: will you see that the Minutes of the Annual and last Executive Business meeting and the last Executive are *very clear and correct*? There has been a difficulty over the minutes two or three times in Committee, and I must say, it makes a very unfavourable impression… *Please* be awfully careful about the minutes.

Nonetheless, Stella concluded

> I think you know that I feel personally a sincere and very warm admiration and affection and respect for you, and *I realise how busy you are, and the amount of valuable and responsible international work you do*. But others perhaps don't realise, as fully as I do, and they only judge by the correctness of minutes and promptitude in despatch of literature.
>
> I do wish I did not feel I ought to say this!
>
> Yours affectionately.[107]

Her continuing trials of health perhaps affected her temper: 'I am suffering from vehement and very painful indigestion and am almost bowled over for the moment';[108] 'My scald has kept me tied up rather'.[109] However, she expressed herself 'very pleased to come to tea' on 21 September.[110] But correspondence with Janet Carson ceased altogether by the end of September 1920. By the following summer, Carson's inefficiency (if no worse) was causing major inconvenience to the BSSSP.

In August 1920, the Communist Party of Great Britain was finally established.[111] It can be assumed with some certainty that Stella would have subscribed herself a Communist from this point. In December, she reviewed *Creative Revolution: A Study in Communist Ergatocracy* by her friends and former colleagues at Federation House, Eden and Cedar Paul, published by her old friend Unwin for *The Communist*. Their synthesis of 'the contributions of Newton, Darwin, Marx, Bergson and Freud towards the modern outlook' was 'one of the best interpretative and creative criticisms I have ever read', and their 'emphasis on human differentiation and diversity' was '[e]qually valuable'. Dedicated to 'the leading exponent of Creative Revolution in Action… our Comrade, Nicolai Lenin', it was 'worthy of his acceptance'.[112] On the one hand, Stella seems swept up in revolutionary enthusiasm, adhering to Party line and accepted formulas, yet there remain hints of her own persistent ideological eclecticism and deep-rooted belief in the virtues of difference and diversity.

Notes

1. Stella Browne to Havelock Ellis, 16 February 1923, Ellis papers in Department of Manuscripts, British Library, Additional Manuscript 70539 [BL Add Ms 70539].
2. Minutes of the 45th (18 January 1918) and subsequent meetings of the Executive Committee, 'BSS Misc', British Sexology Society Archives in the Harry Ransom Humanities Research Center, University of Texas at Austin [HRC].
3. Minutes of the 46th meeting of the Executive Committee, 13 February 1918, 'BSS Misc', HRC.
4. F.W. Stella Browne, 'Ginger', *The Humanitarian*, vol. VIII, no. 187, July 1918, p. 119.
5. Minutes of the 47th meeting of the Executive Committee, 15 March 1918, 'BSS Misc', HRC.
6. Lucy Bland, 'Trial by sexology? Maud Allan, *Salome*, and the "cult of the clitoris" case', in Lucy Bland and Laura Doan (eds), *Sexology in Culture: Labelling Bodies and Desires* (Oxford: Polity Press, 1998), pp. 183–98.
7. F.W. Stella Browne, 'Studies in feminine inversion', *Journal of Sexology and Psychanalysis*, vol. 1, 1923, pp. 51–8.
8. Entry for 22 September 1918, Sheffield City Council Libraries Archives and Information: Sheffield Archives, Carpenter/Mss/261.
9. F.W. Stella Browne, 'Der weibliche Typus inversus in der neueren Literatur: Renée Vivien, Colette Willy, Mary MacLane', *Die Neue Generation*, March/April 1922, pp. 90–6.
10. Sheila Jeffreys, *The Spinster and Her Enemies: Feminism and Sexuality 1880–1930* (London: Pandora Press, 1985), p. 118.
11. Browne, 'Studies in feminine inversion'.
12. F.W. Stella Browne, *Sexual Variety and Variability among Women, and Their Bearing upon Social Reconstruction* (London: British Society for the Study of Sex Psychology, 1917), p. 12.
13. Browne, 'Studies in feminine inversion'.
14. Quarterly Meeting, 11 April 1918, 'BSS Misc', HRC.
15. Edward Carpenter to George Ives, 14 April 1918, Ives papers, Harry Ransom Humanities Research Center, University of Texas at Austin [Ives HRC].
16. Minutes of the 48th meeting of the Executive Committee, 11 April 1918, 'BSS Misc', HRC; Lesley A. Hall, 'Venereal disease in Britain from the Contagious Diseases Acts to the National Health Service', in Roger Davidson and Lesley A.

Hall (eds), *Sex, Sin, and Suffering: Venereal Disease in European Social Context since 1870* (London: Routledge, 2001), pp. 120–36.

17. Minutes of the 4th Annual General Meeting, [? 12 July 1918], 'BSS Misc', HRC.
18. F.W. Stella Browne, 'A slur on women and Malthusianism', *The Malthusian*, vol. 42, March 1918, p. 23.
19. Stella Browne to Miss Carson, 11 July 1920, 'BSS Misc', HRC.
20. Browne, *Sexual Variety and Variability*, pp. 9–10.
21. F.W. Stella Browne, 'Review of *Married Love: A New Contribution to the Solution of Sex Difficulties*. By Marie Carmichael Stopes', *International Journal of Ethics*, vol. 29, 1918/19, pp. 112–13.
22. Havelock Ellis to Margaret Sanger, 20 April 1918, Sanger papers in the Library of Congress, Washington, DC [LC], Volume 4.
23. F.W. Stella Browne, 'Review: *The Erotic Rights of Women*, and *The Objects of Marriage*. Two essays by Havelock Ellis', *The Malthusian*, vol. 42, November 1918, p. 85.
24. Stella Browne to Marie Stopes, 22 August 1918, Marie Stopes papers in the Wellcome Library, PP/MCS/A.42.
25. Browne to Sanger, 4 August 1918, LC, Volume 4.
26. W.F. [sic] Stella Browne, 'One of our liberators: Dorothy Jewson', *Critic and Guide*, vol. 25C/8, August 1925, pp. 316–19.
27. Browne to Sanger, 27 September 1918, LC, Volume 4.
28. Browne to Sanger, 13 January 1919, LC, Volume 4.
29. F.W. Stella Browne, 'Scrapped: the women munition workers of Britain, before and after November 1918', *The Call*, 12 December 1918, p. 7.
30. *The Call*, 13 February 1919, p. 3; 3 April 1919, p. 3; 18 September 1919, p. 5; 13 November 1919, p. 1; 10 June 1920, p. 9.
31. James Klugmann, *History of the Communist Party of Great Britain: Volume 1: Formation and Early Years, 1919–1924* (London: Laurence & Wishart, 1969), pp. 16–17.
32. Electoral registers, Chelsea Local Studies Library.
33. F.W. Stella Browne, 'Havelock Ellis: his view of women's nature and position', *Birth Control Review* (New York), vol. III, no. 2, February 1919, pp. 9–11.
34. M. Lumley Brown (secretary) [? to Miss Carson], 13 February 1919, 'BSS Misc', BSS HRC.
35. Browne to Carson, 21 February 1919, 'BSS Misc', HRC.
36. Browne to Carson, 28 February 1919, 'BSS Misc', HRC.
37. Browne to Carson, 28 February 1919, 3 and 11 March 1919, 'BSS Misc', HRC.
38. Browne to Carson, 14 March 1919, 'BSS Misc', HRC.
39. Browne to Carson, 6 April 1919, 'BSS Misc', HRC.
40. Browne to Carson, 1 March 1919, 'BSS Misc', HRC.

41. Browne to Carson, 11 March 1919, 'BSS Misc', HRC.
42. Browne to Carson, 1 March 1919, 'BSS Misc', HRC.
43. Timothy D'Arch Smith, 'Montague Summers', in *The Books of the Beast: Essays on Aleister Crowley, Montague Summers and others* (London: Mandrake, 1991), pp. 37–45.
44. Minutes of the 54th meeting of the Executive Committee, 8 January 1919, 'BSS Misc', HRC.
45. Browne to Carson, 21 February 1919, 'BSS Misc', HRC.
46. Browne to Carson, 3 March 1919, 'BSS Misc', HRC.
47. Browne to Carson, 7 June 1919, 'BSS Misc', HRC.
48. Browne to Carson, 21 February 1919, 20 March 1919, 'BSS Misc', HRC.
49. Browne to Carson, 6 April 1919, 'BSS Misc', HRC.
50. Browne to Carson, 19 May 1919, 'BSS Misc', HRC.
51. Browne to Carson, 21 February 1919, 'BSS Misc', HRC.
52. Browne to Carson, 20 March 1919, 'BSS Misc', HRC.
53. Browne to Carson, 26 March 1919, 'BSS Misc', HRC.
54. Browne to Carson, 20 March 1919, 'BSS Misc', HRC.
55. Browne to Sanger, 4 March 1919, LC, Volume 4.
56. Browne to Carson, 20 March 1919, 'BSS Misc', HRC.
57. Browne to Carson, 26 March 1919, 'BSS Misc', HRC.
58. Browne to Carson, 27 March 1919, 'BSS Misc', HRC.
59. Havelock Ellis to Françoise Lafitte-Cyon, [n.d. 1919], Howard Gotlieb Archival Research Center, Boston University.
60. 55th meeting of the Executive Committee, 15 January 1919, 'BSS Misc', HRC.
61. Browne to Carson, 6 April 1919, 'BSS Misc', HRC.
62. Browne to Carson, 11 April 1919, 'BSS Misc', HRC.
63. Havelock Ellis to Hugh de Selincourt, 29 April 1919, LC, Volume 7.
64. Browne to Carson, 7 June 1919, 'BSS Misc', HRC.
65. Minutes of 73rd and 74th Executive Committee Meetings, 22 May and 3 June 1920, 'BSS Misc', HRC.
66. George Ives, diary entry for 14 May 1919, 'Notes and Writings', Volume LXXII, Ives HRC.
67. Browne to Carson, 7 June 1919, 'BSS Misc', HRC.
68. Browne to Carson, 7 June 1919, 'BSS Misc', HRC.
69. Browne to Carson, 10 July 1919, 'BSS Misc', HRC.
70. Browne to Carson, 10 and 14 July 1919, 'BSS Misc', HRC.
71. Death certificate of Anna Dulcibella Mary Browne, female, 71 years, widow of Daniel Marshall Browne, retired Lieutenant RN. Obituary of Alice M. Benham, MD, *British Medical Journal*, 1, 1919, pp, 1308–9.
72. Probate Registry Calendar, 27 November 1919.
73. Minutes of Quarterly Meeting, 13 October 1919, 'BSS Misc', HRC.

74. Browne to Sanger, 1 December 1919, LC, Volume 4.
75. Report on R.B. Kerr's talk to meeting of the British Society for the Study of Sex Psychology on 'Probable changes in sexual customs', *The New Generation*, vol. 7, April 1928, p. 40.
76. Browne to Carson, 11 January and 3 February 1920, 'BSS Misc', BSS HRC.
77. Browne to Sanger, 1 December 1919, LC, Volume 4.
78. Browne to Carson, 20 April 1920, 'BSS Misc', HRC.
79. Browne to Carson, 20 September 1920, 'BSS Misc', BSS HRC.
80. For example, F.W. Stella Browne, 'An open letter to the four suspended MPs by a Socialist woman', *The New Generation*, 1923, vol. 2, p. 90.
81. Browne to Carson, 3 February 1920, 'BSS Misc', HRC.
82. Browne to Carson, 11 January 1920, 'BSS Misc', HRC.
83. George Ives, journal entry for 17 January 1920, 'Notes and Writings', Volume LXXIV, Ives HRC.
84. 64th Meeting of the Executive Committee, 18 September 1919, 'BSS Misc', HRC.
85. Browne to Carson, 6 February 1920, 'BSS Misc', HRC.
86. Browne to Carson, 24 March 1920, 'BSS Misc', HRC.
87. Browne to Carson, 28 April 1920, 'BSS Misc', HRC.
88. Browne to Carson, 18 and 22 May 1920, 'BSS Misc', HRC.
89. Postcard from Browne to Carson, 30 May 1920, 'BSS Misc', HRC.
90. Browne to Carson, 11 June 1920, 'BSS Misc', HRC.
91. Browne to Carson, 7 April 1920, 'BSS Misc', HRC.
92. Browne to Carson, [n.d.: probably March or April] 1920, 'BSS Misc', HRC.
93. Browne to Ellis, 12 May 1923, BL Add Ms 70539.
94. F.W. Stella Browne, 'Review of *Pagan and Christian Creeds: Their Origin and Meaning*. By Edward Carpenter', *The Call*, 6 May 1920, p. 5.
95. F.W. Stella Browne, 'Review of *The Paths of Glory: A Collection of Poems written during the War, 1914–1919*. Edited by Bertram Lloyd', *The Call*, 6 May 1920, p. 6.
96. Bertram Lloyd (ed.), *The Paths of Glory: A Collection of Poems written during the War, 1914–1919* (London: George Allen & Unwin Ltd, [1920]), pp. 10, 30–2.
97. Report of Annual General Meeting, *The Malthusian*, vol. 44, May 1920, p. 33.
98. F.W. Stella Browne, 'To the White Eagle of Poland: 7 June 1920', *The Call*, 10 June 1930, p. 9.
99. Browne to Carson, 22 May 1920, 'BSS Misc', HRC.
100. *The Malthusian*, vol. 44, June 1920, pp. 41–2; Browne to Carson, 18 May 1920, 'BSS Misc', HRC.
101. Browne to Carson, 18 May 1920, 'BSS Misc', HRC.
102. Browne to Carson, 30 June 1920, 'BSS Misc', HRC.

103. Atina Grossman, *Reforming Sex: The German Movement for Birth Control and Abortion Reform, 1920–1950* (Oxford: Oxford University Press, 1995), p. 16; Browne to Carson, 11 June 1920, 'BSS Misc', HRC.
104. Browne to Carson, 20 April 1920, 'BSS Misc', HRC.
105. Browne to Carson, 11 July 1920, 'BSS Misc', HRC.
106. Browne to Carson, 12 July 1920, 'BSS Misc', BSS HRC.
107. Browne to Carson, 14 July 1920, 'BSS Misc', HRC.
108. Browne to Carson, 'Tuesday' [July 1920], 'BSS Misc', HRC.
109. Browne to Carson, 8 September 1920, 'BSS Misc', HRC.
110. Browne to Carson, 20 September 1920, 'BSS Misc', HRC.
111. Klugmann, *History of the Communist Party of Great Britain*, pp. 38–49, 64.
112. F.W. Stella Browne, 'Review of *Creative Revolution: A Study in Communist Ergatocracy*. By Eden and Cedar Paul', *The Communist*, 16 December 1920, p. 5.

5

'Strong Red Rag'

The next few years were ones of difficulty and trial. For several of them, Stella remained in the 'House of Bondage',[1] working at the 'Ministry of Disease'[2] (the Insurance Department of the Ministry of Health), a demanding job which she found uncongenial, both the work itself and the long hours.[3] It was possibly there that she encountered bitter sex-antagonism between 'the temporary women clerks and the ex-servicemen'.[4]

In spite of this exhausting and demoralising background, Stella managed to keep up some of her more congenial interests and activities. She assisted Bertram Lloyd in compiling his anthology of humanitarian poetry, *The Great Kinship*, supplying him with a hitherto unpublished translation by John Payne of a poem by Edmond Haraucourt, and her own translation of Léon Cladel's 'My Ass', and in 'other ways' unspecified.[5]

Her article, 'Liberty and Democracy', on Edward Carpenter, for Margaret Sanger's *Birth Control Review*, is a useful counterpart to the article she had already contributed on Havelock Ellis, revealing her response to this other leading figure in British sexology, sex reform, and ethical socialism. She praised the 'gracious balance and proportion' in his 'social message', with its 'fine discrimination between essentials and non-essentials, an equipoise of individual and social rights'. The 'real and wholesome simplification of life' of which Carpenter was 'practical, as well as theoretical exponent', was not 'a mania for self-mortification, or a positively perverted relish in squalor and torment'. It was 'a wonderful demonstration of the possibilities of wholesomeness, refinement and efficiency'. He had 'an intuitive understanding of, and sympathy with the wilder and more primitive manifestations of wonder, awe and love'. She valued the high importance Carpenter gave to the emotional life and to love, as well as his contempt for 'humbug and the "upholstery" and noxious paraphernalia of useless material which clogs and poisons *living*'. Considering him a 'born psychic', she praised his '*intuition* which most men ignore and depreciate' ('men' here can probably be read in a gendered, rather than generic, sense).[6]

She was also managing some kind of social life. She had tea with Havelock Ellis one Saturday in February 1921, on which occasion she told him

> a woman – at all counts an exceptional woman – should not attach her love to one man only. Then she will escape much suffering.

Ellis was 'not altogether sure'. He also passed on to Françoise Laffite-Cyon the 'nice things about Naiad [Françoise's nickname], of whom she has a very high opinion', Stella had said.[7] Françoise responded that 'S. Browne knew me in the dear, charming days of great enthusiasm, when I was bubbling over with dreams and eagerness', the time of the Freewoman Discussion Circle.[8] Stella also seems to have been investigating the possibilities of getting some of Françoise's writing published: 'Enclosed just came from Stella Browne who is not very encouraging about prospects of publication either for herself (though she writes *very* well) or you.'[9]

In July, a tea party at Mrs Capel Dunn's was attended by quite a little band of BSSSP members – George Ives, John Gambril Nicholson, Montague Summers and Stella.[10] She was reading the manuscript of Margaret Sanger's book on birth control, eventually published as *The Pivot of Civilisation*, and providing comments (in hay fever season). Sanger was still 'dearest Margaret' and 'my dearest'. Stella found it 'a *strikingly fresh, alive, and comprehensive* statement of the b.c. case, and is sure to rouse discussion and interest.' Although she liked 'the title and general outlook and the very apt illustrative bits', she felt that 'some of the *opinions quoted* should be omitted' – in particular, the ones which took a somewhat unfavourable slant towards communism. As Sanger was in England on one of her 'whirlwind tours'[11] and Stella was going to be in town until her holiday on 17 September, they '*must* soon meet'.[12] Sanger's continuing respect for Stella's views is demonstrated by a lengthy quotation in this work on the 'class-bias and sex bias', and 'peculiar use of the terms "fit" and "unfit"', in the eugenics movement.[13] Stella exhorted Sanger to 'take great care of herself' and not to 'overdo things'. She also promised '*More* presently:' but this is her last surviving letter to Sanger.[14]

In August 1921, the lingering problems of Janet Carson's secretaryship of the BSSSP blew up into a crisis. There was a question about missing funds: '*if* our money has gone, I know not how it can be replaced. I feel the first call on me now is the Russian Famine.' Stella thought they should take legal opinion if Carson did not return the account book,[15] and was 'very suspicious': none of the trouble would have arisen had Carson followed instructions. She was anxious to get a full Committee meeting to 'examine books, etc.' Without, she added, 'Miss C. present (we don't want the sort of "information" and "explanation" she abounds in)'. Stella moved that the Committee gave her notice by the following month:

> This sort of thing even if (*if!*) there has been no direct dishonesty, is *intolerable*: e.g. I had to have Saturday and Monday off my work owing to *conjunctivitis* yet have had to do a lot of writing in connection with this ... please write *very coolly* and *firmly* to her. Pathos about 'curtailed holidays' won't wash. We want the book at once.[16]

At a Special Committee meeting on 6 September, it was agreed unanimously that Carson be asked to resign, and Stella was to interview Miss Bailey about her willingness to serve instead.[17] A difficulty was that the Society did not have funds to pay a new secretary as well as 'that *unearned and undeserved* £8–15/- to Miss Carson, it is just making things *unfairly* difficult both for other persons and itself', Stella ranted.[18] She could not 'offer to participate' in the collection scheme suggested: 'anything I have to spare just now, goes to Russia'[19] (how little she had to spare is only too apparent from the amounts she sent *The Communist*'s Russian Famine Relief Fund – two shillings [= £4.77 in 2007 values] in September, five shillings [= £7.95 in 2007 values] in November).[20] The problem still muttered on, not assisted, in Stella's view, by the decision to hold over Carson's dismissal until the end of October: she hoped that at least the Committee would ensure that 'papers [are] put into proper order, to save and need less work to her successor.'[21] Stella had no patience with female inefficiency.

This ongoing source of worry and frustration – and the bad state of her eyes – may have lain behind dissension between Stella and Ellis over a project they were undertaking for Sanger: 'The request to draft the letter [on birth control] was the last straw'. Stella was, said Ellis, 'inclined to rebel': while willing to dispatch the letters, she insisted that Ellis would have to draft the text. As a result, Ellis was amused to find himself 'writing a pontifical letter in [Sanger's] name and signing [her] name to it', based on her notes with 'nothing of mine in it', even though he insisted that Stella must approve of the letter or alter it if she saw fit.[22] This was possibly a British version of Sanger's 1921 questionnaire on birth control practices.[23]

Stella did manage to get a couple of weeks' 'much-needed' holiday in the country, at Thorn Farm, Sidley, Sussex, although she continued to correspond with the BSSSP executive about the pressing issue of the secretaryship.[24]

The Executive asked Stella to visit a Miss Enid Chambers,[25] a self-defined 'Uranian' woman, who had contacted Edward Carpenter about forming a club for such women to relieve their loneliness and provide a sympathetic forum where they could speak of their problems.[26] Whether this ever got off the ground is not known, but Chambers was approved for membership of the BSSSP.[27] Stella was also advocating promoting the Society's activities in various directions, and proposed that they should confer Honorary Membership on Margaret Sanger and Alexandra Kollontai (founder of the Women's Department in the Soviet administration and increasingly a left-wing critic of Lenin's regime), seconded by Ives and agreed.[28] In January 1922, she suggested forming a British subcommittee of organisations interested in a forthcoming sexual reform Congress in Rome:[29] the project presumably bit the dust with the establishment of the Fascist regime in Italy.

Ellis was still deploying her as the person who undertook activities on his behalf in the wider field of sex reform, even though he knew that she was 'not strong and hard-worked'[30] (and even though she 'repeatedly tried to make Ellis understand' that certain matters were best addressed directly to the secretary of the BSSSP).[31] She read his paper 'The Play Function of Sex' (Ellis found public speaking anathema) at the BSSSP annual general meeting.[32] When Françoise suggested getting up a 'protest of eminent persons' about Margaret Sanger's latest difficulty with the law, he wrote back 'I will tell Stella Brown [sic] your suggestion.'[33] To their friend the writer Hugh de Selincourt, he wrote that 'I should like to see that paper of yours in print... and it seems quite suitable for the British Society for the Study of Sex Psychology.' However, de Selincourt would have to become a member, and Ellis advised 'Write to my friend (and a great admirer of Margaret) Miss Stella Browne.'[34] De Selincourt was elected to membership in January 1922, proposed by Ellis and seconded by Stella.[35] His paper was given to the Society meeting of 23 May 1922,[36] and Stella reported to Ellis (in a letter which does not survive) that 'they were all very pleased',[37] but it never achieved pamphlet form under the Society's auspices. De Selincourt resigned the following year.[38] He later claimed, 'I never could stand Stella Browne.'[39] Perhaps she had failed to fall for the boyish charms to which so many women in the Ellis/Sanger circle (including Françoise) succumbed.[40]

Early in 1922, she finally left her job at the 'Ministry of Disease' – 'I had the audacity to *resign*, instead of waiting like a sheep till I was quite broken & flung on the scrapheap' – inaugurating a period of considerable financial anxiety. This was exacerbated by the delay in receiving

> my last 3 weeks pay, & have had to write about it! & I have not yet received any "benefit" (at 12/- a week [= c. £23.50 in 2007 values]) though attending at the 'Employment'!! Exchange 3 times a week (& a damned nuisance it is!) [because she had resigned rather than been sacked] ... I shall get it *ultimately* I believe – or I will know the reason why!'

As a result

> with my strong 'red rag' temperamentally (or Mars in Mid-heaven aspecting every other planet, astrologically!) you can imagine that sort of thing develops the attitude of a tricoteuse. I want to clear out Whitehall with a hand grenade – or several.

She was worried that she would not be able to keep on the Chelsea flat.[41] Her sister was residing with her only intermittently[42] and, at some point in the 1920s, went to keep house for their widowed general practitioner uncle, Dr Philip Rashleigh Dodwell, in Battersea.[43] Stella had been eking out finances by taking a lodger, Miss Woodham-Smith, who had left in the previous December, and not been replaced. As a result, 'with *every wish* to give my efforts to the things I believe in', Stella could no longer 'do so on an entirely honorary basis as has frequently been the case in the past'. She was therefore extremely grateful for Ellis's 'kind thought & trouble in recommending me to the "N.G." [*New Generation*, the latest incarnation of *The Malthusian*] people' as a possible reviewer, and also for his suggestion that she might undertake the 'fine & useful work' of translating the poems of Otto Braun, the son of the feminist and socialist Lily Braun, who had been killed in the Battle of the Somme, provided that she could be 'sure of payment at a rate considerably higher than the usual sweated wages of translations'.[44] She was already paying a special (half)-rate subscription to the BSSSP.[45]

These pressures may have influenced her rather rabid comments on Marie Stopes:

> you know it is going to be very difficult for *anyone* to work with her at all. I can't give you a *detailed* description of her behaviour at our recent Birth Control Meeting but I assure it was a *pitiful* exhibition of temper and insolence and made a

> most unfortunate general impression. Moreover she seems to be getting quite unbalanced in her egomania and conceit ... she is making fresh enemies daily.[46]

Stella was not the only person of this opinion within the British birth controller ranks.[47]

Stella found the result of leaving the House of Bondage was that 'I am enjoying the possibility of air & exercise again, & feel already *much* better'.[48] Her sudden flurry of productivity might be attributable to this cause, but two articles and a substantial review (actually published in March) must have been completed before she stormed out and, in addition, she participated in a symposium on Birth Control held by the BSSSP on 23 February. All this could have contributed to the exhaustion. On the other hand, Françoise Lafitte-Cyon remarked that she was looking at her best'[49] rather sooner than one would imagine removal from the treadmill of office routine would account for. Maybe her health was actually better after the lengthy sequence of chills and digestive disorders, although in the summer she did have to cry off a Malthusian tour organised by Bessie Drysdale, due to ill-health.[50]

At the birth control symposium, Stella represented the feminist viewpoint (although incorporating points in favour of Communism). She referred to her earlier 1917 paper for her considered views, and spoke in a rather '"scrappy" and certainly topical, rather than exhaustive' fashion, on recent developments. Although the international picture was not cheering, all was not grim. The war had 'brought more people face to face with economic facts and sexual facts', and had given an impetus to the campaign against VD. Stella then proceeded to make a passionate case and extremely radical case for 'entirely voluntary motherhood', with 'free sexual selection by women ... and communal care of children', thus 'giving freedom and security to her who remains – altho' an individual and free human person – the gate of the race to life.'[51]

She also contributed to a symposium on women and communism published in *The Communist*, 11 March 1922. Her piece on 'The Women's Question' drew angry attention to the contrast between advances made during the war – the paying of a 'decent living wage' to women, the rights of the mother and child '(grudgingly and inadequately, it is true) ... recognised', while subjects such as VD, housing conditions and the 'famous absurdities of the English law of Separation and Divorce' were 'investigated and talked about' in the hope that, after the war, they would be dealt with – and the fact that, now that the war was over, it was 'once more economically a crime to be a woman'. While it was not a 'proud or pleasant task' to say 'I told you so', she pointed out that before the war

> some of us had steadily pointed out that no fair and tolerable conditions for women and the future generations are possible under competitive industrialism and the obsolescent debris of a patriarchal family system which is breaking before our eyes under sheer economic stress.

What, she asked, were the 'ideals in regard to the special work and special nature of women that are unrealisable under Capitalism, but integral to Communism?' First, was the freedom to do any work they were fitted for, to be instructed, to be given responsibility – the realisation of 'The ideal that nineteenth century bourgeois suffragists fought for piecemeal'. Second, came 'Adequate special protection of the child and the child-bearing mother, by the community', and the

> indispensable 'other side of the shield' – *the entire individual responsibility of women in regard to the acceptance or refusal of motherhood, the fundamental human right of the mother to bear life gladly and proudly or not at all, and of the unborn to be wanted and welcomed.*

The third desideratum was 'freedom of sexual relationships from legal or economic coercion'. All these were realised, or on the way to realisation, in Soviet Russia. She concluded by calling upon

> all women who can work, who can think, who want a better world for their children, who want the full dignity and power and beauty of human love and of human life, to join us in the fight for the Communist Commonwealth.[52]

Sue Bruley has emphasised the uniqueness of this article in the interwar Communist press, in its recognition of 'a system of patriarchal social relations existing alongside the categories of class ... within a society whose dominant economic mode was capitalism'. The Party 'line' was always that women were 'oppressed by individual men in family situations solely as a result of "capitalism"', rather than seeing sexual oppression as having a relatively autonomous parallel existence.[53]

In Sanger's *Birth Control Review*, Stella produced a considered response to an anti-birth control article by the respected American feminist and social reformer Charlotte Perkins Gilman. While her pronouncements on birth control 'should be considered with attention and respect'

> Mrs Gilman is ... afraid that under the knowledge and practice of Birth Control, people will be *too* happy and comfortable. She is afraid they may enjoy not only the psychic but the physical side of sex, more frequently and more intensely than now.

To which Stella asked: 'Well, WHY NOT?'

She engaged with Gilman's claim that the spread of psychoanalytic theory (or, as Stella preferred to call it, 'psychoanalytical *dogmatism*') was 'a disintegrating and degrading influence in morals'. In her own view, the case for birth control as a facilitator of sexual freedom would have been quite as strong if 'Freud and his disciples had never lived'. She acutely observed that the 'nonsense ... talked about "complexes"' was a modish fashion of speech among those 'who two years ago did not know the meaning of the word'. But she was firmly convinced of 'the evils of sexual repression from which so many women still suffer'.[54] This critical attitude towards the increasingly dogmatic theories of psychoanalysis recurred elsewhere. She praised the eschewal of 'the total surrender of independent judgement which so often afflicts the Freudian amateur' in R.H. Hingley's *Psycho-analysis* and the inclusion of Jung and Adler's theories. She also found pertinent Hingley's question '"To what society ... is the individual to be reconciled?"'[55]

Stella adduced recent biochemical researches on hormones to counter Gilman's assertion that, while 'the purpose of mating is clear, the accompanying pleasure is not the purpose', that '*sex exists and is determined by the hormones or products of the ductless glands, quite apart from the reproductive functions*'. She took issue with Gilman's assumption that monogamy was 'natural to our race'; in her view, it was '*extremely rare*' and only achievable through 'the strict subjection of women; an alternative which we both agree is intolerable', or else the recognition that it should be 'relieved by variety', in a situation which provided 'a very minimum of coercion or maximum of freedom ... in sexual relationships'. The 'brain and imagination in "homo sapiens"' had 'stimulated and complicated the physical sex functions and the psychic impulse of sex'. While this had had 'hideous and deplorable consequences', economic and social reform would largely remove these. Birth control, Stella concluded, was 'the key to sexual liberty' and, thus, 'logically attacked by the opponents of sexual liberty and sexual equality'.[56]

By April, things were looking up a little: Stella obtained a post with *The New Generation* – 'reviewing and canvassing'[57] but, although this seems to have relieved the immediate crisis, her financial position remained insecure. She continued active in the BSSSP.[58]

Reviewing Ellis's *Little Essays of Love and Virtue*, she detected the downside of Ellis's 'intellectual power and originality' and 'temperament of exquisite sensitivity and balance' in 'slightly excessive caution and a slightly excessive idealism.' In her view, 'direct action of the most thoroughgoing description is necessary, before the lessons he teaches can be assimilated and his ideals "made flesh"'. He was inadequately militant over the necessity for changes in the existing marriage system. But, nonetheless, she considered the work 'brilliant and subtle ... harmonious and profound. '[R]epelled by the notice on the "jacket"', she advised readers to throw away the 'cheap-jack advertisement' typifying 'an increasingly vulgarised and mechanised world.' Such a world, she warned, would never allow the 'aspirations these essays express and the delicate evolutionary developments with which they deal' to come to fruition.[59]

Elsewhere, she found it her

> unpleasant duty to speak plainly about the new 'line' in sexual commercialism. The demi-semi-pseudo-scientific 'popular' work which exploits ignorance and curiosity by its title, imparts very little by the way of accurate information, and less than nothing ethically.

But a pamphlet by her friend and colleague Norah March was 'a breath of fresh air from hill and park after the exhalations of a crowded cinema hall': its 'Moderate Conservative' case for birth control was 'extremely good', and if 'sublimation' was perhaps over-emphasised, on the whole March was 'very fair and sane.'[60]

Stella was now regularly reviewing a very varied selection of publications. She dismissed *The Natural History of the Child* as 'gossip and anecdotage, unsifted folklore and saccharine sentimentalities', not even 'amusing as light reading.'[61] Under the pseudonym of 'Vega', which she employed occasionally for many years, she gave a very favourable notice to Cicely Hamilton's science fiction novel *Theodore Savage*:

> an impressive picture of the material and mental ruin of our present phase of civilisation by scientific warfare and of the infinitely slow and painful process of re-building some form of communal life ... the cumulative effect ... is ominous and disturbing.'[62]

She was far from impressed by the report of the National Council on Public Morals report on *The Prevention of Venereal Disease*: a 'priceless psychological document' revealing 'the breakdown of bourgeois morality in the face of venereal disease, the result of ignorance, poverty and prostitution – the three pillars of bourgeois society', and in spite of itself proving 'the need for sanitary and contraceptive knowledge among the mass of the people'.[63] She was also addressing meetings on birth control: on June 20 she had a 'most instructive and encouraging experience' addressing the Southend branch of the Women's Cooperative Guild (WCG).[64]

She undertook a little reviewing for William J. Robinson's US journal *Medical Critic and Guide*, although this never became a regular outlet. Among the volumes she dealt with was *Die weibliche Eigenart im Männerstaat unde die männliche Eigenart in Frauestaat* (which Stella translated as 'Feminine Peculiarities in the Androcratic State, and Masculine Characteristics in the Gynecocratic State'), by Mathilde and Matthias Vaerting, whom she regarded as 'among the most profound and original investigators of eugenics and sociological problems at present'. She praised their 'use of modern anthropological and historical research', and made an intriguing allusion to Margaret Murray's recently published *The Witch-Cult in Central Europe* (an influential work, although modern scholars of witchcraft do not accept Murray's thesis). Stella claimed that Murray and the Vaertings had 'proved their case for the historical association of phallic worship with a social order on a matriarchal basis, or at least a basis of approximate co-sexual equality'. She also found 'peculiarly interesting' the Vaertings' argument that 'the penalisation of abortion is one of the most signal proofs and accompaniments of the strict subjection of women'. Also praised was Alexandra Kollontai's 'incisively yet gracefully written' *Die Neue Moral und die Arbeiterklasse* ("The New Morality of the Working Class'), which gave 'full value to the psychological factors which are *sometimes* unduly ignored by Marxist writers, but which can only be correctly appraised when we remember the ceaseless pressure of economic environment'.[65]

In July, she participated in the Fifth International Neo-Malthusian and Birth Control Conference at Kingsway Hall in London. As well as attending as a delegate for the BSSSP,[66] she presented a paper on 'The Feminine Aspect of Birth Control'. She spoke 'as a Feminist and a Communist ... a very small minority in the [birth control] movement in this country', for whom birth control signified 'freedom for women, social and sexual' – the reason why it was 'so intensely feared and disliked in many influential quarters'. Alluding to the existing prevalence of self-induced or backstreet abortion by 'drugs or ... violent internal operative methods', she considered that it was not 'beyond the powers of medical and chemical science to invent an absolutely reliable contraceptive!', especially in view of the 'marvels of destruction in the shape of asphyxiating and corrosive gases' all ready for the next war, and the knowledge already attained of the sex hormones. This was almost certainly the first argument on a public platform in Britain for the legalisation of abortion. Stella referred to the 1920 law of the Soviet Republic entitling women to abortion during the first three months of pregnancy, with rest and care at State expense, and to the movements in other European countries for similar legislation. Disclaiming any concern 'to vindicate the moral right to abortion', even though she was 'convinced that it is a woman's primary right', she was prepared to consider the argument that 'abortion is *physiologically injurious* and to be deprecated'. She wondered whether the 'effects of abortion itself have been sufficiently separated from the appalling bad conditions of nervous terror, lack of rest and lack of surgical cleanliness in which it is generally performed', but, if it were the case, 'the demand for effective contraception is all the stronger'.[67]

In July, she reviewed Sanger's *The New Motherhood* and *What Every Girl Should Know* in *The New Generation*, alongside Katharine Anthony's biography of the nineteenth-century American feminist Margaret Fuller. Stella suggested that Fuller would have understood and appreciated Sanger and Alexandra Kollontai – 'the two great living woman-emanicipators of women. She predictably praised Sanger's 'profound and enthusiastic feminism' and 'sanely human outlook'.[68] The following month, she gave very positive notice to Leonora Eyles's *The Woman in the Little House*, although conflicting political sympathies came through in her comment on Eyles's 'unaccountable *optimism* with regard to the possibility of a peaceful "*evolution*" of capitalism into civilisation'.[69]

If she was trying to radicalise the birth control movement, she was also engaged in trying to raise the consciousness of the Communist Party of Great Britain CPGB) regarding birth control, a thankless task which would lead, at least in part, to her resignation from the Party. In the letter column of *The Communist*, she referred to an article by 'Clete' as 'an example of the exclusively masculine point of view on a fundamental human question', pointing out that '*birth control for women is no less essential than workshop control and determination of the conditions of labour for men*'. Birth control as 'woman's crucial effort at self-determination and at control of her own person and her own environment' had been recognised by 'leading Socialists and proletarian women' in 'countries where sex questions are less obscured by cant than in Great Britain'.[70] 'Clete' responded by describing her opinions as 'exclusively feminist', and his response conveys a fearful subtext about 'woman "determining" or dictating her own terms', with a curious anthropological allusion to the 'matriarchal system' and women's control not merely of birth but 'all sex intercourse'. This sits oddly alongside his claim that 'a woman of independent means or capable of earning an efficient wage. .. can make a fair bargain with any male she desires'. Contraception, he averred, was 'a question for individuals'. He also read into Stella's letter a claim that does not appear there – that 'the capitalist's doll needs a knowledge of birth control less than the average working woman'.[71] His position was supported by a letter from S. Francis, 'a woman, who, although a believer in individual birth control, does *not* see eye to eye with Comrade Stella Browne'. Comrade Francis regretted that 'on the subject of sex equality, the majority of my women comrades are as unsound as their capitalist-minded sisters'. Women's 'so-called "slavery" to man ... *can only end when the capitalist regime ends*'.[72]

If Stella or any other 'unsound' women comrades provided any riposte, this was not published. Elsewhere, she commented that on the individual level 'my most effective and able comrades under the Red Flag practice birth control ... intelligently and consistently', but wished that

> revolutionary women would more boldly and explicitly incorporate birth control not only in their individual tactics but in their philosophy: not for an instant as an alternative solution to the mess the world has got into, but as the accompaniment and aid to our view of life.[73]

Sue Bruley has demonstrated that women's issues, of which birth control was only one, were consistently occluded and considered private rather than political matters by Party leadership,[74] while female Party membership was extremely low.[75]

This attitude on the part of the CPGB may have influenced Stella's growing praise for the WCG.[76] The Guild had a remarkable record of campaigning from a perspective both of the needs of the working class and feminism. By autumn 1922, birth control was 'already being discussed in some of the branches',[77] and Stella herself had addressed WCG branch meetings, which she described as a 'rare treat'. These women, 'so tightly bound down to bread-and-butter considerations by material facts', nonetheless took a 'human and social' and sympathetic line on birth control. Although they had 'an ethical standard and a high one, and they consistently live up to it', their minds were free from 'effete formulae in the region of personal conduct'. However, she was only too aware of the extent to which so many of their lives were 'not glorified by any of the sweetness and rapture of sex-love except for a few fugitive glimpses at courting-time'.

Contemplating these 'Working Women who Think' led her a paean to 'one of the dearest friends I have ever known'. This woman, 'child-bearer and homemaker' and 'earner' as well, had had nine surviving children out of fifteen pregnancies. Her second husband infected her with syphilis, leading to the loss of sight in one eye and ulcers. Nevertheless, 'she remained till the day of her death a tower of mental and psychic strength and a source of help and happiness to many distressed and unhappy people'. She had 'gifts' which, in more favourable circumstances, 'would have made her famous ... exquisite tenderness, the most undaunted courage'. This moving tribute to a nameless woman underscores Stella Browne's passionate and unsentimental attachment to women very unlike herself. There is nothing patronising in her account but, rather, profound admiration for women who, in the teeth of adversity, were 'examples of the woman worker who loves and helps and thinks'.[78]

In the *Labour Leader* (published by the Independent Labour Party), she recommended the re-branded Malthusian League to 'all who believe that the knowledge of birth control should be available to all humanity'.[79] This may have been a gesture as much against Marie Stopes and her burgeoning Society for Constructive Birth Control as to promote the New Generation League. In September 1922, dissensions in the birth control movement over Marie Stopes's attempt to assimilate it as her own personal cause (and the growing breach between Sanger and Stopes) came to a crisis when, in a review of Sanger's *The New Motherhood*, Stopes asserted her own priority in recommendation of the female check pessary (occlusive rubber cap). Stella wrote to Stopes, 'call[ing] your attention to a certain erroneous statement', citing Sanger's 1914 pamphlet, *Family Limitation*. She was 'certain you would not wish to leave a serious and demonstrable error uncorrected'.[80] Stopes sent an impersonal note in response, asking 'Miss Browne' to 'mak[e] clear [in] which words of the published quotations any error exists'.[81]

Havelock Ellis alluded to his own exchange with 'naughty Marie Stopes', in which 'it passed through my head to refer to the baseless charge against Margaret Sanger', and he 'wished I had when I ... found the "B.C. News" with no retraction of the statement. Stella Browne will be furious.'[82] Stella arranged for *The New Generation* to publish a note about the Stopes review, and wanted Ellis to cooperate in circulating copies of her correspondence with Stopes, but he diplomatically claimed that 'I am on friendly terms with Marie Stopes and could not work against her behind her back.'[83] Stopes stuck to her disingenuous claim that Stella has 'failed to substantiate any verbal inaccuracy in our quotations' in a note 'ATTACK ON THE BIRTH CONTROL NEWS',[84] described by Stella as 'excited but evasive'.[85]

A hint of future trouble on a different front appeared in the autumn of 1922. Stella was back in economic straits. She was 'out of *regular* work and doing scraps of piece work only', a situation which continued well into the following year.[86] Her writing was proving 'very difficult to place'.[87] Sanger hinted at 'making her the European representative of the B. C. Review.' Stella took this as perhaps rather more definite than it was: Ellis assumed that it was 'an idea you [Sanger] threw out for future consideration should it seem practicable', but advised Sanger that 'being inclined to be neurotic, she might come to consider herself rather aggrieved if you seem to have forgotten it'.[88] During this 'bitter but educative year', Stella 'waited in *sickening* anxiety, & positive hardship' for 'weeks and weeks this autumn', in the hopes of hearing from Sanger with positive news of 'a *part-time* job I could at least rely on'.[89]

Meanwhile, Stella made a new friend through Ellis: Jane Burr, an American writer. There is some evidence that they remained in touch during Burr's travels,[90] but little correspondence from this period of Burr's career survives.[91]

Other correspondence which has not survived is Stella's '9 excited pages in response to my 4' sent to George Ives in November, in which she mentioned (among other things) that she had resigned from the 'Literary subcommittee'.[92] Possibly the commitment impinged on her developing role as a lecturer on birth control under the auspices of the New Generation League, which took her not only to venues within London and its peripheries, but as far afield as Slough.[93] However, she remained active on the BSSSP Executive, in particular in the search for an office, visiting premises under consideration near Hyde Park. Although 'not what one would have *chosen*' (partly due to its location – 'far from the homes of most of our members', although '*by no means further for most than for instance Hampstead and Harper St have always been for me personally*'), she had 'no hesitations in advising the Committee to take it' for an initial six months. She considered an available office to be '*the* key for our future' and that, if an appeal failed to raise sufficient finance, she rather despaired that there was 'not enough backing to keep us alive'.[94]

She was rendered 'quite pleased and happy' by a letter from Sanger in late November,[95] which conveyed the rather surprising news of her marriage to J. Noah Slee, and by a 'magnificent photograph' of Sanger with a 'charming signed inscription'. In addition, at this time Stella was '"up to the ears"' in a passionate love affair with an (unidentified) man who was

> very vital & very attractive, not in the least handsome, though clever, but intensely alive & I sh[d] think as impulsive capricious & jealous as they are made, as well as being *heavily overworked professionally* in his career, & of course, married! – so you see the difficulties of life are considerably added to.

For her, 'love is the sauce of life, but every love has its limitations, & the cure for love is – strictly homeopathic!' On keeping a relationship continuing over a long period of years, she commented, about her still 'very intermittent and occasional' first lover, 'I have known *when & how* to *leave him alone* – that is the secret! & never whined or made scenes.'

This personally optimistic note was somewhat undercut by the arrest of the anarchists Guy Aldred and Rose Witcop for publishing Sanger's pamphlet *Family Limitation*, a cause which was to occupy much of the attention of the birth control community in Britain during the first months of 1923. Stella wondered if 'Stopes may not be behind it'. She had 'written to various Labour MPs', but could 'personally do very little, situated as I am at present'. Other supporters were rallying to the cause, even the Drysdales in a 'peculiarly graceless and grudging manner ... they are both spiritually such – well *oafs*'.[96]

The massing clouds of problems with causes she was committed to and personal relationships in which she was deeply involved were to break into a storm of trouble and upheaval in the early months of 1923, and it would be some time before Stella regained anything like equilibrium.

Notes

1. Stella Browne to Janet Carson, 20 September 1920, 'B.S.S. Misc', British Sexology Society Archives, Harry Ransom Humanities Research Center, University of Texas at Austin [HRC].
2. Havelock Ellis to Margaret Sanger, 22 December 1921, Sanger papers in the Library of Congress, Washington, DC [LC], Volume 7.
3. Browne to Carson, 20 September 1920, 'B.S.S. Misc', HRC.
4. F.W. Stella Browne 'The "women's question"', *The Communist*, 11 March 1922, p. 7.
5. Bertram Lloyd, *The Great Kinship: An Anthology of Humanitarian Poetry* (London: George Allen & Unwin, 1921), pp. xvi, 127, 181.
6. F.W. Stella Browne, 'Liberty and democracy', *Birth Control Review*, February 1921, pp. 6–7.

7. Havelock Ellis to Françoise Lafitte-Cyon, [? 21 February 1921], Howard Gotlieb Archival Research Center, Boston University [HGA].
8. Françoise Lafitte-Cyon to Havelock Ellis, 22 February 1921, HGA.
9. Ellis to Lafitte-Cyon, 31 May 1921, HGA.
10. George Ives, diary entry for 24 July 1921, 'Notes and Writings', Volume LXXXI, Harry Ransom Humanities Research Center, University of Texas at Austin [Ives HRC].
11. Phyllis Grosskurth, *Havelock Ellis: A Biography* (London: Allen Lane, 1980), p. 301.
12. Stella Browne to Margaret Sanger, 14 August 1921, LC, Volume 16.
13. Margaret Sanger, *The Pivot of Civilisation* (New York: Brentano's, 1922), pp. 181–2.
14. Browne to Sanger, 14 August 1921, LC, Volume 16.
15. Stella Browne to S.H. Halford, 19 August 1921, 'B.S.S. Misc', HRC.
16. Browne to Halford, 24 August 1921, 'B.S.S. Misc', HRC.
17. Minutes of Special Committee meeting, 6 September 1921, 'B.S.S. Misc', HRC.
18. Stella Browne to T. Atholl Joyce, 11 September 1921, 'B.S.S. Misc', HRC.
19. Browne to T. Joyce, 13 September 1921, 'B.S.S. Misc', HRC.
20. *The Communist*, 24 September 1921, 19 November 1921.
21. Browne to Halford, 26 September 1921; Minutes of 90th Executive Committee Meeting, 29 September 1921; Minutes of the 91st and 94th Executive Committee Meetings, 13 October 1921, 12 December 1921, 'B.S.S. Misc', HRC.
22. Ellis to Sanger, 13 September 1921, LC, Volume 4.
23. Ellen Chesler, *Woman of Valor: Margaret Sanger and the Birth Control Movement in America* (New York: Simon & Schuster 1992), pp. 202, 203; Emily Taft Douglas, *Margaret Sanger: Pioneer of the Future* (Garrett Park, MD: Garrett Park Press, 1975), pp 164–7: too early to be a protest against the police raid on Sanger's public meeting in New York, or the refusal of a visa for Japan.
24. Browne to Joyce, 18 September 1921, and to Halford, 26 September 1921, 'B.S.S. Misc', HRC.
25. Minutes of the 91st Executive Committee Meeting, 13 October 1921, 'B.S.S. Misc', HRC.
26. Enid M. Chambers to Edward Carpenter, 19 August 1921, Carpenter/Mss/386/355.
27. Minutes of the 92nd Executive Committee Meeting, 27 October 1921, 'B.S.S. Misc', HRC.
28. Minutes of the 93rd Executive Committee Meeting, 17 November 1921, 'B.S.S. Misc', HRC.
29. Minutes of the 95th Executive Committee Meeting, 12 January 1922, 'B.S.S. Misc', HRC.
30. Havelock Ellis to Hugh de Selincourt, 22 December 1921, LC, Volume 7.

31. Stella Browne to Mrs Bailey, 10 March 1923, 'B.S.S. Misc', HRC.
32. Minutes of the 86th Executive Committee meeting, 10 June 1921, 'B.S.S. Misc', HRC.
33. Ellis to Lafitte-Cyon, 22 November 1921, HGA.
34. Ellis to de Selincourt, 9 December 1921, LC, Volume 7.
35. Minutes of the 95th Executive Committee Meeting, 12 January 1922, 'B.S.S. Misc', HRC.
36. George Ives, diary entry for 24 May 1922, 'Notes and Writings' LXXXIII, Ives HRC.
37. Ellis to de Selincourt, 16 July 1922, LC, Volume 7.
38. Minutes of the 109th Executive Committee Meeting, 8 March 1923, 'B.S.S. Misc', HRC.
39. Hugh de Selincourt to Margaret Sanger, 8 July 1924, Sanger papers in the Sophia Smith collection, Smith College.
40. Chesler, *Woman of Valor*, pp. 183–6.
41. Stella Browne to Havelock Ellis, 6 March 1922, Ellis papers in the Department of Manuscripts, British Library, Additional Manuscript 70539 [BL Add Ms 70539].
42. Chelsea Electoral Registers, Chelsea Public Library.
43. Family information supplied by John Dodwell.
44. Browne to Ellis, 6 March 1922, BL Add Ms 70539.
45. Elizabeth Marian Bailey to S.H. Halford, 14 February 1922, 'B.S.S. Misc', HRC.
46. Browne to Ellis, 6 March 1922, BL Add Ms 70539.
47. Bessie Drysdale to Margaret Sanger, 12 May 1923, LC, Volume 21.
48. Browne to Ellis, 6 March 1922, BL Add Ms 70539.
49. Lafitte-Cyon to Ellis, 24 March 1922, HGA.
50. Bessie Drysdale to Sanger, 20 July [? 1922], LC, Volume 21.
51. F.W. Stella Browne, 'Women, birth control and the social order', *Medical Critic and Guide*, vol. 25/6, June 1922, pp. 210–12.
52. F.W. Stella Browne, 'The "women's question"', *The Communist*, 11 March 1922, p. 7.
53. Sue Bruley, *Leninism, Stalinism and the Women's Movement in Britain, 1920–1939* (New York: Garland Publishing Inc., 1986), pp. 77–8.
54. F.W. Stella Browne, 'Birth control and sex psychology: a reply to "Back of birth control"', *Birth Control Review*, March 1922, pp. 33–4.
55. F.W.S.B., 'Review: *Psycho-analysis*. By R.H. Hingley, B.A.', *The New Generation*, vol. 1, no. 8, August 1922, p. 7.
56. Browne, 'Birth control and sex psychology'.
57. Ellis to Sanger, 20 April 1922, LC, Volume 5.
58. Minutes of the 99th meeting of the Executive Committee, 11 May 1922 HRC.

59. F.W. Stella Browne, 'Review: *Little Essays of Love and Virtue*. By Havelock Ellis', *The New Generation*, vol. 1, no. 5, May 1922, pp. 7–8.
60. F.W. Stella Browne, 'Review: *Husbands and Wives*. By Arthur Belville; *Love, Courtship and Marriage*. By Thomas Herne; *Sex Knowledge, with a special chapter on Birth Control*. By Norah March', *The New Generation*, vol. 1, no. 5, May 1922, p. 8.
61. F.W.S.B., 'Review: *The Natural History of the Child: A Book for All Sorts and Conditions of Men, Women and Children*. By Dr Courtenay Dunn', *The New Generation*, vol. 1, no. 6, June 1922, p. 13.
62. 'Vega', 'A novel with a purpose'; 'Review: *Theodore Savage: A Story of the Past or the Future*. By Cicely Hamilton', *The New Generation*, vol. 1, no. 6, June 1922, p. 13.
63. F.W. Stella Browne, 'Reviews: *The Prevention of Venereal Disease. Being the Report of and the Evidence taken by the Special Committee on Venereal Disease*', *The New Generation*, vol. 1, no. 6, June 1922, p. 13.
64. F.W. Stella Browne, 'Women workers who think', *The New Generation*, vol. 1, no. 9, September 1922, pp. 6–7.
65. Stella Browne, 'International reviews: studies in constructive psychology', *Medical Critic and Guide*, vol. 25/6, vol. 25, June 1922, pp. 235–6.
66. Elizabeth Marian Bailey to S.H. Halford, 30 June and 5 July 1922, 'B.S.S. Misc', HRC.
67. F.W. Stella Browne, 'The feminine aspect of birth control', in Raymond Pierpoint (ed.), *Report of the Fifth International Neo-Malthusian and Birth Control Conference,* Kingsway Hall, London July 11th to 14th, 1922 (London: William Heinemann (Medical Books) Ltd, 1922), pp. 40–3.
68. F.W. Stella Browne, 'Reviews: The message of the Margarets', *The New Generation*, vol. 1, no. 7, July 1922, pp. 14–15.
69. F.W. Stella Browne, 'Review: *The Woman in the Little House*. By Leonora Eyles', *The New Generation*, vol. 1, no. 8, August 1922, pp. 12–13.
70. Stella Browne, 'Birth control', *The Communist*, 19 August 1922, p. 2.
71. Clete, 'Birth control'. *The Communist*, 26 August 1922, p. 6.
72. S. Francis, 'Birth control'. *The Communist*, 26 August 1922, p. 6.
73. F.W. Stella Browne, 'Working woman supports birth control', *The New Generation*, vol. 1, no. 11, November 1922, p. 5.
74. Bruley, *Leninism, Stalinism and the Women's Movement in Britain*, pp. 71–81.
75. Andrew Thorpe, 'The membership of the Communist Party of Great Britain, 1920–1945', *The Historical Journal*, vol. 43/3, 2000, pp. 777–800.
76. Browne, 'Review, *The Woman in the Little House*'.
77. Central Council Meeting, 27–28 September 1922, item 12, Women's Cooperative Guild Archives, Brymor Jones Library, University of Hull.
78. Browne, 'Women workers who think'.

79. 'Our letter box: Stella Browne writes', *Labour Leader*, 24 August 1922, p. 7.
80. F.W. Stella Browne to The Editor of the *Birth Control News*, 14 September 1922, Marie Stopes papers, Wellcome Library, PP/MCS/A.42.
81. Marie Stopes to Stella Browne, 19 September 1922, PP/MCS/A.42.
82. Ellis to Sanger, 6 October 1922, LC, Volume 5.
83. Ellis to Sanger, 27 October 1922, LC, Volume 5.
84. Manuscript and typescript drafts of note, PP/MCS/A.42.
85. Stella Browne, 'Letter: Misrepresentative methods', *The New Generation*, vol. 2, no. 1, January 1922, p. 15.
86. Browne to Bailey, 4 April 1923, 'B.S.S. Misc', HRC.
87. Ellis to Sanger, 10 December 1922, LC, Volume 5.
88. Ellis to Sanger, 16 November 1922, LC, Volume 5.
89. Browne to Ellis, 16 February 1923, BL Add Ms 70539.
90. It seems probable that Stella's knowledge of birth control initiatives in Central America – F.W. Stella Browne, 'The art of suppression', *The New Generation*, vol. 4, February 1925, pp. 16–17 – came via Burr, who was travelling there: Havelock Ellis to Burr, 6 April 1925, Jane Burr papers in the Sophia Smith Collection, Smith College, file 14.
91. Jane Burr to Margaret Grierson, 17 August 1949, Jane Burr papers: 'Travelling in suitcases as I did all over Europe I could not allow myself an extra sheet of paper'.
92. George Ives, Diary entry for 14 November 1922, 'Notes and Writings', Volume LXXXIII, Ives HRC.
93. 'Forthcoming meetings', *The New Generation*, vol. 1, no. 10, October 1922, p. 11; 'Reports on meetings', *The New Generation*, vol. 2, no. 1, January 1923, p. 7.
94. Browne to Bailey, 17 December 1922, 'B.S.S. Misc', HRC.
95. Ellis to Sanger, 10 December 1922, LC, Volume 5.
96. Browne to Ellis, 25 December 1922, BL Add Ms 70539.

6

Endings, Beginnings, New Directions in the Middle Way of Life

At the beginning of 1923, Stella quit the Communist Party, but did not announce this for several years, as 'Communists are suffering so much persecution'.[1] It was known among her associates: Bessie Drysdale gloated 'F.W.S.B. has now resigned from the Communists!'[2] The reasons behind her decision (although she remained a passionate 'fellow-traveller')[3] were never explicit. A major factor was the lack of support by the Communists for birth control.[4] Nearly all the 'small leavening of middle-class "intellectuals"' in the Party had fallen away by late 1924.[5]

There was a strong strain of traditional British puritanism among the CPGB.[6] A great deal of active participation in Party work was expected: 'attendance at frequent meetings; activity in trade unions and other outside bodies; membership of "front" organisations; the sale of literature', all of which would have added to Stella's already considerable burdens, as would the relatively high subscriptions.[7] Stella may have been expected to renounce her birth control work in favour of other tasks deemed more politically relevant; and she did not respond well to authoritarian demands. Her 'strongly individual and independent point of view... [was] often as unwelcome to the Communists as to the orthodox "Right Wingers" and "pale Pinks"':[8] idiosyncratic and eccentric as the CPGB might have been in a wider European context, a woman like Stella was unlikely to find it an easy fit.[9] Nonetheless, it must have been a wrench to give up this commitment.

In her work for 'the Cause' of birth control, Stella scored a significant coup in the fight to generate support within the Labour movement. The paper of the Independent Labour Party, *The New Leader*, published her letter condemning the police raid on Guy Aldred and Rose Witcop's Bakunin Press, the confiscation of their stock of Sanger's *Family Limitation*, and its impending prosecution for 'obscenity'. Stella pointed out that 'the knowledge and practice of birth control are absolutely legal in this country'. She also cited the concurrent cause célèbre, the dismissal of Nurse Elizabeth Daniels, a health visitor, for giving birth control advice: 'an urgent wrong for Labour to set right'.[10] (Daniels was involved with the New Generation League and may have been Stella's informant with 'wide nursing experience' who considered abortion '*physiologically injurious*'.)[11] While this was not the first time Stella's letters on the subject had appeared in the Labour press, this time her appeal garnered editorial support. The leader included a paragraph on 'Birth Control', agreeing that 'the business of a Health Authority, so far from suppressing this knowledge, should be to spread it among those who need it most'.[12]

During January, Stella was 'pretty well run off my feet *with the worries of the Aldred case*',[13] and Rose Witcop wrote to Sanger that she had heard from 'your good friend Stella Browne' about Marie Stopes's attack on *Family Limitation*.[14] Stella concluded a talk to Chelsea Labour Party women with an appeal for the Walworth Women's Clinic, started by the Malthusian League late in 1921, and also 'an appeal ... for the Aldreds'.[15] Stella's life became sufficiently hectic that, towards the end of January, she failed to turn up to a lunch engagement with her old friend the lawyer E.S.P. Haynes, who had hoped to discuss some BSSSP matters with her.[16]

In the January issue of *Birth Control Review*, Stella took time out from immediate campaigns to pay tribute to a long-standing heroine, Dr Helene Stöcker and her 'long and splendid record of effort and achievement', as a writer, propagandist, theorist and campaigner both in the field of sex reform and pacifism with feminism as the subtext of her achievements against 'all the iniquities of the "double standard"'. Her question, 'What was its leading note – its chief color ray?'[17] suggests an acquaintance with Theosophy or related belief systems. Stella was not a member of the Theosophical Society,[18] but she certainly seems to have had some sympathy for its ideas.

She continued to produce reviews and columns for *The New Generation* that demonstrate that the fight for birth control was not the sole focus of her interest, even during this intensive phase of the campaign. They also demonstrate the multilingual range of her reading.[19] Her attack on the 'savage persecution of contraceptive information and propaganda' taking place in France demonstrates the extent to which she was keeping up with developments worldwide.[20] While praising Laurence Housman's pamphlet *The New Humanism*, she critiqued his 'idealisation of woman as mother': 'We have all', she suggested, 'known women whose maternal "devotion" or obsession varied from insidious mental tyranny to sheer bullying.'[21]

We have a rare glimpse of Stella engaged in cultural activities even less related to her political concerns during February. Havelock Ellis encountered her at the Phoenix Theatre's production of John Ford's *'Tis Pity She's a Whore*. Stella 'thought it a very fine performance.'[22] She also had two translations, 'Epitaph', and 'Shepherd's Song (Ombre du bois)' from the French poet Pierre Louÿs's 'Les Chansons de Bilitis' published in the American periodical *The Freeman*.[23] She was 'sensitive to beauty & luxury', yet would not compromise her principles in order to achieve these things.[24]

This became very clear in a disenchanted letter she wrote to Ellis in mid-February 1923. While recognising his 'staunch loyalty' to Margaret Sanger she could no longer ignore 'a certain phase in her character – which I will *admit* I had not noticed, or *perhaps had not suffered from*' previously. It was unpleasant 'to have been forced to the conclusion I have been forced to.' Although Stella still 'love[d] the gallant little rebel of 1914 & 15 with her charm and steadfast courage', she was moved to 'criticise the very fashionable, very diplomatic lady of 1922', her public activities in 'the cause' and attitudes towards 'co-workers'. She alluded to some unstated grievance over the Conference, but the main burden of her attack was the disappointment over the *Birth Control Review* job. '*It ought*', Stella considered

> to <u>be intolerable</u> to Margaret in her present circumstances that e.g. I – whose record both for the cause & as her personal friend she knows – sh[d] be as I am now, in such urgent need of opportunity, & of an adequate regular salary, & sh[d] be made a scapegoat of with impunity.

The 'weeks and weeks' spent waiting 'for the news I trusted to receive of a *part-time* job that I could at least rely on (surely £5 <u>*a month*</u> could have been found even if her old Board refused!)' had 'left their mark on me', as had the 'neglect to reply to my letters'. '[*S*]*ome* of us', she concluded bitterly, 'manage not to compromise *quite* so much! Oh this may sound hateful – but alas alas its *true*.'[25] These letters made Françoise literally sick: she thought that Stella must be ill to write in such a way.[26]

Stella may also have been physically exhausted as she rushed around doing 'good work' by her 'lectures … to women's clubs' on the 'theory and practice of birth control',[27] attracting increasingly large audiences.[28] Some evenings she was double-booked. A 'Big Meeting' of the BSSSP in March at 5.30 pm at Princes Gardens 'makes it easier for me to attend as it is ... not half-way across London' and she was addressing the Chelsea Labour Party on 'Housing-Education-Birth Control ("Evolution in Modern Politics")' the same evening.[29] Trying to organise 'tea and a talk' with Mrs Bailey at the 1917 Club in Soho, she could do 'Monday afternoon ... or this Saturday' but couldn't do 'Tuesday or Wednesday ... and am a *bit* doubtful about Thursday', although might be able to manage the afternoon.[30]

The complications of a busy life were not made easier by Ellis's continued use of her as his contact with the BSSSP, introducing additional difficulties and more correspondence for herself, as in the unsuccessful endeavour to arrange at short notice for Maurice Parmalee, an American who had been studying the nudist movement in Germany, to speak to the Society.[31] She 'repeatedly tried' to make Ellis understand that 'these matters ... should come before the Secretary *direct*! but in vain! And we do not, of course, want to offend Ellis.'[32] 'Suffering from 'the usual cold', she was grateful for the secretary, Mrs Bailey's, pleasant comments about her chairmanship at a previous meeting.[33] In spite of all these demands on her time and energies, she wrote to several members of the Committee of the Walworth Women's Clinic concerning 'the selling price of the syringes'.[34]

The various pressures were, however, getting to her, and she wrote to her colleague on the BSSSP Executive, S.H. Halford, that she was no longer able to 'undertake any work in connection with the *office* for B.S.S.P.'. She had been out of regular employment since the previous August; 'occasional writing and speaking jobs are few far between and badly paid'; she was not receiving benefit; and could no longer give 'my time and minor expenses like fares etc ... to any Society'. While remaining on the Executive and attending such meetings as she could, she had given up all her subcommittee work already, and could not 'undertake any detail work of any kind' for the Society. It struck her as unfair that 'willing workers sh^{d} be either rushed off their feet ... or completely "stoney"'.[35] Her finances were in such bad shape – she was doing 'scraps of piece-work only' – that she was unable to pay even her reduced annual subscription to the BSSSP, and pointed out 'the very large amount of honorary effort, literary, propagandist and in routine work which I have *given* in the past.' This had included 'answering a good deal of correspondence of which I enclose a sample ... I feel I have really laid up some treasure in heaven!!' However, she would 'prefer some treasure in the bank occasionally'. Once she was 'earning well and regularly again', she would pay up.[36] In spite of this cutting back on her activities for the Society, she was still being proactive in promoting it.[37]

On 24 April, she addressed 54 women at St Alban's Women's Adult School on 'the economic and national side of birth control': while 'well-received', she had 'the impression that "practical methods" would have been more appropriate and useful', given the 'eagerness with which application forms for our leaflet were demanded'. Two days later, she spoke to St Pancras Labour Woman's Group – 'one of the best and most intelligent meetings' she had ever addressed, and on 9 May to East Islington Labour Women – 'almost equally as good'. She alluded to the birth control resolution raised at the 1923 Conference of Labour Women, and hoped that at the 1924 Conference the issue 'will be even more persistently and widely voiced, until the Party bureaucracy at least see reason'.[38] According to R.B. Kerr of the New Generation League, she was 'getting to be an excellent speaker on practical methods, and only needs to be known about to be in great demand'.[39] Her lecturing, however, was not confined to birth control: in May she was 'speaking at Chelsea on East Galicia & [? the Oil War – a particularly illegible phrase]'.[40]

In spite of this whirl of activity, or maybe because of it, she had not 'been at all well' and was finding the 'extremes of temperature ... trying'. She was also undergoing, once again, 'worry about a lodger'. There were also continuing difficulties over the final stages of the Otto Braun translation project which Ellis had put her way. In the end, she had revised literal translations, rather than retranslating from scratch, and was looking over the 'final notes'. The Braun-Vogelstein family, she informed Ellis, had 'shown a very arrogant & exacting spirit both to the firm of publishers & to Miss Winter: just that fatal tact & tastelessness of the German or the German-Jew which do bring such deserved dislike on them & involve so many excellent other sort of Germans in odium'.[41] (In her article on Helene Stöcker, she had commented on the latter's 'vivacity and geniality ... natural sweetness and buoyancy of temper' characteristic of the Rhinelander, which did not impair 'the two first qualities of the German mind, unflinching intellectual honesty and thoroughness'.[42] Stella could be both very positive and very negative about Germans. It would appear to have been the Germanic quality of the 'German-Jew' she objected to: no other remotely anti-Semitic remark can be traced, although occasionally a degree of racial essentialism can be discerned.)

Problems with Sanger and the *Birth Control Review* continued to nag on, even though Ellis 'repeatedly tried to assure her how much you [Sanger] have wished to be helpful & to generally expound to her your (as I consider it) beautiful psychology'.[43] When Stella sent in a review of American socialist Scott Nearing's book *The Next Step*, commissioned by the *Birth Control Review*, she was told by Annie Porritt that 'they already had one in hand'. This she considered 'either a piece of toadying to a capitalist board, or ... a deliberate affront'.[44] Her review seems fairly mild after this account.[45] She found Mrs Porritt 'totally uncongenial in temperament & opinion', but conceded her to be '*competent and certainly a very loyal employee*' and was convinced that Porritt was 'being *used*' and that Sanger's attribution to her of blame for the various muddles was 'mean "scapegoating" '.[46]

It was not the most apposite time for R.B. Kerr to suggest to Sanger (considering a trip to the UK to address Labour meetings) that 'it might be a good plan to take her [Stella] around with you', and to pass Sanger's letter to Stella for her to 'handle the matter'.[47] Although Sanger had expressed herself 'in the most flattering terms ... on my work among Labor [sic] women' both directly and through Kerr, Stella continued suspicious, feeling that there was a wide gap between this 'gush' and Sanger's actions – 'This running with the hare and hunting with the hounds is neither dignified, honest, nor in the long run very wise'. The proposed lecture tour had not been mentioned in Sanger's letter to Stella herself, while the delay in payment for her work for *Birth Control Review* put Stella 'to excruciating inconvenience by the lack of cash', and she felt that 'I might have starved in the winter for all she cared.' If Sanger and her organisation had money to spare for a European tour ('If the account of the American position given in her paper, is anything like the truth, her post of duty ... is there'), '*more could have been done & with more gracious promptitude, to help the Aldreds, who were good enough to be her friends & hosts in 1914 and again in 1920*'. Stella '*unequivocally and* [?*un*] *conditionally refused*' to organise the lecture tour; and if Sanger did 'come over it will be on a far less triumphal progress than [the] last'.[48]

The whole episode caused her 'a frightful nervous upset', 'a most upsetting psychic "storm" ', although she had been enabled to weather this by her first out-of-town visit for eight months, a weekend with the progressive Montessori-influenced MacMunns at their school at Tiptree Hall in Essex. She had been put in touch with them by Ellis, possibly with a view to employment, but 'I sh^{d} never have been suited for a post in which manual & domestic skill is so essential.' While their 'experiment is extremely promising & creative, if it is to survive – there will have to be not only more cash but more *practical* capacity.' (Doubtless her opinions were influenced by her own experiences.) Norman MacMunn himself combined 'amazing mental fertility & enthusiasm & great independence of mind' with 'that curious rigidity of mind often found in the extreme ideality' – a phenomenon which she was possibly experiencing with her Party comrades. She was '"bucked up"' by the visit, especially the 'most beautiful & fascinating garden & orchard, with a lake'.[49]

The Sanger situation finally came to a head in early August. Sanger had written to Stella in late June claiming that she had no plans to visit Britain before 1925, which Stella considered, in the light of the correspondence with Kerr, a 'gratuitous direct lie', which 'made me too sick' to answer. Sanger wrote again, on 6 August from Denver, 'in most affectionate terms', enclosing a cheque for $100 [nearly £884 in 2001 values] as a 'birthday present' ('my birthday is May 9th – but n'importe') for Stella to 'take & use & say nothing about'. To which Stella's response was:

> Oh, I wish she hadn't done that! not that – if help and service (I won't talk of friendship, *that* is over) are rated on a cash basis, I haven't earned it amply from her: *but* if it were meant like that, *there were eight months to send it in* – months *when I hadn't quite realised facts which of course now make it impossible for me to take any gift from her. I could not do so & <u>then</u> take the independent course of actions which I now see is due <u>both to the movement and to myself</u>*. So, though I have tried to say what I had to say without causing *needless* offence, or being petty or bitter, I fear it means our friendship is over, & I have returned the cheque – & kept a copy of my letter and the original of hers. I'm afraid one almost wonders whether the operation in 1921 had a psychic effect of quite altering her judgement & feeling in some matters. Or is it – too much comfort?[50]

Ellis tried to smooth matters over, writing to Sanger:

> All that you say about Stella Browne I understand already and should be endeavoured to expound to her, and how much you wished to be helpful to her. But it was no good by now – if I write – I say no more, as her neurotic mind clings to her unreasonable ideas and twists everything accordingly.[51]

He was 'quite unable to modify [Stella's] present opinion'.[52] Sanger herself continued to speak kindly of Stella in correspondence and her published works (e.g. as 'that intrepid rebel Feminist'),[53] but the friendship seems to have ended beyond hope of reconciliation, although there is an intriguing hint in Sanger's autobiography, 1938, of some later personal contact.[54]

Added to this upsetting state of affairs, there was trouble within the ranks of the BSSSP Executive over the new office. Open conflict broke out between Stella and Norman Haire, an Australian doctor who had come to England after the war and was determined to make himself a leading figure in the British sex reform movement, which he felt should be under medical control. He had joined the BSSSP in 1920 on Havelock Ellis's referral.[55] He was consulting doctor to the Walworth Women's Clinic until an incident which Stella alluded to obliquely as 'peculiar methods ... Led the Drysdales to request and then compel his resignation'. She complained of Haire's attempt to 'jockey' the Executive into a commitment to a particular office. She conceded that the rooms 'are excellent' but, 'at £15 [c. £613 in 2007 values] a year', rather expensive. Haire had told her over the telephone that Halford approved of taking the rooms, but since he had already inspected them rather surreptitiously with Miss Bailey she was disinclined to take his word.[56]

Haire was furious to hear that Stella had said that 'we would *not* take them' and declared that 'While I am a member of the Committee, Stella Browne will *not* rule as an absolute monarch. She and Lloyd have had everything their own way far too long.' The only reason for the Society's financial straits was 'our membership is too small, and a certain element in the Society far too pronounced.' Therefore, 'Let us more normal people take the wheel, and steer the Society to success.'[57] Haire's plans for the Society verged on the grandiose, and what stood in his way, he believed, was an existing controlling cabal of Lloyd ('carries discretion to extremes'), Stella ('clever and brave, but ill-balanced and indiscreet') and George Ives ('timid as a hare').[58]

Stella had her feet more firmly on the ground: writing about the purchase of cleaning materials and necessary furnishings for the new office, she added '*all this mounts up ... the Committee must realise that expenses constantly accumulate*'. She hoped that 'certain other aspects of our work won't be lost sight of': as a result of galloping German inflation, Helene Stöcker had asked '*pressingly but with the utmost pathetic dignity*' to have the Society's account settled up in banknotes sent by registered post. It would be

> a tragedy if her splendid paper and organisation collapse. God knows if I had the money I would send it to her privately, it has been one of my greatest griefs that I can do nothing for her financially, *but in my present position that is quite impossible*.[59]

The situation was critical: 'every day's delay counts, and Berlin *may* be in flames by now and all its decent progressive people shot or fugitives!'. She conceded that the office '*in itself* seems extremely good'. However, it had become 'a primary obligation' of the Society and, in her view, 'will indeed be too dear in every sense, moral as well as financial, if it prevents our continued support and cooperation with the international movement'.[60] The Society's commitment to the office indeed initiated a period of chronic financial crisis.[61]

Throughout the summer, Stella continued writing for *The New Generation*. Her articles ranged from exuberant tribute to the work of Alexandra Kollontai in the nascent Soviet Union[62] to a scathing attack on Dr Ethel Bentham for shelving 'the mild and moderate resolution' put to the Labour Party Women's Conference in York concerning the giving of birth control advice in welfare centres.[63] The 'Ministry of Disease' also came in for another hammering: 'far too refined to use such gross terms as "*overcrowding*" and "*dirt*"'; 'humbugging'; 'it is well that birth control should keep free from the taint of its sinister and treacherous incompetence'.[64] Curiously, a review of Ellis's *The Dance of Life*, mentioned during August as being undertaken for *The New Generation*, did not appear. She wrote to Ellis of this work that

> I think it is extremely interesting – it's much more abstract & philosophical than most of your work, but although *as a rule* I love not philosophy, I *do very much like* 'The Dance of Life', particularly the Studies of British and Foreign Genius in it, & the description of the psychological process of conversion.[65]

A longer and more analytical account of her reactions would have been interesting.

Against this background of personal turmoil and upheaval, Stella went on a lecture tour in South Wales (Rhondda Valley), 1–7 September, to speak on birth control under the auspices of the local Communist Party Propaganda Committee.[66] The committee was organising hospitality ('which I can only hope won't be *too* primitive') and paying her fares, while the New Generation League was paying her 'the usual London rate per lecture'. She was to give four lectures on birth control and socialism, two lectures to women only on practical methods, and hold one public meeting. This, she hoped, would be 'a really useful & helpful series of lectures, helpful both to the poor people, the Cause, & myself'.[67] It certainly stuck in the community's memory, her visit being recalled in an oral history interview conducted in the area around 1960.[68]

'[T]he glorious mountain air' revivified her, as did encountering those 'in contact with life's grimmest realities' yet with a broad cultural background, who received her with 'a friendliness and a welcome which were both a great honour and a great responsibility' and formed appreciative audiences. Her four mixed-audience lectures, 'synthesising the theory and practice of birth control with Socialist principles', dealt with 'the present position of birth control throughout the most "civilised" countries', 'the proposed remedy of emigration' (which she was 'able to illustrate ... by a fair amount of personal knowledge of Canada'), 'Suggested Alternative Remedies to Birth Control, the Proposals for Employment and Housing Reform', and 'Birth Control as the key to rational and humane sex ethics'. Audiences ran to 250–300. At her lectures on practical methods for women only, 'every foot of floor space was packed, and women, mostly with babies clasped in their arms, stood five deep in rows behind the chairs'. She estimated that about 350 were present, but 'finally lost count'. 'The interest and the passion of gratitude and hopefulness displayed' remained 'one of my best memories and an encouragement to further efforts'. The public meeting, 'Birth Control as the People's Need and Right' had '*comparatively* less satisfactory' an attendance, but achieved a unanimous resolution 'calling for Birth Control Instruction facilities'. While she was in the area, she went down a coalmine – coming up again 'somewhat black with coal dust, but redder than ever!'[69]

R.B. Kerr wrote that

> The League is singularly fortunate in having secured such a speaker. Miss Browne is a highly cultivated woman with a rich vocabulary and an excellent platform voice. She is full of sympathy and has intellectual ability enough to demolish any opponent.[70]

For the next several years, lecturing became one of her predominant activities. The demands on her time and energies from this new turn in her career (eight meetings in the London area during late September and October)[71] led to her resignation from the Executive of the BSSSP in November, citing 'over-pressure of work' as the reason. Her resignation was received with 'the greatest regret and a vote of thanks ... in appreciation of all the arduous work done in the past by her for the Society' and the hope that in future she might once again be free to take a more active role.[72] There is no indication that her decision had been influenced by the recent dissension, rather, that it was 'to devote herself to the work for birth control'.[73]

According to Ellis, she was noticeably 'more cheerful than usual being busy working with the "New Generation"' when she came to tea in early November, although the subject of Sanger was avoided.[74] He also reported that she 'gets on well with [R.B. Kerr] so far'.[75] Bessie Drysdale, however, felt that Kerr and Stella had

> changed the colour of the League's activities and ideas and while losing ground with the old supporters, do not appear to be making a large increase in the numbers of members to whom their socialistic or communistic point of view should appeal.[76]

This presumably reflects not merely longstanding political differences, but also ideas at variance as to the League's role in the changing world of the 1920s. Stella's meetings usually resulted in resolutions to the Ministry of Health demanding the provision of birth control in welfare centres and, in some cases, in a collection for the Walworth Women's Welfare Centre. Numbers of copies of *The New Generation* were sold. But she was not engaged in a membership drive for the League itself.[77]

Following these talks, she was 'honoured with many intimate confidences', and 'confronted again and again with the heart-breaking appeals of unwillingly expectant mothers – more often married than unmarried – which I can only refuse'. Even if she could 'disregard my obligations to the League and the welfare of the movement' and give them the information required, 'in nine cases out of ten they would be unable to take proper care of themselves and would destroy their lives or health'. She had taken to incorporating in her lectures 'warnings against abortifacients, couched in the gravest terms'.[78] It is not however clear whether she was warning against the commercial scam of 'Female Pills' or potentially lethal folk remedies.

A new acquaintance and colleague in 'the Cause' was Dora Russell. Stella had not kept up her earlier contact with Bertrand Russell, but when he stood as a Labour candidate for Chelsea with support for birth control a strong feature, she met Dora, his second wife, herself a passionate feminist and socialist, while working for the electoral campaign.[79] Dora later claimed to have been 'brought into that struggle [for birth control] ... by Miss Stella Browne' around 1922.[80] It may have been this contact which led to her speaking to both Chelsea Labour Women and the whole Chelsea Labour Party. By the autumn of 1923, she seems to have grown closer to Dora Russell but, presumably since they were near neighbours, little correspondence survives. Russell's diaries survive only sporadically, but do mention 'SB to tea' in late October 1923, as well as a 'BC committee' in early November.[81] This was probably to do with the petition presented the following year to the Minister of Health about birth control advice in welfare centres.

Dora Russell's files include a 'Memorandum on Some Considerations affecting Birth Control Propaganda' by Stella – from the date, 5 November 1923, probably prepared for the 'BC Committee'. On the basis of her own experience, Stella began by suggesting that, for 'the poorest class of women (who need it most)... the spoken word tells more than the printed'. Even the simplest pamphlets 'require a certain amount of knowledge & intelligence/to understand & can stand being supplemented by verbal instruction'. She had indeed discovered that 'some women several years married seemed not to understand the different between the *os-uteri*; and the external genital organs' and that many could not 'adjust the caps at all'. While 'Diagrams would certainly help', as 'the Aldred prosecution was based largely on a clear little medical diagram, *great care seems necessary in selecting such diagrams*'. Clinics would provide 'personal attendance & attention which all contraceptive work hitherto shows is indispensable'. Stella's views on variance between women was borne out by the observation that '*the variety in the size shape and angle of the organs*... apparently varies almost as much as the features of the face'; she had 'discussed this very thoroughly with Nurse Daniels'. She believed that clinics should also 'provide care for Infancy and Pregnancy', and keep thorough records: and 'A Centre is *tangible* & rouses confidence & interest'.[82]

She was sufficiently close to Dora Russell to prepare a horoscope for her son John Conrad, born on 16 November 1922 – the notes survive but not the actual chart.[83] A historian of astrology comments that Stella correctly deployed the glyphs for the planets, signs of the zodiac and aspects but used the ephemeris for 1921 rather than 1922 as the basis for her calculations: 'the impression is of a rather slapdash astrologer, doing in haste a chart for a friend's child, and wanting to be encouraging'. There is an intriguing hint that there might be some German influence on her astrological practice.[84] The haste, and concomitant error, are not surprising, given the range of other pressures on Stella.

In a review of Bertrand and Dora Russell's *The Prospects of Industrial Civilisation*, Stella praised them for having 'already done more than any other persons to link up our cause with the Labour movement'. The book had a 'tonic clarity of perception', was 'full of the most vividly suggestive sidelights', 'gripping power and detachment' and 'lit up by an irony worthy of Voltaire'.[85]

Besides her political activities and writing, Stella had several verse translations from the German published in the *New Leader*: one wonders how she found time. 'The Death Parade', a dramatic duologue, the prologue to Ernst Toller's *Wandlung*, recently having been produced in Vienna, was a satirical dialogue between 'Death in War' and 'Death in Time of Peace'.[86] Agnes Miegel's 'Moses' has a revolutionary message:

> Henceforth the comrades of my days are those
> Whose dreams are broken on the merciless street
> Who bear the load but never share the spoil[87]

Short lyrics by Max Barthel ('Sea-Shells')[88] and Agnes Miegel, ('Gesina with the Voice of Gold', and 'That Spring'),[89] strike a different, much more lyric and sensuous, note. Another glimpse into the aesthetic side of Stella's life.

A long article in *The New Generation* for November expressed her concern about legislation under discussion in Parliament. 'Embedded deeply' in a Criminal Justice Bill was a sinister clause concerning 'indecent and obscene articles'. Stella found this 'no laughing matter', since one paragraph was 'expressly framed in order to cover contraceptive devices of any description'. A private member's bill aiming at the protection of children and minors from 'sexual abuse and financial exploitation', contained 'many admirable suggestions', but included to her horror a clause to make causing 'the death of an unborn child' a felony equivalent to homicide. She protested against this '*iniquitous legislation*' when '*safe and legal knowledge is not accessible to the poorest women*'.[90]

During November, she made another propaganda tour in Wales, this time Monmouthshire, based in Tredegar, where the 'side-alleys ... hide their tragedies of unemployment and bad housing behind an Italianate picturesqueness'. She stayed with Mr and Mrs Oliver Morgan, in one of the new council houses, 'on the very crest of the hill, in exquisite mountain air', which she was pleased to see had 'an adequate supply of cupboards.' (As with her concern over cleaning materials for the BSSSP office, Stella demonstrated first-hand knowledge of the practicalities of housekeeping.) Her first lecture, 'Birth Control in its Relation to Socialism', filled the Temperance Hall of the Tredegar Workmen's Institute to capacity – she estimated the audience at 900. She addressed a small, but 'extremely enthusiastic', women's meeting in Ebbw Vale, and, standing on 'a precarious chair', 200 or so women in Tredegar, who 'completely crowded out the Lower Hall of the Institute'. She also spoke to a women's meeting at Bryn Mawr, where 'two great invisible furnaces ... flung a red glare into the sky' which 'rose and fell and shifted constantly', with an effect 'extraordinarily fascinating and menacing', and to both mixed and women's audiences in Oakdale. She commented as to

'How often ... have elderly women not said, "You've come too late to help me, Comrade, but give me some papers for my girls. I don't want them to have the life I've had"'. While the tour was a success, Stella concluded with a plea as to the necessity of practical follow-up, such as providing specialist nurses with midwifery training and experience, as well as 'developed qualities of sympathy and judgement', and 'free from the miasmatic influence of the Ministry'.

While there, she was able to enjoy a number of less cause-focused activities. During a 'restful day at Tredegar', she heard 'the exquisitely selected and rendered music of Mr Morgan's treasure, the most beautiful gramophone I have ever heard – an instrument which quite revolutionised my views on gramophones'. She 'explored the delightful public park' with its 'extraordinary Saurian fossils'. She was 'whirled down the valley in a motor-bicycle sidecar' to Oakdale, with time to appreciate the scenery – 'hedges of bramble, bracken and trees give something of the West of England charm instead of the bare grimness of Gwent', although the 'prosperous and exhilarating impression' of Oakdale could not 'conceal the poverty of the majority'. She encountered new and 'delightful friends', including 'my guide, philosopher and friend at Tredegar, Iris Phillips (aged six)'.[91]

Early in 1924, on top of everything else, Stella was doing her best to assist Françoise Lafitte-Cyon in obtaining a divorce from Russian journalist Serge Cyon, who had vanished into Russia at the time of the Revolution. Françoise's situation was awkward and anomalous: married to a Russian when the British government did not recognise the Soviet state, thus stateless and fearful of deportation. She was also unable to claim a legacy without her husband's signature.[92] Ellis had heard 'from Stella Browne that there is "a brilliant and sympathetic lawyer" who is willing to act for you.'[93] Françoise wrote back confirming that Dr Leslie Burgin had taken over from Haynes.[94] It seems odd that Stella had brought in a replacement for her old friend and colleague, but perhaps he lacked the expertise for Françoise's complicated, never resolved, case.[95] Ellis was also encouraging Françoise to make further use of Stella's good offices in another direction: '*Quite time* you sent the Pellerini translation to the *New Generation*. Better send it to Stella Browne, who is closely associated with the N. G. now.'[96] Françoise did so: 'As I have occasion to write to Stella Browne to thank her, I am sending her the Pellerini poem.'[97]

Ellis also used Stella as the intermediary for the disbursement of money entrusted to him by the wealthy writer Bryher (Winifred Ellerman) for 'work "likely to be of benefit for humanity, such as in connection with birth control"' to a Miss Sanders (whom Bryher was thus discreetly helping out). Ellis informed Bryher that he had contacted Stella and 'asked her if she can indicate useful work for Miss Sanders that would not otherwise be easy to get done'.[98] Initial misunderstandings led to Ellis approaching Norman Haire instead.[99] Haire claimed Stella had set Sanders against him. Ellis conceded that 'Stella Browne sets up violent antipathies' (he usually refrained from commenting on Stella in his letters to Haire, so this presumably reflects his continuing distress at her extreme reversal of feelings towards Sanger). However, she had not to his knowledge met Miss Sanders but had managed to provide some birth control manuscripts for her to type.[100] Miss Sanders had 'received the whole of her £15', fulfilling Bryher's intentions, by April: Ellis hoped that they might find her work on her own account[101] and, by June, Stella was getting the Walworth clinic to offer Sanders 'some literary or clerking work'.[102]

Ellis did not dismiss Stella's indignant letter to him concerning the proposal to 'suppress the "New Generation"' and make Sanger's *Birth Control Review* 'suffice for English news', as yet another manifestation of her neuroticism and Sanger-paranoia. He told Sanger,

> I sympathise with SB! For much as I admire and delight in the "BCR" I think it would be absurd for England not to be able to support a BC [birth control] paper of its own.[103]

Although Stella had resigned from the BSSSP, she was still in demand to chair its meetings,[104] and in contact with George Ives: he wrote to her following a troubling three-hour committee meeting.[105] In May, Stella wrote to him:

> I was so sorry that 'thronging duties' made it impossible for me to have a longer talk with you today, and extremely sorry for all you've had to go through recently. You must take care of your health, however irksome the trouble and restrictions that implies!

Networking again, she took the opportunity to recommend to him a 'typist and duplicator', Miss M.E. Duff, who did excellent work at reasonable terms, 'for B.S.S.P., Penal Reform or your own MSS.'[106]

Although she had broken with Sanger, Stella was still in active contact with other American feminists, radicals and reformers. She was particularly taken with initiatives in the area of dealing with prostitution and 'the delinquent girl'. In April, she was in touch with the biographer and feminist

Katharine Anthony, whose 'scholarship and judgement' were responsible for bringing to her attention William I. Thomas's work *The Unadjusted Girl*, which she reviewed in *The New Generation* in May 1924.[107] She wrote to Anthony that she was 'trying to get it widely known and reviewed' in Britain, and commented on the work of Miriam Van Waters with delinquent girls, 'What splendid work that is ... real reconstructive healing, and in the right spirit too'. She hoped to hear from Anthony 'one of these days', and signed off 'Kindest regards from your friend Stella Browne'.[108]

Stella also wrote to Ethel Sturges Dummer, 'one of the initiators of the Chicago Juvenile Courts', who had provided the introduction to *The Unadjusted Girl*'[109] – to let her know that a copy of *The New Generation* with the review in was on its way, and to 'congratulate you heartily on such an admirable piece of work'. She alluded to a couple of contemporary incidents in the USA, including the 'miserable Tresca case, which appears to have been merely brought in subservience to Fascist bullying' (The Italian-American Socialist Tresca's US citizenship status was being investigated under strong pressure from the Mussolini regime). In the latter case, Stella added that she could not

> hope that the American Birth Control League, which left the English publishers of Mrs Sanger's pamphlet so badly in the lurch last year & which permits its organ to suppress Socialist reviews of books, will do anything; Tresca is neither wealthy nor (obviously) respectable.

But she knew 'some of you' would do something.[110] In a later letter, she noted that although she 'dislike[d] intensively the atmosphere and attitudes of prostitution – I nevertheless regard the prejudice in favor [sic] of strict monogamy as a relic of Puritan ~~prejudice~~/bigotry (for *both* women & men).'[111]

Given her leaning towards 'anarchist individualism', and her contacts with the American Left and other progressive reformers, Stella surprisingly had no recorded contact with Emma Goldman, the American anarchist, feminist, labour campaigner, birth control advocate and sex radical. Goldman was in touch with several individuals in the same circles and a passionate admirer of Ellis, but there is no evidence that she knew Stella. While they might have met in person during Goldman's sojourns in Britain, there are no letters, and her name is startlingly absent from Stella's own writings. Goldman does not seem to have had any interaction with the BSSSP. It is possible that Stella's earlier devotion to Sanger had occluded other US birth control activists. After the Bolshevik revolution in Russia, Goldman became a sharp critic of the regime (from a left/anarchist perspective), which might well have caused differences with Stella.

Stella continued active propagandist work for birth control, mainly in London, but she made another tour to the provinces, visiting Norfolk and Suffolk in early April 1924. This tour was made possible 'through the introduction of my honoured friend Dorothy Jewson', returned as an MP in the recent election which had brought the Labour Party into power. The 'particularly competent and effective organisation and publicity' were the work of a special Committee of the Women's Group of the Labour Party, headed by Dorothy Jewson's cousin, Dr Violet M. Jewson, who acted as Stella's hostess for part of her stay in Norwich. Stella extended particular thanks to the women who provided hospitality, as 'one who realises what sudden visits mean to even the best of housewives and most understanding of professional women!'. She enjoyed her stay in 'that fascinating old city, a veritable treasury, both of architecture and decorative craftsmanship since the Early Middle Ages'. In Norwich, she addressed five women-only meetings, and also a mixed meeting of the Norwich Independent Labour Party. In Ipswich, 'Even after one hour and twenty minutes of my oratory', her mixed audience was 'most keen and inspiring and keen for more proof of the identity of aim between our two causes'.[112]

While inspired by the enthusiasm of grass-roots Labour supporters, Stella was less sanguine about the recently elected government. She doubted that its tenure of office would be lengthy, or that its scope would be 'other than very limited'. But she hoped that the first Labour Minister of Health would at least '*be* a Minister of Health and not of Disease and Death' and allow welfare centres 'to give the information regarding hygienic and reliable methods of birth control'. Unfortunately, there were 'many persons in the Labour Party' whose 'passion to restrict, manage, prohibit, inhibit and generally "boss" other men and women' had 'assumed unhallowed proportions' – quite apart from those who remained 'under the sway of the obsolete, but still paralysing superstitions', or 'some psychic maladjustment, some deep-seated repression', or simply suffered from 'incurable unimaginative stupidity'. Therefore, she called on all those who had heard her speak, the 'over-worked mothers who have confided in me', and the comrades who had given support to the Walworth Centre and the Aldred's Defence Fund, to make unequivocal demands on the Party leaders to raise the ban on birth control knowledge. In conclusion, she claimed that 'the finest brains and most outstanding personalities in the

Labour movement' were those '*who are Socialists because they are such Individualists*', who had

> definitely rejected a social order which puts necessary work, justice, creative art and science, love and breeding on a cash basis, who have resisted class injustice and sex injustice and race injustice.

These men and women, shortly to be under the 'nerve-racking pressure of work and other claims' when Labour took office, were exhorted to 'remember ... that this claim of motherhood to be conscious and voluntary is fundamental'.[113]

In April, she covered the same ground for an American audience in another short-lived publication from Dr William J. Robinson's stable. There is a sense of working off some personal grudges, perhaps because she was writing for a remoter audience. Her comment that 'birth control *among the wealthy* is ... a very paying proposition for some experts in advertisement' sounds like a side-swipe at Norman Haire's plush Harley Street practice. She paid off another score in her reference to the

> fêted and wealthy authoress of the pamphlet for which the Aldreds – her working-class *friends and hosts* in 1914 *and again in* 1920 – suffered prosecution, [who] left the brunt of the agitation for their defence to their British Comrades.

The Webbs, and other antagonists, were the object of diatribe against those of a 'sexually anaemic, anaesthetic or neutral temperament ... combined with a faculty for organisation and an aptitude for management', who, in the 'organized hypocrisy of modern politics' were at 'a considerable advantage over their intellectual superiors of a more full-blooded emotional nature'.

Apart from these divagations into personal points-scoring, she expressed anxieties over the new Minister of Health, Mr Wheatley. While praising his distinguished record, she was concerned 'that he is a devout Roman Catholic' and likely to argue that adequate housing would 'entirely supersed[e] any need for Birth Control'. It was not just the Catholic element which worried her, there was the problem of the 'bureaucratic mind [which] runs in grooves', and the 'deadly influence of Nonconformist pseudo-Puritanism, the deadliest legacy of nineteenth century Liberalism to the Labour Party'. Nonetheless, 'the great rank and file of Labour welcomes Birth Control'.[114] This article has less force and, with its accenting of personal animus, lacks the resonance of the shorter piece in *The New Generation*.

Its impact took some little time to make itself felt, although Stella was already the subject of hostile remarks among Sanger's British circle. In May, Françoise, following a visit to Stella and joint attendance at a meeting, dissociated herself from the opinions of 'S. de J. [Soleil de Joie = Hugh de Selincourt] and [Harold] Child', praising Stella's strong and serious qualities.[115] Ellis commented that 'I can't imagine why you attach the least importance to S de J's dislike of Stella Browne!'[116] As a single mother in a matrimonially complex position, eking a living as an elementary schoolteacher, she may have had some sympathy with Stella's position.

Sanger wrote in aggrieved tones to Rose Witcop in July: 'As Stella Browne seems to take up the cudgels for you, I think it is only fair that you should set her straight on what has been done'. Having 'always had a very high opinion of and deep regard' for Stella, Sanger was 'deeply disappointed at the deliberate way she misrepresents facts these days'.[117] Witcop responded:

> I hope you will believe me Margaret when I say that I knew nothing at all about Stella Browne's article until you mentioned it. I should certainly have considered it my duty to reply to her, had I known of it ... I could show you from Mrs Russell's own letter that she knew of your contribution towards the costs of the case. Stella Browne certainly knew because she made a reference to it when I saw her at the Ministry of Health. But life is too short. And there are some things one must ignore. We will concern ourselves only with the written word of the highly neurotic Miss Browne.[118]

Sanger replied:

> I did not care if what little I did was not acknowledged, but I do not want persons like Stella Browne to say I left you in the lurch and left you to shoulder all the expenses and fight ... but all these small gossipy things go on for ever.[119]

She was perhaps more wounded than this suggests: a letter from Hugh de Selincourt reassured her that

> I could never stand poor Stella Browne. I cannot feel that she is much loss ... But why the hell she should spit venom, except that these poor little devils always do, like the horrid fish which the French call piss-vinaigre. It's her misfortune.[120]

Ellis also wrote soothingly that he was sorry that Sanger had been

> hurt over the eccentric workings of Stella Browne's queer brain. She has many fine qualities & great ability & is doing splendid work, but there is always that neurotic twist liable to come in. Quite suddenly, after all her enthusiasm over your greatness & goodness, *everything* you do is wrong. I have given up trying to make her see things reasonably, it's no good.

He also implied that Aldred and Witcop were far from guiltless in this imbroglio: 'they behaved badly to you ... Even S. B., I believe, admits/[privately] that they are not satisfactory people.'[121] But, as late as November, he was reiterating that 'Stella Browne, with all her good points, is always violent and neurotic, and her changing likes and dislikes will not bear much influence.'[122]

Meanwhile there were developments for 'The Cause'. On 9 May, Stella participated in a deputation to the new Labour Minister of Health to put the case for permitting birth control advice to be given in maternity centres through the Public Health service. Her detailed account for *The New Generation* described it vividly. She set the scene with the deputation being 'ushered upstairs into an enormous room lavishly pillared and carpeted, and certainly provided with the worst acoustic properties I have ever had occasion to suffer from'. While there were many familiar figures from the birth control and Labour causes, there were also 'some new and very welcome faces'. They waited in 'that desiccated atmosphere where the voices of human pity and indignation and intelligence die away, as human effort and suffering die away among the pyramids of dusty files in the Ministry's pigeon-holes.'

The Minister, John Wheatley, 'brisk, capable, dictatorial and rosy-cheeked as ever', and his accompanying officials were 'punctual to the minute'. His party included 'a tall, graceful woman', Dr Janet Campbell

> the author of a *Report on Maternal Mortality*, which is the *pièce de résistance* in our indictment of the present policy. I do not envy, and I do not understand, the author of that report, herself a woman, who could sit unmoved through the evidence and continue service under the Ministry after our deputation.

After some introductory speeches, H.G. Wells rose, and 'the assembly became not only deeply impressive, but dramatic'. Stella, who had criticised Wells in the past, felt that they got all that they could expect from 'genius': he was 'admirable. Intensely serious yet genial, entirely dignified and controlled' and got to the 'core of the matter – the right to knowledge and to freedom of choice'. Further arguments were put by the gynaecologist Dr Frances Huxley, by Dora Russell and by Mrs Jennie Baker, 'well-known in the Labour movement'.

The Minister 'made a condescending acknowledgement ... of the purity and nobility of our motives'. He conceded that he was glad not to have to argue the general case for birth control, 'though he also indulged in a somewhat irrelevant jibe at those who had long employed it'. Then he came to

> the crux: the matter was highly controversial; religious feeling was involved; the centres were maintained from public funds, and no public mandate had yet been received.

Indeed, the Minister was 'amazed at our audacity in demanding an administrative order in this matter without Parliamentary sanction" Wheatley refused '*even to give modified permission in special medical cases*', drawing a 'delicate distinction between permitting access to knowledge and actually supplying it': his answer was 'In short, let Parliament decide. Till then – No.' The deputation left 'that deadly stone sarcophagus of the spirit'. Stella concluded:

> We have had Wheatley's answer. And Labour women mean business in this matter. He will have ours.[123]

On 14 May, 'the largest conference of women of the Labour Party ever yet held in these islands' refused, by an overwhelming vote 'to accept a further shelving and temporising resolution of its executive'. Instead, a motion was passed that

> this conference, while in no way criticising the views of those who for scientific or moral reasons are opposed to the practice of birth control, expresses the opinion that the Ministry of Health should permit public health authorities to provide, for those who desire it, information on the subject of birth control.

As a result of the conference, a new Workers' Birth Control Group was formed (WBCG).[124]

This had been planned at least as early as February 1924. Unlike other birth control organisations, the WBCG was not establishing clinics but, rather, activating public opinion, and lobbying local and central government officials to provide advice in publicly funded welfare centres. Although Stella worked closely with them, her contribution was not formally acknowledged.

The WBCG presented itself as 'representing working mothers':[125] for tactical reasons, 'control of its policy was to be in hands of men and women who had known the responsibility of parenthood'. The only exception was Dorothy Jewson, since 'there was and is, no married Labour woman in the House of Commons', and she was 'untiring and unafraid in her advocacy of the cause of working mothers'.[126] Dora Russell's reminiscences suggest that Stella was nevertheless very much part of the group, although her support for abortion was felt to be counter-productive on grounds of political practicality. But, in spite of their differences, Dora used to 'honour her intransigence, she would get up there with wisps of hair coming from her untidy coiffure and no chairman on earth could get her to sit down'.[127]

The years 1923–4 were a period of major upheaval for Stella, with the breach with Sanger and her departure from the Communist Party, as well as her bowing out from active involvement with the BSSSP and the final laying to rest of the New Freewoman Company (the shareholders' meeting on 28 July, which Stella chaired, agreed to dissolve it),[128] against the background of her struggles for employment and subsistence. But Stella was not disillusioned. In spite of Bessie Drysdale's bitchy prediction 'In 5 years she'll probably be a staunch Tory!',[129] she remained loyal to her existing convictions. She neither became a Tory, converted to Roman Catholicism, got married (unlike several women rebels and activists who eventually, like Sanger, chose husbands well able to support them), or in any way reneged from her existing principles. She remained an ardent fighter for the liberation of women – a campaign so often said to have dwindled after 1918 – and continued to be a 'fellow-traveller' of the far Left, while her exertions for 'the Cause' of birth control, if anything, intensified. Far from dwindling into a disillusioned has-been, for Stella the next several years were filled with ardent activity and significant achievements.

Notes

1. F.W. Stella Browne, 'A French view of us', *The New Generation*, vol. 5, April 1926, p. 45.
2. Bessie Drysdale to Sanger, 24 April [no year: ? 1923/4], Sanger papers in the Library of Congress, Washington, DC [LC], Volume 21.
3. F.W. Stella Browne to Olaf Stapledon, 7 February 1949, Stapledon papers, Liverpool University Library, STAP. H VIII B 9/21.
4. [? William J. Robinson], 'Special article: the most radical British feminist and birth control advocate of today', *Medical Critic and Guide*, vol. 25E/5, May 1927, pp. 192–4; Sue Bruley, *Leninism, Stalinism and the Women's Movement in Britain, 1920–1939* (New York: Garland Publishing Inc., 1986), pp. 71–81.

5. Andrew Thorpe, 'The membership of the Communist Party of Great Britain, 1920–1945', *The Historical Journal*, 43, 2002, pp. 777–800; James Klugmann, *History of the Communist Party of Great Britain, 1919–1924* (London: Lawrence & Wishart, 1969), p. 333.
6. F.W. Stella Browne, 'The European outlook', *The New Generation*, vol. 3, July 1924, p.76; and see Kevin Morgan, Gidon Cohen and Andrew Flinn, *Communists and British Society 1920–1991* (London: Rivers Oram, 2007), especially ch. 4, pp. 143–83, on attitudes towards women and gender more generally in the CPGB.
7. Thorpe, 'The membership of the Communist Party of Great Britain'.
8. 'The most radical British feminist'.
9. See Morgan *et al.*, *Communists and British Society*, *passim*, for the constraints that operated.
10. F.W. Stella Browne, 'Letters to the editor: Cheap children', *New Leader*, 5 January 1923, p. 7
11. F.W. Stella Browne, 'The feminine aspect of birth control', in Raymond Pierpoint (ed.), *Report of the Fifth International Neo-Malthusian and Birth Control Conference,* Kingsway Hall, London, July 11th to 14th 1922 (London: William Heinemann (Medical Books) Ltd, 1922), pp. 40–3.
12. 'Birth control', *New Leader*, 5 January 1923, p. 3.
13. Stella Browne to Havelock Ellis, 12 May 1923, Ellis papers in the Department of Manuscripts, British Library, Additional Manuscripts 70539 [BL Add Ms 70539].
14. Rose Witcop to Margaret Sanger, 12 January 1923, LC, Volume 21.
15. *The New Generation*, vol. 2, no. 2, February 1923, p. 17.
16. E.S.P. Haynes to the BSSSP, 23 January 1923, 'B.S.S. Letters Received', British Sexology Society Archives, Harry Ransom Humanities Research Center, University of Texas at Austin.
17. F.W. Stella Browne, 'Helene Stöcker, defender of motherhood', *Birth Control Review*, January 1923, p. 8.
18. I am indebted to the Theosophical Society for letting me check its membership registers.
19. F.W. Stella Browne, 'The duty of knowledge', *The New Generation*, vol. 2, no. 3, March 1923, p. 39.
20. F.W. Stella Browne, 'An international movement', *The New Generation*, vol. 2, no. 4, April 1923, p. 48.
21. F.W.S.B., 'Review: *The New Humanism*. By Laurence Housman', *The New Generation*, vol. 2, no. 4, April 1923, p. 51.
22. Havelock Ellis to Françoise Lafitte-Cyon, 3 February 1923, Howard Gotlieb Archival Research Center, Boston University [HGA]; according to Timothy D'Arch Smith, *Montague Summers: A Bibliography* (Wellingborough: The

Aquarian Press, 1983), p. 154, The Phoenix Theatre production of John Ford's *'Tis Pity She's a Whore* was performed at the Shaftesbury Theatre on 28 and 29 January 1923.
23. 'Poetry', *The Freeman*, 28 February 1923, pp. 594–5.
24. Browne to Ellis, 16 February 1923, BL Add Ms 70539.
25. Browne to Ellis, 16 February 1923, BL Add Ms 70539.
26. Françoise Lafitte-Cyon to Havelock Ellis, 19 February 1923, HGA.
27. R.B. Kerr of the New Generation League, Letter to the Editor, *Birth Control Review,* March 1923.
28. R.B. Kerr to Margaret Sanger, 27 March 1923, LC, Volume 21.
29. Stella Browne to Mrs Bailey, 8 March 1923, 'B.S.S. Misc', HRC.
30. Browne to Ellis, 10 May 1923, 'B.S.S. Misc', HRC.
31. Browne to Ellis, 10 and 14 April 1923, 'B.S.S. Misc', Havelock Ellis to BSSSP (copied to Stella Browne), 9 April 1923, 'B.S.S. Letters Received' HRC, Browne to Ellis, 12 May 1923, BL Add Ms 70539.
32. Browne to Ellis, 10 March 1923, 'B.S.S. Misc', HRC.
33. Browne to Ellis, 14 March 1923, 'B.S.S. Misc', HRC.
34. Minutes of the Walworth Women's Clinic Committee, 4 April 1923, Walworth Clinic records in Family Planning Association Archives, Wellcome Library, SA/FPA/X.8/1.
35. Stella Browne to S.H. Halford, 14 March 1923, 'B.S.S. Misc', HRC.
36. Browne to Ellis, 4 April 1923, 'B.S.S. Misc', HRC.
37. Browne to Ellis, 6 May 1923, 'B.S.S. Misc', HRC.
38. *The New Generation*, vol. 2, no. 6, June 1923, p. 71.
39. R.B. Kerr to Margaret Sanger, 29 May 1923, LC, Volume 21.
40. Browne to Ellis, 6 May 1923, 'B.S.S. Misc', HRC.
41. Browne to Ellis, 12 May 1923, BL Add Ms 70539.
42. Stella Browne, 'Helene Stöcker, defender of motherhood', p. 8.
43. Havelock Ellis to Margaret Sanger, 12 June 1923, LC, Volume 5.
44. Browne to Ellis, 12 May 1923, BL Add Ms 70539.
45. F.W. Stella Browne, 'Review: *The Next Step: A Plan for Economic World Federation*. By Scott Nearing', *The New Generation*, vol. 2, no. 5, May 1923, p. 62.
46. Browne to Ellis, 7 June 1923, BL Add Ms 70539.
47. Kerr to Sanger, 29 May 1923, LC, Volume 21.
48. Browne to Ellis, 7 June 1923, BL Add Ms 70539.
49. Browne to Ellis, 7 June 1923, BL Add Ms 70539; an entry on Norman MacMunn can be found in the *Oxford Dictionary of National Biography*.
50. Browne to Ellis, 25 August 1923, BL Add Ms 70539.
51. Ellis to Sanger, 17 July 1923, LC, Volume 5.
52. Ellis to Sanger, 28 August 1923, LC, Volume 5.

53. Margaret Sanger, *My Fight for Birth Control* (London: Faber & Faber Ltd, 1932), p. 98.
54. Margaret Sanger, *An Autobiography* (London: Victor Gollancz Ltd, 1939), p. 126.
55. Havelock Ellis to Stella Browne [1920], 'B.S.S. Letters Received' HRC.
56. Browne to Halford, 20 June 1923, 'B.S.S. Misc', HRC.
57. Norman Haire to S.H. Halford, 20 June 1923, 'B.S.S. Misc', HRC.
58. Norman Haire to Havelock Ellis, 20 August 1923, BL Add Ms 70540.
59. Browne to Halford, 10 August 1923, 'B.S.S. Misc', HRC.
60. Browne to Halford, 12 August 1923, 'B.S.S. Misc', HRC.
61. Lesley A. Hall, '"Disinterested enthusiasm for sexual misconduct": the British Society for the Study of Sex Psychology, 1913–1947', *Journal of Contemporary History*, vol. 30, no. 4, 1995, pp. 665–86; Entry for 3 January 1924, George Ives 'Notes and Writings', Volume LXXXVI, Harry Ransom Humanities Research Center, University of Texas at Austin [Ives HRC].
62. F.W. Stella Browne, 'Light from the East: a great birth controller', *The New Generation*, vol. 2, no. 6, June 1923, p. 66.
63. F.W. Stella Browne, 'An open letter to Dr Ethel Bentham, By a Socialist woman', *The New Generation*, vol. 2, no. 7, July 1923, p. 84.
64. F.W. Stella Browne, 'An open letter to the four suspended M.P.s, By a Socialist woman', *The New Generation*, vol. 2, no. 8, August 1923, p. 90.
65. Browne to Ellis, 25 August 1923, BL Add Ms 70539.
66. 'South Wales tour', *The New Generation*, vol. 2, no. 9, September 1923, p. 107.
67. Browne to Ellis, 25 August 1923, BL Add Ms 70539.
68. Interview with Ben Davies, *c.* 1960, South Wales Miners' Library, University of Swansea, AUD/168.
69. F.W. Stella Browne, 'Birth control in Taff Vale: a Socialist synthesis', *The New Generation*, vol. 2, no. 10, October 1923, pp. 116–17.
70. Editor's leading column, *The New Generation*, vol. 2, no. 10, October 1923, p. 113.
71. F.W.S.B., 'Our education propaganda: London lectures', *The New Generation*, vol. 2, no. 11, November 1923, p. 129.
72. Minutes of the 115th Meeting of the Executive Committee, 1 November 1923, 'B.S.S. Misc', HRC.
73. 'The most radical British feminist'.
74. Ellis to Sanger, 13 November 1923, LC, Volume 5.
75. Ellis to Sanger, 8 December 1923, LC, Volume 5.
76. Bessie Drysdale to Sanger, 9 January [192?], LC, Volume 21.
77. F.W.S.B., 'London lectures', *The New Generation*, vol. 2, no. 12, December 1923, p. 138.
78. F.W. Stella Browne, 'The price of liberty', *The New Generation*, vol. 2, no. 11, November 1923, pp. 130–1.

79. Transcript of interview with Dora Russell, 16 February 1986, Russell Archives, McMaster University, Hamilton, Ontario [RA].
80. 'World League for Sexual Reform', *The New Generation*, vol. 11, December 1932, pp. 137–8: Russell said she had been brought into the birth control campaign 'ten years ago, by Miss Stella Browne'.
81. Dora Russell's diary for 1923, Dora Russell papers in the International Institute of Social History, Amsterdam [DR], file 2.
82. F.W. Stella Browne, 'Memorandum on some considerations affecting birth control propaganda', 5 November 1923, DR, file 402.
83. DR, file 6.
84. Information from Annabella Kitson, to whom I am much indebted.
85. F.W. Stella Browne, 'Reviews: *The Prospects of Industrial Civilisation*. By Bertrand and Dora Russell', *The New Generation*, vol. 2, no. 11, November 1923, p. 134.
86. Ernst Toller, 'The death parade', (Translated by F.W. Stella Browne), *New Leader*, 26 September 1924, p. 13.
87. Agnes Miegel, 'Moses' (Translated by F.W. Stella Browne), *New Leader*, 14 December 1923, p. 11.
88. Max Barthel, 'Sea-shells' (Translated by F.W. Stella Browne), *New Leader*, 28 September 1923, p. 10.
89. Agnes Miegel, 'Gesina with the voice of gold' (Translated by F.W. Stella Browne), *New Leader*, 28 December 1923, p. 9; Agnes Miegel, 'That spring', (Translated by F.W. Stella Browne), *New Leader*, 25 April 1924, p. 11.
90. Browne, 'The price of liberty'.
91. F.W. Stella Browne, 'My tour in Monmouthshire', *The New Generation*, vol. 3, no. 1, January 1924, pp. 8–9.
92. Françoise Delisle, *Friendship's Odyssey: In Love with Life* (London: Delisle, 1964), pp. 247–8.
93. Ellis to Lafitte-Cyon, 'Thursday evening' [n.d. 1924], HGA.
94. Lafitte-Cyon to Ellis, 27 January 1924, HGA.
95. Delisle, *Friendship's Odyssey*, p. 247.
96. Ellis to Lafitte-Cyon, 'Tuesday' [n.d. 1924], HGA.
97. Lafitte-Cyon to Ellis, 27 January 1924, HGA.
98. Havelock Ellis to Bryher, 15 January 1924, Bryher papers in the Beinecke Library, Yale University, GEN MSS 97/10/413-420.
99. Havelock Ellis to Norman Haire, 6 February 1924, Norman Haire papers in Fisher Library, University of Sydney.
100. Ellis to Haire, 6 February and 17 February 1924, Norman Haire papers.
101. Ellis to Bryher, 15 January 1924, Bryher papers, GEN MSS 97/10/413-420.
102. Ellis to Bryher, 26 June 1924, Bryher papers, GEN MSS 97/10/413-420.
103. Ellis to Sanger, 17 February 1924, LC, Volume 5.

104. Minutes of 118th meeting of the Executive Committee, 3 January 1924, 'B.S.S. Misc', HRC.
105. Entries for 3 and 4 January 1924, George Ives 'Notes and Writings', Volume LXXXXVI, Ives HRC.
106. Stella Browne to George Ives, 5 May 1924, 'B.S.S. Misc', HRC.
107. F.W. Stella Browne, 'Review: The unadjusted girl', *The New Generation*, vol. 3, May 1924, pp. 57–8.
108. Stella Browne to Katharine Anthony, 28 April 1924, Ethel Sturges Dummer papers in the Schlesinger Library, Radcliffe College [ESD], A-127, folder 465.
109. Browne, 'The unadjusted girl'.
110. Stella Browne to Ethel Sturges Dummer, 2 May 1924, ESD, A-127, folder 465.
111. Browne to Dummer, 12 June 1924, ESD, A-127, folder 465.
112. F.W.S.B., 'Miss Browne tours East Anglia', *The New Generation*, vol. 3, May 1924, p. 51.
113. F.W. Stella Browne, 'The philosophy of the free spirit', *The New Generation*, vol. 3, February 1924, p. 17.
114. F.W. Stella Browne, 'Birth control and the British Labour Party', *Humanity*, vol. 1, no. 2, April 1924, pp. 73–6.
115. Lafitte-Cyon to Ellis, 6 May 1924, HGA.
116. Ellis to Lafitte-Cyon, 7 May 1924, HGA.
117. Margaret Sanger to Rose Witcop, 8 July 1924, LC, Volume 21.
118. Witcop to Sanger, 8 August 1924, LC, Volume 21.
119. Sanger to Witcop, 25 July 1924, LC, Volume 21.
120. Hugh de Selincourt to Margaret Sanger, 8 July 1924, Sanger papers in the Sophia Smith Collection, Smith College, Northampton, MA.
121. Ellis to Sanger, 25 July 1924, LC, Volume 5.
122. Ellis to Sanger, 26 November 1924, LC, Volume 5.
123. F.W. Stella Browne, 'Mr. Wheatley's reply – and ours', *The New Generation*, vol. 3, June 1924, pp. 63–4.
124. F.W.S.B., 'Women vote for birth control', *The New Generation*, vol. 3, June 1924, p. 65.
125. Circular of February 1924, Workers' Birth Control Group files, DR file 402.
126. 'Report of the founding and work of the Workers Birth Control Group and the attitude of the English Labour Party towards birth control', [1925], Workers' Birth Control Group files, DR, file 403.
127. Dora Russell: The Human Factor: Speech 16 February 1986 (actually, an interview by 'Kieran'), RA.
128. Minute Book, the New Freewoman Ltd, Harriet Shaw Weaver papers in the Department of Manuscripts, British Library, Add Ms 57358.
129. Bessie Drysdale to Sanger, 24 April [no year: ? 1923/4], LC, Volume 21.

7

Activism and Other Interests

After the series of political and personal upheavals, Stella's work for 'the Cause' of birth control continued with unabated, even increased, vigour. For the next several years her columns in *The New Generation* recorded the slow progress of the campaign. Stella was acutely aware of the need to keep fighting, even when gains appeared to have been made, until the desired changes had been achieved. By this stage of her career, she had abandoned her earlier 'Forward, Charge!' approach, and had settled into the trenches for a long struggle. However, quotidian immersion in this struggle and the minutiae of Labour Party politics did not blind her to broader contemporary topics. In spite of a hectic round of activity, she remained interested in and responsive to a wide range of interests, and even managed to have some kind of personal life.

In April 1927, R.B. Kerr claimed that in the previous four years she had 'addressed about 150 meetings of Labour Women':[1] in fact, a far greater variety of organisations. Although she personally thought herself 'better as a writer than a speaker', her abilities as a speaker were clearly remarkable. Others considered her 'extremely impressive, direct, emphatic, totally unembarrassed, with a fine vocabulary and a speaking voice of unusual range and power – a deeper rather musical alto'.[2] Probably her largest meeting was 'Birth Control and Modern Politics', under the auspices of the New Generation League at Caxton Hall, Westminster, on 18 November 1924, reported in the Labour national newspaper, the *Daily Herald*. Given the recent change of government, she argued that

> from a Conservative point of view birth control would be an excellent thing to take up, because the giving of information

> at the maternity centres would add nothing to the taxes, and would, on the contrary, save a great deal of money.

The Labour Party had a duty to bring up the subject 'on all ... possible occasions'. She compared a Brighton doctor's claim that 'the death-rate among the children of the poor [was] "selective" to 'the time when pious and patriotic Carthaginians piled living children into the furnace to propitiate their idol, Moloch' (a comparison she deployed elsewhere).[3] Lively discussion followed.[4]

While she spoke mainly on practical methods, most of her meetings concluded with the sending of letters or resolutions to the Ministry of Health, and other sources of influence. Her message was usually well – even enthusiastically – received, even though she was warned that 'the discussion of a birth control resolution would be prevented by violent, or even indecent, interruptions'. Although she 'invite[d] opponents to do their worst', the threatened 'objectionable behaviour' only materialised on a couple of occasions. At Slough Women's Section of the Labour Party in February 1925, 'an elderly lady in the audience ... before the lecture began, rose and denounced "this propaganda of birth control" as "an outrage" ', and after citing medical opinions (to which Stella provided counter-arguments) 'fell back on the "Christian" and "moral" argument'. Stella riposted as to whether 'organised Christianity in 1500 years, had a record inspiring confidence as regards poverty, prostitution and war', and appealed to the audience, who expressed their unequivocal wish to hear her out. The lady in question left, 'announcing that she was a member of the Catholic Women's League'.[5] In April, speaking at the Feltham Labour Women's Guild, she encountered 'a curious instance of the survival of a slave scale of values in a woman aiming at freedom', who was 'disturbed at the thought of birth control information being given by "A Spinster"!'. Stella's response, to audience applause, was that she 'had no apology to offer either for my status or my work" '[I]n more pretentious quarters', she had encountered 'attempts to raise prejudice on this score', and wondered if the campaign for the endowment of motherhood was troubled by 'similar irrelevant and impertinent questions' concerning Eleanor Rathbone, the independent MP and tireless campaigner for family allowances as well as many other causes.[6]

In January 1927, she made another speaking tour, in the Hampshire/Surrey area. As the guest of the Eclipse Study Circle and Lecture Group at Aldershot, her first lecture took place on a Sunday afternoon in Odiham Assembly Hall, on the 'national and international significance of birth control'. The audience included 'two ladies well known in the district as prominent Conservatives' whose 'persistent interrogations... raised points of great importance as to emigration'. At the end of the discussion, they 'appeared to have overcome their suspicions of the subject'. In the evening, Stella spoke on 'Birth Control and Socialism' at the Labour Hall, Aldershot, to a 'keen and varied audience', and on practical methods to women only the next day, garnering 'eager and detailed questions'. She also engaged in a public debate before the Farnham Wranglers, 'one of the oldest-established and best-known debating societies in the South of England': the first time a woman had debated in this 'assembly of professional and business men'. Stella, proposing the motion, 'That Birth Control Information should be given free by Doctors at Welfare Centres to All Women Desiring Such Information", gained a majority in its favour. She considered this, of all these meetings, 'the most stimulating and successful in provoking thought'.[7]

A tour of the West Country in the autumn of 1927 was less rewarding. Ross-on-Wye had initially 'enthusiastically asked for a meeting, and offered hospitality', then regretted that 'owing to opposition' the plan would have to be abandoned. Shrewsbury and Cheltenham also avoided 'anything so "unsettling"'. A meeting at Hereford did take place but, owing to 'the incessant deluge' and 'the peculiar methods of the local Trades Council and Labour Party, who... took no steps to organise or publicly advertise it!', was 'disappointing as propaganda'. The episode was redeemed from complete disaster through the organisation of a Drawing Room Meeting at St Leonard's Vicarage, where 'the women showed keen interest and absolute agreement', under the 'splendidly inspiring' chairing of Mrs Davis. She and her husband, Canon Davis, were described by Stella as in the 'fine tradition of social courage and idealism' associated with other socially concerned members of the Established Church, the more meritorious as this was continued 'against opposition and obstruction which only those who know the English countryside and small towns can realise'. Stella did find her stay in Hereford 'personally most interesting and refreshing' but the experience was not a triumph for the cause.[8]

In December 1927, she made a three-day 'propaganda journey' to Lincolnshire, and addressed four meetings: 'a tiny, but pathetically eager group of women' in Hibbaldstow, a 'spirited and satisfactory mixed meeting' in Scunthorpe, a women's meeting in Grimsby, and 'the best of the bunch' of Lincoln (Labour Party) Women's Sections. She did not meet the expected 'storm of criticism', although there were 'underhand attempts to sabotage' the meeting in Grimsby (but no details of what these were). With Mrs G. Jervis, her hostess in Grimsby, Stella attended a lecture and reception at the Town Hall, and met 'various influential social workers' of the area. Stella had 'pleasant memories of the courteous hospitality of her many kind hosts' – staying in a different place on each of the four nights covered by her visit.[9]

In the autumn of 1928, she made two tours under secularist auspices. During a visit to Durham mining districts suffering severe industrial depression, she had substantial, mixed, audiences at Chester-le-Street and Hetton and, 'although questions were keen, *no* difference of opinion was expressed on principle'. She found it 'gratifying…that local Spiritualist groups combined with the Secularists to give her a platform', in Hetton.[10] On 28 October, she gave two lectures to members and friends of the Manchester and Salford Secular Society. The Engineers' Hall was 'well-filled in the afternoon and packed in the evening' for her address on 'The New Code of Sexual Ethics'. Although the chairman called out after each lecture for any opponent who wished to speak against her, none appeared, although there was 'particularly animated discussion'.[11] She also visited Liverpool in January 1929.[12] During a repeat visit to Durham in April, she addressed six 'animated and satisfactory' meetings in four coalfields constituencies. An 'entirely civil and dignified protest' by the Anglican priest at Brandon was 'in marked contrast to the time-honoured Romanist methods, of incitement to violence and offensive abuse'.[13]

In the autumn of 1929, there were several other engagements through secularist connections. In October, Stella spoke at the 'historic Secularists' Hall at Leicester', to an audience, 'in spite of heavy rain', of nearly 300. Her given subject was 'Birth Control Problems and Humanist Ethics', with a 'brief supplementary speech' on the World Congress for Sexual Reform following a question in discussion.[14] Her longstanding audience of Labour women was not neglected: she spoke on the Congress, 'by request', to the Southall Labour Party women's section, 'one of the most eager and enlightened groups of women in the London area', in November, and also to Charlton Women's Ward of Greenwich Labour Party, and Hanwell Labour Party Women's Section, where the 'audience were much in agreement, not only with birth control, but with the wider and deeper implications of modern ethics'.[15] In November, she returned to Manchester to give a lecture to the Manchester Branch of the National Secular Society on the World Congress. Compressing this 'into a single lecture might daunt any lecturer, but it was successfully accomplished' – in fact, 'an excellent example of how such things may be done'. Instead of giving 'a dreary list of papers', Stella outlined 'the principal subjects dealt with day by day, and epitomis[ed] the arguments', and clearly distinguished her own views from the ones she was summarising. On the evening of the same day, she gave an address on 'The Government and Humanism', including a scathing, and well-documented, attack on the Government's 'pusillanimous attitude'. Manchester 'look[ed] forward to further doses of Miss Browne's strong medicine'.[16] In the same busy month, she also found time to speak to the Peckham Labour Party women's section on 'Birth Control and Public Health',[17] and to the South London branch of the National Secular Society at Brixton, on 'The Right to Free Motherhood', where the 'audience, which filled the hall, was greatly impressed by the lecturer's treatment of the subject'. A further visit from her in January was 'eagerly awaited'.[18]

The 'most encouraging feature' that she found in this work was 'the increasingly frank and intelligent interest in sex among working women.[19] From the summer of 1926,[20] as a result of the 'interest ... displayed and so many personal difficulties [being] brought forward for solution', she began speaking on 'Some Health Problems of Women',[21] in order to 'explain some of the difficulties facing the average – and often the exceptional – woman, throughout her life',[22] and to deal with the 'preservation of physical and mental health and joy and looks in the critical periods of women's lives'.[23] 'Great enthusiasm was displayed' by her audiences.[24] It was a shocking revelation that 'the problems of health – physical and mental – and of happiness – so far as happiness is within the power of individual reason and effort – which affect every women' formed an area 'in regard to which the medical advisers of the women present had apparently thought fit to leave them in total ignorance!'[25] These 'active, intelligent, high-spirited working women' were in 'total ignorance of even such normal general hygiene as the wholesome management of diet during puberty, periodicity, pregnancy and the menopause'. This Stella attributed to the 'vested interests in women's ignorance and helplessness'.[26] These lectures proved – 'If anything could further prove [it,] the need for wider and deeper sex enlightenment, even among women so alert and public-spirited as the majority of Guildwomen!'.[27] Among the subjects she touched on were 'Health Problems of Puberty and Sex Education': at a meeting at Plaistow on this topic, 'many of those present disagreed with the lecturer's view of how much children should be told', but nevertheless agreed with her that 'total silence, as a policy, was cruel, disastrous and ineffectual'.[28] She referred to these lectures as dealing with 'difficulties which the medical profession, whether out of moral scruples or, shall we say, Trade Union solidarity? has generally refused to help solve'.[29]

She continued critical of medical institutions and medical orthodoxy,[30] as the report by the 'Ministry of Disease' revealed the huge extent of maternal morbidity.[31] Stella declared that 'The medical profession will do well not to persist in attempts at dictature in this matter [birth control]. Their own low birth rate is widely known'. 'As a worker who has for years been extending to the poor the information which their accredited healers mostly refuse', Stella

> protest[ed] against medical monopoly under pretext of 'safeguards,' hygienic or 'moral.' This knowledge is the *right* of every adult human being.[32]

While conceding that it would be desirable to obtain information on 'many, hitherto obscure, physiological and psychological complications of pregnancy', she emphasised strongly that these '*can be and must be obtained without offensive interference* with the most intimate human liberty and dignity'.[33] (Stella Browne, pioneer of the concept of patient consent in human clinical trials?)

Housing issues continued to concern her: in 1929, she described 'the most inhuman, indecent and insanitary slums', in a 'winding street that writhed down to the Severn like a slimy reptile', a stone's throw from a Trollopean vista of 'architecture and scenery, a thousand glories of history and poetry, wealth and security, and green English turf and trees', in a Cathedral city where she was 'a humble helper of a most gallant forlorn hope' in the General Election.[34] This image seems to have haunted her: a couple of years later, she recalled this 'long writhing street' of a 'noisome foulness ... not jerry built, but the accumulation of centuries', whose 'troll-like inhabitants had grown into their present state in the shadow of the Cross'.[35] Might 'time and energy and public money' now be diverted from 'persecuting serious artists and suppressing their work' to 'making life in this country cleaner and happier and more valuable?'[36]

Stella continued to find that 'a very painful part' of her duty was to refuse entreaties for abortion. While she conceded that many of those requesting help were 'fairly worthless persons', who, when refused assistance, 'degrade themselves by hypocritical lies about the wickedness of abortion', others were 'women worthy of all respect: humble heroines of that drab, ceaseless grind, the common people's daily life and work.' She was sure that with the 'increased number of educated and public-spirited women' active in the birth control movement, converts must be coming to believe in the 'fundamental urgency of women's right to terminate an undesired pregnancy', but recognised that she was still 'a heretic' on this question.'[37]

Abortion, 'the next Woman's Right that needs vindication',[38] began to surface in her writings (and presumably her talks) with greater frequency. She pointed out, 'people who disapprove of legalised or illegal abortion ... *are bound in reason to support effective and reliable birth control*'.[39] Early in 1929, she reported receiving 'fresh expressions of approval for the effort to get this right on to the statute book: much of it entirely disinterested and very distinguished [but alas unidentified] approval'.[40] While she was pleased to note that there were sympathisers among the medical profession,[41] she observed sinister demands from other doctors to curtail illegal abortion. She saw this as 'a modern witchhunt' with 'more prohibitions, penalties, foul spying, denunciations, blackmail, agony and death' and despaired of 'the type of person who would volunteer for such detective service'. This was 'facing abortion with what I can only call the psychology of Torquemada – or Peeping Tom?'[42]

She gained a considerable audience for her ideas at the World Sexual Reform Congress in London in September 1929, where she presented a paper on 'The Right to Abortion', as 'the further logical implication' of the separation between 'the fulfillment of the sexual impulse [and] the procreation of children.' Her case was 'absolute freedom of choice on the woman's part in the early months of pregnancy.' She pointed out that the various limited cases for legal reform (e.g. unmarried mothers, raped women) were unsatisfactory and unworkable; moreover, 'it is probably that the majority of enforced and unwilling conceptions take place within the marriage tie'. On the eugenic arguments, she advanced her very strong view on 'the racial damage caused by unwilling maternity and pregnancy' ('nervous wrecks ... embittered, and yet half-hearted, mortals'), conceding that it could not 'be scientifically proved'. She accepted that, as a result of the 'physical processes of gestation', many women 'soon become entirely reconciled to the prospect', but argued that, if the 'woman's refusal is still definite and passionate' after three months, 'the case for relief is overwhelming'. She also pointed out that, given the enormous genital diversity of women, existing forms of contraception (barrier or chemical) could in many cases 'destroy or impair pleasure'. She concluded, 'Not abortion, but forced motherhood, is the crime.'[43]

Her position on eugenics remained aloof to hostile, as she forcefully repudiated the 'presumptuous and slap-dash panaceas advocated by certain so-called eugenists' and 'any *wholesale* sterilising or segregating':[44] 'The most recent work in biological chemistry' exposed 'the superficial and misleading nature of popular concepts of the trivial rôle of environment and of the popular belief that environment cannot greatly modify the quality and possibilities of the developing living creature – whether *in utero* or later.'[45]

'Race' in the interwar years could mean debates around the differences and distinctions between the various 'strains' making up the British nation. In a letter to Ellis about his 'superb piece of work', *Studies in British Genius*, his discussion of the 'Celtic vs Nordic', she stated, 'helped me personally'. She commented that the 'Nordic type exists with all its limitations as well as its achievements, just as marked today as when we climbed out of the long vessels with our battle axes in the 800s and 900s.' (We may deduce that Stella identified as Nordic rather than Celtic.) As for the contrast he drew between (Celtic) 'bright sensations … restless invention' and (Nordic) 'profound human passion with all its painful and stupid limitations', 'Oh don't I just know that!!'[46]

In spite of continued resistance by the Labour Party Executive, by 1926 there were a number of indications that entrenched opinions about birth control were beginning to shift. The 34th Independent Labour Party Easter Conference passed a very wide-ranging resolution – 'amid scenes of intense enthusiasm' and by an overwhelming majority – in favour of birth control.[47] The feminist National Union of Societies for Equal Citizenship threw 'its immense political ability and experience' behind Lord Buckmaster's House of Lords motion on the subject.[48] 'Labour bureaucrats … failed in their attempt to suppress mention of birth control' at the Party's Annual Conference in Margate, October 1926: Dora Russell and Dorothy Jewson stood on chairs to address 1100 delegates, 'crowded galleries and Press table', 'against the wide light space of the Winter Gardens, with the sea as a background', and their 'two contrasting heads and voices – hazel brown and clearly chiselled treble, silvery black and resonant mezzo – focussed eyes and attention'. In spite of Ramsay MacDonald's 'formidable weapons of … oratory, personal prestige and skill in side-tracking main issues', a narrow majority vote left the 'question free for discussion next year'.[49] Ernest Thurtle's 'plucky initial effort' to introduce a private Bill enabling birth control information by local authorities, though defeated, roused 'great public interest'. Clinics had been opened in Salford, in spite of vociferous Catholic opposition, in Stepney, East London, and in Aberdeen. Stella summed up 1926 as 'a Golden Year for our Cause.'[50]

All was not well, however, within the movement. In April 1927, Stella became troubled about the internal politics of the Malthusian League:

> The latest news of the Mal: League's affairs has an absolutely ludicrous side, though it is also, in some ways intensely serious.

> Kerr has been for some time on very bad terms with the Drysdales & has treated them as rudely as he generally treats people he can't bully with impunity.

Supporters of birth control were directing their efforts towards clinics, while their resources were depleted as a result of the General Strike. The Drysdales urged

> that on the occasion of the League's 50th Anniversary in July, *it must be disbanded, regardless of whether we have got any concessions from the Govt. for women at Welfare Centres or not!* It has not yet been submitted to a general meeting... My relations with the Ds are perfectly friendly, they show me courtesy & consideration & I am in no way implicated in the Kerr v D. row, though it may of course have a most disastrous effect, not only on the b.c. cause here, but also on my personal affairs.

She begged Ellis that 'if you are directly or indirectly consulted in the matter you will *stress* the awful humiliation & fiasco of disbanding with our work unfinished'.[51]

Stella pursued this point in *The New Generation*, threatened by this dissension. Nothing, she warned, could be 'more deceptive than the general appearance of acceptance and approval'. With

> every movement for enlightenment and liberation, there comes a time, after unremitting toil and steady battle against odds, when even the keenest fighters tend to feel that they may rest and let their turning of the tide carry the cause to victory.

This was such a moment. None of the three major political parties had yet incorporated birth control into its programme. The recently formed 'League of National Life' had 'concentrated and crystallised' Catholic opposition. She was rather paranoid about this body, believing it 'command[ed] large financial resources'.[52] It had a relatively small and aging membership, including a few well-known medical and political figures, and by no means extensive financial resources,[53] but it embodied inchoate forces ranged against birth control. The movement was in danger of resting 'content with the superficial freedom of today, which is still a freedom of discussion rather than action'.[54]

At the Malthusian League's dinner to celebrate fifty years since its founding, Stella encountered an almost mythic figure in British birth control history, the extremely elderly Annie Besant. This 'dignified, white-robed figure' with her 'splendid massive, silver-haloed head', sent Stella's mind 'back to her great revolt and the courage and vision that revolt implied, in mid-Victorian days'. Although C.V. Drysdale emphasised the 'growing popularity and diffusion of birth control', Stella's answer to the question 'Is the League's work done?' was that, in spite of 'great interest, of pressing and increasingly acknowledged need... the cause is not yet victorious'.[55]

There were some encouraging developments. Lady Rhondda's influential 'vigorous and vivacious weekly' feminist journal *Time and Tide*, which Stella had earlier accused of 'sexphobia' for prioritising political equality over 'pre-occupation with birth control',[56] was rendering 'the best service to birth control' through a series of articles.[57] A conference on Maternal Mortality at Central Hall Westminster on 22 October, made 'no attempt to rule out birth control in discussion', and Stella herself raised 'the *bête noire* of these conferences, the undeniable fact that abortions need not be fatal to women, or even dangerous'.[58]

Stella was beginning to pursue a strategy of seizing on some newsworthy item as a peg on which to hang a short but punchy letter to a suitable periodical, arguing for birth control or abortion. A letter to *Time and Tide* in September 1929 pointed out that the maternal mortality rate in the just-published vital statistics for 1928 was the worst since 1911, and that for 'every recorded death, there are several more cases of injury – often serious and life-long'. Her solution was, of course, 'give those who desire it, wholesome and reliable birth control knowledge and help, at Maternity Welfare Centres'.[59]

Bessie Drysdale's prophecy of a sharp move rightwards on other political fronts remained unfulfilled. Stella remained an ardent left-winger, becoming a fairly active member of the Fabian Society.[60] In August 1924, she (with R.B. and Dora Kerr) attended the Fabian Summer School at The Downs School, Seaford. In the Visitors' Book, Stella described herself as 'journalist and lecturer... articles in New Generation, Socialist Review, German and Am[erican]: papers'.[61] During her stay, there were lectures on 'Some Difficulties of the Labour Party' and 'Some Aspects of the Population Problem', although walking and bathing were also on the agenda.[62] She spent at least one day at the 1928 Summer School at Cirencester,[63] and also managed to attend the Summer School on 'Indian Problems'[64] at Bexhill-on-Sea on 30 August 1929 (under interests she put down 'Human nature, justice').[65] She regularly took a vociferous part in the discussions arising at Annual General Meetings,[66] and was an habitue of the Fabian Common Room at Tothill Street in Westminster, where she occasionally entertained guests.[67]

She was honorary secretary of the Chelsea Labour Party from around 1924 until 1926,[68] and Secretary of its General Strike Committee (the General

Strike, in defence of miners' wages and hours, under threat from the mine-owners, took place in May 1926).[69] Although 'hardly prepared', they 'did some useful work' in 'carry[ing] out the decisions of the Trades Union Congress insofar as they affected Chelsea. Reviewing the situation in 'a somewhat more peaceful atmosphere', it was possible that 'they could have done better'[70] than this 'triumph of improvisation'. In the immediate aftermath, she was 'raw with anger and pity, dazed with the implications of the defeat one had foreseen'.[71] She represented the Women's Section at the London Labour Party Women's Advisory Conference and the International Class War Prisoners' Aid. Presumably she was also involved in organising 'jumble sales, socials and raffles'.[72]

On 28 July 1926, the National Labour Party Executive disaffiliated Chelsea Trades Council and Labour Party for not adhering to rulings concerning the admission of Communists.[73] Stella protested vociferously, inferring that '*one* reason for our excommunication is our defence of the rights of working women to control their essential job':[74] Chelsea had sent in a resolution to the National Party Conference demanding birth control information in Maternity Centres and Clinics.[75] In spite of their 'lengthy' protest,[76] by November 'new Labour Parties[were] being formed in the Divisions recently disaffiliated'.[77] A decade later, Stella commented that Leslie Paul's novel *Men in May* had 'done to the life' the 'struggle between Right Wingers and Left, the Party Meetings, the struggles of the Chairman, the descent of the suave and dapper organiser, threatening disaffiliation from Eccleston Square' (i.e. that the local party would no longer be recognised by the national party).[78] Possibly as a result of the differences between the local party and HQ – not to mention internecine rifts between a left-wing group (with which Stella was identified), and another antagonistic and even obstructive group which saw itself as representing the 'real' Chelsea Labour Party[79] – Stella 'left Chelsea'.[80]

She was by no means complacent about women's position, which had not yet 'advanced half way towards economic justice'.[81] With the 'tardy and grudging concession' of extension of the female suffrage,[82] Stella suggested that the vote had 'gained in respectability as it has lost in efficacy'.[83] Early in 1928, she conveyed her 'best wishes to the under thirties', with the hope that they might use this 'overrated but often helpful weapon of the franchise, not to shackle and forbid, but to liberate and help!'[84] She perceived one positive result:

> It is now common form, politically, or shall I say electorally, to stress the need to reduce maternal mortality... Baby's bottle

> and the kitchen sink are no longer trifles beneath the serious consideration of statesmen.[85]

She found much to praise in Eleanor Rathbone's plea for the endowment of motherhood (family allowances), *The Disinherited Family*. But she protested against Rathbone's advocacy of placing the children of unmarried parents in Poor Law care, if its 'progenitors refuse to turn a brief – though possibly worthwhile – illusion into a permanent incompatibility'. Otherwise, she found Rathbone's work 'notably competent and substantial', 'illumined by that instinct for generally neglected facts and values ... yet ... based on adequate documentation'.[86] She retained a certain wariness, even amounting to hostility, towards 'the organised women's movement's 'smugness'.[87]

She exempted from this criticism Alison Neilans, the Secretary of the Association of Moral and Social Hygiene – founded by the great Victorian feminist Josephine Butler. Stella greatly admired her expression of 'the great objection to prostitution in general and licensed houses in particular'.[88] At the time of Josephine Butler's centenary, Stella expressed her admiration of this important figure in the struggle for an equal moral standard. '[T]hose of us' who believed that 'no sexual acts should take place which are not desired and enjoyed by both partners' were surely entitled to bring Butler their own tribute, in memory of her 'proclamation of individuality and individual worth' and 'enormous courage and against odds'. She conceded that the equal moral standard was being worked out along lines different from those Butler's 'colleagues and followers anticipated', but there was not 'so much steadfast courage or so much honest sex pride or solidarity among women' that Butler's work could be forgotten.[89] But 'That old fear that women should know and dare to be free!' was

> percolating even into our [birth control] movement, oh, so anxious to demand marriage lines, and dictate the quota of children to be produced before help can be given![90]

Her own views on the problem of prostitution remained what they had always been, that

> *the commercialisation of sex outside the marriage tie*, was the inevitable accompaniment of its commercialisation *within* legal marriage, and that both are part and parcel of civilisation on a cash basis.

'Prostitution and procuration' would only be reduced or abolished 'by giving light instead of that ignorance, and freedom instead of that subjection'. The League of Nation's report on the Traffic in Women and Children 'glossed over'

> the whole vast network of psychological and physiological motives, the effects of ignorance, of the hideous boredom of much modern work, of the increased mechanisation of much modern leisure, of the inadequacy and disharmony of most modern marriage, of the vast individual range of sexual tastes and 'twists', of the fear of the unwanted child.[91]

She commended 'the main recommendations of the Street Offences Committee', 1928, since 'the necessary degree of public order and safety in our cities must be based on fair play and a certain respect for individual freedom'.[92] The 'theory of a rightless class or a rightless sex' could not 'with any logic, decency or comfort' be acceptable to 'a modern community', as the

> two stereotyped feminine patterns of the sheltered wife and the chivvied outlaw are merging into a more various and spontaneous humanity.

Stella noted, however, with some cynicism, that

> the woman of the transition so often wants to have it both ways – to enjoy the privileges of subjection and the rights of freedom![93]

She posited much more radical changes in sexual institutions, arguing that as marriage became 'more fluid and more differentiated', so would 'its shadow sister', prostitution, change.[94] She also continued to plead for 'the right to effective means of preventing venereal disease, for all adult persons, *without discrimination against class or sex*'.[95]

She was depressed by the 'many cruel and absurd anomalies' following the 1923 Divorce Act'.[96] But, while arguing that conditions of release should be improved, she remained sceptical about marriage and monogamy:

> We are working out standards and codes with pain and stress, with mistakes, no doubt, but with an unalterable 'No' to the lies and fears of the former dispensation.[97]

Although 'the failure of old prohibitions and promises was now evident to all, it did not follow that there was no distinction between things worthy and unworthy'. There was a need for 'rules of behaviour which modern individuals, with their scientific and democratic background, could respect and accept'. In her vision of the 'rational humanist attitude to marriage, parenthood, prostitution, and sexual abnormalities', birth control was essential and 'Free love was the ideal'. This implied both responsibility and freedom for both partners, and she wondered 'how many professed free lovers' were ready to admit these implications. A new ethics would take into consideration the 'immense variety of quality and indeed even of structure' between individual human beings: 'Life and love [have] enough difficulties and tragedies in themselves, without gratuitous persecution.' Young children, and mothers engaged in child-bearing and rearing, would need special protection (she mentioned Soviet Russia as an example).[98] Legal change was still necessary with regard to divorce, 'the public attitude towards commercialism in sex, and the treatment of the sexually abnormal'.[99]

Similarly, she argued that 'economic changes are absolutely necessary before honestly adequate sexual institutions and a wholesome and dignified *atmosphere* in these matters can exist', although such changes would not 'automatically produce such customs and atmosphere'.[100] Many persons knowledgeable 'in modern medical and biological research, and without theological and conventional superstitions' had a 'fatal flaw in their vision and treatment of sex': seeing 'sexual relationships [as] entirely physical, an error only less deep and devastating than its opposite, the denial of the body'. This ignored the 'immense range of complexities and semitones' among both modern women and 'the more intellectual and complex men': it was possible (a theme which Stella constantly reiterated) 'to utterly repudiate (both by instinct and by conviction) cast-iron compulsory monogamy, yet at the same time to be rigorously selective'.[101]

As might be anticipated, she spoke out against the attacks on Radclyffe Hall's pioneering novel on lesbianism, *The Well of Loneliness* (1928)[102] – 'a decent (and to tell the truth, rather dull) novel on inversion',[103] written

> in a spirit of the most earnest idealism, not wholly escaping sentimentality, but certainly without any stress on the physical aspects of her theme, and with far more reticence than the average novelist now observes.[104]

She contrasted the shock manifested towards this novel in the press with the lack of similar concern towards

> A married woman, aged 41. Twelve live births, four children dead, eight surviving. Three bad miscarriages. Motherhood in all its sacredness![105]

She protested 'equally against the minority who idealise inversion and the mob who insult and persecute it'. Certainly, 'the social order which wrecks so much normal sex life has no right whatever to condemn the abnormal *as such*'. The subject-matter of Hall's novel was, she argued

> unknown in its conscious and developed phases, to most women in this country, till the vigorous missionary efforts of Mr Douglas [James Douglas, of the *Sunday Express*, whose vicious attack on *The Well of Loneliness* led to its notoriety and eventual prosecution] and Sir William Joynson Hicks ['Jix', the Home Secretary] so effectively advertised its existence!

'Congenital, conscious and exclusive homosexuality', was 'very rare'. But it could not be eradicated, 'even by the avenging flames so lavishly lighted in the ages of faith and chivalry'. It was

> up to all of us, men or women, inverts or normal, to love bravely and finely, but we cannot choose *whom* to love.[106]

She expressed related concerns over censorship:

> How much money goes to the Public Prosecutor's staff and to the sort of people who enjoy opening and confiscating other people's letters and manuscripts? How much scientific research and artistic creation is at the mercy of Comstock [the notorious USA persecutor of 'obscenity'] cads? If the Government disapproves of all forms of sexual abnormality, why should *voyeurism* alone be privileged and immune?[107]

It is possible that her emotions on this subject were particularly aroused: her translation of Theodor Van de Velde's *Ideal Marriage* had been cautiously issued by the publishers as for sale to the medical profession only,[108] which cannot have pleased her. Would the anticipated 'next Labour Government'

> raise the ban on the science and the poetry of sex, in the great work of Havelock Ellis, and what is reported to be the finest book of D. H. Lawrence [presumably *Lady Chatterley's Lover*]. Will it even make knowledge which is available to peeresses, equally available to working women?[109]

Although she retained her interest in all questions of sexual reform, she refused the BSSSP's invitation to address it in 1925. While 'obliged ... for their kind invitation', she did not see her way to accepting:

> There must surely be many members of the Society who are able to contribute essays and lectures of value in subject and outlook, and there are certainly vast tracts of the Society's subject, which have not been touched on.

She added:

> During my membership of the Society, for eight years, I did a considerable – and perhaps disproportionate – share of its work in various directions. I feel that it would now be more graceful on my part, to leave that work to others – and incidentally, fairer to my already overworked self![110]

However, she remained in touch with them,[111] and continued to attend meetings and contribute to discussion,[112] and to promote it to interested individuals.[113] In March 1929, E.B. Lloyd persuaded Stella to speak on 'Legalized Abortion',[114] resulting in 'quite a good meeting' on 18 April.[115]

In September 1929, she found the week-long 3rd International Congress of the World League for Sexual Reform, held at the Wigmore Hall, London, a very stimulating and enjoyable occasion.[116] The 'diversity of views' all 'proved the injustice and inadequacy of merely traditional codes'. Her only suggestions for future improvements were that 'more time for *discussion* of the many absorbing themes' should be allowed, 'if possible – more stress on the *anthropological* aspects of sex', and more efficient handling of the resolutions. But it had been an 'encouraging and memorable historical landmark' and had 'given considerable impetus to public discussion over here'.[117]

Besides her interest in the anthropological approach to sexuality, she engaged intelligently but critically with Freud and psychoanalysis, applying a degree of scepticism to this new approach to the mysteries of the mind and of sex. She did not 'bolt [it] whole'.[118] She praised Paul Bousfield's 'admirably close and detailed criticism of Freud's androcentric view of sex and mis-interpretation of the sexual impulse in women'.[119] She was well up in the various different strands of psychoanalytic thought and, while 'the general concept of the Unconscious is extraordinarily suggestive and important', there was neither 'harmony nor finality in [the] conclusions' of the various schools,[120] and 'Freudian dogma has expanded, if not shifted, not only through the researches of Adler, Jung and Stekel, but in the mind of its founder.' Her own preference was for Stekel, probably the most politically radical and activist of Freud's disciples and his 'most illuminating and helpful contribution to the sum of psychological knowledge and creative experiment'.[121]

She considered it possible for the unconscious to be 'a powerful ally of Tyranny': Freudian '*dogma*, adopted by ignorant and unevolved minds, may be made a justification for obsolete institutions and customs', even for 'attacks on birth control': assumptions about '"*a stratified and static Society*"' were implicit in some psycho-analytic thinkers.[122] Mary Chadwick, a trained nurse and a qualified Freudian analyst, won Stella's praise for balancing and supplementing her 'devout Freudian ... command of psycho-analytic theory' by 'experience of life and work in her chosen profession'. In Stella's opinion

> some such independent first-hand experience and opinions are necessary in order to extract what is of value and help from psycho-analytic doctrine. The mind which has never faced realities or formulated its own working theory of life, before meeting Freud's, is apt to be utterly overwhelmed, and to uncritically accept or to reject equally *in toto*.

However, she considered that 'So many people nowadays, when the psycho-analytic vocabulary is "in the air," think that to call any emotion a "neurosis" or a "complex" settles it for ever', and 'thus take cover from life's intricacies and surprises under the aegis of Freud!'[123]

She found R.E. Money-Kyrle's *Aspasia: The Future of Amorality* 'a concisely persuasive and stimulating application of Freudian psychoanalysis to modern conditions', including how 'the international scene becomes one gigantic paranoia'.[124] She continued to refuse to 'resign my critical faculty about psycho-analysis or anything else', and during the 1930s was impressed by

> the admirable work of Dr. Wilhelm Reich, both in analysing the stress and suffering of young people in ignorance and poverty, and in exposing the results of sexphobia and dogmatic pedantry among those in authority.[125]

She praised the work of his 'Sex-Pol' group, even though 'it appears ... sometimes to accept as final what is so far experimental only', and particularly admired Reich's showing up of the 'totally patriarchal and one-sided approach to the material' in Geza Roheim's *Psychoanalysis of Primitive Cultures*. Roheim ignored 'the importance of matriarchal customs' and treated 'passivity and dependence of women as obvious and desirable', and even found 'excuses for the hideous mutilations whereby certain East African tribes ensure the subjection of their women'[126] (she had long been concerned about the 'painful mutilations' inflicted upon girls in those regions).[127]

In her view, psychoanalysis was only one of two 'lines of specialised investigation in sex matters' which had 'profoundly influenced modern – after-war – thought'; the other was 'the transcendent powers attributed to – "monkey gland"'. '[E]fforts at Rejuvenation through physiological experiment' had 'failed to produce a happy uniformity of success' and, indeed, 'offer[ed] painful facilities to the charlatan.' But 'the very *possibility* ... [had] psychical value' through encouraging 'boldness of speculation and action in regard to sexual conditions' and being in 'direct antagonism to the slavish and despairing apathy enforced by poverty and ignorance.'[128]

Life was not all work and no relaxation. In February 1925, Stella had a break, 'gone to get strength at a cottage in Oxfordshire'.[129] She found her 'best medicine and recreation' in Nature, 'in animals, in trees and the sea'. Although she had no 'athletic aptitudes', she was fond of 'walking and swimming' within the 'severe limitations' imposed by her 'strained heart'.[130]

She had various social contacts during the late 1920s. William J. Robinson, American sex reformer and indefatigable publisher of journals, dined with her at least once during a visit to England in 1925.[131] She saw two of her heroines, veterans of the international women's cause, during that summer when both Alexandra Kollontai and Helene Stöcker visited the Walworth Centre. Stella was keeping up not only with Stöcker's journal, *Die Neue Generation*, but with her articles in 'other German papers of progressive views and high literary standing', her 'two psychological studies in modern literature and history', and a long novel.[132] Stöcker paid tribute to Stella and her campaigns in *Die Neue Generation*, but it is not entirely clear how well they were personally acquainted.[133] Stella contributed to *Die Neue Generation* occasionally from at least 1922, mostly accounts of the progress of the British birth control movement.[134]

Stella also encountered members of the Scandinavian birth control movement. Early in 1926, she wrote to Ellis about 'two interesting Norwegians' visiting Britain: Professor and Dr Mohr, the latter 'an advanced Socialist, daughter of the leading Norse feminist Fru Anker', who ran a birth control bureau '& believes in & advocates right of abortion'.[135] This enabled Stella to produce an article on 'the movement to give birth control knowledge to the Norwegian workers'. The active support given by the Norwegian Labour Party was emphasised: although, even within Norse Labour, there was 'need for vigilant and vigorous defence' of women's right to birth control.[136] Stella maintained contact with these Norwegian colleagues.[137]

In 1927, Stella and other British feminists were 'stimulated by a brief visit from Miss Doris Stevens, of the National Women's Party of America, who 'view[ed] birth control as part of a coherent philosophy of sex and life' and was 'appl[ying] the New Psychology to the presentation of the feminine case'.[138] During her visit to Hereford, the 'busy wayfarer' would always remember 'the hospitable kindness and beautiful music' she enjoyed with Canon and Mrs Davis at St Leonard's Vicarage.[139] She also received 'delightful hospitality during her first visit to Manchester',[140] and never failed to comment on the hospitality received on her other lecture-tours.

At the World Congress of Sexual Reform in 1929, Stella was delighted at the opportunity to meet 'so many of the pioneers and real spade workers of the movement, British and foreign', although she regretted that certain 'international stalwarts', including Kollontai, were absent, and mentioned the 'shadow' of the news of the death of Aletta Jacobs, 'active and consistent champion of free motherhood'.[141] But she also appreciated the associated 'motor excursions' and 'a thoroughly enjoyable Conversazione and soirée at the Hotel Cecil, at which Sex Reformers laughed, gossiped, danced and absorbed light refreshments just like ordinary mortals!'[142] Later the same year, she published a sixtieth birthday tribute to Stöcker, 'one of the most courageous, enlightened and distinguished persons now living'.[143]

A new friend was cosmopolitan internationalist Bertha Lorsignol.[144] Old friends included Dorothy Jewson. In a eulogistic article in *Medical Critic and Guide* in 1925, Stella described her as 'one of the finest fighters' for the birth control cause. While the article concentrated on Jewson's political career, it also mentioned that she was 'tall and slender' and 'walks quickly and with something of an athlete's spring', her 'delicate though resolute chin', 'brown eyes with straight brows, and hair 'originally that *brun cendré* which also touches black' now 'grey at the front and sides', giving 'an eighteenth century *poudrée* touch to her straight clear features'. She had 'an extremely keen though quiet sense of humour'.[145]

Stella presumably remained close to Dora Russell, although they had something of a falling out in March 1926 over Stella's publication in *The New Generation* of a list of sympathetic MPs that Russell claimed had been for internal Workers' Birth Control Group circulation only.[146] A review by Stella of Russell's *Hypatia: Or Women and Knowledge* a little earlier, however, suggests pre-existing tensions. Although praising Russell's 'clarity of and rapidity of thought and mastery of graceful and pointed phrase', Stella pointed out the amazing omission of the work of *The Freewoman* group. Also, she felt that 'the denunciation of marriage ... would come with better taste from one who had not accepted the marriage contract'[147] – somewhat unfair to Russell, who had been prepared to live in free union with Bertrand Russell, but once she became pregnant was pressured by him into marriage.[148]

But, at some point after Stella had left the Chelsea Labour Party, she wrote to Russell about consulting the London Association for the Care of the Mentally Defective about 'Mrs Baker's boy Charlie' (possibly their Labour Party and birth control movement colleague Jennie Baker?), in whom they were both taking an interest.[149] This indicates that they were still managing to work together and cooperate, although Russell mentioned in later life that 'Some of us were hesitant about [the demand for abortion] and anyway we were very worried because we were trying to get birth control on the way and we didn't want a disturbance to our work'. However, she did 'honour [Stella's] intransigence ... no chairman on earth could get her to sit down'.[150]

It would be interesting to know how Russell responded to comments by Stella's old antagonist, Norman Haire, as they organised the World League for Sexual Reform Congress. Haire wrote to her that R.B. Kerr had 'wished on us Stella Browne, who wants to read a paper on the "Right to Abortion". They are both difficult people, and we must give them no opportunity of stirring up strife.' Stella managed to scrape up a guinea for the Conference subscription and four shillings towards expenses and sent these in early January 1929, but this promptitude and generosity did not ameliorate Haire's animus. He complained that 'I dislike Stella Browne intensely but I do not quite see how we can stop her reading a paper', and feared that, if offended, she and Kerr would 'attack the Congress or ignore it'. He suggested that the length of their papers could be limited and they could be allocated 'the most inconspicuous and unfavourable position' on the programme.[151] There are no copies of Russell's responses to Haire's Machiavellian paranoia in her files. In spite of any negative feelings towards Haire which she may have entertained, Stella was clearly strongly committed to the idea of the World Congress, not only singing its praises in *The New Generation* and *The Medical Critic and Guide*, but speaking about it in a very positive fashion in her lectures. This was one of a number of instances where, whatever her personal feelings about colleagues in 'the Cause', she was prepared to praise their achievements on its behalf – there may have also been a feeling that it was necessary to 'close ranks' in the face of the opposition.

A relatively new figure in Stella's circles was the novelist and journalist Winifred Holtby, whom Stella reported in summer 1928 as doing 'very effective publicity work'.[152] She gave glowing reviews to Holtby's *Eutychus: or the future of the pulpit* – 'Her satire is never savage, it is scrupulously impartial, and it is certainly comprehensive!',[153] and her *A New Voter's Guide to Party Programmes: Political Dialogues* which applied 'alert and continuous candour ... to all political parties'.[154] It is a pity that no more personal evidence survives about the relationship of these two strongly feminist women of different generations: possibly personal contacts obviated the need for correspondence.[155]

She had a high opinion of Cicely Hamilton and her incisive way of putting things – 'I wish we could send Cicely Hamilton to Geneva next year'.[156] She praised her 'independent and balanced enquiry' into 'the vice we call unnatural' [lesbianism] and congratulated *Time and Tide* 'on their courage in writing and publishing this penetrating piece of social diagnosis'.[157] Lis Whitelaw claims in her biography of Hamilton that there can have been no real relationship between the two women, because they 'had very different views' even if they agreed 'on the need for birth control'. Whitelaw posits complete dichotomy between an older generation of 'social purity', 'Old' Feminists on the one hand, and a younger generation of 'sex reform', 'New' Feminists on the other.[158] Even if this existed, personal ties might transcend partisan allegiances. In fact, Stella had enormous admiration for social purity heroines such as Josephine Butler, and considered the exploitation of women through prostitution an evil to be eradicated, while Hamilton had been the first woman to join the BSSSP, in 1914, and had translated a German pamphlet for it.[159] They had broader mutual sympathies than simply joint interest in birth control and abortion.

Stella was interested, it sometimes seems, in anything and everything, even the wonders of 'modern metallurgical chemistry'.[160] She had a strong appreciation of aesthetics, although 'more interested in life than in literature'. '[A]s a critic', she was 'extremely fastidious, with a palate for pungent flavours and for "*nuances*"', and had an 'almost hypercritical sense of language'. Her 'literary ideal [was] the chisel or the stiletto', and she aimed, herself, at 'brevity and concentrated significance'.[161] Praising Theodore Dreiser's *An American Tragedy* as 'powerful and poignant', she suggested that it suffered from excessive length and seriousness.[162] In Calverton and Schmalhausen's *Sex in Civilisation,* 'Even those [authors] convinced of the desirability of brevity in love, fail to appreciate the case for brevity in literature.'[163] She was 'too much interested and too busy to have ever, as yet, written the book of which' she admitted, 'she occasionally dreams'. As for other arts, she was 'extremely susceptible to music – or rather to melody, for this susceptibility is almost purely emotional – and to color'.[164]

She wrote a long appreciative letter to Ellis about his *Sonnets and Spanish Folksongs*. 'Unfinished Symphony' 'convey[ed] just that extraordinary sense of expansion & intense yet as it were *rarefied* emotion that some music always brings me'. She approved of the production of the book: 'How beautiful (without being gaudy) & appropriate the binding is, & the type & "get up" so fine and appropriate.' Receiving the book was 'a great joy ... & an encouragement ... after a damnable Tuesday & most depressing Wednesday.'

He was 'a great consoler and strengthener'. She was suffering, yet again, from 'a horrid internal chill.'[165]

She was still finding time for the occasional verse translation herself: in February 1926, *The New Leader* published her version of Theodor Storm's 'Consolation'. She also undertook the challenging task of translating Helena Stöcker's novel, *Liebe* (Love) into English but, although it seemed likely to be published by Thomas Seltzer,[166] an idealistic young New York publisher, presumably his bankruptcy from fighting prosecutions for obscenity halted operations.[167]

There were occasional theatre visits: early in 1926, she went to see Cicely Hamilton's play 'The Old Adam' at the Kingsway Theatre, a science-fictional treatment of the 'problem of modern warfare *versus* civilisation'. Hamilton's 'unflinching vision of disaster [had] become tinged as much with irony as despair', in a play which 'probe[d] too deeply for either the conventional patriot or the conventional pacifist', asking what outlet a future society would provide for 'the deepest and most permanent instinct of the majority of men: that love of a good fight'. Stella praised both the play – 'the movement ... is swift and direct from the biting satire of the first act to the futile pathos of the last' – and the 'triumphs of characterisation' achieved by the cast.[168]

Stella seldom mentioned the 'mass media' of the day, although she did comment that

> Broadcasting and the cinema have the advantage of 'immediacy' in propaganda, but they appeal to the fancy rather than to the deeper instincts, and are instruments of recreation rather than controversy; of mass-suggestion rather than exposition.[169]

She continued to respond much more acutely to the written word, perhaps especially when this gave 'a vivid sense of the pathos and beauty of animals and the special magic of trees'. Sylvia Dunn's short stories embodied 'the direct yet sensitive vision of an artist and the sturdy courage of a woman of action', and had 'the effective economy of a good line drawing', a comparison which suggests that Stella also had a taste for the visual arts.[170]

She was also enthusiastic about Alexandra Kollontai's three stories, published 'in an inadequate translation under the title "Red Love"',[171] noting in particular how '*the deprivation of leisure*' during the years of 'fierce hunger and effort', causing 'strange, unanalysed changes in the chemistry of bodies and souls', created problems in relationships.[172] (Perhaps a note of personal resonance from someone who seems to have enjoyed little leisure herself.) Among other literary works (in at least three languages) which she praised were Victor Margueritte's *Ton Corps Est À Toi* and the concluding volumes of H.G. Wells's *The World of William Clissold*. Margueritte's book could almost have been written at Stella's dictation, it covered so many of her pet issues.[173] She considered *The World of William Clissold* as a 'study of the contemporary position of women ... an enormous advance on "The New Machiavelli" with its 'blurring obsession with Motherhood', about which she had written him a critical letter in 1911.[174] (She also admired 'Wells' great imaginative short stories, with their amazing vividness and precision and their pathos of weirdness or macabre horror'.)[175]

Her awareness of history and, in particular, women's history was continually manifested: 'women have been home-makers since the Stone Age, wage-earners since the Industrial Revolution'.[176] In her review of Katharine Anthony's biography of Catherine the Great, she appreciated 'the years of minute original research and of sifting and clarifying such research' that went into 'this study of the greatest stateswoman of recorded history'. Anthony treated her heroine 'as an all-round human being': the 'legendary 300 lovers' were reduced, 'on investigation, to 13 ... not a surprising number in a life so long, so busy, and so full of imperial opportunity!'[177]

What was happening in her own erotic life at this time is not clear. She wrote to Ellis of 'an extraordinarily vivid physically intense – coitus dream – the most realistic I have ever had, which seemed to make me very strong & happy too'.[178] In a review of the anti-feminist Antony Ludovici's *Man: An Indictment*, she considered that he had 'missed the opportunity of a really thorough and independent study of the distinctive masculine brain and emotions'. Such a study would include, she suggested,

> that most interesting and delightful minority of human beings, whose existence he ignores: the men whose creative vigour and intelligence is supplemented by sympathy and imagination, who do *not* need to be perpetually fussing about their powers of mind or body; who do *not* need to fetter and further handicap women as workers, who can attract and satisfy women as mates, without attempts at bribery or bullying.

It would be nice to know if this were written from close personal experience of such a delightful figure.[179]

There are the usual recurrent tantalising hints about the diversity of her own sexual life: she quoted approvingly the statement that 'If two people love one another any conceivable form of intercourse they have a fancy for is normal and enobling.'[180] She also made the intriguing statement that 'Liberty – which includes other people's liberty as well as one's own – is a stringent and selective discipline.' Even in an ideal world, individual diversities would persist, and 'with them, the difficulties as well as the charm and thrill of emotional relationships'.[181] Were her own relationships 'garden-groves – Edens of subtle movement and various colour and above all – *distance*', rather than 'straitjackets or prison cells'? Did she condemn 'the incessant clutch on a man's soul and life' by monogamy-indoctrinated women because it was alien to her – or because she had felt the temptation?[182]

William J. Robinson suggested that her 'personal history, like her public activity, [had] few "half-tones"'. It had been 'intensely vivid and strenuous, and its most salient events [had] been the result of actions and decisions of her own, against considerable pressure of opposition'. Her 'likes and dislikes [were] intense and lasting' and she was 'about as neurotic a woman as one wants to meet'.[183] A tantalising comment in her review of Robinson's *A Doctor's Views on Life* suggests that they 'differ[ed] sharply' on the subject of telepathy.[184] Unfortunately, she did not expand on this and her views on psychic phenomena remain passing allusions.[185]

About to turn fifty, at the close of the 1920s Stella Browne was in one of the more obviously successful phases of her life. In spite of the upheavals and disappointments of the earlier part of the decade, she was doing relatively well. She had a steady outlet for articles and reviews with *The New Generation*.[186] She was an increasingly sought-after lecturer. She had received credit as the translator of van de Velde's *Ideal Marriage* (although she considered his 'fine sympathy and immense proficiency both clinical and technical' was '"unequally yoked" with traditional ethics'):[187] it is improbable that she shared in the financial rewards gained by this popular marriage manual, which sold in thousands over the following decades.[188] She was (presumably) preparing her translation of Müller-Lyer's *The Family*, which would appear in the following year. She had assorted fora for her views, and the causes to which she had dedicated herself had increasingly likely prospects of success. In the absence of much private correspondence for this period of her life, we cannot tell if there was a price in health problems or emotional turmoil to pay for her hectic activity or, indeed, how she was managing to earn a living; what we can see is the activity.

Stella might also have felt that there was reason for optimism about the prospects of 'the Cause'. Birth control was increasingly discussed and debated. A Labour government had been returned, albeit with a 'dingysouled clique ... busily engaged in haggling and shoving and boot-licking'[189] strongly represented, and women's interests still being given less than their due. Progress had been slower than she would have wished, but it was gradually being made.

Notes

1. Editorial, *The New Generation*, vol. 6, April 1927, p. 37.
2. [W. J. Robinson], 'The most radical British feminist and birth control advocate of today', *Medical Critic and Guide*, vol. 25/E no. 5, May 1927, pp. 192–4.
3. F.W. Stella Browne, 'Friends and foes of birth control', *The New Generation*, vol. 3, December 1924, p. 135.
4. 'Miss Browne's lecture', *The New Generation*, vol. 3, December 1924, p. 137; 'No burden on rates: birth control knowledge would cost nothing', *Daily Herald*, 19 November 1924, cutting in Dora Russell papers, International Institute of Social History, Amsterdam [DR], file 497.
5. F.W.S.B., 'Catholic interrupts Miss Browne', *The New Generation*, vol. 4, March 1924, p. 28.
6. F.W.S.B., 'Miss Browne's meetings', *The New Generation*, vol. 4, June 1925, p. 62.
7. 'Miss Browne's southern tour', *The New Generation*, vol. 6, March 1927, p.30.
8. F.W.S.B., 'Miss Browne's meetings', *The New Generation*, vol. 6, October 1927, pp. 117–18.
9. 'Miss Browne in Lincolnshire', *The New Generation*, vol. 7, January 1928, p. 8.
10. 'Miss Browne in Durham/Miss Browne's lectures', *The New Generation*, vol. 7, November 1928, p. 125.
11. 'Miss Browne in Manchester', *The New Generation*, vol. 7, December 1928, p. 137.
12. 'Miss Browne in Liverpool', *The New Generation*, vol. 8, February 1929, p. 20.
13. 'Miss Browne in Durham', F.W. Stella Browne, 'Notes on Durham tour', *The New Generation*, vol. 8, May 1929, pp. 52, 59.
14. 'Miss Browne at Leicester', *The New Generation*, vol. 8, November 1929, p. 128.
15. *The New Generation*, vol. 9, January 1930, p. 2.
16. Edward Shiel, 'Miss Browne and Manchester', *The New Generation*, vol. 8, December 1929, p. 137.
17. 'Miss Browne's meetings', *The New Generation*, vol. 8, December 1929, p. 136.
18. A.H., 'Miss Browne at Brixton', *The New Generation*, vol. 8, December 1929, p. 134.
19. 'Miss Browne's meetings', *The New Generation*, vol. 5, December 1926, p. 126.
20. 'Miss Browne's meetings', *The New Generation*, vol. 7, December 1928, p. 139.

21. 'Miss Browne's meetings', *The New Generation*, vol. 5, August 1926, p. 74; 'Southall Meeting', *The New Generation*, vol. 7, August 1928, p. 88.
22. 'Miss Browne's meetings', December 1926.
23. 'Miss Browne's meetings', *The New Generation*, vol. 7, December 1928, p. 139.
24. 'Miss Browne's meetings', December 1926.
25. 'Report of meeting', *The New Generation*, vol. 6, April 1927, p. 38.
26. 'Plaistow meeting', *The New Generation*, vol, 6, May 1927, p. 52.
27. 'Report of meeting', April 1927.
28. 'Miss Browne's meetings, *The New Generation*, vol. 6, February 1927, p. 26.
29. 'Miss Browne's meetings', December 1926.
30. 'Plaistow meeting'.
31. F.W. Stella Browne, 'Some damning statistics', *The New Generation*, vol. 4, December 1925, pp. 135–6.
32. F.W. Stella Browne, 'Critics and champions at Westminster', *The New Generation*, vol. 5, June–July 1926, pp. 67–8.
33. F.W. Stella Browne, 'Progress of the movement: no obstetric inquisition!', *The New Generation*, vol. 7, July 1928, p. 76.
34. F.W. Stella Browne, 'An American tragedy with British versions: a cathedral and a slum', *The New Generation*, vol. 8, July 1929, p. 79.
35. F.W. Stella Browne, 'The "Freethinker", Mr Justice McCardie, and the "Church Times"', *The Freethinker*, [? December 1931], 'Sir H M McCardie: press-cuttings', Eugenics Society Archives, Wellcome Library, SA/EUG/C.217.
36. Browne, 'An American tragedy with British versions'.
37. F.W.S.B., 'Political notes', *The New Generation*, vol. 6, May 1927, p. 57.
38. F.W.S.B., 'In the front line', *The New Generation*, vol. 5, June–July 1926, p. 70; 'Mrs Malone's lecture', *The New Generation*, vol. 5, December 1926, p. 124; F.W.S.B., 'Reviews: *Sex, Love and Morality. A Rational Code of Sex Ethics*. By William J. Robinson, MD', *The New Generation*, vol. 7, July 1928, p. 78.
39. F.W. Stella Browne, 'The progress of birth control', *The New Generation*, vol. 7, September 1929, pp. 99–100.
40. F.W. Stella Browne, 'A modern programme: medical progress', *The New Generation*, vol. 8, April 1929, p. 41.
41. 'B.S.S.S.P. meeting', *The New Generation*, vol. 8, May 1929, p. 55.
42. F.W. Stella Browne, 'How the fight goes', *The New Generation*, vol. 8, October 1929, p. 113.
43. F.W. Stella Browne, 'The right to abortion', in Norman Haire (ed.), Sexual Reform Congress, London 8–14: IX: 1929. *World League for Sexual Reform: Proceedings of the Third Congress* (London: Kegan Paul, Trench and Trubner & Co. Ltd., 1930), pp. 178–81.
44. F.W. Stella Browne, 'Review: *Where Girls Go Right: Some Dynamic Aspects of State Correctional Schools for Girls and Young Women*. By Miriam Van Waters', *The New Generation*, vol. 3, July 1924, p. 82.

45. F.W.S.B., 'A book on heredity', *The New Generation*, vol. 5, January 1926, p. 10.
46. Stella Browne to Havelock Ellis, 3 April 1927, British Library Department of Manuscripts, Additional Manuscripts 70539 [BL Add Ms 70539].
47. F.W. Stella Browne, 'I.L.P. for birth control', *The New Generation*, vol. 5, May 1926, pp. 51–2.
48. 'N.U.S.E.C. Meeting', *The New Generation*, vol. 5, May 1926, p. 52; F.W.S.B., 'Our movement: the "new feminism"', *The New Generation*, vol. 5, May 1926, p. 53.
49. F.W. Stella Browne, 'Labour demands birth control: official "misadventures at Margate"', *The New Generation*, vol. 5, November 1926, pp. 111–12.
50. F.W. Stella Browne, 'Britain's great year for birth control', *Medical Critic and Guide*, vol. 25E/2, February 1927, pp. 61–3.
51. Browne to Ellis, 3 April 1927, BL Add Ms 70539.
52. F.W. Stella Browne, 'Victory – or compromise?', *The New Generation*, vol. 6, April 1927, p. 39.
53. Emma Chewter, 'The League of National Life', BA History Dissertation, University of Reading March 2002. I am grateful to Emma Chewter and Dr Helen King of Reading University for making this available to me.
54. F.W. Stella Browne, 'Progress of the movement: are we half-hearted?', *The New Generation*, vol. 6, May 1927, p. 52.
55. F.W. Stella Browne, 'The Jubilee and the end of a great pioneer organisation', *Medical Critic and Guide*, vol. 25E/11, November 1927, pp. 473–5.
56. F.W. Stella Browne, 'Birth control in Parliament: the obsession of the ballot box', *The New Generation*, vol. 5, August 1926, p. 76.
57. F.W. Stella Browne, 'Progress of the movement: a new open forum', *The New Generation*, vol. 7, July 1928, p. 76.
58. F.W. Stella Browne, 'Notes on the way', *The New Generation*, vol. 8, November 1929, p. 124.
59. Stella Browne, 'Maternal mortality and official futility', *Time and Tide*, 13 September 1929, p. 1091.
60. Membership records, Fabian Society Archives, London School of Economics, LSE/Fabian Society.
61. Summer School Visitors' Book, LSE/Fabian Society/G.11.
62. Summer School Log Book, LSE/Fabian Society/G.15.
63. Summer School Visitors' Book, LSE/Fabian Society/G.11.
64. Summer School Log Book, LSE/Fabian Society/G.15.
65. Summer School Visitors' Book, LSE/Fabian Society/G.11.
66. Minutes of Annual General Meetings, 16 June 1927, 14 June 1928, 13 June 1929, LSE/Fabian Society/C.42.
67. Fabian Common Room Visitors' Book, LSE/Fabian Society/C.44.

68. Annual Report of the Labour Party 1924, Labour Party Archives, Manchester [LPA].
69. F.W. Stella Browne to Olaf Stapledon, 7 February 1949, Stapledon papers in the Special Collections, Liverpool University Library, STAP. H.VIII B 9/21.
70. 'Chelsea Labour Party: a lively annual meeting: appeals for unity', press-cutting from unidentified periodical, 1926, in DR, file 496.
71. F.W. Stella Browne, 'Reviews: *Men in May*: By Leslie Paul', *Plan: for world order and progress*, vol. 3 no. 3, March 1936, pp. 18–19.
72. 'Chelsea Labour Party: a lively annual meeting'.
73. Labour Party National Executive Committee Minutes, 28 July 1926, LPA; F.W. Stella Browne, 'Chadband as Mussolini?', *The New Generation*, vol. 5, September 1926, p. 90.
74. Stella Browne, 'Chelsea Labour Party', *Lansbury's Labour Weekly*, 'What our readers think', 28 August 1926, p. 2.
75. F.W. Stella Browne, 'Birth control in Parliament: Chelsea's birth control resolution', *The New Generation*, vol. 5, August 1926, p. 76.
76. Browne, 'Chelsea Labour Party'.
77. Labour Party National Executive Committee Minutes, 22 November 1926, LPA.
78. Browne, 'Reviews: *Men in May*'.
79. 'Chelsea Labour Party: a lively annual meeting'.
80. Stella Browne, 'Private' postscript to Dora Russell [n.d.], DR, file 402.
81. F.W.S.B., 'Reviews: Mr Joad's book', *The New Generation*, vol. 5, March 1926, p. 32.
82. Browne, 'Victory – or compromise?'.
83. F.W. Stella Browne, 'Marking time', *The New Generation*, vol. 6, August 1927, p. 89.
84. F.W. Stella Browne, 'Current political notes', *The New Generation*, vol. 7, April 1928, p. 44.
85. F.W. Stella Browne, 'Parliamentary notes', *The New Generation*, vol. 7, June 1928, p. 68.
86. F.W. Stella Browne, 'Reviews: Endowment of motherhood', *The New Generation*, vol. 4, February 1925, p. 22.
87. F.W. Stella Browne, 'Stocktaking', *The New Generation*, vol. 6, September 1927, p. 102.
88. Browne, 'Stocktaking'.
89. F.W. Stella Browne, 'Current notes', *The New Generation*, vol. 7. May 1928, p. 53.
90. F.W. Stella Browne, 'A year of indiscretion', *The New Generation*, vol. 8, January 1929, p. 7.

91. Browne, 'Victory – or compromise?'
92. F.W. Stella Browne, 'A year of indiscretion', *The New Generation*, vol. 8, January 1929, p. 7.
93. Browne, 'A year of indiscretion'
94. F.W.S.B., 'Review: A plea for fair play', *The New Generation*, vol. 9, April 1930, p. 47.
95. F.W. Stella Browne, 'A modern programme': monogamy and the melting pot', *The New Generation*, vol. 8, April 1929, p. 41.
96. Stella Browne, 'Progress of the movement: are we half-hearted?', p. 52.
97. F.W. Stella Browne, 'A modern programme'.
98. 'Miss Browne in Manchester'.
99. 'Miss Browne in Liverpool'.
100. F.W. Stella Browne, 'A standard bearer of twenty-five years of progress in sexual science', *Medical Critic and Guide*, vol. 25E/4, April 1927, pp. 158–62.
101. F.W. Stella Browne, 'Book review [*A Doctor's Views on Life*. By William J. Robinson]', *Medical Critic and Guide*, vol. 25E/7, July 1927, pp. 297–300.
102. F.W. Stella Browne, 'Letter to the editor: A secret censorship', *The New Generation*, vol. 7, September 1928, p. 107.
103. F.W. Stella Browne, 'A year of indiscretion: the innocence of a magistrate', *The New Generation*, vol. 8, January 1929, p. 7.
104. Browne, 'A secret censorship'.
105. Browne, 'A year of indiscretion: the innocence of a magistrate'.
106. F.W. Stella Browne, 'A year of indiscretion: a triumph of imbecility', *The New Generation*, vol. 8, January 1929, p. 7.
107. Browne, 'A modern programme'.
108. According to the review in *The Lancet*, vol. 2, 1929, p. 177.
109. F.W. Stella Browne, 'A modern programme'.
110. Stella Browne to Lewis H. Plummer, 21 March 1925, 'B.S.S. Misc', British Sexology Society Archives in the Harry Ransom Humanities Research Center, University of Texas at Austin [HRC].
111. Minutes of the 157th Meeting of the Executive Committee, 2 June 1927, 'B.S.S. Misc', HRC.
112. Report on R.B. Kerr's paper to the British Society for the Study of Sex Psychology, 'Probable changes of sexual customs', 8 March 1928, *The New Generation*, vol. 7, April 1928, p. 40.
113. Marie Barquet to the British Society for Study of Sex Psychology, 13 February 1929, 'B.S.S. Letters received K', HRC.
114. Minutes of 176th Meeting of the Executive Committee, 7 March 1929, 'B.S.S. Misc', HRC.
115. George C. Ives, entry for 18 April 1929, 'Notes and Various Writings', vol. 93, HRC; 'B.S.S.S.P. Meeting', *The New Generation*, vol. 8, May 1929, p. 55.

116. F.W. Stella Browne, 'How the fight goes', *The New Generation*, vol. 8, October 1929, p. 113.
117. F.W. Stella Browne, 'Impressions of the Third International Congress of the World League for Sexual Reform', *Medical Critic and Guide*, vol. 27, December 1929, pp. 438–86.
118. Browne, 'A standard bearer ... of progress'.
119. F.W. Stella Browne, 'Reviews: Concerning women and children', *The New Generation*, vol. 4, March 1925, pp. 33–4.
120. Browne, 'A standard bearer of ... progress'.
121. F.W. Stella Browne, 'A book on Freud', *The New Generation*, vol. 3, November 1924, pp. 130–1.
122. Browne, 'Book review [*A Doctor's Views on Life*.]'
123. F.W. Stella Browne, 'A modern programme'; Browne, 'A book on Freud'.
124. F.W.S.B., 'Review: Through science to justice', *The New Generation*, vol, 11, December 1932, p. 140.
125. F.W. Stella Browne, 'Reply to Mr Preece', *The New Generation*, vol. 13, September 1934, p. 106.
126. F.W.S.B., 'Books: through science to justice', *Plan: For World Order and Progress*, vol. 2, no. 1, January 1935, pp. 15–16.
127. F.W.S.B., 'Is it well with the child?', *The New Generation*, vol. 4, September 1925, p. 105.
128. Browne, 'A standard bearer of ... progress'.
129. Havelock Ellis to Françoise Lafitte-Cyon, 24 February 1925, Howard Gotlieb Archival Research Center, Boston University.
130. 'The most radical British feminist'.
131. 'A little trip to England impressionistically described', *Medical Critic and Guide*, vol. 25C/4, April 1925, pp. 143–4.
132. F.W. Stella Browne, 'Helene Stöcker, Ph.D.', *The New Generation*, vol. 4, July 1925, p. 80.
133. Lesley A. Hall, 'Stella Browne and the German radical sex reform tradition', in Willem de Blécourt (ed.), *Sisters of Subversion: Histories of Women, Tales of Gender: A Festschrift* (Amsterdam: AMB, 2008), pp. 152–61.
134. Helene Stöcker, 'Eine Kämpferin für Gebrutregelung in England: Stella Browne', *Die Neue Generation*, vol. 22 no. 2, February 1926, pp. 52–4.
135. 'Miss Browne's meetings', *The New Generation*, vol. 5, February 1926, p. 17.
136. F.W. Stella Browne, 'The Norwegian pioneers', *The New Generation*, vol. 5, February 1926, p. 15.
137. Binnie Dunlop to Norman Himes, 2 May 1928, Norman Himes papers in the Boston Medical Library in the Francis. A Countway Library of Medicine, BMS C77 Box 35 folder 396.

138. F.W. Stella Browne, 'Current political notes: a distinguished American birth controller', *The New Generation*, vol. 6, March 1927, p. 29.
139. 'Miss Browne's meetings', October 1927.
140. 'Miss Browne in Manchester'.
141. F.W. Stella Browne, 'How the fight goes', *The New Generation*, vol. 8, October 1929, p. 113.
142. Browne, 'Impressions of the Third International Congress of the World League for Sexual Reform'.
143. F.W. Stella Browne, 'Homage to a pioneer', *The New Generation*, vol. 8, December 1929, p. 142.
144. F.W. Stella Browne, 'Madame Samuel Lorsignol', *The Eugenics Review*, vol. 47, April 1955, pp. 14–15.
145. F.W. Stella Browne, 'One of our liberators: Dorothy Jewson', *Medical Critic and Guide*, vol. 25C/8, August 1925, pp. 316–19.
146. Dora Russell, Letter to the Editor, *The New Generation*, vol. 5, March 1926, p. 35.
147. F.W. Stella Browne, 'Review: *Hypatia: Or Woman and Knowledge* – By Mrs. Bertrand Russell', *Medical Critic and Guide*, vol. 25C/8, September 1925, p. 369.
148. According to Ray Monk, *Bertrand Russell: The Spirit of Solitude* (London: Vintage, 1997), p. 308, she was distressed by it as a 'betrayal of principle', but Russell, who was anxious to have children, was insistent.
149. Stella Browne, 'Private' postscript to Dora Russell [n.d.], DR, file 402.
150. Dora Russell: The Human Factor Speech, 16 February 1986 (actually an interview by 'Kieran'), in Russell Archives, Division of Archives and Manuscripts, McMaster University Library, Hamilton, Ontario.
151. Norman Haire to Dora Russell, [n.d. 1928 or 1929], 14 and 15 January 1929, DR, file 407.
152. F.W. Stella Browne, 'Progress of the movement: the rebound from Portsmouth', *The New Generation*, vol. 7, July 1928, p. 76.
153. F.W.S.B., 'On preaching', *The New Generation*, vol. 7, December 1928, p. 140.
154. F.W.S.B., 'A guide to voters', *The New Generation*, vol. 8, May 1929, p. 56.
155. No letters from Stella have been located among the copious Holtby papers in Hull City Library.
156. F.W.S.B., 'Is it well with the child?'
157. F.W.S.B., 'A courageous diagnosis', *The New Generation*, vol. 7, December 1928, p. 137.
158. Lis Whitelaw, *The Life and Rebellious Times of Cicely Hamilton: Actress, Writer, Suffragist* (London: The Women's Press, 1990), pp. 202–3.
159. Minutes of 5th meeting of the Executive Committee, 10 January 1914; 7th meeting, 20 February 1914; 11th meeting, 8 June 1914, 'B.S.S. Misc', HRC.

160. F.W.S.B., 'Two good books', *The New Generation*, vol. 12, December 1933, p. 143.
161. 'The most radical British feminist'.
162. Browne, 'An American tragedy with British versions'.
163. F.W.S.B., 'Review of *Sex in Civilisation: Essays by Thirty-One Writers*. Edited by V. F. Calverton and S. W. Schmalhausen', *The New Generation*, vol. 8, October 1929, p. 116.
164. 'The most radical British feminist'.
165. Browne to Ellis, 9 January 1926, BL Add Ms 70539.
166. 'Eine Kämpferin für Gerburtenreglung in England: Stella Browne'.
167. For Seltzer and his context, see Jay A. Gertzman, *Bookleggers and smuthounds: the trade in erotica, 1920–1940* (Philadelphia: University of Pennsylvania Press, 1999).
168. F.W.S.B., 'Miss Hamilton's play', *The New Generation*, vol. 5, February 1926, p. 18.
169. F.W.S.B., 'A sheaf of pamphlets', *The New Generation*, vol. 5, September 1926, pp. 93–4.
170. F.W.S.B., 'A merciful dryad', *The New Generation*, vol. 6, February 1927, p. 22.
171. F.W. Stella Browne, 'Two books that live', *Medical Critic and Guide*, vol. 25E/11, November 1927, pp. 475–80.
172. Browne, 'Two books that live'.
173. F.W.S B., 'Reviews: A birth control novel', *The New Generation*, vol. 6, August 1927, pp. 92–3; Browne, 'Two books that live'.
174. F.W.S.B., 'Modern love'; Stella Browne to H.G. Wells, (n.d. [? 1911/12]), H.G. Wells Archive, Rare Book and Special Collections Library, University of Illinois at Urbana-Champaign.
175. F.W.S.B., 'Six windows on the modern world', *The New Generation*, vol. 11, October 1932, pp. 113–14.
176. Browne, 'Some damning statistics'.
177. F.W.S.B., 'A feminist in action', *The New Generation*, vol. 5, April 1926, pp. 46–7.
178. Browne to Ellis, 9 January 1926, BL Add Ms 70539.
179. F.W.S.B., 'Reviews: A brilliant boomerang', *The New Generation*, vol. 6, March 1927, pp. 33–4.
180. Browne, 'A book on Freud'.
181. F.W. Stella Browne, 'A standard bearer of ... progress'.
182. Browne, 'A modern programme: monogamy and the melting pot'.
183. 'The most radical British feminist'.
184. Browne, 'Book review. *A Doctor's Views on Life*'.
185. 'Miss Browne in Durham'.
186. 'Two leading feminists', *The New Generation*, vol. 10, December 1931, p. 134.

187. F.W.S.B., 'Review: The finest art', *The New Generation*, vol. 12, July 1933, pp. 81–2.
188. On Van de Velde and the outstanding success of *Ideal Marriage*, see Edward M. Brecher, *The Sex Researchers* (London: André Deutsch, 1970), pp. 82–103.
189. F.W.S.B., 'Political notes: a plague on both!', *The New Generation*, vol. 8. April 1929, p. 40.

8

Milestones on the Long Road to Freedom

The year 1930 opened with what looked like business as usual. Arrangements were in hand for a large conference on birth control and public health services. Additional birth control clinics were being organised. '[L]egalisation of abortion, at the woman's request in the early stages of gestation', had been recommended by the National Association of Surgeons of Norway.[1]

Towards the end of January, Stella paid her return visit to the South London Secular Society in Brixton. 'Attendance was good in spite of atrocious weather', for her talk on 'The New Code of Sexual Ethics'. She was pleased to note that 'the women in the audience took more part than on the previous occasion'.[2]

In spite of personal animosity, Stella gave Stopes's *Mother England* a lengthy and glowing review. It was 'a master-stroke' to 'confront the decorous deliberations of the Maternal Mortality Conferences' with 'a transcript of letters in her 1926 clinic file', and 'a few pages of annihilating indictment' by Stopes herself. The letters showed the medical profession 'in a most unfavourable light', but also revealed 'striking cases of chivalry and decency among the women's husbands'. Stella noted that most of the women whose letters were included 'have been driven to complete indifference to intercourse – or to active dislike and nightmare dread' – this was 'what Church and State have combined to do to Love in Marriage'.[3] Stopes was moved to write a letter of thanks for this 'stimulating and perceptive' review.[4] Another, younger, colleague in the struggle whom Stella praised was Janet Chance. Her article in January's *Socialist Review* was

> a direct yet entirely dignified and objective indictment of the sexphobia – the ignorance of and prejudice against the physical

> side of sex which is still so prevalent among our countrywomen in all walks of life.

Chance was 'doing most urgent work with fine taste and fearless courage'.[5]

While there was cause for rejoicing – the 'popular and vocal demand' being generated by the Shoreditch circular calling on Medical Officers of Health to use powers under the new Local Government Act to implement birth control advice in welfare centres, for example – Stella was still on the attack against 'Catholic hooligans from across the Irish Sea' (and those politicians terrorised by them).[6] These 'exiles of Erin' were always ready to 'mount the high horse and dictate to the natives of this – not wholly unprofitable – island, what they shall do and shall not do', such as the 'two women councillors with unmistakeably Hibernian names' at St Helen's who voted against accepting the circular. Nonetheless, she gloried in the circular's 'spectacular' success in both St Helen's and Bootle, which had, Stella claimed, 'long disputed the palm of Catholic piety as "the most religious industrial town in England"'.[7]

In early February, Stella addressed the Birmingham Branch of the National Secular Society on 'The New Code of Sex Ethics': 'good attendance ... extraordinarily keen attention and discussion'. The visit was a 'pleasure and a success', organised by John Dobson, a 'stalwart of Free Thought' in his eighties, who kindly showed Stella his 'most valuable and interesting library'. She also had the opportunity to visit the Birmingham birth control clinic: 'splendidly equipped and organised' with generous funding from local philanthropist Sir John Sumner,[8] who conveyed to Stella his approval for abortion law reform. She found his 'quiet courtesy and generosity ... like clear fresh water on many dusty ways.'[9]

Lella Florence's analysis of the first three hundred cases at the Cambridge Birth Control Clinic confirmed Stella's belief that there was 'clamant need for further research and a much more varied armamentarium of methods', given the 'extremely wide range of variation among women in all sexual matters, whether organs, functions or emotions'. The 'precise and painstaking analysis' of this relatively small number of cases was, she considered, much more valuable and convincing than less meticulous accounts of larger samples.[10] This was probably a dig at Stopes, who had published reports based on five, and then ten, thousand cases at the Mother's Clinic, and who certainly took it as such.[11]

Stella was not entirely surprised at the negative reactions of women to the various internal pessaries on offer:

> when to their physiological ignorance we add the systematic sexual stultification which has been and still is the training of

> the majority of women in these matters, it is not surprising that a woman with no bathroom and, of course, no separate bedroom, nor any decent provision for privacy in her home, should fail to apply the pessary.

As always, Stella was sensitive to intertwined mental and physical environmental factors: 'defective housing and no hot water supply' were as significant as women's fear and uncertainty about their own sexual organs. Further 'acceptable and reliable methods' were needed, but so was 'a complete change of mental attitude towards sex relationships'.[12]

During March, Stella addressed the Northwood Women's Cooperative Guild on 'Birth Control: in Politics and in Practice', and the Dulwich Independent Labour Party on 'The New Code of Sex Ethics', with special reference to parenthood. For the former, the 'room [size unspecified!] was filled to capacity' and the keenly sympathetic audience asked 'very helpful and illuminating questions'.[13] Speaking engagements seem to have been rather fewer: one in April to the Surbiton and District Branch of the Railway Women's Guild, and a couple in May to the Greenwich and Plaistow Women's Cooperative Guilds, although (except for Plaistow) attendance was 'good and enthusiastic'.[14]

In April, the Birth Control Conference was 'a conspicuous success', with an attendance of nearly 700, delegates from local authorities, national and local organisations, and visitors from abroad, among them the Norwegian socialist and birth control activist Dr Tove Mohr. However, even 'the Press friendly to birth control', apart from *The Nation*, had 'suppressed *all* mention of the very brief plea for the right to abortion, put forward by me and seconded by Mrs Russell' – this suggests that Dora Russell was already moving into Stella's camp.[15] Stella found 'the organised feminist movement and birth control movement in England ... still so afraid of or averse to radical sex reforms.'[16] Although 'the Cause' was gaining political credibility

> The movement in English-speaking countries is full of the oddest contradictions and compromises: of 'social workers' who would refuse information to the unmarried; of professional feminists who try to suppress discussion of the case for abortion.[17]

Naomi Mitchison's *Comments on Birth Control* (based on her paper at the World League for Sexual Reform Congress), however, met with approval, both for the matter, and for 'the vigour and rich colour of her mind and her wide-ranging Rodinesque style'. While Stella found 'disputable' the claim that many women would want '*lots* of children', she admired Mitchison's 'essential and direct courage; no pretty-pretty or playing down to the Mothers' Union', and her very radical opinions on abortion also endeared her.[18]

In July 1930, the Ministry of Health issued circular MCW/153, allowing, but not requiring, local authorities to give birth control advice in welfare centres. This apparent victory was described by Stella as 'a set of grudging concessions and niggling restrictions'.[19] That advice might be given solely 'on *medical grounds* in cases where further pregnancy would be detrimental of health', should, Stella warned, remind her comrades that although the '*immediate* objective of the movement' had been achieved, 'a *battle* has been won – but not a *campaign*'.[20] Stella had no intention of letting her sword sleep in her hand just because some milestone along the road to Jerusalem had been reached.

During October 1930, Stella persuaded Plaistow ASLEF Women's Section and the East Ward Women's Section of the Mitcham Labour Party, to ask their local authorities local council to provide birth control instruction, under the Ministry permission now granted.[21] Speaking to the local branch of the National Secular Society in Birmingham, she urged them to agitate for municipal provision of the facilities already available in the privately run model birth-control clinic in the city.[22]

She had an audience of over 400 for her talk on 'Some Sex Problems from the Freethinker's Point of View: Present Conditions and Future Tendencies' to Leicester Secular Society: delighted to be where the Ministry circular had been implemented while 'most boroughs were still shuddering on the brink', she paid tribute to the Medical Officer of Health, Dr Killick Millard. As chair at the April Birth Control Conference, Millard had 'fairly and wisely given a hearing to minority views' (such as her own, presumably), 'which the conventionalists would be falling over each other to greet and accept, in another century or so'. After 'eager questions', there was a 'social gathering, conversation and refreshments', and 'beautiful music' from Miss Ensor, whom Stella thanked specifically.[23] In early December, she spoke on 'The Right to Abortion', at the Sex Education Centre in Archer Street, where she was given 'a graceful and generous welcome' by its founder, Mrs Janet Chance.[24]

The further victory of the decision by the Lambeth Conference of Anglican bishops 'by a large majority to give qualified tolerance to birth control' was also strictly limited. She described the *Encyclical Letter, with Resolutions and Reports* as a 'classic of climbdown ... a general retreat from the claims and the certitudes of tradition'. To the claim that 'the human equality and partnership of women' was a specifically Christian ideal, she suggested that 'the only fitting comment is more forcible than polite', noting that, while the need for more candidates for ordination was urged, women could only become deaconesses. The resolution was 'a tardy and ungracious concession'.[25] The subject cropped up again in many of the talks she gave around this time. Addressing the South London Secular Society at Clapham Public Hall, Stella pointed out the 'tardy concessions to modern ethics' and exhorted freethinkers to 'show up these inconsistencies' in the Church's arguments.[26]

Her extensive review of Katharine Bement Davis's *Factors in the Sex Life of Twenty-two Hundred Women* (1929), in *The New Generation*, illuminates in detail Stella's contemporary thinking about sexual matters – in particular, on female sexuality – which can otherwise only be gleaned through tantalising and frustrating hints in the reports of her speaking engagements. About two thirds of the unmarried women in the sample 'had practised or were practising some form of auto-erotism', and around 40 per cent of the married sample. Stella quoted Bement Davis's suggestion that it might be 'a symptom of a type of personality', but argued herself that

> In the light of science and everyday experience, it is intolerable that it should be treated as a disease, a disgrace, or a crime. It is probably a normal human experience.

She found the 'investigation equally clear and courageous' on homosexuality, providing 'much food for thought'. Bement Davis found a very large percentage, married and unmarried, who reported intense emotional relationships with other women. A smaller but still significant number had had overt homosexual experience. A surprising correlation was discovered concerning the unmarried who admitted some form of sexual relationship with one or more men: the percentage was highest amongst the overt homosexual practice group. Stella gave this a highly positive (and perhaps personally inflected?) spin:

> There is undoubtedly a type of articulate, vigorous and adventurous, woman, who is inherently bi-sexual. She is active and positive, yet a sexual epicure as well. In art and letters this strain can give brilliant results.

The moral she drew from Bement Davis's study was the '"infinite variety" of human nature', and she found that the conclusions corroborated the suggestions of her own *Sexual Variety and Variability in Women* pamphlet.[27]

During 1930, Stella was, presumably, working on two substantial pieces of translation, both published during 1931: Franz Carl Müller-Lyer's *The*

Family, first published in German in 1912, and Theodor Van de Velde's *Fertility and Sterility in Marriage*, the third volume of his 'trilogy on marital problems' begun with *Ideal Marriage*. Van de Velde was clearly very taken with her skills, and in his preface to the English edition thanked Stella 'for the extraordinary care she devoted to the translation' (it is not clear why she was not commissioned to translate the middle volume, *Sex Hostility in Marriage*).[28]

On the whole, she kept herself out of *Fertility and Sterility*: her comments tended to be points about the British system for comparison with continental law and practice,[29] clarification and emphasis, and cross-references to material dealt with in more detail in *Ideal Marriage*. A personal note did creep into her elucidation of the term 'lordosis': 'the peculiarly graceful and extremely sexual inward curve of the spine at the waist and just above the hips and nates.'[30] Curiously, or perhaps not, the final section, 'Author's view on the Problem of Artificial Termination of Pregnancy', was translated by another hand. Given the difference which quickly becomes apparent between Van de Velde's position on the subject – 'Artificial abortion is to be condemned, although it is unavoidable in certain cases in order to avert the greatest evil'[31] – and Stella's own, the reason was doubtless conveyed by her later comment that, although the book contained 'interesting and novel material on all aspects of its theme', she 'regret[ted] the attitude on abortion'.[32] She found some contradiction generally between Van de Velde's 'fine sympathy and immense proficiency both clinical and technical' and his support for 'traditional ethics'.[33]

While Van de Velde's work doubtless appealed to the campaigner for birth control and the right of women to knowledge of their own bodies, the Müller-Lyer book seems to have been almost a labour of love, especially in the context of her plea for 'more stress on the *anthropological* aspects of sex' at the World Congress on Sexual Reform.[34] Her translation includes many of her own notes, which reveal the broad extent of her reading and how very up to date she was in a wide range of subjects. Some flagged up the social and political changes which had occurred since the book's publication two years before the upheaval of the Great War and subsequent developments.[35] Her reading in and knowledge of contemporary developments in archaeology and anthropology was manifested throughout with allusions to more recent theories and discoveries.[36] She appended a long list (impressive testimony to her own reading) of 'English, German, French, Scandinavian and American' writers who bore out Müller-Lyer's contention that 'most writers of any merit who express themselves on sexual problems now are individualists'.[37]

Some comments reveal personal quirks and biases, such as the 'ignorant and prejudiced denunciations of Christian zealots' obscuring the facts about women's position in the later Roman Empire,[38] and the plaint that since the Great War 'the younger generation of women are in danger of taking their rights too much for granted'.[39] Occasionally, she contradicted or modified Müller-Lyer's own remarks, suggesting, for example, that 'instinct', applied to the sexual emotions of humanity, was 'not correct as applied to anything so protean in its manifestations and so intermingled with mental imagery and suggestion'.[40] To his arguments that children needed the society of others, she riposted that 'Human beings grow in solitude – if they have any depth or force – as well as in society of others', and asked 'Do we not know the types who can never bear to be alone?'[41] While she clearly approved of the work's feminism and liberalism, she dissented from the author's belief in freely entered monogamous relationships as the highest form of human relationship.[42]

She took further issue with Müller-Lyer's statement that '"crossing" between races ... probably has not very favourable results', given that 'there is hardly any European society in which such persons ... do not meet artificial handicaps and prejudice', and alluding to 'brilliant artists and writers with a streak of African'.[43] Elsewhere, she had touched on 'the changed attitude of official Christianity towards other races and religions',[44] and praised Constance Malleson's 'words of burning urgency – well documented – on the treatment of the black folk in Africa'.[45] Her own views on questions of race and colonialism were seldom expressed in much detail, but she did indicate an awareness of the issue: for example, commending R.B. Kerr's 'case for the coloured races' which had 'never been stated with less sentiment and more power'.[46]

In spite of any contribution to her personal exchequer that these translations may have made, financial problems remained. In the autumn of 1931, the Treasurer of the British Sexological Society (BSS) (formerly the British Society for the Study of Sex Psychology – BSSSP) raised the 'question of Stella Browne's status', but the Executive decided to take no formal action as she 'had rendered such great service in the early days of the Society's existence'.[47] Either she was not paying a subscription at all, or still, perhaps, the lower rate agreed on years before.[48] A note in *The New Generation* towards the end of the year indicated that 'Miss Browne ... has long contributed her articles gratuitously to this paper.' She was also 'becoming very popular as a lecturer',[49] but a list of the organisations does not suggest that this was remunerative.

The issue of the Papal Encyclical 'Casti Connubii' early in 1931, stressing the sanctity of marriage but specifically prohibiting artificial birth control, led her to warn 'let no one dream that our work is done – or half done, yet'. It was 'an appallingly lengthy document, and a psychological curiosity', if 'at least, consistent' in 'denouncing and attacking all modern efforts at sexual enlightenment and happiness'. Catholic couples, Stella suggested, 'must not even enjoy each other occasionally... at least, not too much'.[50]

In February, there was a return visit to the Sex Education Centre in Archer Street, at which she spoke on 'Sex and Mental Health', dealing mainly with 'the adjustments of middle life'. She laid special stress on two factors: 'the humble but immensely important choice of diet, and the general emotional tone towards life and other persons'. She also considered 'various aesthetic points, some brought forward by her in lectures to women's groups... and some which had not been publicly discussed before' (about which we might wish she had gone into more detail). In the same month she addressed the Women's Ethical Union on 'Birth Control and the Right to Abortion', in which she revealed how abreast she was with the latest scientific developments, mentioning that 'modern biochemical technique could establish the fact of impregnation at an extremely early date' (the Aschheim–Zondek test, developed in 1928), which ought to obviate 'the weeks of anguished uncertainty so many women endured', if the knowledge could only be made more available.[51] She was also up to date with the latest developments in obstetric analgesia.[52] As she commented,

> If all women had access to the best modern knowledge in medicine and hygiene, if all women had means and leisure, and minds freed from fear and medievalism – *how* different things would be.[53]

A taboo was broken in March 1931 in the influential weekly feminist journal *Time and Tide* when a debate on abortion broke out in its correspondence columns: 'the feminists of *Time and Tide* are of the free-minded variety, which is still quite rare'.[54] Stella managed to get quite a lengthy letter accepted, emphasising the amount of 'suicides, hideous injuries, blood poisoning, permanent invalidism, madness and... secret blackmail', resulting from the denial of the right of women to chose termination. 'What the qualified and skilled surgeon is forbidden to do', she pointed out, 'the "*outsider*" will do at a price – without necessary equipment, or knowledge, or asepsis'. Contraception was not an alternative: '*no method... is infallible, nor universally applicable*'.[55]

A short notice of Cicely Hamilton's *Modern Germanies* shows Stella already alert to the nature of Nazism, while not underestimating its potential appeal. She praised Hamilton highly:

> She has a directness of vision and breadth of judgement which brush aside trivialities and give due weight to unwelcome facts; and these qualities help balance her passionate pity for, and belief in women's special sufferings and intimate rights, and to make her one of the sanest, as well as bravest, of our champions.

She found Hamilton's 'estimate of the new German nationalism' of considerable interest: 'not one of the people who think a movement must be negligible nor wholly ignoble because it is extremely regrettable and reactionary'.[56]

Although the Workers' Birth Control Group was disbanded in March 1931, following official concession of birth control advice in welfare centres,[57] Stella continued her round of talks to assorted groups and to promote the cause. In February, she 'presented her case with skill and eloquence to the Ethical Society Women's Group'. Although, or because, 'her views are more "advanced" than those of most persons', she had a 'full room' and received a 'volley of questions.'[58] She was clearly moving on to promote 'The Right to Abortion' much more extensively, speaking on this subject to the Kilburn Women's Cooperative Guild in March: they 'listened with rapt attention' and 'passed a brief and carefully worded resolution on the subject' to send to the local MP and the Minister of Health.[59]

She continued to be concerned with wider questions of sex within modern society: suggesting to the Secretary of the BSS that she did 'not wish to be too closely tied to the one subject of birth control, however great its importance undoubtedly is'.[60] In May 1931, she lectured on 'Some Modern Problems' to the South London Ethical Society, 'suggest[ing] lines of thought' rather than analysing conditions. Arguing that 'modern biological and psychological knowledge could and should be assimilated both in art and in moral codes', she perceived three main lines of advance: 'Economic, Educational and Eugenic'. The last, she thought, was 'the least explored but the most radically effective, and of course, included birth control'. As always, what Stella meant by eugenics is hard to assimilate to the doctrines and programmes of the organised eugenics movement in contemporary Britain. At a time when sterilisation of the 'unfit' was being widely debated, she remarked that

> 'Compulsory sterilization' was often an excuse for the poverty of mind and spirit which refused either to improve institutions

> or liberate individuals from obsolete sex standardizations. Voluntary and temporary sterilization, on the other hand, had magnificent possibilities.

She generated 'keen and wide-ranging questions' and was invited to come again.[61]

She gave a similarly wide-ranging lecture, 'Three possible alternatives in Social Evolution' to the International Circle of the Labour Club in Westminster on 2 July. Right at the beginning she expressed her hope that the audience would 'take for granted ... that she postulated economic changes and circumstances, as the basis of administration and ethics'. She envisaged three possible futures for contemporary Britain. First, 'Decline and Disintegration', brought about by 'supine, unimaginative, slovenly "letting things slide"'. The second was 'Ossification, or Systematic reaction', which would

> tighten up existent, unjust, legal survivals and/or enact new ones, on Fascist lines, and would be characterized by co-operation with organized Christianity, on the lines of the recent Papal encyclicals.

But the

> third possibility – for which she worked and hoped – would realize that you cannot combine twentieth century economics with medieval ethics, and would try to reconstruct laws in harmony with facts.

Much discussion followed, and there was a 'hearty vote of thanks to the speaker'.[62]

In July, she defended Mrs Grocott, who had pleaded guilty at Manchester Assizes to a charge of manslaughter after causing a woman's death by performing 'an illegal operation' and received a four-year sentence, even though she 'admittedly acted in many cases without pecuniary profit to herself and in true helpfulness to over-burdened and distraught fellow-women'. Laws had and could be changed, Stella asserted, 'by the effort of ceaseless agitation, and by the refusal to accept injustice as immutable'.[63]

On a lighter note, Stella found great pleasure in reading Naomi Mitchison's 'epic novel' *The Corn King and the Spring Queen*. Mitchison had achieved

> something very big and individual ... with the wide sweep and sustained power to which even the women writers who excel in concentrated, exquisitely jewelled flashes, seldom attain.

The book's 'many-facetted richness of content' created 'a world' with 'deep, but not doctrinaire' feminism, 'pictorial vividness' and 'clear-sighted courage'. And, most difficult of all, 'the witchcraft theme has been treated with masterly insight and sympathy'. Stella liked best of the characters 'the adorable Metrotimé, who might have walked out of the Eiffel Tower Restaurant *en route* for Chelsea, any evening of 1931'.[64] Stella also admired Mitchison's 'vivid and well-documented picture' of a 'primitive ritual group merging' enough to mention it several years later in a footnote to Max Hodann's *History of Modern Morals*.[65]

Early in October 1931, Stella spoke to the South London Ethical Society on 'Thinking at First Hand', with 'a few thoughts on present conditions which would have the merit of being the fruit of some observation and of genuine conviction'. She stressed 'the danger of any rigid system of thought': the world 'was full of rigid systems, many admirable and helpful but none of them quite big enough to fill the whole of reality'. The present economic situation, she feared, would result in inflation and 'all that inflation means'.[66] But there were other equally urgent and important matters – for example, land and population. Laws relating to sexual matters demonstrated a '"time-lag" which might cover decades or even centuries', so that they were 'quite irrelevant to real life today'.[67] She did not think it possible 'to build up a new social system and retain a cast-iron marriage system',[68] and was scathing about the 'preposterous infamy' of a divorce law which compelled couples who had both 'repeatedly and publicly committed adultery and who felt such detestation for one another that they each did all they could to cause the other expense and trouble to remain legally bound'. She also alluded to the 'refusal of early, cleanly and safe abortion to any woman who wanted it'.[69] She addressed them again in late November on 'Three Possibilities of Social Evolution', when 'despite the fog a keen audience was assembled' and there was 'animated discussion'. Although 'a Catholic priest rose and strongly protested against both title and substance of the address', he 'failed to carry the audience with him and left the meeting attended by a solitary disciple'.[70]

Because of the quite inadequate take-up of the opportunities enabled by circular MCW/153, Stella (presciently) cautioned against

> the assumption that municipal or civic birth control work – however essential and competent – is going to supersede private generosity, private initiative, and individual ability in organising and propaganda. There will probably always be scope for the private birth control Clinic, and certainly there is immense scope for it today.

She went on to warn that 'the need for economy and reconstruction will be interpreted in some quarters, as arguments for cutting down what little is spent on women's intimate health and needs!', in spite of the 'economic argument for birth control' which seemed so obvious at the present time. But she went on to point out

> the futility of assuming that population and sex problems can be solved by contraception alone, even with a little marriage law reform, and the compulsory sterilization of obscure and unpopular persons! There are thousands of entrapped and frantic women in our country today: what are we going to do about them?[71]

Another young feminist entered 'the battle for human dignity and happiness' when Janet Chance published *The Cost of English Morals*, to Stella's hearty approval. Chance's indictment was 'stated with extraordinary ability, and documented with shattering effect', as well as 'highly civilised in its standards and sensibilities'. Chance was firmly in Stella's camp, with her accounts of 'sex evasion', and her support for the legalisation of safe abortion.[72] Admiration appears to have been mutual: Chance described Stella as one of the 'few intellectual heroes' of the day who was '*honest in regard to sex*'.[73]

Abortion became even more widely discussed as a result of the controversial and widely reported remarks of Mr Justice McCardie from the bench at Leeds Assizes in December, highly critical of the existing law.[74] In a letter to *The Freethinker*, Stella praised his 'brave and humane remarks', which 'some of our conventionalist-contraceptionists ... have already tried to smother'.[75] At this apposite moment, Stella produced the first part of an article on 'The Right to Abortion'. This first of an apparently uncompleted series was mainly a brief history of the campaign for reform, taking in the work of Helene Stöcker and other German feminists, Stella's own advocacy of legalisation, and the resolution in favour of revising the laws passed at the World Congress for Sexual Reform in London in 1929. Naturally, for Stella, it was paramount that '*the woman should decide*', but she conceded that '*to implement her decision, she needs medical knowledge, and medical skill*'.[76] She lost no opportunity in her lectures and writings to point out that, without a change in the law

> there would continue to be thousands of women die of septic and unskilled abortions, more would continue to take loathsome and harmful concoctions and to act in ways inviting physical

> disaster, whilst unwanted, unloved offspring would continue to multiply and grow to be ... anti-social and deficient citizens.[77]

At the beginning of 1932, although 'very rushed', she hoped to attend J.C. Flugel's lecture to the BSS, and found the secretary's account of the current state of the Society 'interesting and heartening'.[78] She mentioned later in the year that, 'being a fairly busy person', she experienced 'the difficulty of doing half the things one wants to do' [without details].[79] On January 28, she spoke under the auspices of its Sexology Group to the Promethean Society on 'Three Fundamentals of the New Sexual Ethics'. As usual, Stella stressed 'the need for a complete revision of our present abortion laws', and also demanded 'a thorough revision of the laws of divorce', pointing out that 'it should be a point of honour among feminists to remove the present injustices and inequalities of the marriage laws, against the male partner'. In conclusion, she

> urged the need to take differences of emotional trend and emotional texture among human beings into account, and to recognise concurrent moral codes.

'Illuminating and stimulating discussion over a wide range' and 'valuable comments' followed: the Prometheans were 'alive and useful allies'.[80] Her concern about the impact of contemporary social mores on men as well as women also surfaced in her comment about an 'episode of attempted blackmail' in Cicely Hamilton's novel *Full Stop*, 'over an utterly trivial and irrelevant week-end episode ... for which in the past, men of proved ability and achievement have been cast aside!'[81]

In early February, she was off to Manchester to address the local branch of the National Secular Society again. On the afternoon of 7 February, she dealt with 'Some Human Mental Types'. She outlined 'the biological and endocrine bases of temperament, which were as independent of the conscious will as, for instance, colour of hair or shape of profile. These could, she suggested 'be controlled to some extent, modified or sublimated, though not radically reversed'. It was 'one of the problems of a civilization based on science and freedom to develop a sense of social responsibility in abnormal persons, as well as to cease systematic persecution of such people'. She referred to a recent instance of the 'persecution of an intermediate type',[82] that of Augustine Hull, a young man who had passed for some considerable time as a woman and lived with another man as his common-law wife, and eventually prosecuted.[83] The case had been taken up by various progressive interests, and Stella among others signed a petition protesting against his sentence of eighteen months hard labour.[84] The case embodied for Stella 'the actual operation of the Law towards such abnormal persons as had neither wealth nor intellectual and social position and influence'. In the evening of the same day, she spoke on 'Lambeth and Rome: some recent capitulations': she 'traced the very real but uneven progress of recent years' (the concessions by the Ministry of Health and the Lambeth Conference in favour of birth control, and the Pope's vigorous repudiations of it), and, as always 'stressed the need for constant vigilance and vigour in agitation' rather than complacency. While in Manchester, Stella was again the guest of the Greens, 'these sensitive artists in life', and met once more 'other staunch friends' as well as making new ones.[85]

Ten days later, she spoke on 'The Present Sexual Situation: Achievements and Difficulties' to the BSS.[86] The title she had originally suggested was 'Achievements and Difficulties: footnotes to a pamphlet of 1915' (i.e. *Sexual Variety and Variability*)[87] but, on reflection, she considered that

> as the address I propose to give will deal with the present position of sex laws and habits, and not rescind or negate my pamphlet (which on the contrary, I think has been confirmed by the developments of the last decade) – I think that it would be best not to mention the pamphlet in the title, but only to refer to it in the course of my address.[88]

She added 'unless we are all bombed to chaos by someone's battle plan[e]s by then!'[89]

The meeting was well attended, including old friends such as George Ives as well as old adversaries like Norman Haire.[90] While the changes since 1915 were 'welcome and significant ... she wished to warn against too rosy a view of what had been done and was still to do'. There had been an immense increase in freedom of discussion, and even in publication, but 'was there any *generally commensurate* freedom in action?' Laws relating to 'inversion' remained unaltered. 'Organized feminism ... apparently preferred to consolidate the position and privileges of the legal wife, rather than to make birth control knowledge available to all women', while, on the subject of abortion, until 'Justice McCardie broke the Taboo', she 'knew no stronger argument for women's innate inferiority than the manner in which all but the tiniest brave half-dozen or so, had avoided discussing or publicly claiming that right'. However, looking forward, Stella suggested that, even when the 'necessary economic basis and the minimum of legal interference' had been achieved, psychological differences would remain. A major cleavage existed between those 'whose attitude to sex was casual and incidental' and those to whom 'sexual experience was intertwined with imagination and affection and one of the greatest things in their life'. Both kinds 'existed and had a right to exist', and there were also those who 'were capable of both light love and deep, according to personality and circumstances'. There was (as she has been reiterating for nearly two decades by this time) 'no one formula' which would 'solve sex problems'. A lively discussion followed.[91] As Deighton, the then Chair of the British Sexology Society Executive, wrote afterwards,

> Not only was the lecture itself of quite exceptional interest, but it also evoked a discussion of a very high standard – and that, perhaps, is the surest proof of success.
>
> Everybody obviously enjoyed it thoroughly.[92]

A letter from Dora Kerr to Deighton passed on a friend's comment that 'she enjoyed Stella Browne's lecture very much' and 'had not realised before the importance of the problem of abortion'.[93] However, the 'most interesting, enlightened and helpful discussion' which Stella had '*without exception*' been present at, was, she stated, that which followed her lecture to the Wembley and District Branch of the National Secular Society during April, reported in some detail by the *Wembley News*.[94]

R.B. Kerr, editor of *The New Generation*, claimed that

> Miss Browne is the most complete and logical of all women sex reformers. She is rapidly becoming a national figure on the lecture platform, and ... contributes valuable articles to this paper.

He exhorted any societies which desired 'to learn something about the future of the women's movement' to get Stella to lecture to them.[95]

Stella's belief in variety and difference, and the need to eschew rigid formulae emerged again in her contribution to a symposium on 'Sex Education' in April 1932 in *The New Generation*. She did not doubt 'the need for knowledge', and did not uphold 'the mixture of ignorance, blundering, crude terrorism and dishonest sentimentality in which the Victorians were reared'. But she was unable to convince herself that '*one and the same presentation of sexual facts is equally helpful, equally enlightening, balancing and encouraging, to all children*'. Although 'the superiority of co-education' had always been 'one of my fervent articles of faith ... having suffered from the older system!', while it might be 'an excellent sedative and tonic to certain natures', it was by no means so in all cases. She also wondered whether methods of enlightenment took adequate account of 'the "contrareity," the self-assertion of all vigorous and active natures at and after puberty'. The adolescent might 'react violently against an acceptance of sex that seems too facile and commonplace'. Any child who had 'formed *conscious* habits of its own [was] apt to treat adult allusions, however "tactful" or matter-of-fact, as outrages to be repelled and frustrated by any means': sex-experiences were 'precious individual achievements'. Her plea was for 'more Light and Elasticity of Method' and 'more individual variation', and not merely shifting from *'Terrorism into Trivialization!'*[96]

Sex education was generally on Stella's mind around this time, as part of her broader agenda for an improved society: she was far from a single-issue fanatic obsessing about abortion law reform to the exclusion of all else. Any 'honest or helpful study of sex' for any age-group, should not

> talk scare stuff about masturbation or any autoerotic activities, unless it is prepared to explicitly recommend definite heterosexual relationships as more beneficial and preferable: a very moot point, and one depending on individual temperaments and circumstances.

Neither would it

> pretend that permanent monogamous marriage is easy to make a success of, or even possible in many cases, quite apart as its complete inadequacy as a rigid rule for all![97]

She argued that birth control should be taught to 'every young man and woman as soon as maturity was reached ... irrespective of whether they were married or not'.[98] Her thoughts about the problems of sexual enlightenment and adolescence were strongly influenced by her very wide reading and her understanding of cross-cultural research. For example, she cited data on Tibetan women gathered by Alexandra David Neel, and Margaret Mead's work in Samoa and Melanesia, which suggested that

> much physical pain and debility are due to mental distress, and that the whole periodic function has been as misunderstood and mismanaged as the maternal.[99]

Stella was a great admirer of Mary Ware Dennett's work – which may have appeared to her as continuing the American radical sex reform tradition which Sanger had abandoned. In August 1932, she finally managed to write a long letter to Dennett, to 'congratulate you on two admirable pieces of work', her 'study of the sex attitudes & sex education of both the older & the younger generation', and her 'analysis of the struggle for birth control in your country, & the masterly plea for *real reform* instead of tinkering!' (Take that, Margaret Sanger!) She supposed that Dennett already knew Janet Chance's 'splendid book' (*The Cost of English Morals*) and

> all the latest attempts to teach to modern Western humanity, something of the mechanism of physical love-making, which in animals is instinctive, in Orientals imaginative, but in many of our people apparently non-existent!

She sent 'all best wishes to your great fight, and hoping to meet', signing off 'yours cordially'.

She appended a postscript, placing their common struggle within the contemporary world political situation, expressing her own anxieties 'as to the risk of an authoritarian – I won't say an *ascetic* – reaction, in the immediate future, which *may disperse all* our hard fought for gains'. The British Labour Party's failure to 'operate a consistent & comprehensive sexual policy' was 'simply deplorable and disgraceful', while the 'very brave & consistent humanists of Central Europe are now at *Hitler's* mercy!'[100]

Fears of political reaction were very much on Stella's mind. In her review of Cicely Hamilton's *Modern Italy*, Stella suggested that the question that had to be addressed was 'why the Fascist régime has managed to inspire a certain amount of disciplined enthusiasm and to achieve a certain degree of efficiency' while 'ideals which to some of us appear so infinitely greater and better' remained 'well shall we say – *unrealized*?' Although she had some differences of opinion with Hamilton's conclusions, she praised her as

> *one of the band of less than a dozen women in this country*, who have ventured in public to question and reject the view of abortion proclaimed by celibate priests, and *either definitely accepted or implicitly connived at by all the official feminist organizations of this country*.[101]

While there were certainly no grounds for complacency, Stella continued to welcome what she saw as promising developments. She was impressed by the findings of the Pioneer Health Centre in Peckham.[102] This touched on many concerns of hers: she noted the 'devitalization and loss of selective instincts about food', and that very few Centre members aged over 25 years had nothing at all wrong with them, while many had 'frank disease'. Although 'their emotional scale of values seems rather obsessed with Parenthood!', they were 'carrying out a brave and wholesome adventure with ability and sympathy'.[103] In a letter published in *The Week-end Review*, she praised Dr J.R. Baker's 'invaluable and urgent work in contraceptive research': but '*why* does he deprecate the legalisation of abortion?' She deplored 'Dr Baker's serenity' towards the fact that 'to evolve ideal contraceptives' involved 'the method of trial and error' and wanted to know 'What about the errors?'[104]

There were moderate grounds for rejoicing in July, when the British Medical Association (BMA) adopted 'a definite forward move' in the shape of a resolution to call on the BMA Council to set up a special committee to considered modification of the law on abortion. Stella exhorted 'all those who believe in the right to freedom of choice in motherhood' to continue

> keeping the full measure of justice which is the measure of our demand, steadily in view, while making the very most of all and any concessions in our direction.[105]

In a letter to *The Week-end Review*, she exhorted all those who felt that some reform of the existing abortion laws was needed to express their views to the BMA secretary. She also expressed her hope that the forthcoming meeting of the National Council of Women in Norwich would recommend abortion law reform: 'In the past, persons urging such reforms have been termed "scarlet women" and "village atheists"'.[106]

A significant advance in the struggle to get abortion law reform on the agenda took place in the autumn of 1932, involving a startling shake-up of existing alliances, as Norman Haire publicly declared himself converted to Stella's point of view.[107] A meeting to discuss 'the present laws concerning abortion' was organised under the auspices of the British Section of the World League for Sexual Reform (WLSR), a body strongly identified with Haire. In October, he invited the leading women activists on the issue (Dora Russell, Janet Chance, and Stella herself) to lunch to discuss the forthcoming meeting, go over the points of their speeches and ensure that the various lines of attack were not duplicated.[108] Around the same time Stella formally subscribed to the WLSR (this cost her five shillings – the equivalent of over £12.50 in 2007 values, so probably a not insignificant amount in her budget).[109]

The meeting took place at the London School of Hygiene on 3 November, with Haire in the chair, and Mme Berty Albrecht, a leading French feminist and birth control advocate, as a speaker besides Stella, Dora Russell and Janet Chance. Stella cautioned against 'undue optimism and moderation'.

She dissented from Haire's introductory comments that 'any explicit radical reform of the law was far off, but that we should welcome small mercies and minor alleviations'. In her view, 'if we demanded *much*, we might get something; if we asked *little*, we should certainly receive less'. Her demand continued to be that '*the woman should decide, in the early months of pregnancy*'. The 'position of merciful doctors under the present law should be intolerable to women'. Finally, she touched on 'an important aspect of the case':

> Sexual relationships are intricate and delicately poised processes. We know now the toxic effect of perpetual fear, and we know we have as yet no sovereign and infallible contraceptive. We modern people do not apologise for sex, knowing how beautiful, educative, liberating, and satisfying an experience it can afford. Quick and safe relief from unwelcome parenthood would help men and women to greater mutual understanding, enjoyment, and tenderness.

While no formal resolution was passed, 'it was decided to take every opportunity of bringing the urgent need for reform into public discussion'.[110]

'Needless to say, the meeting was not reported in the daily Press', Stella commented in a letter to *The Week-end Review*.[111] An interested party who had not attended the meeting, Marie Stopes, had nonetheless sent along an observer. As a result, she wrote to Stella concerning her mention of 'the exclusion of the import of an abortifacient. Would you mind telling me about it?'[112] (No response can be traced). Stella was further gratified to note, as 'symptomatic of the changing outlook', a meeting of the Eugenics Society on 20 December, at which Dr H. Harris spoke on the Abortion Laws of Soviet Russia, in theory and practice.[113] Matters had clearly moved on since she first raised the question of abortion at a Eugenics Society meeting, and 'her remarks were received in a silence that could be felt'.[114]

In spite of this increase in the momentum of the movement for abortion law reform, Stella retained her more general interests in sexual reform. At the annual general meeting of the BSS, she apparently asked to be added to the Committee[115] but, due to constitutional confusion, it does not look as though she rejoined them.[116] In late November, she once again addressed the South London Secular Society, this time in Clapham, on 'The Message of Three Modern Writers'; the chair introduced her as 'one who championed the frank and intelligent examination of all human problems'. On this occasion, she examined 'the present national and world situation' from the angle of J.M. Keynes's theories on sound finance, H.G. Wells's ideas on regulated population and Freud's illumination of the 'inhibitions and distortions of basic impulses'. As usual, there was a lively discussion session.[117]

By this time, Stella had passed her half-century. She had somewhat, perhaps, modified her 'Forward, Charge!' approach to the matter of reforming society, but remained extremely radical. She had, as it were, settled in for the long haul of the job of bringing about change, gladdened by signs of progress but refusing to become complacent or to forget the need to ensure that laws were implemented, promises fulfilled, knowledge spread beyond a small circle. Her constant reiteration of the need for legalised abortion as part of the wider strategy of the birth control movement was shifting from an embarrassing fringe extreme to a degree of acceptance as the subject became opened up for public debate. But taboos still operated, and Stella was aware of the need to keep hammering away.

Notes

1. F.W. Stella Browne, 'How the fight goes', *The New Generation*, vol. 9, June 1930, p. 5.
2. 'Miss Browne at Brixton', *The New Generation*, vol. 9, February 1930, p. 17.
3. F.W. Stella Browne, 'Dr. Marie Stopes's masterstroke', *The New Generation*, vol. 9, January 1930, p. 7.
4. 'Correspondence: from Dr Marie Stopes', *The New Generation*, vol. 9, February 1930, p. 23.
5. F.W.S.B., 'Mrs Chance's indictment', *The New Generation*, vol. 9, February 1930, p. 16.
6. F.W.S.B., 'Clinic reports', *The New Generation*, vol. 9, February 1930, p. 17.
7. F.W. Stella Browne, 'How the fight goes', *The New Generation*, vol. 9, February 1930, p. 19.
8. 'Miss Browne at Birmingham', *The New Generation*, vol. 9, March 1930, p. 34.
9. F.W.S.B., 'A true knight', *The New Generation*, vol. 13, June 1934, p. 62.
10. F.W.S.B., 'Review: A milestone', *The New Generation*, vol. 9, March 1930, pp. 33–4.
11. Marie Stopes, Letter to the Editor, *The New Generation*, vol. 9, May 1930, p. 59; Marie Carmichael Stopes, *"The first five thousand": being the first report of the first birth control clinic in the British Empire, "The mother's clinic" for constructive birth control* (London: J. Bale, Sons, & Danielsson, Ltd, 1925), and *Preliminary notes on various technical aspects of the control of conception: based on the analysed data from ten thousand cases attending the pioneer Mothers' Clinic, London* (London: Mothers' Clinic, 1930).
12. F.W.S.B., 'A milestone'.
13. *The New Generation*, vol. 9, April 1930, p. 38.

14. *The New Generation*, vol. 9, June 1930, p. 64.
15. F.W. Stella Browne, 'How the fight goes', *The New Generation*, vol. 9, May 1930, p.53.
16. F.W. Stella Browne, 'At home and abroad', *The New Generation*, vol. 9, April 1930, p. 41.
17. F.W.S.B., 'Review: Twitterings from a backwater', *The New Generation*, vol. 9, May 1930, p. 58.
18. F.W.S.B., 'Reviews', *The New Generation*, vol. 9, June 1930, p. 67.
19. F.W. Stella Browne, 'Letters to the editor: bureaucrats, bishops and women', *The New Leader*, 22 August 1930, p. 2.
20. F.W. Stella Browne, 'How the fight goes: the Ministry climbs down – half-way', *The New Generation*, vol. 9, August 1930, p. 88.
21. *The New Generation*, vol. 9, November 1930, p. 122.
22. 'Miss Browne in Birmingham', *The New Generation*, vol. 10, January 1931, p. 5.
23. 'Miss Browne at Leicester', *The New Generation*, vol. 9, December 1930, p. 142.
24. 'Sex education centre', *The New Generation*, vol. 10, January 1931, p. 5.
25. F.W. Stella Browne, 'Lambeth and Whitehall', *The New Generation*, vol. 9, September 1930, pp. 102–3.
26. 'Secular Society meeting', *The New Generation*, vol. 9, November 1930, p. 124.
27. F.W. Stella Browne, 'Women bear witness', *The New Generation*, vol. 9, November 1930, pp. 127–8.
28. Theodor H. Van de Velde, *Fertility and Sterility in Marriage: Their Voluntary Promotion and Limitation* (London: William Heinemann Ltd, 1931), p. vii.
29. Van de Velde, *Fertility and Sterility*, p. 101.
30. Van de Velde, *Fertility and Sterility*, p. 156.
31. Van de Velde, *Fertility and Sterility*, p. 430.
32. F.W. Stella Browne, 'The birth control position', *The Week-end Review*, 24 October 1931, p. 512.
33. F.W.S.B., 'Review: The finest art', *The New Generation*, vol. 12, July 1933, pp. 81–2.
34. F.W. Stella Browne, 'Impressions of the Third International Congress of the World League for Sexual Reform', *Medical Critic and Guide*, vol. 27, December 1929, pp. 438–86.
35. F.C. Müller-Lyer, *The Family* (translated by F.W. Stella Browne) (London: Allen & Unwin, 1931), pp. 197, 285, 312, 382.
36. Müller-Lyer, *The Family*, pp. 32, 113, 115.
37. Müller-Lyer, *The Family*, pp. 379–80.
38. Müller-Lyer, *The Family*, pp. 198, 204.
39. Müller-Lyer, *The Family*, p. 237.
40. Müller-Lyer, *The Family*, p. 304.

41. Müller-Lyer, *The Family*, p. 334.
42. Müller-Lyer, *The Family*, p. 362.
43. Müller-Lyer, *The Family*, p. 307.
44. 'Secular Society meeting', *The New Generation*, vol. 9, November 1930, p. 124.
45. F.W.S.B., 'Reviews: An authentic person', *The New Generation*, vol. 10, August 1931, pp. 94–5.
46. F.W.S.B., 'Six windows on the modern world', *The New Generation*, vol. 11, October 1932, pp. 113–14.
47. Minutes of 202nd meeting of the Executive Committee, 8 October 1931, 'B.S.S. Misc', British Sexology Society Archives, Harry Ransom Humanities Research Center, University of Texas at Austin [BSS HRC].
48. Elizabeth Marian Bailey to S.H. Halford, 14 February 1922, 'B.S.S. Misc', BSS HRC.
49. 'Two leading feminists', *The New Generation*, vol. 10. December 1931, p. 134.
50. F.W. Stella Browne, 'How the fight goes', *The New Generation*, vol. 10, February 1931, p. 17.
51. 'Miss Browne's meetings', *The New Generation*, vol. 10, March 1931, p. 29.
52. F.W.S.B., 'Reviews: Motherhood without fear', *The New Generation*, vol. 10, June 1931, p. 70.
53. F.W.S.B., 'Miss Browne replies', *The New Generation*, vol. 10. September 1931, p. 99.
54. F.W.S.B., 'A taboo broken!', *The New Generation*, vol. 10, April 1931, pp. 41–2.
55. F.W. Stella Browne, 'Modern Germanies', *Time and Tide*, 21 March 1931, p. 351–2.
56. F.W.S.B., 'Germany today', *The New Generation*, vol. 10, April 1931, p. 44.
57. F.W.S.B., 'Workers' Birth Control Group', *The New Generation*, vol. 10, April 1931, p. 39.
58. *Ethical Societies Chronicle*, vol. VIII, no. 59, March 1931, p. 4.
59. *The New Generation*, vol. 10, April 1931, p. 40.
60. Stella Browne to E. Lonsdale Deighton, 30 June 1931, 'B.S.S. Misc', BSS HRC.
61. *The New Generation*, vol. 10, June 1931, p. 62.
62. 'Miss Browne's lecture', *The New Generation*, vol. 10, August 1931, p. 88.
63. F.W.S.B., 'Crimes committed out of charity: judge and the gravity of illegal operations', *The New Generation*, vol. 10, July 1931, p. 76.
64. F.W.S.B., 'Reviews: An epic novel', *The New Generation*, vol. 10. July 1931, p. 88.
65. Max Hodann, *History of Modern Morals* (London: William Heinemann Medical, 1937), p. 288.
66. *Ethical Societies Chronicle*, vol. VIII, no. 63, November 1931, p. 3.
67. 'Miss Browne in South London', *The New Generation*, vol. 10, November 1931, p. 128.

68. *Ethical Societies Chronicle*, vol. VIII, no. 62, October 1931, p. 3.
69. 'Miss Browne in South London'.
70. *The New Generation*, vol. 11, February 1932, p. 17.
71. F.W. Stella Browne, 'How the fight goes', *The New Generation*, vol. 10, October 1931, p. 114.
72. F.W. Stella Browne, 'Mrs Chance's indictment', *The New Generation*, vol. 10, November 1931, p. 123.
73. Janet Chance, 'The Sex Education Centre', *The New Generation*, vol. 11, April 1932, pp. 39–40.
74. 'Sir H. M. McCardie: press-cuttings', Eugenics Society Archives, Wellcome Library, SA/EUG/C.216-217.
75. F.W. Stella Browne, 'The "Freethinker", Mr. Justice McCardie, and the "Church Times"', *The Freethinker*, [?] December 1920, SA/EUG/C.217.
76. F.W. Stella Browne, 'The right to abortion', *The New Generation*, vol. 11, January 1932, p, 4.
77. Lecture to the Wembley branch of the National Secular Society, report in the *Wembley News*, reprinted in *The New Generation*, vol. 11, May 1932, pp. 52–3.
78. Stella Browne to E. Lonsdale Deighton, 18 January 1932, 'B.S.S. Misc', BSS HRC.
79. F.W. Stella Browne to Mary Ware Dennett, 18 August 1932, Mary Ware Dennett papers in The Arthur and Elizabeth Scheslinger Library on the History of Women in America, Radcliffe College, Cambridge MA, MC 392, Folder 34 (Reel 2) General correspondence B 1932–34.
80. 'Promethean Society', *The New Generation*, vol. 11, February 1932, p. 14.
81. F.W.S.B., 'Reviews: An original novel', *The New Generation*, vol. 11, February 1932, p. 20.
82. 'Miss Browne at Manchester', *The New Generation*, vol. 11, March 1932, p. 29.
83. The case is discussed in greater detail by Angus McLaren in *The Trials of Masculinity: Policing Sexual Boundaries, 1870–1930* (Chicago: University of Chicago Press, 1997), pp. 208–13.
84. 'Hull, Augustine Joseph: papers concerning his conviction and imprisonment', 1931–1932, 'B.S.S. Misc', BSS HRC.
85. 'Miss Browne at Manchester'.
86. 'British Sexological Society', *The New Generation*, vol. 11, March 1932, p. 26.
87. Browne to Deighton, 18 January 1932, 'B.S.S. Misc', HRC.
88. Browne to Deighton, 3 February 1932, 'B.S.S. Misc', HRC.
89. Browne to Deighton, 1 February 1932, 'B.S.S. Misc', HRC.
90. Entry for 16 February 1932, George Ives, 'Notes and Writings', Volume 96, HRC.
91. 'British Sexological Society'.
92. E. Lonsdale Deighton to Stella Browne, 18 February 1932, 'B.S.S. Misc', HRC.

93. Dora F. Kerr to E. Lonsdale Deighton, 26 February 1932, 'B.S.S. Letters received', HRC.
94. 'Miss Browne at Wembley', *The New Generation*, vol. 11, May 1932, pp. 52–3.
95. Leader column, *The New Generation*, vol. 11, April 1932, p. 37.
96. F.W. Stella Browne, 'Standardized sex enlightenment: a laywoman's question', *The New Generation*, vol. 11, April 1932, p. 40.
97. F.W. Stella Browne, 'Some books that help', *The New Generation*, vol. 11, June 1932, p. 65.
98. Lecture to the Wembley branch of the National Secular Society, report in the *Wembley News*, reprinted in *The New Generation*, vol. 11, May 1932, pp. 52–3.
99. F.W.S.B, 'The age of bewilderment', p. 80.
100. F.W. Stella Browne to Mary Ware Dennett, 18 August 1932, MWD, Folder 34 (Reel 2).
101. F.W.S.B., 'Reviews: A feminist looks at fascism', *The New Generation*, vol. 11, July 1932, p. 78.
102. Lesley A. Hall, 'The Archives of the Pioneer Health Centre, Peckham, in the Wellcome Library', *Social History of Medicine*, vol. 14, 2001, pp. 525–38.
103. F.W.S.B., 'Achieving health', *The New Generation*, vol. 11, May 1932, p. 58.
104. F.W. Stella Browne, 'Letter to the editor: medicine and contraception', *The Week-end Review*, 23 June 1932, p. 796.
105. F.W. Stella Browne, 'British Medical Association on abortion', *The New Generation*, vol. 11, August 1932, pp. 89–90.
106. F.W. Stella Browne, 'Letter to the editor: hushing-up sex crimes', *The Week-end Review*, 1 October 1932, p. 371.
107. 'World League for Sexual Reform', *The New Generation*, vol. 11, December 1932, pp. 137–8.
108. Ruby Lockie (Haire's secretary) to Dora Russell, 20 October 1932, Dora Russell papers in the International Institute for Social History, Amsterdam [DR], file 412.
109. R. Lockie to Mrs Harrington re new annual subscriptions to the WLSR, carbon copy, 24 October 1932, DR, file 408.
110. 'World League for Sexual Reform', *The New Generation*, vol. 11, December 1932, pp. 137–8.
111. F.W. Stella Browne, 'Sexual reform', *The Week-end Review*, 12 November 1932, cutting in DR, file 408.
112. Marie Stopes to Stella Browne, carbon copy, 8 November 1932, Stopes papers, Wellcome Library, PP/MCS/A.42.
113. Vega, 'Aspects of population control', *Time and Tide*, 14 January 1933, p. 33.
114. Alice Jenkins, 'Obituary: Miss F.W. Stella Browne', *The Eugenics Review*, vol. 47, 1955/56, pp. 78–9.

115. Private report to Marie Stopes on the meeting, Notes on back of notice of British Sexological Society meeting of 15 November 1932, 'General Correspondence', Marie Stopes papers in the British Library Department of Manuscripts, Add Mss 58712.
116. Minutes of Annual General Meeting, 15 November 1932, 'B.S.S. Misc', HRC.
117. *The New Generation*, vol. 11, December 1932, p. 134.

9

Progressing

The international political situation, and its potential repercussions, was continuing to concern Stella. She saw Nazism as the 'Dragon's harvest' of the Treaty of Versailles:[1] the resulting injustice and exploitation had produced a 'natural reaction of the pride and power of a virile and able race'. But Hitler's regime was 'sweeping away ... all the achievements of opportunity and equality for German women after the war';[2] its 'meanly unjust' constraints were a 'wastage of ability and capacity and varied knowledge'.[3] A 'blistering example' of the 'official attitude' of the Nazis 'towards the knowledge of sex and its rights to recognition and expression' was the burning of the Library of the Berlin Institute of Sexual Science. Some of the foremost fighters were known to be safe outside the borders of Germany, but what of others 'who brought light and help to the slums of Berlin and Frankfurt', and 'What of the creative work in art and literature ... A *culture* has been wrecked.' How, asked Stella, should 'we British birth controllers and sex reformers' face 'what our comrades in Central Europe, Hebrews or Gentiles, Liberal pacifists or Communists are enduring now?' Who was to say that 'a Right Wing revolution, with its return to the values and the methods of the thirteenth century – or earlier – can never cross the strip of sea which, in the past, has guarded us so well?'[4] She had herself 'emphasized the danger of reaction on Fascist lines, as no vigorously and consistently constructive policy had as yet been put in hand'.[5] '[I]n the face of the prolonged muddle and disintegration which our present rulers apparently prefer to any sort of action', hopefulness 'was not easy to maintain'.[6]

Stella's own views on race and ethnic questions were expressed following an 'interesting and controversial' lecture to the Eugenics Society on 'Race Mixture' by Dr K.B. Aikman. She reported that he 'hardly touched at all on the recently discovered "Blood Groups" which are by no means coterminous with the three primary races'. (*When* did Stella get the time to keep up with advanced technical writings in modern science and medicine? Not to mention the familiarity with developments in modern art and literature also revealed in her response to this lecture. And how did she gain access to these resources?) Aikman 'strongly deprecated any ethnic "crossing"': each race should 'stay in its own place'. 'To at least one listener' (surely Miss F.W.S.B.),

> this ideal, while not lacking in dignity, beauty and value, seemed wholly impracticable; is Dr Aikman prepared, in the interest of ethnic homogeneity and nationalist culture, to scrap not only long distance transit, large scale commerce, the Trust, but even the Town?

During the vigorous discussion, she mentioned 'the increasing and already valuable contribution to distinctively modern thought and art' being made by 'the coloured races': her 'remarks roused lively dissent'.[7]

Later the same year, she reported sympathetically on a Conference on Birth Control in Asia, at which India 'was particularly well-represented', as well as 'students and experts from "the most Eastern East"'. Helena Wright's remarks about avoiding 'unwise suggestion of dictation and interference', and the desirability of training local women as doctors and nurses met with her approval.[8] In her 1935 essay 'The Right to Abortion', Stella remarked that

> Western Europe and America have brought much knowledge, much expansion – even very painful expansion – of experience to the coloured races and the Ancient East; some of their gifts have been dragon's teeth, and of that harvest we have not yet seen the end.

However, there were good things, such as 'modern sanitary and contraceptive science' and, in return for that, perhaps the West was beginning to realise, and 'even here and there to acquire, something of the Asiatic and Pacific peoples' art of love'.[9] Stella's enthusiasm for the potential of ethnic diversity and mingling was a logical outcome of her belief in the importance and value of human differences, a topic she continued to emphasise in articles and reviews.

Stella's Norwegian friend Dr Tove Mohr was amazed that only two women at a British birth control conference 'ventured to claim the right to *real* birth control'. However, early in 1933 'a larger and very active band of supporters and agitators' including Stella, joined in a discussion 'full of animation and practical information', when Dr J.H. Leunbach of Copenhagen addressed the World League for Sexual Reform, British Section on 'Abortion and Birth Control in Scandinavia'.[10]

'Much can be done by writing to the papers':[11] she achieved a 'hat-trick' of three letters published in one week of February 1933. One under her occasional nom-de-plume 'Vega', mentioning the 'archaic survivals in our present criminal law' in *Time and Tide*;[12] another in *The Spectator*, suggesting that 'abortion law reform, *plus* adequate housing, would perhaps be of more benefit to suffering humanity' than the proposed forty-five new churches;[13] and one on the case of Mrs Minnie Weaving, aged 37, with an unemployed husband and seven children, who had died 'by voluntary slow starvation, so that her children might live',[14] in *The Week-end Review*.[15] Stella achieved a certain amount of mileage out of the French amnesty on women imprisoned for performing illegal abortions on themselves, with a letter to *Time and Tide* in March tying it in neatly in with Cicely Hamilton's 'brilliantly independent' *Modern France*.[16] In a letter to *The Week-end Review*, she asked why this example could not be followed in recent British cases.[17]

Stella continued to address a range of audiences on varied subjects. On March 6 she spoke to the North Battersea Cooperative Women on 'Birth Control and Unemployment'.[18] On 12 April, the Highgate Women's Cooperative Guild heard a talk on 'The Reform of the Abortion Law' with 'keenest interest', and followed it with stimulating discussion. This resulted in a resolution to be forwarded to the Ministry of Health, 'demanding reform, *in harmony with modern needs and views*' and that the convicted abortionists Mrs Lee and Mrs Grocott be released.[19] On 23 April, it was the South London Ethical Society again, this time on 'Primitive Thought Through Modern Eyes'. Stella gave them the benefit of her extensive reading in modern anthropology, commenting on the 'wider sympathy and juster appreciation' of 'primitive achievements and outlooks in Communal life', being brought about by science, 'combined with a respect for the individual'. Initiation rites at puberty might be 'crude and painful', but 'honest and dignified in comparison with the subterfuges of certain later phases'. The ideal was to 'aim at a realism as honest as the primitive, but more sensitive, and at a bolder and more balanced vision of human possibilities'.[20] Stella had been very impressed by Malinowski's study of the Trobriand Islanders, and 'what the White West has still to learn from the South Seas'. She hoped that they might, 'untainted by traders, unterrified by missionaries', retain their 'joy and pride, and escape the fate of exploitation, hatred and debasement which has overtaken Hawaii'. 'One of the requisites of civilization', she considered, was 'a biological and anthropological conscience'.[21]

For Stella, knowledge was still provisional, still being worked out. She was interested

> to observe the large of number of women who are now taking up psycho-analytical doctrine and practice. They may throw light on aspects of personality, hitherto obscured by a somewhat arbitrary and eccentric system of value and deductions.[22]

Mary Chadwick's *Women's Periodicity* bore 'honest witness to the amount of knowledge and liberation still needing to be won', given the 'pitiful ignorance which still aggravates the difficulties of women's lives'. If Stella would have preferred more case histories and 'fewer psycho-analytic interpretations', she was intrigued by Chadwick's suggestion of a 'recurrent rhythm ... long after the climacteric'.[23]

Her concern over the inadequacy of the laws of marriage and divorce continued active. At one of the weekly debates at the Lyceum Club (founded for women writers and journalists in 1904, in rather splendid premises in Piccadilly), on 'Divorce by mutual consent was the only solution to the matrimonial tangle', Stella claimed during discussion that 'a complete social and economic change would alone provide a remedy'.[24] She wrote approvingly of A.P. Herbert's campaign to reform the existing law,[25] and she praised the 'urbane mastery, the documentation, pathos and humour',[26] of *Holy Deadlock*, his 'modern divorce novel', even though

> many people will ask themselves, is the thing worth tinkering at? Is it worth the risk of having one's life and love messed about, and of hurting the people one cares for, beyond repair? No. Keep out of the trap.
>
> And so say more and more of us.[27]

It sometimes seems as though Stella's life was one long round of attending meetings, participating in debates, giving lectures (in November, she addressed the South London Secularists yet again, this time on 'The Mechanisms of Agitation in politics and sociology'),[28] reading widely and multilingually to keep up with modern scientific and political developments (e.g. the 'admirable quarterly' *Le Problème Sexuel* edited by Mme Berty Albrecht, a 'public-spirited and efficient enterprise'),[29] writing letters to the press and paragraphs, reviews and articles for *The New Generation*. However, she did have some lighter pleasures; for example, an eye which could be charmed by the 'special note of colour and grace' given to the Conference on Birth Control in Asia by the 'Indian ladies in their *saris*'.[30] She 'rejoice[d] at G. Farleigh's illustrations' to Cicely Hamilton's *Little Arthur's History of the Twentieth Century*, 'especially those cats!'[31]

Yet another organisation was now making claims upon her time and energies. In 1932, with 'fairly extensive support among a number of prominent intellectuals', the Federation of Progressive Societies and Individuals (FPSI) was inaugurated.[32] The Sex Reform Group represented 'an essential feature of Federation policy'. Janet Chance was initially its 'esteemed leader' but, in October 1933, the secretary of the FPSI wrote to Vera Brittain, the well-known writer and journalist, inviting her to take over.[33] Brittain's response does not survive but, by December, Stella and her old friend Ashton Burall were the joint leaders of the Group. They were already aiming at organising a public meeting, and 'the systematic writing of letters to the Press',[34] as well as attending 'as many committee meetings as convenient', directing the group's policy and any campaigns it might undertake, attending the monthly Council meetings of the Federation, and chairing public meetings of the group.[35]

Other groups were less welcoming. Early in November, Stella wrote to Dr Carlos Paton Blacker – one of the 'enlightened and distinguished medical men now at the head of the Eugenics Society and the Birth Control Investigation Committee'[36] – to request information about the deputation to the Ministry of Health contemplated by the Eugenics Society and the National Birth Control Association (NBCA). She congratulated him on 'the work you are doing & have already accomplished'.[37] Blacker, who regarded Stella as 'one of the most fanatical women I have had the pleasure of meeting [a remarkable statement from a close friend of Marie Stopes!], the legalisation of abortion being the consummation she desires to see realised', forwarded her letter to Miss Holland of the NBCA, remarking that 'if she is fishing for an invitation to take part in your delegation I should, if I may suggest it, not give her encouragement'.[38] Holland, in 'quite a non-committal manner',[39] informed Stella that there was 'at present no definite decision about a deputation' although 'authoritative information' was being gathered.[40] This correspondence rather substantiates some of Stella's scathing remarks about the more respectable wing of the birth control movement.

Another issue engaging Stella's interest at this time was the debate around the potential legalisation of voluntary sterilisation for the 'unfit'. It has been alleged that she was an advocate of compulsory eugenic sterilisation of the mentally defective.[41] Far from it: she praised the Report of the

Committee on Sterilisation for its express repudiation of compulsion and its stress on the 'very complex nature of heredity'. Her major criticism was, instead, that voluntary sterilisation should be 'applicable to all those physically and mentally healthy persons *who ask for it*', whereas the report still 'struggles in the grip of an obsolete standard of morality and system of economics'[42] She smacked down Cora Hodson's *Human Sterilization To-day* for ignoring 'the grave difficulties incidental to any eugenic legislation on lines convention would as yet approve', and pointed out that, since the researches of Mendel and Bateson, heredity was hardly the 'perfectly simple straightforward matter' Hodson assumed.[43] She was concerned lest even voluntary sterilisation might be used as a weapon against the poor.[44]

Stella gave what appears to have been the last of her several lectures to the South London (or, indeed, any other) Ethical Society on 18 February 1934, on 'The State as Biologist'. Arguing that 'modern communities were being compelled (sometimes much against the grain) to recognize biological facts as well as economics': some states followed 'some form of Plan, in accordance with some type of Ethical theory' (she cited as contrasting models the German Sterilization law of 1933 and the Soviet legalisation of abortion), while others succumbed to 'a planlessness ... which soon became chaotic, without really respecting individual liberty'. An exemplar of this was British policy towards birth control and divorce law reform.[45] The reason for the end of an apparently successful period of lecturing to ethical and secularist organisations is not clear, as a number of colleagues associated with similar progressive causes continued to address meetings of ethical societies.[46]

She was still finding an audience in the Women's Cooperative Guild (WCG). In February, she spoke to the Elmers End Guild on 'The Unwanted Child', referring particularly to 'the recent crop of infanticide cases', and a resolution was unanimously passed for submission to the Annual Conference.[47] In March, she spoke to the Penge and Biggin Hill Guilds on a similar theme, and they approved the resolution already formulated by Elmers End. She also addressed the Peckham Women's Adult School: 'more conventional in outlook but keenly interested and anxious for further information'.[48]

She continued to attend and participate in the debates at the Lyceum Club. At a debate on the reform of the House of Lords, she argued from the floor that 'the imbecile waste of time and neglect of vital facts in the present House of Commons procedure' were not necessary characteristics of Single Chamber Government.[49] On March 12, she herself proposed the motion that 'the relationship of the sexes is better under Communism than Fascism', against William Joyce of the British Union of Fascists (later notorious for broadcasting Nazi propaganda as 'Lord Haw-Haw' during the Second World War). While admitting that Fascism might be 'honouring and providing for women as mothers', she contended that this was 'exalting their maternity at the expense of their full humanity'; whereas Communism 'admitted women to a full share in industry, the professions and administration', while providing for the child-bearer, abolishing illegitimacy, making divorce accessible and respecting women's right to refuse to bear children. It had broken with 'the tradition that founded the sheltered and sacred home on the indispensable services of a despised and outlawed class'. Joyce claimed that the British Fascists meant to raise women's status and promote their interests, while preserving tradition and religious standards and sentiments: 'above all [they] would preserve the family'. Following the discussion and the final summing up by both speakers, the result was exactly equal at fourteen votes each.[50]

She attended a symposium on birth control at the annual meeting of the Eugenics Society on 17 April. To Stella, this

> left a most obstinate and uncomfortable questioning: how far is it possible to carry out adequate and detailed tests of contraceptives – for ultimately it is the *clinical test* that counts, however important and significant the laboratory's role – *so long as any failure of a contraceptive is irreparable and there is no lawful second line of defence?*

Stella herself reminded the meeting of the 'disaster of rubber goods that tear and chemical preparations that liquified into green vinegar'.[51]

Besides monthly discussion meetings, the FPSI Sex Reform Group held a conference jointly with the Education Group at Digswell Park, Welwyn Garden City, 9–11 June. A programme of lectures included the educational methods of Homer Lane, Ashton Burall on René Guyon's *Sex Life and Sex Ethics*, and a report on women and children in Soviet Russia.[52] It is unfortunately not clear whether Stella attended – it took place very shortly after the epoch-making meeting at West Hartlepool, at which she was present, when the WCG Congress passed a resolution in favour of abortion law reform.

This Congress brought, on 7 June, 'a lesson for the half-hearted, the temporizers and trimmers', passing a resolution (only twenty contrary votes in an assembly of 1360 delegates) for the legalisation of abortion. This asked for revision of the 1861 law to bring it

> into harmony with modern conditions and ideas, thereby making of abortion a legal operation that can be carried out

> under the same conditions as any other surgical operation. It further asks that women now suffering imprisonment for breaking these antiquated laws, be amnestied.

Two 'timid qualifying amendments' (to omit the amnesty and to require women to 'show good cause') were decisively rejected.[53] A report in *The New Generation* suggested that Stella and Mme Lorsignol were to be congratulated 'for gaining the adhesion' of this important and successful women's organisation.[54] Stella contrasted the vigour of the WCG's declaration for 'the woman's right of choice', with the continued evidence that the BMA was 'determined to shirk' the task of initiating its proposed enquiry.[55]

Shortly after the Congress, she spoke on 'The Unwanted Child', to Oxted Cooperative Women and, later in June, returned to Elmers End. She congratulated them for 'their great work at Congress' (they had seconded the resolution), and lectured this time on 'The Hygiene of Middle Life', in which she emphasised 'the wealth of neglected knowledge and possibilities of health and happiness in this particular field'. She argued that 'we are neither mentally civilised nor biologically sound if our life is crippled half-way through'.[56] (Her own attitude to the middle years of life?)

In September, *Plan* published her article 'The Constructive Case for Abortion Law Reform'. She made her usual allusions to the inadequacy of contraception, the fact that 'doctors who take a humane and courageous view of their rights and responsibilities in this matter, do so under the shadows of prison and ruin', the various recent desperate cases which had been in the news, the success of the Soviet experiment. But her final argument was 'emotional, aesthetic and feminist': abortion formed one 'aspect of our whole modern movement for the control of life and the rehabilitation of sex and its emotions'. It was 'the basis of any real eugenics', and she did not see it 'fitting very easily into the framework of an economically unequal and artificially ignorant community'. While it was part of 'the socialist ideal' for 'a socialism which does not ignore biology', 'for women's freedom, for anything like an equal chance for women to taste and experience and conquer life – this right of refusal is absolutely essential'. The twentieth century had 'discovered ... a whole science of parenthood' and that there was

> also an erotic and coital art, in which many primitive races, untouched by either Christianity or mechanization, as well as some more elaborate eastern civilisations are adepts.

The younger generation was 'learning to try to accept and harmonize its sex life, not to deny or bury it' and were in 'revolt against the imbecility of compulsion in sex life and parenthood'. She concluded by asking for their 'support and help in this agitation for the most urgent sex reform today'.[57]

She gave a resoundingly favourable review to Winifred Holtby's *Woman and her place in a changing civilisation* (which thanked her in its introduction),[58] referring to Holtby's 'breadth of view and sensitive chivalrous courage'. She had 'a steady grip on the ceaseless interaction of women's emancipation with economic justice, education and international peace', and 'her knowledge of contemporary history supplie[d] the aptest and often most unexpected ammunition'.[59]

C.P. Blacker of the Eugenics Society continued to be snarky about Stella, writing to J.R. Baker that 'She is a passionate propagandist in favour of legalising abortion. I regard her as a very difficult type and moderately mad, so do not let her bother you too much.'[60] He was more tactful in writing to Janet Chance: 'Miss Browne seems to feel very strongly on the subject'.[61] But Stella, more generously, found praiseworthy the recent addition of (limited) legalisation of abortion by the Eugenics Society to its aims and objects in the summer of 1935. Although this was restricted to cases 'where there is probability of inherited physical or mental defect, and also in cases of rape, criminal assault and incest', she gave them her 'sincere and cordial congratulations' on a 'step forward which will have influences in many far from radical circles!'[62]

Stella's association with *The New Generation* seems to have more or less ceased at the end of 1934. No explanation can be found in its columns and any breach is not mentioned elsewhere. It was almost the end of her relationship with this forum for her views and writing, which had lasted for nearly twenty years. To some extent, *The New Generation*'s role in her life was superseded by *Plan*, but this did not provide quite such a broad stage for her to ventilate her ideas and report on the progress, or lack of it, of 'the movement'. However, it did perhaps have a greater and more up-to-date commitment to her general agenda of sex reform.

In January 1935, *Plan* published the FPSI Sex Reform Group's Memorandum on 'The Reform of Sexual Law and Convention', in which Stella must surely have had a large hand. It emphasised that, under the existing economic system, 'no solution of many sexual problems is possible', and that 'All branches of social reform are interdependent'. Some of the existing issues arose from economic factors, others from current laws, and others fell within the realm of educational needs. The ideal was the elimination of 'the obscurantist view of sex' by 'the deliberate adoption of a scale of values based upon reason and knowledge as distinct from superstition'. Legal and economic equality between the sexes should be established. The provisos concerning birth control, legal abortion, voluntary sterilisation, the simplification of divorce laws, the provision of better education and facilities for treatment in venereal diseases, the decriminalisation of homosexual 'voluntary associations between responsible adults', the destigmatisation of the unmarried mother and the illegitimate child, better and universal sex education on enlightened lines, and the recognition of masturbation as a normal characteristic about which feelings of guilt should not be inculcated: all these were reforms about which Stella had already expressed herself strongly in a variety of places over the years. However, the advocacy of nude sunbathing, which should be 'given every encouragement', features nowhere in Stella's known writings.[63] It does, however, seem to have been a particular interest of Ashton Burall's.[64]

In February, she spoke to the Sex Reform Group on 'Varieties of Sexual Trend',[65] and on 8 April was one of the speakers at a Symposium on Sex Reform, a 'highly successful' FPSI public meeting of the 1934–5 session.[66] The FPSI was not, however, the only venue in which Stella's views were being expressed: in February 1935, she gave 'one of her characteristically stimulating lectures on the question "Should Abortion be Legalised?"' at one of the informal Wednesday evening talks at the Birth Control International Information Centre.[67]

Dr Max Hodann, formerly Magnus Hirschfeld's assistant in Berlin, was endeavouring to establish 'an international bureau for information and research on sex subjects' in Britain, and the Sex Reform Group and the Federation as a whole were 'doing all they could to help'.[68] Stella wrote a personal letter on Hodann's behalf to the Academic Assistance Council of the Society for the Protection of Science and Learning (SPSL), a body which tried to find suitable work for academic refugees from Nazi Germany. She had 'put Dr Hodann in touch with various persons of knowledge and high reputation in these matters'.[69] Esther Simpson of the SPSL was non-committal about Hodann's prospects.

On Magnus Hirschfeld's death in 1935, Stella contributed a brief obituary to *Plan* – 'one of the most consistently courageous humanitarians and most learned specialists of our time'. His 'statesmanlike vision [had] included *all* the aspects of a sane and tolerable treatment of sex'. He had, she said, 'a fund of geniality, sociability and wit; his sombre Assyrian features would light up when he discussed the cause that moved him most', which suggests that they had had some personal contact.[70]

The Sex Reform Group was 'on the whole well-supported', and the attendance at its monthly meetings was 'gratifyingly high', with 'keen interest' shown in the discussions. It was regretted that 'directly propagandist activities ... have not been greater' (e.g. 'the useful field of letters to the press'). The Federation was giving 'special prominence and attention to [the] urgent matter' of abortion law reform, in which growing interest was evident. Members of the Group were taking 'an active part in the preliminary steps for the formation of a society specially devoted to Abortion Law Reform', keeping in touch with international developments, and supplying material for discussion at conferences.[71] She was cheered by the report of the Committee on the Reform of the Norwegian Abortion Laws,[72] writing to Havelock Ellis that it was about the only part of the world from which the news could be said to be good – 'from human cruelty and folly may humanity be saved'.[73]

A new ally in the abortion law reform struggle was the young socialist doctor Joan Malleson. Stella praised Malleson's handbook *The Principles of Contraception* in *Plan*: 'written with acute and delicate insight and with a fluid grace of expression, very easy and individual'.[74] Malleson was instrumental in organising a conference in 1935 on the legalisation of abortion – in Janet Chance's chronology of abortion law reform, the first event of note between the '1861 Offences Against the Person Act', the period in between being the years during which 'STELLA CAMPAIGNS ALONE'. Details of this meeting are tantalisingly frustrating. It seems to have taken place in February, since a list of individuals invited bears a handwritten note: 'The ALRA formed one year after in Feb. 36.'[75] Malleson referred in a private letter to 'my "Abortion" society I started',[76] but she was surely working with Stella and the other women who had already been promoting the cause. This theory is borne out by the list of invitees, on which the names of none of those already active appear, although a handwritten note adds 'Also present Janet Chance Alice Jenkins Others?'[77] This suggests it was a wider sweep for support: a discussion early in 1936 involved the core group of stalwarts – Stella herself, Frida Laski, Gerda Guy, Berthe Lorsignol, Alice Jenkins, Dora Russell and Janet Chance[78] (Malleson herself did not attend, her father having suddenly died).[79]

Stella had not abandoned her connection with the Fabian Society. As usual, she spoke up during discussions at the annual general meeting.[80] In August, she spent at least one day at the Fabian Summer School at Frensham Heights School near Farnham, describing herself as a journalist, writer, lecturer, with articles in American and foreign press, in *Plan* and *New Generation*, and translations.[81]

There was excellent news for the cause at the Conference of the National Council of Women held at Leicester in October. This was the largest women's organisation in Britain, and '*not* a subversive organization!', being 'mainly, though not entirely, middle-class and professional'. It had not committed itself to the question of birth control in welfare centres until the relatively late date of 1929. But it moved a resolution urging the government to appoint a committee to enquire into the incidence of abortion, the existing law and what measures might improve the existing position. This was passed unanimously, and a further resolution was moved to amend the Offences Against the Person statute of 1861, in order to make it lawful for medical practitioners to terminate pregnancy in cases of conception resulting from criminal assault in girls aged under fourteen: although hardly radical, at least 'this tragic wrong' had been brought 'into public discussion'.[82]

A major personal achievement for Stella during 1935 was the publication of the symposium *Abortion*, containing essays by herself, the doctor Harry Roberts and her old adversary, the flamboyant misogynist reactionary Antony Ludovici. It is not clear whose was the initial stimulus for producing this: the only relevant file of correspondence with the publishers is with Roberts alone.[83] However, a couple of years later Robert Latou Dickinson, mentioning the possibility of an American edition, referred to it as 'Stella Browne's Abortion with the Ludovici handicap'.[84] George Allen & Unwin considered that discussion of the subject was desirable, but the 'commercial outlook speculative'.[85] Indeed, the publishers would 'not be despondent if we do no more than cover our costs', since it was 'the sort of work with which we like to be associated'.[86] Stella and Ludovici both saw each other's contributions and incorporated response to them in their own chapters, but it is not clear if Roberts was quite as interactive.[87] A certain amount of delay was caused by Roberts's other commitments: in September, Stella phoned him 'in rather a state because the Abortion book isn't appearing earlier ... she seemed to think it of vital importance'.[88]

A first edition of 1,500 copies was printed – the publishers believing that 'we shall be very lucky if we sell it out' – of which 100 review copies were sent out.[89] Stella received an advance of ten guineas (equivalent to £523 in 2007 values) against royalties[90] although, unbeknownst to her, Roberts got an advance of fifteen guineas. It seems probable that the publishers were anxious to get a medical opinion mid-way between the extremes represented by Stella and Ludovici.[91]

Stella's essay 'The Right to Abortion' made no concessions or compromises. She started from

> the (as yet still rather unpopular) assumption that women are really human beings, and that freedom of choice and deliberate intention are necessary for them in their sexual relations and

> their maternity, if they are to make anything of their status and opportunities in certain communities today.[92]

She then went on to provide an overview of the law in Britain and the reformed laws of various European countries, and the history of the struggle or, rather, the refusal of the authorities to even consider the subject, in Britain, to date.[93] She was adamant that 'the woman's right to abortion is an absolute right... up to the viability of her child'. It was not contingent upon threats to health or sanity, potential genetic defect in the child, upon economic hardship, proven contraceptive failure, marital status, or being the victim of a crime. Stella regarded these cases – pregnancy through rape or incest – as 'peculiarly pitiful', and the suffering caused

> an indictment of the whole social system that tolerates its infliction and... the ultimate expression of the view of women as vessels – of 'honour' and 'dishonour' as the case may be – for men's use and as automatic breeding machines.

While suggesting that 'laws justifiably treat as second only to murder' these 'crimes which the conventions of romantic tradition deem worse than death', she also acutely asked

> how far the reprobation of rape is a defence of women's dignity and personality, and how far it is subconscious 'compensation,' communal jealousy, and property defence.

Abortion should be 'the key to a new world for women, not a bulwark for things as they are', and available 'without insolent inquisition... ruinous financial charges... tangles of red tape.'[94] She pointed out the impracticability of many of the controls and limitations which were being mooted.[95]

She argued that skilled surgical abortion under hygienic conditions, 'not scrambled through' in fear of detection or having to be concealed, would 'save thousands of lives'. It would also 'encourage *constructive* research' in 'chemistry and psycho-biology'. She argued that, although most traditional remedies were only effective when taken in dangerous dosages, in various parts of the world 'a highly skilled and carefully guarded technique... attains results without slaughtering and crippling women', attested by anthropologists. Whether based on this ancient knowledge or not, 'a perfectly reliable and otherwise tolerable abortifacient... would be the greatest gift science could give to women.' (But this was a less 'lucrative and respectable a branch of research and industry' than 'high explosives and poison gases'.)[96]

She dismissed the appeal to 'the cant of contraception': 'No contraceptive at present accessible to the public is 100 per cent reliable... cheap, easy to store and to apply, otherwise non-injurious and aesthetically satisfactory.' Manufacturers indulged in 'almost incredible profiteering,' and inadequate housing and hot water supplies militated against the effective practice of contraception. If the control of reproduction was accepted, 'the exact method becomes a matter of individual preference and/or expediency,' and a 'sure second line of defence' would spare 'the racked nerves of thousands' and 'prevent the shipwreck of much mutual joy and affection.'[97]

She envisaged a future society moulded by 'human brain and will' in which 'children will be welcomed and created as achievements, and not flung into life with fear and anger as disastrous accidents.' But, as things were, women who would have preferred to have children were driven by economic necessity to procure miscarriages. In the ideal future, such maternal women would 'not be sterilized,' while 'the woman of variant endocrine blend and psychological trend will not be obliged to have nervously unbalanced and devitalized children whom she neither wants nor understands.' And there were women who were

> not primarily maternal, who love their own vanity or their own dreams, or some creative call of work; or a man, or more than one man, or another woman, more than any child. These women exist. Their exact percentage may be small – I do not think it is – but their total number is large.[98]

Stella went on to make an argument that, for some women (perhaps herself among them?), abortion was 'erotically preferable to any current and available form of contraception,' which disturbed 'the essential rhythm, the crescendo, climax, and diminuendo of the communion of sex.' This most 'intimate and individual' function was the one to which convention granted 'least scope for diversity,' an ignorance exacerbated by 'the still prevalent lack of erotic knowledge and skill.'[99] She also touched on religious objections: she denied that the right to abortion contravened 'any belief in either the possibility of human survival or the mystery of human consciousness and human personality,' adding that 'those who support the case for reincarnation or continuation' ought to regard 'human parental responsibility as an important factor in the sifting of souls': a point she considered 'worth the consideration of those who take the theosophical – or other angles of the mystical – view of human destiny and cosmic forces.'[100]

She concluded with a plea for the 'inestimably precious and significant' fusion of sex and love, 'whether or not the fruit of love should result'. Even 'experimental and casual' relations had 'use and value', although 'our modern consciences are apt to shrink from linking children to casual and impersonal sex contacts'. Parenthood was 'a responsibility, or, if you will, a privilege for the sanest, finest, and most vital yet altruistic'.[101]

The volume appeared in the autumn and, as she commented in a letter to Havelock Ellis, 'the line adopted by a large section of the Press is the much more difficult one of smothering by silences' – even advertisements were 'not appearing, even in places where it might be hoped for'. She hoped for the '*honour & help* of some public mention' by Ellis, and requested both him and Françoise to do what they could to push the book.[102] Ellis did produce a 'generous review', which, however, the Hearst Press in the USA refused to print – although it was not at the root of his 'row' with them, Stella was glad to hear.[103] She suspected that the concurrent prosecution of Edward Charles's *The Sexual Impulse* would 'intimidate publishers and booksellers not to speak of the timid & tender editorial species!' However, Allen & Unwin were 'taking a very sensible line'.[104] A few years later, however, she strongly advised Max Hodann not to offer his work to Unwin, although without saying why.[105]

Allen & Unwin found that 'the Browneites appear to have rallied well' in getting attention drawn to the volume, and they were 'endeavouring to interest the Ludovicians', but 'the ordinary mid-way readers still seem conspiciously absent'.[106] There were perhaps predictable good reviews in *The New Generation* and *Plan*. *The New Generation* remarked on her 'very able statement of the case' in a work 'very ably written by all three writers ... makes lively as well as profitable reading', commenting that, as Stella has 'frequently stated [her] case in *The New Generation*, we need not enlarge on her argument'.[107] Alec Craig, in *Plan*, referred to Stella as 'a courageous pioneer who was not afraid to speak up in less happy times when to bring information and reason to bear on this issue was to court misrepresentation and social obloquy'. He coupled her name with Mr Justice McCardie's as sharing 'the bulk of the honours won to date in this fight'.[108] T.F. Fox (himself a doctor, and one who was, at least some while later, extremely active in the Family Planning Association) reviewed the book for *The Spectator*. Although he conceded the sincerity of both Stella's and Ludovici's positions, he found it 'a relief to turn to Dr Roberts and his plea for "more latitude" for doctors to 'do what they feel right'.[109]

The book also received positive notices in the *British Medical Journal* and *The Lancet* – the latter, indeed, deeming it 'well worth reading'.[110] Both journals conceded that 'the whole position is more than ripe for careful consideration',[111] and 'adjustment of the present law is probably inevitable'.[112] There was a positive notice by E.F. Griffith, a leading figure in the British birth control and sex education movement, in the international journal *Marriage Hygiene*. While he clearly felt professional solidarity with Roberts's point of view, and considered that 'there are very few medical men ... who would endorse Miss Browne's plea', he conceded that this 'well known supporter of the case for the Legalisation of Unrestricted Abortion at the discretion of the woman ... presents her case lucidly and convincingly'.[113] The book also received a very positive notice in an unexpected quarter: 'M.N.', writing in *The Shield*, the journal of the Association for Moral and Social Hygiene, stated that 'the publishers are to be congratulated on presenting this subject'. The reviewer found Stella's essay 'well-argued, and presents the case for legalised abortion in a straightforward and readable manner', and concurred with her reading of the existing law that 'all abortion here is illegal and therapeutic abortion by doctors is not legal though in practise it may be recognised'.[114]

There was sad news around the time that the book was published. Winifred Holtby, still under 40, died of a 'lingering illness, mid tiring bouts of pain'. But Stella found that 'neither fatigue nor pain' had 'blurred the swift lucidity, nor upset the balance and breadth of vision of her remarkable mind'. Neither had they 'chilled the kindness and courage that made her so beloved'. Holtby's 'varied abilities and achievements' included her work 'as a champion of the coloured races, especially the African natives, of woman's full human dignity and opportunity' and in the quest for international peace. Stella wished to 'acknowledge and record' her 'rarest [of] gifts'; she was '*chivalrous* to an amazing degree, generous with time and brain and sympathy, to her own hurt'. Holtby's 'Sagittarian gaiety and good fellowship' were blended with 'ethereal refinement and detachment'; she had been a 'civilized and merciful and sensitive valkyrie'. (This sounds as though Stella had done Holtby's horoscope in order to discern this 'Sagittarian' element, going beyond the simple 'sun-sign': Holtby was born on the cusp of Gemini and Cancer, not in Sagittarius.)[115]

The wider political situation continued to be worrying. While in Britain, there was 'no law explicitly prohibiting the discussion or recommendation of such reforms as the liberation of marriage or the civilization of marriages – *as yet*': but, she asked, 'Do we understand the peril that encroaches, and its interactions, even in an – as yet – non-Fascist England?' She wondered if her compatriots had grasped that 'the suppression of unwelcome truth in speech or print... without noise or fuss, in a perfection of silent gravity – is still the favourite method in our country of perpetuating old injustice and ignorance'. Or that 'to utter some questions, to state some cases, is in effect to make it impossible to return to the slavery of tradition'.[116]

Friends and allies had died; the wider political situation did not conduce to optimism. Nonetheless, the struggle for abortion law reform was discernibly moving forward, and Stella was still energetically devoting herself to this and the broader cause of liberation in which she believed.

Notes

1. F.W.S.B., 'Woman in Germany', *The New Generation*, vol. 12, September 1933, pp. 99–100.
2. F.W. Stella Browne, 'Are we safer?', *The New Generation*, vol. 12, June 1933, p. 64.
3. F.W.S.B., 'Woman in Germany'.
4. Browne, 'Are we safer?'
5. F.W.S.B., 'Woman in Germany'.
6. Browne, 'Are we safer?'
7. F.W.S.B., 'Eugenic problems and programmes', *The New Generation*, vol. 12, July 1933, p. 75.
8. F.W.S.B., 'Birth control in Asia', *The New Generation*, vol. 12, December 1933, p. 135.
9. F.W. Stella Browne, A.M. Ludovici, and Harry Roberts, *Abortion* (London: George Allen & Unwin Ltd, 1935), pp. 43.
10. F.W. Stella Browne, 'How the fight goes', F.W.S.B., 'Birth control in Scandinavia', *The New Generation*, vol. 12, February 1933, pp. 17–18, 29–30.
11. 'A zealous correspondent', Editorial, *The New Generation*, vol. 12, March 1933, p. 26.
12. Vega [F.W. Stella Browne], 'Aspects of population control', *Time and Tide*, 14 January 1933, p. 33.
13. F.W. Stella Browne, 'Housing and racial tragedies', *The Spectator*, 10 February 1933, p. 185.
14. Browne, 'How the fight goes'.
15. F.W. Stella Browne, Letter to the editor, *The Week-end Review*, 11 February 1933, p. 144.
16. Vega [F.W. Stella Browne], 'Modern France', *Time and Tide*, 25 March 1933, p. 355.
17. F.W. Stella Browne, 'A French example', *The Week-end Review*, 29 April 1933, p. 475.
18. 'Battersea meeting', *The New Generation*, vol. 12, April 1933, p. 38.

19. 'Highgate meeting', *The New Generation*, vol. 12, May 1933, p. 56.
20. 'South London Ethical', *The New Generation*, vol. 12, May 1933, p. 56.
21. F.W.S.B., 'Love's history', *The New Generation*, vol. 13, January 1934, p. 2.
22. F.W.S.B., 'Review: The child', *The New Generation*, vol. 12, May 1933, p. 56.
23. F.W.S.B., 'Review', *The New Generation*, vol. 12, August 1933, p. 90.
24. F.W.S.B., 'Eugenic problems and programmes', *The New Generation*, vol. 12, July 1933, p. 75.
25. F.W.S.B., 'Who is for liberty?', *The New Generation*, vol. 12, September 1933, pp. 103–4.
26. F.W.S.B., '*Holy Deadlock*: by A. P. Herbert', *Plan: for world order and progress*, vol. 1, no. 4, July 1934, p. 14.
27. F.W.S.B., 'The great divorce novel', *The New Generation*, vol. 13, July 1934, p. 76.
28. 'The psychology of agitation', *The New Generation*, vol. 12, December 1933, p. 134.
29. F.W.S.B., 'An international quarterly', *The New Generation*, vol. 12, December 1933, p. 134.
30. F.W.S.B., 'Birth control in Asia'.
31. F.W.S.B., 'Looking backwards', *The New Generation*, vol. 12, December 1933, p. 134.
32. 'Cosmopolis: historical' *c.* 1937, material relating to Cosmopolis in the Peter Wells papers, British Library Department of Manuscripts, Additional Manuscript 71235 [BL Add Ms 71235].
33. J. Stanley Eggleston, Organising Secretary, Federation of Progressive Societies and Individuals, to Vera Brittain, 14 October 1933, Vera Brittain papers, Archives and Research Collections, McMaster University Library, Hamilton, Ontario.
34. 'F.P.S.I.: Sex Reform Group' duplicated notice, *c.* December 1933, kindly given to me by Leslie Minchin.
35. Eggleston to Brittain, 14 October 1933, Brittain papers.
36. F.W.S.B., 'A report and a discussion', *The New Generation*, vol. 13, May 1934, pp. 54–5.
37. F.W. Stella Browne to Dr C.P. Blacker, 5 November 1933, 'NBCA: Deputation (to Ministry of Health) Subcommittee' (Miss Holland's files), Blacker papers, Wellcome Library, PP/CPB/C.3/3.
38. C.P. Blacker, Eugenics Society, to Miss Holland, National Birth Control Association, 'Confidential', 6 November 1933, PP/CPB/C.3/3.
39. Miss Holland, Acting Secretary, National Birth Control Association, to C.P. Blacker, Eugenics Society, 9 November 1933, PP/CPB/C.3/3.
40. Miss Holland, Acting Secretary, National Birth Control Association, to Miss F.W. Stella Browne, 9 November 1933, PP/CPB/C.3/3.

41. Jane Lewis, *Women in England 1870–1950* (Brighton: Wheatsheaf Press, 1984), p. 105.
42. F.W.S.B., 'How the fight goes', *The New Generation*, vol. 13, February 1934, p. 19.
43. F.W.S.B., 'Sterilization', *The New Generation*, vol.13, November 1934, pp. 126–7.
44. F.W. Stella Browne, 'Books', *Plan: For World Order and Progress*, vol. 2 no. 10, October 1935, p. 23.
45. 'The State as Biologist', *The New Generation*, vol. 13, March 1934, p. 29.
46. *Ethical Societies Chronicle*, 1930s.
47. F.W.S.B., 'Elmers End meeting', *The New Generation*, vol. 13, March 1934, p, 31.
48. 'Penge, Biggin Hill and Peckham meetings', *The New Generation*, vol. 13, April 1934, p. 39.
49. F.W.S.B., 'Lyceum Club debate', *The New Generation*, vol. 13, March 1934, pp. 28–9.
50. F.W.S.B., 'Lyceum Club debate'.
51. F.W.S.B., 'A report and a discussion', *The New Generation*, vol. 13, May 1934, pp. 54–5.
52. 'F.P.S.I. announcements', *Plan: For World Order and Progress*, vol. 1, no. 3, June 1934, p. 13.
53. F.W. Stella Browne, 'Cooperative women demand legalization of abortion', *The New Generation*, vol. 13, July 1934, pp. 76–7.
54. *The New Generation*, vol. 13, August 1934, p. 88.
55. Browne, 'Cooperative women demand legalization of abortion'.
56. *The New Generation*, vol. 13, July 1934, p. 80.
57. F.W. Stella Browne, 'The constructive case for abortion law reform', *Plan: For World Order and Progress*, vol. 1, no. 6, September 1934, pp. 8–10.
58. Winifred Holtby, *Women and a Changing Civilisation* (London: John Lane, The Bodley Head, 1934), p. [viii].
59. F.W.S.B., 'Review: *Women*: by Winifred Holtby', *Plan: For World Order and Progress*, vol. 1, no. 8, November 1934, p. 6.
60. C.P. Blacker to J.R. Baker, 17 April 1935, Eugenics Society Archives, Wellcome Library, SA/EUG/C.10.
61. C.P. Blacker to Janet Chance, 7 October 1935, SA/EUG/C.65.
62. F.W. Stella Browne, 'Real eugenics in Britain and Denmark', *Plan: For World Order and Progress*, vol. 2, no. 9, September 1935, pp. 15.
63. F.P.S.I. Sex Reform Group, 'The reform of sexual law and convention', *Plan: For World Order and Progress*, vol. 2, no. 1, January 1935, pp. 3–6.
64. For example, 'Solicitor', 'The FPSI Conference, as seen by a Conservative', *Plan: For World Order and Progress*, vol. 2, no. 9, September 1935, p. 6.
65. *Plan: For World Order and Progress*, vol. 2, no. 1.

66. 'Meetings', *Plan: For World Order and Progress*, vol. 2, no. 10, October 1935, pp. 10–11.
67. *The New Generation*, vol. 14, March 1935, p. 29.
68. 'Groups, branches and affiliations: Sex Reform Group', *Plan: For World Order and Progress*, vol. 2, no. 10, October 1935, p. 15.
69. Stella Browne, joint Group Leader of the Sex Reform Group of the FPSI, to the Society for the Protection of Science and Learning, 7 September 1935, Max Hodann file, Archives of the Society for the Protection of Science and Learning, Bodleian Library Oxford, file 501/4.
70. F.W. Stella Browne, 'Magnus Hirschfeld, Scientist and Humanitarian', Plan: For World Order and Progress, vol. 2 no. 7, July 1935, p. 15.
71. 'Groups, branches and affiliations: Sex Reform Group', *Plan: For World Order and Progress*, vol. 2, no. 10, October 1935, pp. 14–15.
72. F.W.S.B., 'News from Norway', *Plan: For World Order and Progress*, vol. 2, no. 10, October 1935, p. 23.
73. Stella Browne to Havelock Ellis, 25 November 1935, Havelock Ellis papers in the Department of Manuscripts, British Library, Additional Manuscript 70539 [BL Add Ms 70539].
74. F.W. Stella Browne, 'Books', *Plan: For World Order and Progress*, vol. 2, no. 10, October 1935, p. 22.
75. 'Names of those invited to Dr Joan Malleson's Conference, 1935 ...', 'ALRA pre-1949 material', Abortion Law Reform Association Archives, Wellcome Library, SA/ALR/A.2/1. Janet Chance's chronology of abortion law reform in her scrapbook mentions '1935 Joan Malleson's meeting' but no further details, SA/ALR/B.1.
76. Joan Malleson to Miss Tuker, 12 April 1936, The Women's Library, London Metropolitan University.
77. 'Names of those invited to Dr Joan Malleson's Conference, 1935 ...', 'ALRA pre-1949 material', SA/ALR/A.2/1.
78. 'Summary of Discussion held at Ridgeways 24th January 1936', SA/ALR/B.1.
79. Malleson to Tuker, 12 April 1936.
80. Minutes of the Annual General Meeting 13 June 1935, London School of Economics, LSE/Fabian Society/C.42.
81. Fabian Summer School: Visitors' Book, 17 August 1935, LSE/Fabian Society/G.11.
82. F.W. Stella Browne, 'Light at Leicester', *The New Generation*, vol. 14, November 1935, pp. 124–6.
83. Correspondence between George Allen & Unwin Ltd and Harry Roberts, author, concerning publication of *Abortion* by Stella Browne, Roberts and others, Allen & Unwin Archives, University of Reading Library, RUL MS 3282 AUC 46/13.

84. Robert Latou Dickinson to Stella Hanau Bloch, 7 November 1937, Stella Bloch Hanau papers in the Sophia Smith Collection, Smith College, Northampton MA, Box 1 folder 51.
85. George Allen & Unwin Ltd to Roberts, 13 February 1935, RUL MS 3282 AUC 46/13.
86. George Allen & Unwin Ltd to Roberts, 19 February 1935, RUL MS 3282 AUC 46/13.
87. George Allen & Unwin Ltd to Roberts, 24 May 1935, RUL MS 3282 AUC 46/13.
88. Harry Roberts to George Allen & Unwin, undated, received 21 September 1935, RUL MS 3282 AUC 46/13.
89. George Allen & Unwin Ltd to Roberts, 18 March 1935, RUL MS 3282 AUC 46/13.
90. Browne to Ellis, 26 April 1936, BL Add Mss 70539.
91. Roberts to Unwin, 14 March 1935, and receipt for advance on royalties, 29 October 1935, RUL MS 3282 AUC 46/13.
92. F.W. Stella Browne, A.M. Ludovici, and Harry Roberts, *Abortion*, (London: George Allen & Unwin Ltd, 1935), p. 13.
93. Browne *et al.*, *Abortion*, pp. 13–29.
94. Browne *et al.*, *Abortion*, pp. 29–32.
95. Browne *et al.*, *Abortion*, pp. 34–6.
96. Browne *et al.*, *Abortion*, pp. 33–4.
97. Browne *et al.*, *Abortion*, pp. 37–8.
98. Browne *et al.*, *Abortion*, pp. 40–1.
99. Browne *et al.*, *Abortion*, pp. 43–4
100. Browne *et al.*, *Abortion*, p. 45.
101. Browne *et al.*, *Abortion*, pp. 44–6.
102. Browne to Ellis, 25 November 1935, BL Add Mss 70539.
103. Browne to Ellis, 26 April 1936, BL Add Mss 70539.
104. Browne to Ellis, 25 November 1935, BL Add Mss 70539.
105. Stella Browne to Max Hodann, 25 July 1946, Max Hodann papers in the Swedish Labour Movement Archives and Library, Stockholm.
106. George Allen & Unwin Ltd to Roberts, 24 December 1935, RUL MS 3282 AUC 46/13.
107. Editorial Leader, *The New Generation*, vol. 14, December 1935, pp. 133–4.
108. Alec Craig, 'Books', *Plan: For World Order and Progress*, vol. 2, no. 12, December 1935, pp. 17–18.
109. T.F. Fox, 'The legalisation of abortion', *The Spectator*, 24 January 1936, ALRA early press-cuttings, 1932–1939, SA/ALR/E.39
110. 'Abortion', *The Lancet*, vol. 2, 1935, p. 1446.
111. 'Abortion', *British Medical Journal*, vol. 1, 1936, p. 161.
112. 'Abortion', *The Lancet*, vol. 2, 1935, p. 1446.

113. Edward F. Griffith, 'Reviews of books. *Abortion*, by Stella Browne, A.M. Ludovici, and Dr Harry Roberts', *Marriage Hygiene*, vol, II, no. 3, February 1936, p. 345.
114. M.N., 'Review: *Abortion* by F.W. Stella Browne, A.M. Ludovici and Dr. Harry Roberts', *The Shield*, 5th series vol. IV, no. 4, July 1936, pp. 188–9.
115. F.W. Stella Browne, 'Winifred Holtby: in memoriam', *Plan: For World Order and Progress*, vol. 2, no. 11, November 1935, p. 21.
116. F.W. Stella Browne, 'Do we English understand?', *Plan: For World Order and Progress*, vol. 2, no. 12, December 1935, pp. 15–16.

10

The Years of Triumph

The abdication crisis may have been in full swing, but Stella seems to have paid it little heed. By the beginning of 1936, abortion law reform had moved from being shunned even within the birth control movement to a widely discussed issue. The BMA Committee Report recommended legalisation of abortion in certain clearly defined therapeutic circumstances.[1] The Joint Council on Midwifery set up a committee to investigate illegal abortion, although its agenda was prevention rather than changing existing law.[2] These developments opened up a space into which Stella and her colleagues could advance their own more radical opinions.

On 24 January, a discussion took place at Ridgeways' Café between the group of long-term lay women campaigners for abortion law reform: Stella, Frida Laski, Gerda Guy, Bertha Lorsignol, Alice Jenkins, Dora Russell and Janet Chance. While sensible of the need for medical backing, they were taking the initiative and proposing to ask Joan Malleson and Maurice Newfield, socialist doctors sympathetic to their cause, to call, or authorise the group to call, 'a delegate conference before which shall be laid proposals for the basis of the proposed Abortion Society'. The group were agreed that their aim was to repeal the existing law and to substitute one 'freeing the medical profession from all legal restrictions except those required by medical or humanitarian considerations'. The only restriction on which they were clear was to forbid 'all unqualified persons' from performing abortions. Other issues, such as a second medical opinion and where abortions should take place, were discussed, but the group felt that the 'case for making these part of a law did not commend itself', leaving these requirements to 'the gradual education of the profession and the public by experience'.

The meeting conceded that they would consider compromise if it would 'bring substantial gain in exchange', but they were determined to press their policy, both because it represented their true case, and because it was 'good policy to ask in excess of present opinion; one can always compromise later'. The gathering of 'statistics of the amount and dangers of illegal abortion' from various sources was recommended, and 'the present racketeering in abortion should be exposed'.[3]

The group got moving very rapidly. A circular letter was sent out at the beginning of March by the 'provisional executive committee', consisting of Janet Chance (Chairman), Stella (Vice-Chairman), Alice Jenkins (Secretary), Eleanor Hawarden, Bertha Lorsignol, Frida Laski, Dora Russell, Gerda Guy and Hilda Browning. This proposed founding the Abortion Law Reform Association (ALRA) to advocate the reforms discussed at the Ridgeways meeting: repeal of the existing law, legalisation of abortion by the medical profession subject to medical and humanitarian considerations, and the penalisation of abortion by the unqualified.[4]

Even at this critical moment in the fortunes of the campaign for abortion law reform, it was part of the wider struggle to which Stella was devoted. She had been present at 'A True Feast of Reason' at the annual dinner of the Eugenics Society, at which Professor Julian Huxley spoke on 'Eugenics and the Social Environment'. In this 'epoch-making' speech, he addressed

> eutelegenesis, sterilization, social reconstruction, drastic Divorce Law Reform, international peace; for how can the most sensitive, intelligent and responsible people be persuaded or compelled to produce children to die in clouds of fluorine or torrents of thermite or in the possible *sauve-qui-peut* of a few maddened and crippled survivors?

While Stella still did 'not agree on certain details' with the Eugenics Society, she found its 'efforts and influence ... among the most encouraging symptoms in the world today'.[5]

Unfortunately, as Stella wrote to Havelock Ellis in April, 'work for Causes, though not I hope & trust, fruitless for the Causes, does not bring in cash, & the world is on a cash basis'.[6] She was in her usual financial straits, possibly even more severe than usual. Hodann asked the editors of *Marriage Hygiene*, 'Can you, of course, pay something to Miss Browne if she is translating?'[7] (they could not).[8] It is thus hardly surprising that she 'dressed in aggressively unfashionable clothes'[9] – she probably did not have much choice.

Because of these straits, Stella was sitting 'among the debris of a – *move*' in late April when she wrote to Ellis. She was leaving the flat in King's Mansions, Lawrence Street, Chelsea, where she had been living since before the First World War, and moving 'quite nearby' to 45 Paulton Square, where, however, she would be 'in *very exiguous*' conditions, '*with my sister* (!!) – for some months at least.' The new accommodation would not have 'these unspeakable 53 stairs', and it did have 'a decent warm water supply', plus 'a fine tree-y garden to the Square', but 'if I had been in a position to go anywhere on my own I would *never* have *agreed, for a month even*, to this arrangement! ... Well – I hope I can stand Sylvia until I can find some other place.' Just one of the difficulties caused by this domestic rearrangement was that 'my sister refuses utterly to have a telephone installed at 45! At this juncture in the work!'. Even in these adverse conditions, she added a postscript concerning 'the new Icelandic law on Abortion',[10] on which she reported at the ALRA Committee meeting the next day.[11]

On 15 May, the planned conference took place at Conway Hall. A number of distinguished figures in medicine, politics, feminism and the birth control struggle were present, and letters of support read from well-known names. During the first question session, Dr Binnie Dunlop of the Malthusian League queried the inclusion of 'humanitarian considerations' as a potential restriction on abortion. Stella pointed out that, first

> It might be that a woman, and probably an unmarried woman, who seriously wished to bring her child to term and have it, might have undue pressure put on her by relatives and others to have an abortion performed.

Second, 'many women in the pregnant state are unstable'; having induced 'humane and kindly doctors' to meet their 'frantic wish', they then turned around and said 'Oh why didn't you leave me alone?' She therefore considered that women should have a period of grace to think over the decision.[12]

In her own speech from the platform, Stella opened by remarking 'What a great satisfaction it is today, after 21 years of effort, to find this cause has come into the Daily Press and public discussion.' She gave a brief overview of 'the definite advance' made by some other countries. She hoped that no one present would say '*"Do not rush the M.P.s". My friends, if we ask very little, we shall get very much less.*'

She then went on to argue that there were two groups of women concerned. First, those who 'would prefer to have a child or children, but for serious disadvantages'. If civilisation wanted the children, it would have to 'provide that better state of things'. Second, there were the women who did not want children, even though 'we have been told again and again that there are no such women!' It was 'a crime against humanity to force them to become mothers'. '*Let them choose*', Stella demanded:

> For what is this ban on abortion? It is a sexual taboo, it is the terror that women should experiment and enjoy freely, without punishment. It is a survival of the veiled face, of the barred window and the locked door, of burning, branding, mutilation and stoning; of all the pain and fear inflicted ever since the grip of ownership and superstition came down on women, thousands of years ago.

Even in the present day, there were women who were 'such slaves in their souls, that when they hear our demand, their first thought is – "Oh, but every woman would become immoral if they were permitted to have this relief"'.

It was not a 'struggle between men and women, but between the prisoners of the past and the forward-looking minds'. Stella appealed

> Will you help, so that this terror shall be lifted from women, from love and from sex which should be beautiful and inspiring, but cannot be when two people have this ghastly shadow of undesired conception at the back of their minds the whole time. Will you help to make the world more fit to live in, and humanity better worth life and love?[13]

Following this meeting the committee moved ahead with further plans for action. A subcommittee (including Stella) was formed to edit the proceedings of the conference. Potential sympathisers were solicited for support. Press-cuttings were to be sent to Stella for replies to be composed where appropriate (Mme Lorsignol would type these up, which suggests that typing was not among Stella's skills). Meetings were to be arranged with appropriate organisations, and a list of ALRA speakers (including Stella) was made available.[14] While various distinguished men were vice-presidents or on the Medico-Legal Consultative Committee, the latter was purely consultative: 'the *direction* of our policy is to be in the hands of a committee of laywomen, who are, after all, those most concerned in the great cause'.[15]

The picture was not all rosy. There was 'news of a definite stage in officially sanctioned reaction in the U.S.S.R',[16] unanimously deplored by the ALRA Executive,[17] although also the introduction of 'new, constructive and comprehensive laws in Iceland'. This retreat from women's rights to abortion in Russia would, Stella surmised, 'be given full publicity' by 'reactionaries and enemies of women', while the more progressive trends in Iceland and Latvia would be ignored.[18] She expressed herself even more forcefully in a private letter: 'the disaster (for it is nothing less!) of the Russian *volteface*', she hoped would 'spur our cause on to victory though greater awareness & efforts'.[19]

ALRA kept Stella busy. In June, she met Dr Aleck Bourne, a sympathetic gynaecologist involved with the Socialist Medical Association.[20] She produced a report on cases of criminal abortion and the sentences imposed and, at the July meeting of the ALRA Executive, put forward a list of suitable Parliamentary questions to ask on the topic.[21] Presumably, it was with this support that Mrs Tate, MP, spoke 'admirably in the House' on the issues.[22] A Parliamentary subcommittee consisting of Stella and Mrs Cobb was formed. Stella was also tagged to participate in a debate arranged by the Women Citizens' Association.[23]

Stella remained active in the Fabian Society, speaking up at the annual general meeting in June on a variety of administrative matters.[24] She also attended the Society's summer school at Normanhurst Court, near Battle in Sussex, for a whole week in August, describing herself in the visitors' book as 'journalist, translator, agitator'.[25] Although her name was not specifically mentioned, the Summer School Log Book records that on 20 August, during a talk on Sweden's Labour Government', there was 'a long digression on the Population Policy of the Swedish Socialist Party', which 'prompted a most interesting and restrained discussion of "Community Control over Population"'.[26] It seems unlikely that Stella sat silent while this was in progress. She also retained her connection with the BSSSP,[27] much regretting that she could not attend their At Home in early October as she was 'so very rushed'. A suggested speaking date of 23 March 1937 was impossible for her – her only free Thursday in the second half of the month would be the 30th.[28]

News of ALRA was reaching across the Atlantic: Margaret Sanger wrote to Janet Chance about this 'new organization of which you are chairman', commenting that

> As Stella Browne has long been interested in such and has watched the types of reforms in different countries she doubtless knows more than any other woman, and is informed as to both abuses and possible harmfulness.[29]

Stella herself wrote to Norman Himes, the American birth control historian, expecting that he would 'have heard of this new organization of ours', of which a report was being sent to him personally. She conveyed her '*sincere gratitude & admiration*' for his magnificent work', *The Medical History of Contraception* (1936). She wanted to tell him 'how very much I admire it, & what a service it is, not only to the special movement which interests us both, but also to the general enlightenment of the world & the appreciation of actual human evolution'. It was 'good to see the way your country is going ahead in sex matters, in spite of all your economic & political troubles': it seemed to her that 'You will be able to carry on a bigger torch than we could, if – as seems "not unlikely"!! Europe *is* done for!'[30] (The recent outbreak of civil war in Spain must have added to Stella's gloom at international political prospects.) Himes, who had known Stella many years before during his 'student days in England', was very pleased to receive her 'high opinion ... after so long a silence'. He suggested getting a news report about ALRA into *Marriage Hygiene*, and also hoped to meet the following year when he expected to visit England.[31]

Even given her absorption in the setting up of ALRA and the various activities that involved, it seems unlikely that Stella would have not been doing something for Spain following the outbreak of the Civil War, but no evidence has been uncovered of her participation.

ALRA activity continued at a brisk pace. By September 1936, Stella was reporting on the formation of a Library;[32] in the following month, a Publications subcommittee was set up and Stella herself was to prepare a pamphlet on 'foreign aspects of abortion law'.[33] By the November meeting of the Executive, she had made a visit to Bristol resulting in 'successful contacts & meetings'[34] (and the publication of an article by her in *Bristol Labour Weekly*),[35] and also produced 'an interesting translation from "Isvestia" on Abortion'.[36] She also produced a brief report for *The New Generation* about the achievements of ALRA in the less than a year it had been going, in which she paid generous tribute to her co-workers and allies, and exhorted sympathisers to write letters to the Press and their MPs, and to suggest speaking engagements. 'Much, very much, is still to do', she concluded.[37] Her strenuous activities were not without adverse repercussions on her health: the National Council for Equal Citizenship held an Education Conference on Abortion Law Reform in Liverpool on 3 December at which 'Miss Browne's address was read, owing to her absence through illness.'[38]

In spite of this flurry of activities on behalf of ALRA, Stella clearly had other demanding commitments, leading to a delayed arrival at the October meeting of the Executive.[39] The FPSI was undergoing various upheavals during the autumn of 1936 and, on 14 November, she was elected to the Council of what had become the Federation of Progressive Societies and Individuals (FPSI) being the British section of Cosmopolis (an organisation set up to promote the ideals expressed in the works of H.G. Wells – in particular, internationalism).[40] However, early in the following January she wrote to the Chairman that 'she wished to resign from the Council, as she had little time to attend meetings', but the Executive asked her to reconsider.[41] Her election to Council and the reluctance to accept her resignation suggest that she was not merely a marginalised agitator for a specific and not entirely acceptable cause. Although some may have found her 'eccentric, somewhat weird in appearance ... aggressively unfashionable', indeed, a 'caricature "bluestocking"', there were clearly circles in which she commanded respect, in which her alleged 'propensity to tell dirty stories in a voice like a foghorn' might have been easy to overlook, or even an asset.[42]

The pace of her activities for ALRA did not let up. In January, she reported that she had managed to persuade both Cicely Hamilton and H.N. Brailsford to become vice-presidents. She had helped the sympathetic Conservative MP Robert Boothby draft a Parliamentary question. She promised to arrange for the typing of twelve copies of her summary of Foreign Laws of Abortion, and to organise the addition to the Library of duplicate copies of cheaper books. With Alice Jenkins, she had an interview with Mrs Wignall, the North Regional Secretary of the National Council for Equal Citizenship, during which they heard a debrief about the Liverpool conference. There was a promise to try to arrange an autumn tour of abortion law reform lectures.[43] In February 1937, she and Janet Chance opened a discussion at the Sex Education Centre founded by Chance in King's Cross, on the subject of 'The Disciplines implicit in Sexual Freedom'.[44] At the end of March, she was scheduled to speak to the BSSSP, although the day before she wrote to the Secretary that 'I have a very tiresome internal chill – I don't think it is flu but of course it may be', and it is not certain that she was able to fulfil this commitment.[45]

Following *Tribune*'s offer to publish something on abortion law reform, Stella shortly completed a 700–1000 word piece:[46] which does not seem to have appeared, although a similar piece eventually featured over Janet Chance's name.[47] Stella did get a letter into the *Tribune* in May greeting the setting up of the Interdepartmental Committee on abortion under the chairmanship of Norman Birkett.[48] She also managed to get a report about the latter into the Bombay-published international journal *Marriage Hygiene*. In this, she pointed out that 'wide terms of reference ... afford great opportunities of public education and humane agitation'.[49] She spoke at Norwich sometime during the spring of 1937, and at meetings of the Friday Club and the South London Secular Society, and had also had an interview with Ernest Thurtle MP, about a question in Parliament on the Maternal Mortality Report.[50] She was also firing off letters to the press:[51] the *Spectator* published one on the appointment of the Birkett Committee, which, 'After years of effort for reform' she 'welcome[d] ... with congratulations and thanks',[52] although in private correspondence she commented that 'Investigation and Action don't necessarily hang together!'[53] She and Robert Boothby were in correspondence about the Committee, to which she had applied to give evidence as a private person, while suggesting a suitable official ALRA delegation. Besides all this, she was in touch with international sympathisers.[54]

Her renown was such that Margaret Sanger included Stella in a list of British luminaries of the birth control and sex reform movements whom she hoped that Edith How-Martyn of the Birth Control International Information Centre could arrange for the American gynaecologist and sex researcher Dr Le Mon Clark to meet.[55] There is a hint that the two women had had some personal contact after the bitter breach of 1923. Sanger described Stella's 'faintly florid face, hair never quite white, and indefatigable vivacity' as being the same 'a quarter of a century later' as at their first meeting in 1913: 'Many women in causes are like that: something in their spirit keeps them forever young.'[56] Perhaps they met during one or other of Sanger's visits to London in the mid-1930s,[57] although no details are recorded.

In spite of this whirlwind of activity, Stella somehow managed to keep up reviewing for *Plan*,[58] and to translate Max Hodann's *History of Modern Morals* (never published in German) into English for publication by Heinemann. It was no rushed hack job and more than just a translation. Hodann expressed 'particular thanks to Miss Stella Browne of London, not only for the English translation of my work, but also for her many valuable annotations and information on the movement in Great Britain.'[59] These not only added a good deal from her knowledge of the British birth control movement and its struggles, but included mentions of her wider interests in sexual research and reform. Reference to recent researches on the prevalence of masturbation, she noted, vindicated her 1915 comments in 'Sexual Variety and Variability among Women' on 'self-excitement and solitary enjoyment' as 'inevitable in any strongly developed sexual life.'[60] She also included some comments on the divorce law and the state of marriage.[61] One reviewer commented 'the English rendering of the text is admirably accomplished (usually a rare achievement in a translation of German scientific books)'.[62] Alec Craig, in his review in *Plan*, remarked that the 'translator's notes containing a good deal of "late wire and stable-door" information are a valuable addition'.[63]

Meanwhile, matters were getting ever more hectic on the abortion law reform front. In a letter to *The Yorkshire Observer*, Stella emphasised that, up to twelve weeks from conception, the operation was 'comparatively safe', '[t]he terrible toll of disease and death ... was largely due to delay'. She emphasised the class and economic angle: increasing legal penalties would not eradicate abortion but only make it more expensive.[64]

She applied to the Birkett Committee to give evidence in person.[65] The Committee invited ALRA to send a memorandum and report, and the Executive set up a subcommittee, while Stella was to continue to make contact with MPs.[66] She was evidently having considerable success since, on 10 June, she organised a House of Commons meeting on abortion with Robert Boothby in the chair, to consider evidence to be given.[67] During June, she addressed meetings at Lambeth and East Willesden (both enthusiastic)[68] and, in the following month, she spoke in St John's Wood and West Leyton.[69]

There was a 'special discussion meeting' of members of ALRA on 28 June,[70] followed by the annual general meeting on 29 June,[71] a day on which Stella also managed to fit in dinner with Norman and Vera Himes, who were in London.[72] She was 'look[ing] forward greatly to a talk' with them, and was also hoping for 'a few minutes' private talk ... just to you both', and looked forward to thanking them, for some unspecified favour,[73] unless she simply meant what they were 'doing across the Atlantic for sex reform'.[74] Social engagements clearly had to be carefully carved out of a busy life: 'I am engaged tomorrow and Wednesday evening',[75] 'I don't think I can be with you as early as 5 that day'.[76] In spite of her concern, expressed to the Himeses, that 'we and Europe' might 'blow up before your departure!',[77] Stella continued the immediate struggle. During August, she managed a single day at the Fabian Summer School at Normanhurst Court.[78]

The Birkett Committee informed her that

> the Committee wished to raise no objection to her submitting memoranda adding a few further comments on the view presented in her book, on the situation as regards foreign countries, and the situation as it affects individual women today.[79]

Stella's memorandum was typed and circulated to the Committee on 30 October. While her essay 'The Right to Abortion' contained 'the main substance of the case', the intervening two years had seen 'events – some unfavourable to the recognition of that right, and others strongly favourable – which made it desirable to face certain objections, and to emphasise certain facts'.

She contrasted 'the *volte face* of Soviet Russia', the new anti-abortion decree of June 1936, with the recent Catalonia reformed law on abortion, which gave 'frank and emphatic recognition of the individuality of the woman and the quality of motherhood'. She argued that

> we are only now beginning to understand and experiment with either surgical or pharmaceutical abortion, under conditions of cleanliness and care, unhampered by secrecy, illegality, or the influence of fear. *We cannot be sure that terminations of pregnancy on social grounds or for reasons of individual psychology... are necessarily always or generally harmful in themselves.*

Opponents of reforming the law had claimed 'mental and emotional injuries produced by abortions'; but what, asked Stella, 'of the mental and emotional injuries of profoundly unwanted motherhood?' She pointed out the distinction between 'maternity feared and avoided on account of external things' – for which the solution was changes in social attitudes, and financial provision for mother and child – and 'maternity which is repugnant in itself'.

Stella mentioned three cases well-known to her, in which 'repeated terminations of pregnancy have not lead to the physical and mental ruin so often predicted'. The second case was 'past the climacteric', had had an 'intellectually and sexually active life', had 'borne no children, but has had at least three early terminations of pregnancy', yet had 'suffered neither peritonitis, nor septicaemia, nor melancholia as a result'. (This case was surely Stella herself.) Other women, Stella argued,

> especially among those self-supporting in professions and skilled occupations, or of inherited independent means, who could give similar instances of the benefits of skilled and voluntary abortion, to their whole subsequent lives, were they not deterred from testifying, by a convention which itself creates misery and mortality.

She concluded by mentioning that she had been studying the question of abortion for twenty years.[80]

On 13 October, the ALRA delegation – consisting of Stella, Janet Chance, Joan Malleson, and ALRA's legal advisor, Gerald Thesiger – gave evidence to the Birkett Committee at the Ministry of Health, and discussed questions arising from ALRA's pre-submitted memoranda.[81] Lady Rhys Williams of the National Birthday Trust Fund (not in sympathy with the aims of ALRA) wrote at the top of her 'Points re Abortion Law Reform Assn. Memo', 'Unexpected appearance of Miss Browne'.[82] This may simply reflect the fact that Stella was not originally part of the suggested ALRA delegation. Or it may indicate that Stella did not look like Lady Rhys Williams' previous image of a wild sex-radical.

At the Committee's next meeting, 17 November, she attended alone for interview. The formal panoply and the prospect of speaking alone before a committee of the great and good, most of them relatively or extremely hostile to her position, did not cow her. She was, of course, used to addressing audiences and dealing with hostile responses. The Chairman of the Committee, Norman Birkett, was a judge, who appears to have been generally sympathetic to many of the reforms which Stella herself advocated. However, whatever his personal sentiments, he conducted the proceedings, and the writing up of the Report, with appropriate judicial impartiality.[83]

The first point was to establish Stella's qualification for speaking on medical matters. She conceded that she had 'no first-hand medical knowledge' and had 'never practised medicine' or 'trained as a doctor'. However, she did have 'a certain amount of knowledge by personal experience of what modern medicine can do', as well has having 'received the confidences of a great many women of all classes and ages'. Their experiences, and information from medical professionals, indicated to her that 'the operation is not necessarily fatal or even injurious'. She then played her shocking trump card as to her right and her qualifications to speak on abortion:

> I have also – and I say this as a matter of public duty – the knowledge in my own person that, if abortion were necessarily fatal or injurious, I should not now be here before you.

The transcript of the interview does not record gasps or horrified silence, but surely some response intervened before Norman Birkett resumed the interview with the phrase 'You will quite understand that nobody would challenge the sincerity of your motives', before moving on to elucidate her points about the inadequate state of medical knowledge.

After a mutual agreement had been reached that her point was that 'the data upon that topic from the medical point of view is inadequate to form a conclusion at the moment', Birkett moved on to ask 'what first excited your interest in the subject of the right to abortion?' Stella responded 'the unnatural sufferings and complications in the lives of women', both 'working women, and women of the professional class', which she had encountered when librarian at Morley College. He then suggested that in her book and her memorandum she struck 'what I may term the ethical note': 'Yes, absolutely', Stella replied. She was also, she went on, coming at the problem from 'the side of human happiness, or, if you like to call it so, the hedonistic side, because I think happiness is a very important element in human life'. When presented with the 'absurd case' of all women refusing to have children and the race dying out, Stella commented that it 'rather depends on the prospects before the race ... if all women were unwilling to bear children it would be much better that no children should be born'. Birkett then returned to establishing her qualifications for discussing abortion in other countries: Stella admitted that she had never been to Soviet Russia, Catalonia, or Uruguay, but knew 'conditions in Germany very well, and ... a certain amount about the conditions in Scandinavia'.

Mr de Montmorency (secretary to the Committee, representing the Ministry of Health) asked what prospect of success she thought a Parliamentary Bill would have. Stella, realistically, thought 'at first it would undoubtedly be defeated, but it would arouse great interest, and ... a large amount of more or less inarticulate support'. She thought it hard to judge 'how much steam' there was behind the movement, but that 'it is astonishing how much steam does gather when people are able to speak freely, and not by any means among women alone'.

Following further inquisition by Committee members as to her knowledge of developments abroad, she displayed great familiarity with the situation in Iceland, the Chief Medical Officer there ('writes English very well'), and how to contact him. She also offered to endeavour to obtain further information about Catalonia, prompting Sir Ewan to ask 'Is the argument that what is good enough for Catalonia is good enough for us?' To this, Stella returned the question 'Are you asking me to wave the Red Flag, because I am quite willing to do so, but I am afraid it may be a little irrelevant.' She added 'But please do not let me face an anti-red pact, ladies and gentlemen.' The discussion moved on to Scandinavia, and then to Stella's own views on women's 'right to love', married or unmarried, and on their right to bear children even if unmarried: 'I stand by every word I have written', Stella replied.

'I dare say', Birkett went on, 'that you have considered very carefully what an amendment of the abortion law might do to what I will call, for want of a better term, the ordinary morality of the sexes.' 'That is a very wide question', Stella answered. 'Does the Committee wish me to state my definition of the term "morality"? I shall be delighted to do so, but it might take up a good deal of your time.' 'You tempt us very much', Birkett responded (is it fanciful to detect an almost flirtatious note here, or merely the skilled elicitation of a brilliant advocate?) However, to clarify, he understood that 'the ordinary accepted standard in that regard has no meaning or weight with you at all?' Might she, Stella responded, 'answer that a little more widely?'

In response to his permission, she gave her credo:

> I think there is a virtue of sexual dignity, which, incidentally I may say, is a very rare thing. I think also there is a virtue of sexual modesty, which is a rare and a beautiful thing. I do not think that to refrain from sexual intercourse out of fear, whether fear of the unknown, fear of venereal disease, fear of a baby, fear of ridicule, or fear of damages in the Divorce Court, or anything like that, is in any way a virtue. I think that sexual intercourse between those who love each other and understand each other is the most beautiful and valuable thing in life.

– a statement which seldom can have been heard in the context of a government enquiry.

Lady Baldwin (founder of the National Birthday Trust Fund, wife of the former Conservative Prime Minister Stanley Baldwin) asked whether she was not 'debasing the word "love"'. Stella responded:

> I do not think I am debasing the word, but I will admit that love is probably rather rare. It is a very big thing, and rather rare. I should perhaps use instead the expression, 'the right to happiness in a mutual sexual relationship which involved affection and respect'. Unfortunately one cannot have affection and respect to order.

Lady Rhys Williams and Sir Comyns Berkeley (distinguished medical man who had served on the BMA abortion investigation) interrogated her about the hypothetical financial practicalities of provision.

Birkett then asked whether, if 'the common weal of the community – demanded that the abortion law ... should not be so extended because of the evils which might attend it, would you be quite content or would you go on agitating?' Quite predictably, Stella replied that 'I should definitely go on agitating' and asked to make a personal statement. She wanted to make it entirely clear that what she was advocating was 'a change in the law, and not a breach of the law', as she had seen 'so much ... dreadful harm done to women by illegal abortions'. In addition, 'all those present will know that the severe laws which exist do not prevent constant breaches'. Birkett was concerned at the potential effect 'from a racial point of view, the community point of view, and the national point of view' of making any wide extension of the law. Stella pointed out that other things might also be included in the picture she envisaged, such as 'wiser and fairer marriage laws', the removal of the stigma of illegitimacy, and 'much wider provision for contraception'. Birkett suggested that 'activity upon those lines might achieve success rather more quickly than the lines you are now advocating': 'Well', responded Stella, 'I rather like the most difficult task.'

Mr Bentley Purchase (Coroner for London Northern District) queried whether a stigma could be removed by Act of Parliament: no, agreed Stella, 'that was a clumsy expression ... But the expression of a stigma can be removed by Act of Parliament, can it not?' She concurred with Purchase's suggestion that it would take time to change public opinion, as well as the law.

Returning to abortion, Mr de Montmorency asked whether she had any idea of the extent to which advantage would be taken of the legislation she advocated. At first, she thought, the uptake would be among 'a certain number of more or less intelligent and responsible women' but that, as downtrodden working women 'became aware that they were entitled to the operation', they would 'take advantage of it with gratitude, as they are doing in respect of birth control facilities'. Dr M'Gonigle (Medical Officer of Health for Stockton-on-Tees, and a Labour sympathiser) brought up the lurking spectre of population anxieties: might not such an Act finally 'lower appreciably the birth rate?' Stella did not think so: under the existing situation, many women were in fact 'rendered sterile by clumsy and dirty attempts to procure abortion'. Lady Rhys Williams enquired as to what might Stella's response be 'if it were shown fairly conclusively that it may be harmful': '"harmless"', Stella commented, was 'a very relative term ... a great many operations – not necessarily abortions or even operations on the generative system – are not harmless, but are probably the lesser evil'.

Mrs Thurtle, an old colleague from the days of the Workers' Birth Control Group, and wife of the sympathetic Labour MP Ernest Thurtle, asked Stella whether it really was, in her view, 'only women driven quite desperate' who sought illegal abortion, or might some women resort to 'these attempts ... just because they did not want another child'. Stella replied that 'probably the largest number of abortions take place among women who are in a pretty desperate economic situation', but that statistics on the matter could not be obtained while it was 'under the shadow of the criminal law'.

Would it not be better, argued Lady Ruth Balfour (vice-president of the National Council of Women), to spend the money on 'better social amenities ... creches, day nurseries, family allowances'. Stella concurred that, if these pressures were removed, 'a great many women who now resort to abortion would gladly have children'. However, even so, there would remain 'a residue of women who would definitely not want children'. While she had encountered cases of women who, having tried to get rid of a child when they became pregnant, were glad to have it once it was born, she also know of women who bore a continued grudge against the child.

Dorothy Thurtle intervened once more to point out that 'nature, left to itself, will produce far too many children, more children than an ordinary mother now-a-days will bear'. Stella felt that Thurtle had put 'the case of the average married woman' so well that she did not need to say more, but added

> may I say this? I know it is a dreadful confession, but I have never met the normal woman. I have seen a lot about her in print, and heard a lot about her on platforms and even in conferences, but I have never met her. Women are different from one another in so many ways.

Lady Ruth Balfour came back to ask whether 'every woman wished to limit her family?' Stella had actually heard 'women say that they were sorry that economic considerations made it impossible for them not to have eight children' – but did not know whether they were telling the truth.

Norman Birkett then pointed out that 'our time is almost done', and wanted to ensure that Stella did not go away without mentioning any other matter about which she would like to say a word. Stella responded that she very much appreciated his kindness, and would like to make just one point very briefly. She understood that there had been suggestions of 'getting some sort of mass evidence regarding the non-injurious or injurious effects of abortion on large numbers of women'. She did not think that, under the existing law, this would be possible. While women would 'speak very frankly in privacy to those whom they feel they can trust, the average working woman before a distinguished assembly of this kind would be struck absolutely dumb.'

Birkett thanked her for sending in her book and memorandum, and coming to give evidence, and Stella withdrew. The subsequent exchanges among the Committee members are not recorded.[84] Stella and Janet Chance both spoke at the ALRA members' meeting in early December on their impressions of their hearings by the Committee, but no details remain.[85]

Meanwhile, Stella was continuing the struggle in other directions. It was suggested that she might publish a pamphlet on the legal position of abortion in other countries, and she undertook to approach Allen & Unwin.[86] However, this turned out to be one of several doomed publishing possibilities. American gynaecologist and sexologist Robert Latou Dickinson rejected a proposal for the US publication of 'Stella Browne's Abortion with the Ludovici handicap'.[87] In November, the ALRA Executive was approached by Dr David Glass of the London School of Economics about his book in preparation on foreign abortion laws. Stella 'was willing for material she had collected to be at Dr Glass's disposal'.[88] She may have reckoned that a book by someone with Glass's institutional credibility might have wider circulation and achieve a greater impact than a pamphlet by someone already identified with the most radical of positions on abortion.[89]

She was keeping busy in other directions, being appointed to the ALRA Constitution subcommittee,[90] and undertaking to draft a resolution for Labour Women's Sections addressed by ALRA to send to headquarters for the Annual Conference scheduled for June 1938. She also, rather curiously, became a member of the Eugenics Society in February 1938.[91] This may have represented some kind of strategic alliance-cum-representation for ALRA on this influential body, although it is not mentioned in the ALRA minutes. It rather suggests that, in the late 1930s, progressive opinion did not see much similarity, if any, between the policies and activities of the British Eugenics Society (which had condemned Nazi antisemitic policies several years previously) and what was happening in Hitler's Germany, especially as there were no links between the society and the parties of the extreme Right such as the British Union of Fascists. Stella had not discarded her critical stance to some of the attitudes and proposals within the eugenics movement, but may well have been persuaded by C.P. Blacker's policy of strategic alliances and fostering of common interests with a wide range of groups, including the birth control movement, that it might prove a useful ally. Her membership was fairly transient, lapsing early in 1942,[92] possibly for financial rather than ideological reasons.

The world situation was weighing heavily on her. In March 1938, she wrote to Norman Himes:

> I so want to urge *all* our friends outside Europe, to keep on with the good work of general & social reform, all the harder. We here, are probably doomed – in this generation anyway. But let us at least feel we've lighted a torch!

She sent with this letter – 'for your information & your archives' – the ALRA Quarterly Newsletters for October and February, and (to be held as 'entirely *private & confidential until the Birkett Committee issues its report*') a copy of her own memorandum to the Committee. She feared that

> a lot of evidence will not reach them: *namely, material which could be supplied by women who have had the pluck & wits & the sheer good luck to experience what can be done by modern science for women, when science is used by dependable & humane doctors*.'[93]

There was an invitation from an old comrade, Dora Russell, to attend the Open Day of Beacon Hill, her progressive school, on 2 April. Stella regretted that she would be unable to come, 'much as I should have enjoyed it' (which may be a polite social convention, or indicate that Stella retained her earlier interests in educational experiment).[94]

Stella continued to add to her responsibilities in ALRA, being appointed to the finance subcommittee,[95] and elected Chairman of the Executive.[96] She also spoke at a public meeting in Conway Hall, 'That the present Abortion Law requires reform', along with Cicely Hamilton and Joan Malleson, on 17 March. Stella's contribution focused on various foreign examples: the year-old Catalonian law – 'Barcelona might be pounded to ruins by Fascist planes, but this wise and generous example would be a light for the future, how distant' – the extension of the existing Icelandic law, and an improved law recently passed in Denmark. She also asked:

> How many woman leading worthwhile lives and enjoying public respect, owed their survival, in health and peace of mind, to the humanity of doctors, whose humane action was technical crime?[97]

The very next day, the National Council for Equal Citizenship passed 'with no dissentients' a far-reaching resolution including 'the legalisation of abortion under adequate safeguards'.[98]

While ALRA occupied a good deal of Stella's time and energies, including travelling with Alice Jenkins to Leamington to hold a teatime meeting at the Labour Party Women's Section Annual Conference,[99] she was not neglecting other organisations. In April, she addressed the FPSI Forum on the intriguing title 'The Mirror of Venus: some reflections'.[100] In August, she managed to spend some time at the Fabian Summer School at Dartington Hall in Devon (describing herself in the Visitors' Book as 'writer, speaker and agitator').[101] A resolution was passed at the Summer Conference of the FPSI, held at Dora Russell's Beacon Hill School on 22 August, asking 'that some speaker such as Stella Browne, Dr Joan Malleson, Dr Greta Graff or Dr [Edward Fyfe] Griffith be invited to speak'.[102]

But abortion remained the principal cause. She and Mrs Cobb were in touch with MPs, and a panel of professional writers was to be formed. However, ALRA was not going to be drawn into the Bourne case concurrently in the news.[103] Aleck Bourne was a distinguished gynaecologist on ALRA's Medico-Legal Council. Early in 1938, Joan Malleson drew to his attention the case of a pregnant girl aged 14, gang-raped by soldiers at Kensington Barracks. Bourne performed an abortion, and then sent the relevant documents to the police, in order to initiate a test case of the parameters of the existing law.[104]

Even though ALRA were keeping a low profile organisationally, the case stimulated great public interest. Stella herself was interviewed at length for the Birmingham *Sunday Mercury* by Ormsby Lennon. A rare photograph appears with this. Stella, described as 'one of the best known figures in London intellectual circles', looks the epitome of an Englishwoman of a certain class and a certain age dedicated to a Good Cause. Her hair, although not actually coming down, is dressed in such a way that it looks as though it might.

Stella covered the usual points: that parenthood should be a 'free, willing and joyfully undertaken experience'; that the Soviet Union had made abortion illegal on military, rather than medical grounds; that abortion carried out by competent surgeons, instead of under 'most disadvantageous conditions', was a safe operation. Ormsby Lennon seemed to think that if abortion were to become legal, 'the number of marriages would decrease': only, Stella pointed out, forced marriages were likely to end in disaster. Neither did she think that the French system, which Lennon cited, of young girls who became pregnant being allowed to marry the man responsible, was any solution: life-partnership 'founded on the misuse of a "very young girl's" ignorance or fear or dependence' would be 'a mockery and degradation'. She also dismissed the argument from the falling birth rate and the dangers of making it easier for women to 'evade motherhood': 'there is a natural desire for motherhood which can be released if it is found wise to release it'.

Lennon also introduced the historical argument that relaxation of the law on abortion might lead Britain to the fate of Greece and Rome. Stella argued that 'no-one knows the real reasons for the decline of the Roman Empire', and suggested that 'constant warfare, reliance on slave labour and a gradual decrease in the general sense of responsibility' were more relevant than 'the refusal of a minority of patricians to have children'. As for Greece, 'many authorities' now attributed its decline to 'epidemics of the malarial type'. Anyway, it was 'useless to compare these remote historical processes with our very different machine civilisation'.

Those figures who haunted debates on abortion – 'healthy married women quite capable of having children, who, from selfish motives, do not want a family' – were brought into play. Stella suggested that, before deciding that their motives were selfish, the 'reasons for refusing motherhood should be fully explored'. Even if there were 'self-centred and shallow people' – who she would have thought 'were the last people [to be] compelled to bear children against their will' – the vast majority of married working mothers were actuated by 'love of the living', and a recent survey had found that the reasons for refusing motherhood were not the much cited car and luxurious lifestyle but 'POVERTY AND WAR'. The leader writer concurred with her views ('provocative of deep thought').[105]

The fear of war continued to hover: in September, as tension mounted over the situation in Czechoslovakia and the demands of Nazi Germany, and war seemed imminent, Stella suggested to the other members of the Executive that 'in view of the international situation ... copies of all ALRA literature should be forwarded for record purposes' to sympathisers in North America, Australia and New Zealand. And, in the case of war being declared, a subcommittee would 'deal with situation in regard to office, etc.'[106]

Stella was not reassured by the Munich Pact. In November, she wrote to Himes that she and her colleagues found themselves 'amid international tension & a rapidly developing first-class internal political crisis!',[107] and alluded in the following month to 'these dark days' in a metaphorical rather than literal sense.[108] In spite of this looming menace of war, ALRA continued its struggle.

Stella 'put the case for radical reform' at the New Fabian Research Bureau conference in Maidstone in October on the future of the Health Service,[109] and she reported on the National Council of Women conference, at which a large number had been in favour of a resolution for the reform of the abortion laws. During this month or so, Stella also addressed the Leaside Section of Hackney Labour Party and the Downham National Unemployed Workers' Movement.[110]

She also produced a 'Memorandum regarding certain suggestions for the reform of the abortion laws', published by ALRA late in 1938 and sent to the Vice-Presidents, the Medico-Legal Council and the Speakers and

Writers Panel with a covering letter composed by Stella and Janet Chance.[111] The copy in the ALRA archives has been annotated by Alice Jenkins with the comment 'Important'. It drew attention to two proposals made at meetings and elsewhere, and which ALRA members 'would do well to study carefully' in order to be clear about which policies they supported and which they would oppose. The first of these was 'Notification', either of abortion, induced or spontaneous, or of the fact of pregnancy. Stella argued that better ante-natal care involving 'improved conditions all round', including 'Diet', was 'the true remedy'. The BMA had 'expressed the opinion that this was likely to deter women from seeking necessary medical attention. It was also 'a grave infringement of the freedom of the subject, and the privacy which women's feelings generally demand in such matters', and would bear more heavily on the poor. And how could non-compliance be penalised?

The other suggestion often made was to set up 'local or regional Committees' to adjudicate on pleas for abortion, including 'lawyers, social workers, and even clerics of some religious denominations'. Stella outlined the impracticability of such schemes. The 'women concerned would be reluctant to reveal the facts. Investigation would need to take place with great rapidity to ensure that any operation took place while it was still safe, and how could 'the complete privacy due to the women's feelings ... be secured and preserved?' Would really poor women be able to afford the time to attend, even if their expenses were met, and would they be able to 'keep their affairs private?' And how would committees' composition and decision-making processes be determined? '[A]ny whose sexual lives did not accord with the accepted tradition' (i.e. the unmarried or the divorced or separated) would most likely be 'especially and doubly penalized' under such a system.

The conclusion was that 'Both notification and *ad hoc* Committees are attempts to evade the need to do something effective.' There were 'two separate, but convergent ways' to achieve something 'effective, adequate, just and humane'. One was more efficient mother and child welfare services, including contraception; plus 'rehousing ... economic changes ... education ... international peace'. The other way was 'through co-operation with the individual; acceptance of the individual woman's right of choice ... and the use of modern knowledge and science to help her equally, whether her answer be "Yes" or "No".'[112] Stella summarised the memorandum in a letter to Havelock Ellis, 'A memorandum of certain suggested *remedies*, which are no remedies': she expressed herself glad to hear any comments he might have, and whether he concurred.[113]

She also managed to get two letters into the Press in late 1938. In November, while 'still waiting ... for the publication of the Birkett Report',[114] she wrote to *The Spectator* pointing out that, although the Bourne case has 'received wide publicity and approval ... *the Law remains on our Statute Book*'.[115] The following month, her letter (over the soubriquet 'Vega') in *The News Chronicle*, praising Mrs Horsbrugh, MP's 'excellent Bill to amend the Law of Adoption', suggested that 'So many of her arguments might be extended and applied to the present Abortion Law', which was 'an even more prolific cause of disease and misery'.[116]

She also found time to read Norman Himes's *Practical Birth Control Methods* (written jointly with his wife), finding it 'clear, comprehensive and practical ... a vast amount of relevant & useful information'.[117] She described it to Havelock Ellis as 'encourag[ing] hope based on solid achievement'.[118] The *New Generation* published her review of this 'admirable compendium'.[119]

Himes liked her notice and, in the New Year, actually suggested, concerning a projected British edition, that Stella herself 'might collaborate in the additional or different chapters'. Stella felt 'honoured', and told Gollancz, the publishers initially proposed, that she would be willing to do so, 'if a suitable financial arrangement can be made.'[120] By February, Himes had accepted an offer from Allen & Unwin, and 'would be glad if [Stella] would assist with the abortion chapters', for 'some nominal payment'. Himes would be 'very pleased to have you gather material from your wealth of information and submit to me a fairly finished draft'.[121] At some point, these plans appear to have fallen through, as the English edition of *Practical Birth Control Methods*, published in 1940, did not include any acknowledged contribution by her.[122]

In the light of the British response to the European political situation, Stella envied her US friends 'a country that does *not* crawl to barbarism'[123] and President Roosevelt. She wrote to Ellis 'Thank God for Roosevelt's country',[124] and commented to both Himes and to Robert Latou Dickinson that she wished that Britain could 'borrow F. D. Roosevelt for a while',[125] 'but we probably wouldn't return him!!'[126] 'Franco [was] almost in that heroic Barcelona', while 'our British National Government still evades doing anything about systematic underground shelters (I suppose Chequers has been supplied with one, so THATS [Sic] all right)' and 'As for Czechoslovakia I can't write – I am *too ashamed*.')[127] Besides these observations on the wider situation, she also informed these North American colleagues about progress towards the report of the Inter-Departmental Committee.[128]

In spite of fears about the situation, Stella and ALRA did not abandon the more immediate struggle. In January, Stella went to Nottingham to speak at a conference arranged by the local Labour Women's Association.[129] She was scheduled to speak to the FPSI Forum on Sex early in March on 'The Third Person' but was unable, at the last minute, to speak on account of illness, and was re-invited for April:[130] 'a successful meeting' was reported.[131]

There are occasional hints of the old Stella in her letters to Dr Robert Latou Dickinson: in June, she congratulated him on 'those wonderful gynaecological & embryological models' he had made for the World's Fair. She found in Britain

> still a regrettable tendency even on the part of the Eugenics Society (in some ways so admirable) to assume that reproduction is performed by documents & Committees.

From the Press accounts of the Birkett Report (which she was anxiously awaiting), it sounded to be '*a most timorous and regrettable performance*', and even Dorothy Thurtle in her Minority Report 'has been conventional about the "married" woman as against the "unmarried"'.[132]

Stella was still unwell in mid-March, sending her apologies to the annual general meeting of ALRA.[133] However, she was fit enough a month later to attend the April meeting of the Executive Committee[134] and, by May, was even expressing willingness to speak at open-air meetings,[135] although they were '*waiting* over here – waiting for something that *perhaps* may never happen??'[136] A conference on the Birkett Report at Conway Hall was planned,[137] but 'the shadow of another fight hangs over everything', and events overtook them ('*the mess ... that we & Europe have made ...!*').[138] The minutes of the next Executive meeting on 10 July were only retrospectively recorded by Alice Jenkins:

> There is no record of the Meeting which was evidently held on 10 July, & if my memory serves me correctly the proposed conference was abandoned, Mrs Garrett's agreement terminated and the office vacated.
>
> Mrs Chance, Miss Browne and I agreed to form a 'skeleton' Committee, and kept the ALRA alive during the war years.[139]

Although war was not formally declared until Hitler's invasion of Poland in September, the German violation of the guarantees given at Munich over Czechoslovakia meant that the arrival of European war was no longer a matter of if, but when.

Notes

1. Barbara Brookes, *Abortion in England, 1900–1967* (London: Croom Helm, 1988), pp. 67–9.
2. James Thomas and A. Susan Williams, 'Women and abortion in 1930s Britain: a survey and its data', *Social History of Medicine,* 11 (1998), pp. 283–309.
3. 'Summary of discussion held at Ridgeway's, Jan 24th 1936', ALRA Minute-book 1936–1952, Abortion Law Reform Association Archives, Wellcome Library, SA/ALR/A.1/2/1.
4. Duplicate copy of circular letter dated 2 March 1936, Janet Chance's scrapbook, SA/ALR/B.1.
5. F.W. Stella Browne, 'Ministers and eugenists', *Plan: For World Order and Progress*, vol. 3, no. 3, March 1936, pp. 3–4.
6. Stella Browne to Havelock Ellis, 26 April 1936, Havelock Ellis papers in the Department of Manuscripts, British Library, Additional Manuscript 70539 [BL Add Ms 70539].
7. Max Hodann in Oslo to Dr A. Pillay, 7 April 1936, *Marriage Hygiene* files in the Norman Himes papers, Boston Medical Library in the Francis A. Countway Library of Medicine, BMS C77 Box 58 folder 654.
8. Norman Himes to A. Pillay, 14 May 1936, BMS C77 Box 58 folder 654.
9. Keith Hindell and Madeleine Simms, *Abortion Law Reformed*, London, Peter Owen, 1971, p. 59, citing Mrs Garrett, paid secretary to ALRA during its early years.
10. Browne to Ellis, 26 April 1936, BL Add Ms 70539.
11. Minutes of meeting, 27 April 1936, SA/ALR/A.1/2/1.
12. *Proceedings of a Conference on Abortion Law Reform, 15th May 1936*, pp. 13–15, SA/ALR/B.1, another copy in Dora Russell papers, International Institute of Social History, Amsterdam [DR], file 344.
13. *Proceedings of a Conference on Abortion Law Reform*, pp. 26–9.
14. Minutes of meeting, 18 May 1936, SA/ALR/A.1/2/1.
15. Stella Browne to Norman Himes, 20 September 1936, BMS C77 Box 32 folder 364.
16. F.W. Stella Browne, 'Freedom's debit and credit', *Plan: For World Order and Progress*, vol. 3, no. 7, July 1936, pp. 11–13.
17. Minutes of meeting, 15 June 1936, SA/ALR/A.1/2/1.
18. Browne, 'Freedom's debit and credit'.
19. Browne to Himes, 20 September 1936, BMS C77 Box 32 folder 364.
20. Minutes of meeting, 15 June 1936, SA/ALR/A.1/2/1.
21. Minutes of meeting, 20 July 1936, SA/ALR/A.1/2/1.
22. Browne to Himes, 20 September 1936, BMS C77 Box 32 folder 364.
23. Minutes of meeting, 20 July 1936, SA/ALR/A.1/2/1.

24. Minutes of Annual General Meeting, 11 June 1936, London School of Economics, LSE/Fabian Society/C.42.
25. Summer School Visitors' Book, LSE/Fabian Society/G.11.
26. Summer School Log Book, LSE/Fabian Society/G.15.
27. Secretary of the British Sexological Society to Stella Browne, 9 January 1936, 'B.S.S. Letters Out', British Sexology Society Archives, Harry Ransom Humanities Research Center, University of Texas at Austin [HRC].
28. Stella Browne to Mr Bennett, 10 September 1936, 'B.S.S. Letters received', HRC.
29. Margaret Sanger to Janet Chance, 13 July 1936, Margaret Sanger papers in the Library of Congress, Washington, DC, [LC], Volume 23.
30. Browne to Himes, 20 September 1936, BMS C77 Box 32 folder 364.
31. Norman Himes to Stella Browne, 1 October 1936, BMS C77 Box 32 folder 364.
32. Minutes of meeting, 21 September 1936, SA/ALR/A.1/2/1.
33. Minutes of meeting, 19 October 1936, SA/ALR/A.1/2/1.
34. Minutes of meeting, 16 November 1936, SA/ALR/A.1/2/1.
35. Minutes of meeting, 15 March 1936, SA/ALR/A.1/2/1, also mentioned in Janet Chance's scrapbook, SA/ALR/B.1. It has not been possible to trace this article.
36. Minutes of meeting, 16 November 1936, SA/ALR/A.1/2/1.
37. F.W. Stella Browne, 'The ALRA', *The New Generation*, vol. 16, January 1937, p. 5.
38. ALRA Newsletter, February 1937, SA/ALR/B.1.
39. Minutes of meeting, 19 October 1936, SA/ALR/A.1/2/1.
40. 'Progressives unite: The F.P.S.I.-Cosmopolis merger', *Plan: For World Order and Progress*, vol. 3, no. 12, December 1936, pp. 23–4.
41. Minutes of meeting of the Executive Committee of the Council for the Federation of Progressive Societies and Individuals (British Isles Section of Cosmopolis), 8 January 1937, 15 January 1937, London School of Economics, LSE/Progressive League/1
42. Hindell and Simms, *Abortion Law Reformed*, p. 59, citing Mrs Garrett, paid secretary to ALRA during its early years.
43. Minutes of meeting, 11 January 1937, SA/ALR/A.1/2/1.
44. 'Diary for February', *Plan: For World Order and Progress*, vol. 4, no. 2, February 1937, rear cover.
45. Browne to Bennett, 29 March 1937, 'BSS Letters Received', HRC.
46. Minutes of meeting, 15 March 1937, 19 April 1937, SA/ALR/A.1/2/1.
47. List of publications in back of Chance's pamphlet, *The Case for the Reform of the Abortion Laws*, and cutting from *The Tribune*, 7 May 1937, SA/ALR/B.1.
48. F.W. Stella Browne, 'One step forward', *The Tribune*, 21 May 1937, p. 14.
49. F.W. Stella Browne, 'British Government enquiry into abortion', *Marriage Hygiene*, vol. IV, no. 1, August 1937, p. 48.

50. Minutes of meeting, 15 March 1937, SA/ALR/A.1/2/1.
51. Minutes of meeting, 24 May 1937, SA/ALR/A.1/2/1.
52. F.W. Stella Browne, 'The Birkett Committee', *The Spectator*, 21 May 1937, pp. 951–2.
53. Browne to Norman and Vera Himes, 21 May 1937, BMS C77 Box 32 folder 364.
54. Minutes of meeting, 24 May 1937, SA/ALR/A.1/2/1.
55. Carbon copy from Mrs Sanger's secretary to Edith How-Martyn, 12 May 1937, LC, Volume 23.
56. Margaret Sanger, *An Autobiography* (London: Victor Gollancz, 1939), p. 126.
57. Ellen Chesler, *Woman of Valor: Margaret Sanger and the Birth Control Movement in America* (New York: Simon & Schuster 1992).
58. F.W. Stella Browne, 'Reviews, *Plan: For World Order and Progress*', vol. 4, no. 3, March 1937, pp. 27–8.
59. Max Hodann, *History of Modern Morals* (London: William Heinemann Medical, 1937), p. 325.
60. Hodann, *History of Modern Morals*, p. 255, n. 2.
61. Hodann, *History of Modern Morals*, p. 307, 'Postscript to Chapter IX', p. 325.
62. V.R. Khanolker in *Marriage Hygiene*, quoted in *The New Generation*, vol. 16, October 1937, p. 113.
63. Alec Craig, 'Reviews: Men and morals', *Plan: A Constructive Review*, vol. 4, no. 6, June 1937, pp. 28–31.
64. F.W. Stella Browne, 'The population question', *The Yorkshire Observer*, 22 May 1937, p. 6.
65. Minutes of preliminary meeting of the Interdepartmental Committee on Abortion, 9 June 1937, The National Archives MH71/20.
66. Minutes of meeting, 14 June 1937, SA/ALR/A.1/2/1.
67. Browne to Norman and Vera Himes, 21 June 1937, BMS C77 Box 32 folder 364.
68. Minutes of the first Annual General Meeting, 29 June 1937, SA/ALR/A.1/2/1.
69. Minutes of meeting, 19 July 1937, SA/ALR/A.1/2/1.
70. Binnie Dunlop to Norman Himes, 23 June 1937, BMS C77 Box 35 folder 396.
71. Minutes of the first Annual General Meeting, 29 June 1937, SA/ALR/A.1/2/1.
72. Browne to Norman and Vera Himes, 21 and 22 June 1937, BMS C77 Box 32 folder 364.
73. Browne to Norman and Vera Himes, 22 June 1937, BMS C77 Box 32 folder 364.
74. Browne to Norman and Vera Himes, 21 June 1937, BMS C77 Box 32 folder 364.
75. Browne to Norman and Vera Himes, 21 June 1937, BMS C77 Box 32 folder 364.

76. Browne to Norman and Vera Himes, 22 June 1937, BMS C77 Box 32 folder 364.
77. Browne to Norman and Vera Himes, 21 June 1937, BMS C77 Box 32 folder 364.
78. Fabian Summer School Visitors' Book, 1922–1938, LSE/Fabian Society/G.11.
79. Minutes of three meetings of the Interdepartmental Committee on Abortion, 28 July 1937, TNA MH71/20.
80. Memorandum for Presentation to the Inter-Departmental Committee on Abortion from Miss F.W. Stella Browne, A.C. Paper no. 16, TNA MH71/21.
81. Minutes of the 4th Meeting of the Interdepartmental Committee on Abortion, 13 October 1937, TNA MH71/21.
82. Birkett Committee papers, personal papers of Lady Rhys Williams, National Birthday Trust Fund Archives, Wellcome Library, SA/NBT/U.10/2.
83. H. Montgomery Hyde, *Norman Birkett: The Life of Lord Birkett of Ulverston* (London: Hamish Hamilton, 1964); John Chandos, *Norman Birkett: Uncommon Advocate* (London: Mayflower, 1963).
84. Evidence of Miss F.W. Stella Browne, Wednesday, 17 November 1937, A.C. Paper no. 51, TNA MH71/23; Brookes, *Abortion in England*, p. 107.
85. Members meeting, 2 December 1937, SA/ALR/A.1/2/1.
86. Minutes of Executive Committee meeting, 25 October 1937, SA/ALR/A.1/2/1.
87. Robert Latou Dickinson to Stella Bloch Hanau, 7 November 1937, Stella Bloch Hanau papers in the Sophia Smith Collection, Smith College, Northampton MA, folder 51.
88. Minutes of Executive Committee meeting, 29 November 1937, SA/ALR/A.1/2/1.
89. Minutes of Executive Committee meeting, 20 December 1937, SA/ALR/A.1/2/1.
90. Minutes of Executive Committee meeting, 20 December 1937, SA/ALR/A.1/2/1.
91. Minutes of Council Meeting, 14 February 1938, Eugenics Society Archives, Wellcome Library, SA/EUG/L.10.
92. Minutes of Council Meeting, 14 April 1942, SA/EUG/L.11.
93. Browne to Himes, 3 March 1938, BMS C77 Box 32 folder 364.
94. Stella Browne to Dora Russell, 19 March 1938, DR, file 344.
95. Second annual general meeting, 25 March 1938, SA/ALR/A.1/2/1.
96. Minutes of Executive Committee meeting, 28 March 1938, SA/ALR/A.1/2/1.
97. Janet Chance's scrapbook, SA/ALR/B.2; F.W. Stella Browne, 'Abortion law reform', *The New Generation*, vol. 17, April 1938, pp. 40–1.
98. Minutes of Executive Committee meeting, 28 March 1938, SA/ALR/A.1/2/1; Browne, 'Abortion law reform'.

99. Janet Chance's scrapbook, SA/ALR/B.2; Minutes of Executive Committee meeting, 2 April 1938, SA/ALR/A.1/2/1; 3rd Annual Report of ALRA, 1938–1939, SA/ALR/A.1/3.
100. *Plan: A Progressive Review*, vol. 5, no. 3, March 1938.
101. Fabian Summer School Visitors' Book, LSE/Fabian Society/G.11.
102. Circular letter to the Executive Committee, 22 August 1938, LSE/Progressive League/1.
103. Minutes of Executive Committee meeting, 4 and 25 July 1938, SA/ALR/A/1/2/1.
104. Brookes, *Abortion in England*, pp. 69–70.
105. 'Stella Browne questioned for the *Sunday Mercury* by Ormsby Lennon', *Sunday Mercury and Sunday News* (Birmingham), 21 July 1938, p. 8.
106. Minutes of Executive Committee meeting, 20 September 1938, SA/ALR/A/1/2/1.
107. Browne to Himes, 25 November 1938, BMS C77 Box 32 folder 364.
108. Browne to Ellis, 5 December 1938, BL Add Mss 70539.
109. ALRA Annual Report, 1938/39, SA/ALR/A.1/3.
110. Minutes of Executive Committee meeting, 26 October 1938, SA/ALR/A.1/2/1.
111. Minutes of Executive Committee meeting, 21 November 1938, SA/ALR/A.1/2/1.
112. F.W. Stella Browne, 'Memorandum regarding certain suggestions for the reform of the abortion laws' [1938], 'Pre-1949 papers', SA/ALR/A.2/2.
113. Browne to Ellis, 5 December 1938, BL Add Mss 70539.
114. Browne to Himes, 25 November 1938, BMS C77 Box 32 folder 364.
115. F.W. Stella Browne, 'The need for abortion law reform', *The Spectator*, 25 November 1938, p. 906.
116. 'Vega', 'Two laws', *News Chronicle*, 21 December 1938, p. 4.
117. Browne to Himes, 25 November 1938, BMS C77 Box 32 folder 364.
118. Browne to Ellis, 5 December 1938, BL Add Ms 70539.
119. F.W. Stella Browne, 'Norman Himes on contraception', *The New Generation*, vol. 17, December 1938, p. 137.
120. Browne to Himes, 26 January 1939, BMS C77 Box 32 folder 364.
121. Norman Himes to Stella Browne, 10 February 1939, BMS C77 Box 32 folder 364.
122. Norman E. Himes, *Practical Birth-Control Methods* (English edn revised by Margaret Hadley Jackson; introduction by Robert L. Dickinson; foreword by Havelock Ellis) (London: G. Allen & Unwin, 1940).
123. Stella Browne to Robert Latou Dickinson, 26 January 1939, Robert Latou Dickson papers, Boston Medical Library in the Francis A. Countway Library of Medicine, BMS C72 Box 1 folder 15.

124. Browne to Ellis, 5 December 1938, BL Add Ms 70539.
125. Browne to Dickinson, 26 January 1939, BMS C72 Box 1 folder 15.
126. Browne to Himes, 26 January 1939, BMS C77 Box 32 folder 364.
127. Browne to Dickinson, 26 January 1939, BMS C72 Box 1 folder 15.
128. Browne to Dickinson, 26 January 1939, BMS C72 Box 1 folder 15; Browne to Himes, 26 January 1939, BMS C77 Box 32 folder 364.
129. Minutes of Executive Committee meeting, 23 January 1939, SA/ALR/A.1/2/1; 'ALRA News', February 1929, SA/ALR/B.1.
130. *Plan*: *For World Order and Progress*, vol. 6, no. 2, February 1939; Minutes of meeting of 17 March 1939, LSE/Progressive League/1.
131. Minutes of meeting of 19 May 1939, LSE/Progressive League/1.
132. Browne to Dickinson, 9 June 1939, BMS C72 Box 1 folder 15.
133. Minutes of Annual General Meeting, 17 March 1939, SA/ALR/A.1/2/1.
134. Minutes of Executive Committee meeting, 18 April 1939, SA/ALR/A.1/2/1.
135. Minutes of Executive Committee meeting, 15 May 1939, SA/ALR/A.1/2/1.
136. Browne to Dickinson, 22 May 1939, BMS C72 Box 1 folder 15.
137. Minutes of Executive Committee meeting, 10 June 1939, SA/ALR/A.1/2/1.
138. Browne to Dickinson, 9 June 1939, BMS C72 Box 1 folder 15.
139. Note made 7 February 1959, SA/ALR/A.1/2/1.

11

Exile and Twilight

There is little record of Stella's activities or feelings during the first years of the war. ALRA had gone into limbo for the duration, although the Executive 'dealt with enquiries, took any opportunities that offered of small meetings, and kept a watch on press reports and correspondence'.[1] She did not abandon her own efforts, but it was not 'easy to get a hearing ... in wartime.' She failed to get Parliamentary questions asked, 'even when there was a very obvious peg to hang them on to', such as 'Service Women's conditions, maternal mortality from T.B., the Royal Commission [on Population] & its work, the increase in V.D., & the recent cases of doctors struck off the register & sentenced to varying terms of imprisonment'.[2] Press contacts were slightly more successful. On 9 October 1942, *Tribune* published her letter on the recent conviction of Dr de Caux, a qualified anaesthetist, for procuring miscarriages. It was time, Stella suggested to take 'profiteering out of these operations by permitting doctors to perform them for any woman either unfit or unwilling to bear children'.[3] This generated 'a very able critical article' by Cedric Dover, and additional correspondence.[4] The *News Chronicle* published her letter pointing out that, compared to Nazi population policies, 'our own laws are neither merciful nor consistent ... A humane and adequate policy would be both positive and negative, encouraging and supporting parenthood, while avoiding compulsion.'[5] In both letters, she invoked 'other freedoms, more subtle and emotionally imponderable, besides Roosevelt's famous Four!'[6]

For the first years of the war, she was still living in Chelsea. Early in 1941, George Ives sent her the prospectus of his book *Obstacles to Human Progress*,[7] calling a few days later to give her a copy.[8] Her subsequent letter sufficiently impressed Ives for him to copy it in its entirety into his diary. She regarded it 'as a companion to your classic Penal Methods [*A History of Penal Methods*, 1914] on the emotional side, expressing your own individual approach to the greatest problems of life'. She praised its 'noble passages blending poetry and science', and his 'testimony as to the value of mysticism'. Stella was still, it would seem, networking: she mentioned that Ives might have 'received an invitation to address a group of Conway Hall members and friends (including several refugee intellectuals and professional people) on some of the themes interwoven in your latest book'[9] – which was, indeed, the case.[10]

Some time after this, Stella and her sister Sylvia left London for Liverpool. This does not seem to have been a wished-for removal on Stella's part: over a dozen years later she remarked that provincial towns had all the urban problems found in London, without 'London's positive advantages and charms'.[11] Family tradition has it that they were obliged to go there to care for an invalid relative, and that Sylvia (and, given her linguistic skills, possibly Stella as well) worked in official censorship.[12] By May 1942, Stella was residing in the Mildmay Hostel, Blackthorne Place, Liverpool, where she and Sylvia remained until around 1945.[13] While there, she wrote to Julian Huxley, congratulating him on 'the defeat of what seems to a spectator from afar off a persistently mean & organised attempt to oust you from your post [as Secretary of the London Zoological Society]'. She hoped that he would continue his 'admirable independent work'. She also hoped to hear him again on the wireless 'in individual talks, unhampered by what you will perhaps allow me to call the *antics* of some of your colleagues of the Brains Trust'.[14] Presumably, she had some acquaintance with Huxley through moving in similar circles, and he was related to the Hayneses.

In March 1943, Stella returned to an issue about which she had been articulate and concerned during the previous war, that of venereal disease:

> *Why is such instruction not given to members of the female services*? It is an adult right and an adult duty to know how to prevent disease and the duty of any civilised government to supply the knowledge and the means. Venereal diseases cannot be extirpated by knowledge for men only, supplemented by chivvying the poorer prostitutes.[15]

Stella was still recognised in sex reform circles: she was named as a Patron and later Vice-President of the Society for Sex Education and Guidance set up in 1943 by progressive doctor Eustace Chesser.[16] There were several crossovers and connections between this new Society and the circles in which Stella had moved.[17] Chesser himself was dedicated to abortion law reform.[18] Other old friends had not forgotten her, although they might have lost touch. In May 1944, Bertram Lloyd wrote to Ives 'Have you heard aught of say, Stella Browne of recent years?'[19]

In March 1944, the appointment of a Royal Commission on Population stimulated a flurry of activity. Stella had a letter (as 'Vega') printed in the *News Chronicle*, 'on the significance of the appointment & the large proportion of women on the Commission'. She also wrote to the Commission with suggestions of 'various women suitable for appointment as co-opted members ... but none/of those put forward were appointed'.[20] At her suggestion, ALRA composed a letter to the press, suggesting that 'those interested in post-war decisions on these spheres' should bear in mind two things. First was 'The extent of self-inflicted abortion and its possible reduction by legal reform'; the second was 'The inner dignity and pride in motherhood to be based on voluntary as contrasted with haphazard motherhood.' Reforms permitting 'medical advice to the woman who considers her pregnancy in some special circumstances disastrous ... should be included in all population policies'. The letter was not published by any of the 25 leading papers and magazines to which it was sent, and finally appeared in *Plan*.[21]

An informal meeting of ALRA was held at Brown's Hotel on 13 July 1944. Stella sent her apologies and a statement.[22] She did not 'wish to *oppose* but to *supplement* the proposal of ... Mrs Janet Chance, that the British Medical Association be invited to give evidence on the harm done by unskilled and septic interference'. Indeed, she was all in favour of encouraging 'all likely enlightened and responsible bodies (e.g. the Eugenics Society, the Women's Cooperative Guild etc) to come forward'. But, 'surely the women's case in the matter is specially our affair and we cannot make it theirs?' There was 'ample material in our files to compile a case with many modern instances'. She added that 'propaganda for Abortion Law Reform should have a good hearing in the press just now, when public attention is turning to conditions after the War', and regarded 'the more systematic use of the Press as a *main activity*'.[23]

In May 1945, as she was unable to attend the June ALRA Executive Committee, she sent them a substantial report describing her activities during the war years. She was 'sorry ... that I cannot be with you', having 'hoped it might be possible to arrange an E.C. Meeting in April', but 'bow[ed] to the majority's convenience'. Besides her account of her 'efforts & attempts in the time under review', she noted that

> of late, there has been a most encouraging and significant development, in cases of sentences for abortions: *local &*

> *spontaneous petitions signed by those who knew the doctors implicated, for a remission of their sentences.*

During the war years, she had 'had a fairly voluminous correspondence on A.L.R. & relevant cases', and thus did not feel justified in sending in 'more than six shillings (to cover some of the postal expenses in steps advocated by me) towards funds'. (Money was presumably still tight.) Looking towards the future, as the war came to an end, she 'firmly believe[d] that with the right outlook & plan, there is a big field of work for us now, in association with the more positive side of women's rights as mothers'.[24]

In August 1945, Stella wrote to Alice Jenkins, enclosing Janet Chance's '*most generous wise & true tribute*' to Aleck Bourne on his resignation from ALRA's Medico-Legal Committee. She was continuing to keep busy, since the letter ends, rather tantalisingly, 'In a great hurry as ever.'[25] She sent her apologies to the ALRA Members' Meeting held at Conway Hall in October, with various proposals for parliamentary action, and asking that 'a warm vote of thanks be moved to Mrs Chance for her work during the war years'.[26]

Early in 1946, it gave the editor of *Plan* 'great pleasure to publish ... a letter from an old and valued member of our organisation', Stella. One of the writer's 'early and most vivid recollections of the League is of a talk she gave ... on "Jealousy"', and he hoped that they might 'once again have the pleasure of listening to her in the not too distant future'.[27] Stella was responding to an article 'deprecat[ing] and deplor[ing]' the inclusion of abortion law reform in the new Basis of the League's policies.[28] She congratulated the editors on publishing this, as 'it is necessary that advocates of the reform ... should be quite clear in their minds, as to possible objections, and convinced of the justice and reason of their cause'. The arguments made had been 'ingeniously phrased and ingeniously attacked', but the writer had 'miss[ed] the argument that there should be termination of pregnancy if so desired by the woman, until the child is capable of independent existence and survival'.[29]

It was with 'great pleasure' that Stella heard that Janet Chance had seen Max Hodann (now living in Sweden), and received his 'kind messages & greetings'. In Britain, 'all our work is rather backward, having been much held up', although she had 'managed to keep the light burning during the war'. In conclusion, she asked Hodann, if he replied – 'which I should very much appreciate' – '*please address as to a private individual, not mentioning ALRA on envelope*'.[30] By this time, she and her sister were living in lodgings in Hawarden Avenue, Liverpool, a suburban area, and the owners, 'though very friendly, [had] quite different views' from Stella's own.[31]

A month later, she wrote at greater length (heading her letter 'STRING PRIVATIM' – very private). She had received Hodann's 'encouraging news of our Scandinavian co-workers & friends'. She had 'urged the need for *active* & adequate support of your efforts & publicizing of the very significant Swedish material', but problems arose because of paper-rationing and currency restrictions over paying him some kind of remittance. Janet Chance's views were rather less sanguine than Stella's. And, as Janet Chance was '*Chairman, Treasurer AND Secretary* rolled into one, of ALRA – AND contributes about ⅔ A.L.R.A.'s funds, if not more!!' Stella was sure that Hodann would appreciate that it was 'a delicate & difficult matter' to get funding for him in the circumstances – 'Unglaüblich aber wahr!! – Ehrenwort! '[Incredible, but true!! Word of honour!]. She dropped entirely into German to claim that '[T]he management and administration of A.L.R.A.' had become more than ever an autocracy, not to say a tyranny of the severest kind. Individual initiative was treated coldly or as a personal insult, younger fellow-campaigners were not joining, old and trusted friends and members were dropping off silently. On top of this, there were the difficulties of a transition period. She assured her dear comrade that she was doing her best but was unable to hold out much hope of success. She herself was tightly fettered to Liverpool for an indefinite period, and her health was going downhill. Returning to English, she suggested that 'the wider the scope of any book on Scandinavia – e.g. marriage laws as well as b.c. – the better the chance', but warned him '*don't let it be offered to Stanley Unwin*', recommending Heinemann or Cassell as alternatives.[32]

Nearly a fortnight later, Janet Chance reported that the Bank were favourable towards sending a short-term monthly remittance to Hodann. However, groused Stella, Chance had not forwarded to her Hodann's information on proposed changes in the Swedish law which she was '*most* anxious to have.'[33] This, as well as her previous vituperative comments, may have been generated by Stella's sense of isolation from her former comrades, dependent upon correspondence to keep her informed. It also recalls, in its blending of authority issues and resentments around money, the mounting tension and final breach in her relationship with Margaret Sanger, over twenty years previously.

Stella was, however, able to be present at the ALRA meeting on 12 October at Conway Hall. In her introduction, the Chairman, Janet Chance, mentioned that Stella had 'started the movement in England, and was indeed in the field long before anyone else'. At Chance's request, the meeting 'stood in silence for two minutes in homage to these two pioneers' (Binnie Dunlop of the Malthusian League had recently died).[34] This tribute did not relieve her antipathy to Chance, who by late October had 'still not sent ... [Max Hodann's] report on the exact changes effected in 1938, in 1946, & now further proposed in Sweden, and *for quotation I must have the exact particulars*.'[35]

Hodann wrote back with a German version of the new Swedish law on abortion for possible translation into English, as he found the legal language too difficult himself.[36] Stella must have received this very quickly, since his letter was dated 22 November, and on 28 she was writing enclosing 'the final portion of my English translation', having sent off the first part by airmail, 'as I understood promptitude is wished for'; adding, after raising some points about the translation, 'At least it now reaches your hands, after you had raised the matter with our mutual acquaintance, *early in July*.' She also asked if Hodann could let her have a typed copy of the translation at his convenience – 'I do not think there is *any* likelihood of my having one from J.'[37]

In 1946, Stella's connection with the Fabian Society ceased: she was struck off their lists, presumably as her subscription was in arrears as a routine measure by the Society. She does not seem to have become involved with any local group.[38]

In an article in *John Bull* in August 1947, Alice Jenkins paid tribute to Stella's pioneering endeavours, describing her as 'a founder member of the Association, [who] has done much to try to dispel the obscurity and prejudice that has long surrounded even the discussion of abortion'.[39] She continued to make contacts and agitate on behalf of the cause. Her letter (as Vega) in *The News Chronicle*, concerning a recent case of child-cruelty, wondered how many readers realised 'that it would be a *crime under the present law* for a doctor to have relieved Mrs Agar of any of her seven pregnancies in seven years?'[40] Janet Chance suggested that Stella should write to Mrs Margaret Sanger, 'about objectionable questions ... to applicants for visas, by representatives of the USA Embassy'.[41] There is no record of whether Stella ever did so, but a few years later Sanger disclaimed precise knowledge of her present whereabouts.[42]

Although it may have seemed to her co-workers in London that abortion law reform was the only thing on Stella's mind, her concerns continued wide-ranging. Some time during the autumn of 1948, she heard Olaf Stapledon, the left-wing thinker and science fiction writer, address the Liverpool Modern Quarterly Discussion Circle on the Wroclaw Congress[43] ('World Congress of Intellectuals in Defence of Peace').[44] Responding to his emphasis on 'the need of brain workers to unite for peace', Stella wrote to him early in 1949, as if to a stranger, although one would have thought that they would have encountered one another, at least by repute. Current events – 'discussions in & about Scandinavia, the rejection of Stalin's peace offer (*even if a trap* it should surely have been differently handled?!) & the Mindzentky show up in Hungary' – seemed to her 'signs that there is no time to lose'. If he could 'spare the time to indicate whether any written public protest or manifesto is being drawn up about the war drive, or any other measures taken', she would be 'deeply grateful'.

She listed her activist credentials, which are of considerable interest in revealing how she was defining herself at this stage of her life. She described herself as 'a Socialist & "extreme" Left-Wing feminist since 1911', although adding that 'I am not a member of the Labour Party (*one lives & learns!*) *NOR* a Communist, but a "fellow-traveller"', subscribing to the *Daily Worker* and the *New Statesman and Nation*. She gave prominent place to her birth control activism and the fact that she had been 'the first Englishwoman to protest publicly & systematically against our archaic & cruel abortion laws & helped to found the Abortion Law Reform Association'. Her involvement with the Progressive League and the Fabian Society, as well as her work with the Chelsea Labour Party Strike Committee in 1926, were mentioned, as were her writing, speaking, and translations. Rather surprisingly, she did not mention her work for suffrage or for pacifism during the First World War. The selection may be attributed partly to the need to establish her position without going on at too great length, and to indicate the common ground she shared with Stapledon, as well as, perhaps, the connections in which he might have heard of her.[45]

Although she was 'now hampered by lameness & failing eyesight', she told Stapledon that she 'would gladly help, within [her] physical & financial limitations'. She hoped that 'these few details will enable you to judge whether I can be of use', subscribing herself, 'Yours fraternally'. She added a postscript, regretting that she was unable to offer any premises for meetings.[46] There is no evidence that anything came of this contact.

In March 1949, ALRA held a 'Private Conference', which Stella was unable to attend: the statement that came out of it, however, followed her own passionate beliefs:

> The founders of the Society, including the indomitable pioneer and Vice-Chairman, Stella Browne, look forward to the time when the operation of abortion will be treated like any other operation ... the medical profession be free to advise for and against as doctors.[47]

At the September annual general meeting a 'message of greeting' from her was read, and 'her absence owing to domicile in Liverpool was regretted'.[48] During 1950, Stella continued to make suggestions for actions – in June 1951, these were even being carried out.[49]

In apparent contradiction to her cavilling remarks to Hodann in 1946, in June 1951 Stella's latest letter to the ALRA Executive 'included the expression of admiration – heartily endorsed by all Committee members – for Mrs Chance's invaluable work'.[50] This may indicate a change in her feelings, with those of 1946 being the product of immediate stresses and tensions, or simply mark the difference between the requirements of working with someone in the same cause, and the blowing off of steam to a neutral observer. She was writing genially enough to Chance in August, thanking her for 'the notices of & invitations to the receptions to meet Elise Ottesen-Jensen [the leading left-wing Swedish campaigner for birth control and sex education][51] on 28th.' To her great regret 'I cannot be present. But she sent 'hearty congratulations & regards', signing off 'In haste, as ever.'[52]

However, all was not smooth sailing, as a result either of differences of personality and over policy, or of Stella's sense of being at a distance and out of the inner circle. In September 1951, Janet Chance wrote (in response to correspondence which does not survive):

> I am puzzled by your letter and should like to understand it. I value more than I can say having as complete understanding and as full agreement between Exec. members as we can. That has been the great strength of ALRA; or one of its strengths, that since our first meeting we were whole-hoggers and had no need to discuss half the things that others bogg[l]ed at. Now why are you afraid that I need to reflect on the Marylebone case?

She went on 'What then is it in me that somehow disappoints you?', and surmised that 'it must be that you think the E.L. [Enquirer's Leaflet] is a statement of our full aims and outlook', rather than for 'desperate women who *may* get a legal helper thereby'. She exhorted Stella, 'Now for the sake of Auld Lang Syne, tell me where you want something.' One source of dissension would appear to have been the question of Parliamentary action. Stella stressed this, but Janet Chance had 'reasons for thinking that *as things are in 1951*, it is wiser to continue our present surprisingly successful line'. However, she had 'NEVER HAD YOUR CRITICISMS OF MY VIEWS. Do let me have them', and offered to write out her case again.

Would Stella, Chance suggested, 'like the idea which I have in mind of another conference to thrash all this out?' And, while there were those within ALRA who 'may feel there is no reason for re-opening it at this juncture, there are others whose views I should very much like to have'. She then asked Stella whether she had any spare copies of 'leaflet on BOARDS' (presumably her 1938 Memorandum). Chance feared that 'our unthoughtful supporters are going to advocate that [tribunals] in a bill ... That I should oppose tooth and nail. So would you.' She would be grateful for any remarks from Stella, and in a postscript asked her for 'your wording of a Bill for such a conference, if others agree it wd. be useful'.[53] No reply exists.

In December, Stella wrote amiably (although perhaps over-ambitiously) to Janet Chance that

> I think it would be difficult to exaggerate the impression made by the Pope's two pronouncements on British opinion:[54] I mean the everyday, middle-class and lower-middle class opinion, which prides itself on '*moderation*' but this time has been shaken out of its complacency. I would suggest we ask all the Societies formed to represent and defend women's interests in these matters, to get together – so far as their diversity permits – in a carefully thought out, brief, official protest with all the publicity that can be attained. I wish to move this, for the consideration of the next E.C. which I take it will be held shortly.[55]

Presumably one of these was the Pope's reminder to midwives and obstetricians that, in childbirth, saving the child's life should be privileged over the woman's survival.[56]

On the subject of a Private Member's Parliamentary Bill (Joseph Reeves was to propose one the following year as a result of his success in the Private Members' Ballot),[57] she suggested 'a brief yet comprehensive formula such as: "Nothing in any Act shall be held to prejudice the right of a woman to ask a physician to terminate a pregnancy which is unwelcome to her, or the right of a physician to terminate such a pregnancy." ' She went on

> It is not ALRA's business – in my humble view – to raise objections and suggest limitations to the right of maternal choice. Other persons and organizations will do that soon enough. Moreover a private bill will probably be a *ballon d'essai* [trial balloon] and any serious objections or alterations will be voiced in debate and can be considered afterwards.

In addition, she wondered whether ALRA was 'going to collaborate in offering evidence to the Divorce Commission'. She concluded, on a more personal note, with the hope that Chance had good news about her sister.[58] A fortnight later, she returned a draft of a Bill to Chance with comments and suggestions.[59]

In the New Year, she sent Chance '[b]est wishes for 1952 to you and to your very hard work for ALR', returned a batch of press-cuttings, and a contribution of three shillings towards postal expenses. She signed off 'In haste as ever', in a postscript asking Chance to 'please excuse haste and blots. I gather you want this in time for an early EC.'[60]

There was further discussion over the drafting of a Parliamentary Bill. She did not mind whether her proposal was 'worded as an amendment or an Act (or Bill) ... the essential is the substance'.[61] Gerald Thesiger wrote to Janet Chance just over a week later to say that, as he had 'told Stella Browne a fortnight ago', he had advised their current legal advisor, Gerald Gardiner, that as his draft Bill was pre-war, it would be better for them to draft a new Bill.[62] Janet Chance subsequently wrote to Stella of her distress at finding that she and Thesiger had already been in correspondence: 'I am apologising for troubling him twice.' She went on:

> Stella, I have a feeling that you do not trust Alice and me to report and discuss yr suggestions. I hope I am wrong in this for we must work *as a team*. I have [word illegible] more than once given up strongly-held opinions of my own in deference to the views of colleagues because we are a team ...
>
> Of course, if we have lost your trust, the position may require further investigation but I trust not ... It is not a private matter but one that concerns the welfare of ALRA.[63]

This crossed with a letter of Stella's expressing gladness that 'you made it very clear that ALRA was opposed to any reference of such a private matter to any "Board" ... on individual cases'. She was awaiting 'your further account of responses and progress, which, I expect, will explain some items in the minutes which I do not understand quite'.[64] In response to Chance's distressed letter, she proceeded to the crux of the tensions:

> Perhaps you forget that not being present at these ECs, I am wholly dependent for my impressions & opinions of them, on the minutes sent me. In the past, on more than one occasion, I have found in the relevant minutes, NO mention of resolutions submitted by me; after most careful consideration, & in what I

> truly believed to be the best interests of the cause. I do not want to dwell on these occasions, as I too quite understand the need for give & take in all associated effort, & I think I have proved this on various occasions during our years as colleagues. *I too have set aside quite strong feelings & views on various points, in order to continue a cooperation which means so much to me.* Certainly if the minutes & reports sent me in future are as comprehensive & clear as what was sent me on the 22nd, I shall have no cause for doubt & complaint.

She was sorry to hear Chance's disapproval of her asking Thesiger 'whose intellect & services to our cause I greatly respect' for his opinion. In conclusion, she mentioned that she had 'a severe chill & such rheumatism that I think it shows in my writing', hoping that Chance could decipher it.[65]

Multi-directional correspondence had created confusion. So Chance asked Stella, 'will you not in future, share with the Exec. any important opinion such as this, and so obviate the possibility of double correspondence'. She was 'very sorry that adequate information on your resolutions has not reached you ... to write fully to all absent Exec members is at the moment a complicated task'. She concluded by expressing her 'great relief that we are working together for ALRA'.[66]

Stella thanked her for this 'most welcome letter', and reiterated her plea for information as to whether she was to forward accumulated press-cuttings to Janet Chance herself or to Alice Jenkins.[67] She also sent a postal order for two shillings and sixpence (bringing her contributions to ALRA for the year to ten shillings and sixpence), intending this for postal expenses of Parliamentary Bill correspondence.[68]

ALRA's Annual Report for 1951–2 made the, by now ritual, comment that Stella's 'enthusiasm for our cause has never flagged'.[69] In May 1952, she suggested to Alice Jenkins a few additional names of MPs to approach. Stella was not discouraged by the news that Robert Boothby recommended postponing a projected House of Commons meeting; rather, this delay 'would allow full time for circularization ... with the pamphlet'. She concluded with a request for more ALRA headed paper, as she was 'almost through with existing stock'.[70] Either this request was not complied with, or she undertook a great deal of ALRA-related business in the next couple of months as, early in July, she wrote to Alice Jenkins for more official paper as she had 'no more left'.[71]

Janet Chance, suffering from severe depression,[72] sent a 'very moving letter of resignation' as Chair, which was 'dignified, and practical', and included a 'most generous offer' of continued financial help.[73] Stella seconded:

> any resolution that will certainly be moved of thanks and appreciation for what Janet has done, for the Association and the cause, and of good wishes and hopes for the future.

Returning some cuttings to Jenkins, she retained others, as 'a splendid basis for agitation at the local NCW [National Council of Women] occasion' (one of the few allusions to Stella's local activities).[74]

Early in 1953, an article by Chance in *Plan* on 'The Abortion Law Reform Association' paid tribute to 'the pioneer of the movement in this country, Stella Browne, who for many years was its only outspoken advocate', and had done so much to generate the 'first stirrings of interest in reform of the Abortion Law'.[75] The Annual Report for 1952–3 noted that 'our Vice-Chairman, Miss Stella Browne, has continued to exercise her influence in our cause from her Liverpool home, and has sent valuable letters to the Press'.[76]

Stella was engaging in activities and interests outside the constant round of ALRA work. In May 1953, she wrote again to Julian Huxley, this time to thank him for 'the interest & great encouragement' she found in his *Evolution in Action*. 'Its condensation of so much detailed knowledge & its clarity' seemed to her 'masterly'. In particular, she liked his 'treatment of population problems & of eugenics', and she hoped that the book had been widely read. Sending her best wishes, she conveyed these also for 'Unesco's battle for sanity and justice'.[77]

In July, she commiserated with Alice Jenkins, declaring herself 'very much distressed, but not one bit surprised' at the latter's illness, and recommended her to give herself 'all the rest possible'. She declared 'As to finance, I can afford what I have just sent – not habitually but on a special occasion, – or I should not have sent it', and pointed out that they could 'not run a Parliamentary campaign on £50'. Going through a draft document Jenkins had sent her in which she 'kindly mention[ed] my name as pioneer': Stella commented, 'please add "*in Britain*", for Scandinavia and Central Europe were before us'.[78] Writing again within the week, she hoped that the 'suffocatingly hot' London weather had '*not caused a relapse*' in Jenkins's health, and declared herself 'ready to undertake to approach five well-to-do & enlightened people with personal letters and literature to ask for their definite & appreciable support for the Pass the Bill campaign in the autumn'. Thus, she would be glad to see an up-to-date list of members and supporters.[79]

Over August Bank Holiday, she had 'a busy weekend with guests calling' and, thus, had been unable to attend to the 'letter, report, draft and enclosure from D Houghton [Douglas Houghton MP]' sent to her by Jenkins. They were indeed fortunate, she remarked, in him and his wife Vera, and in their other Parliamentary supporters.[80] She returned the materials in question a couple of days later, mentioning Janet Chance's resignation and suggesting a suitable form of words:

> To our great regret and concern our Chairman, Mrs Janet Chance, who has led and mainly financed our Association since our foundation in 1936, has had to resign her office, owing to prolonged illness. She ~~has let us know that she~~ intends to retain her interest in our efforts ~~and has most kindly consented to honour us, by accepting our Presidency~~.

She added that in her previous letter, she had made a mistake in a name – 'not Somers but RIVERS!'[81]

A few days later, she thanked Jenkins for the revised edition of the draft report and '*entirely concur*[*red*] *with what Dorothy Thurtle has said* and add my wish to hers that it should NOT in any way be minimized or watered down'. Promising to return it with any further suggestions the following day, she explained 'At the present moment, I am greatly rushed by other matters, for I too have other duties *besides* those of our great reform and cause.' (What these were is not indicated.) She signed off 'affectionately and in haste.'[82]

In spite of Stella's expressions of warm appreciation, it would appear that Alice Jenkins was not feeling very sanguine. On 26 August she was depressed at the lack of new supporters – ALRA was 'the same old faithful band and very few others' – and thought that the annual general meeting in the autumn 'should be entirely devoted to the subject of "Future Plans"'. She also thought that Stella should attend 'if at all possible'. The previous year, Jenkins had 'found it very depressing' and even thought that the 'very great difficulties of such an unpopular subject' had played a role in Chance's breakdown.[83]

Stella responded to this *cri de coeur* with an invigorating and optimistic letter. Was not Jenkins, she suggested,

> inclined to be too pessimistic – doubtless the result of anxieties & fatigues, after all your efforts – about the future prospects of the Assn. for which you have done so much – ? Remember that *every* civilising cause & agency is short of funds, just now, owing the national & international situation. Remember also, that we have just had a Parliamentary debut which has broken the ice so to speak: & that in '51 & '52 ALRA made contact with

> a large number of organizations & persons all over the country engaged in medical & social work. I agree, on the whole, that further Parliamentary work had probably best be postponed, till after the AGM. But surely you did not expect us to win *in the first round??* My goodness! When I remember the fights for Contraception, even in my time, long after the mid-nineteenth century initial struggles – not to mention the first years after a public demand for legalized abortion by qualified persons. – ! also, the fights for suffrage, divorce reform, etc.[84]

This may or may not have heartened Alice Jenkins, who considered that 'there is much more complex difficulty in abortion law reform than there was in either the *vote* or *divorce law reform*'.[85] Nonetheless, it was a remarkable position statement from an elderly woman in increasingly poor health, who might well have considered, with Jenkins, that their cause was in decline.

Early in October, Stella wrote on personal financial matters:

> In the past I have habitually paid an annual *subscription* of 5/- [five shillings – just over £5 in 2007 values], making up to £1 [just over £20 in 2007 values] – or sometimes – as in 1947 – more, by small donations of a few shillings each, in the course of each year. I now herewith send my annual subscription for the current 1953–54 year, made up to £1, in one crossed postal order. *It is up to all of us who know the amount of work AND cash which Janet & yourself have put into our cause* to pay *promptly* what they can at this decisive time. The £1 I sent in July was a special donation.[86]

She suggested to Jenkins that

> *When you have more time, I hope you will* consider putting our case to the Press in such articles as you contributed to the *New Statesman* in 1946 and *John Bull* in 1947. You have such journalistic ability and *flair* that it is a great pity not to use it – *time and other duties permitting*.[87]

Following the annual general meeting (at which her 'regards and good wishes' had been conveyed to officers and members),[88] Stella wrote that she was 'more than ever sorry that I could not hear the speeches of our helpful friends', but also commented in some puzzlement, 'I do not quite understand, from your very interesting account of the 21st October meetings, who is now Chairman of ALRA'.[89]

She had been 'sending letters and literature to various possible sympathisers and suggesting that they write to you, if they want further information or wish to contribute financially'. However, she was in some confusion 'about *what was decided* at the joint ES [Eugenics Society] and ALRA meeting and hope to hear further and in detail'. The question of legalising termination of pregnancy in cases of rape had apparently surfaced again, and Stella's comment was (as ever):

> NB. There is a marked difficulty in any legislation to legalize Termination of preg. in cases of rape, *as I pointed out in the symposium on Abortion, in 1934. Nothing could be more just and right: but it may be extremely difficult to ascertain what actually happened, unless* the woman complains at once, which many wd. be too ashamed, afraid or ignorant to do. *Will the juries always accept her word?* This is just *one* of the many snags which arise when legalization is made to depend on special circumstances.[90]

Although her tone does not reveal it, it must have been depressing for Stella to see the same old arguments being brought up yet again, and the objections yet again having to be reiterated.

Stella was, perhaps, feeling neglected and out of the loop: she asked that 'When the proposed leaflet is in rough draft, may it be sent me please, for any comments or suggestions?', and also requested that 'if the headed paper on which it is to be printed, is to include officers and MLC please may I be included – my name was omitted in the "Note by EC" printed heading'.[91]

There was tragic news in December of 1953 of Janet Chance's suicide. She had been 'very ill with a depressive attack'. Although two special nurses were with her day and night, 'The nurse only left the room for less than a minute' and Chance 'jumped out of the window'.[92] Stella commented, 'what a year of grief and effort' for Rachel Conrad (Chance's daughter). The loss would also 'sadden Xmas and New Year very much' for Alice Jenkins, although she '*hope[d]* you will not let it knock you out. She exhorted Jenkins to

> Just remember that thanks mainly to her efforts and yours of recent years, in work and cash and provision of premises, ALRA has become *established* as a factor in public life and agent for most necessary reform ...

When Stella thought of 'Janet's pride and force' and compared it 'with the feeble pusillanimity of some of *the women MPs* on this subject, I feel grieved and disgusted'. She exhorted Jenkins to take care of herself, 'Keep your heart up ... And write me after the solstitial feast.'[93]

Whatever Stella's personal issues and conflicts with Janet Chance, she recognised her as a valuable colleague and a major loss to the cause. In her obituary, she referred to Chance as 'one of the most forceful and interesting individualities I have ever met', who 'combined an electrical energy of mind and body, with a deep interest in philosophical theory and problems'. Not only did she have remarkable administrative ability, but she had 'mastery of a stately, rhythmic and distinctive prose'. While Stella admitted that 'we occasionally differed profoundly, as to the best methods of furthering our aims', she 'always fully realized that [Chance] was as ready to give time and effort, as to spend her money for the cause' – indeed, along with Alice Jenkins, 'gave a good deal of sheer *grind*, as well as peak effort, in writing and speech, in the service of a most just and necessary reform'.[94]

But this loss did not discourage Stella; rather, it incited her to argue that there was 'great need for wider and more many-sided active support *if* we are to be able to stand up to the R.C.s and their satellites. Especially since the gap left by Janet's loss.' Alice Jenkins was also engaged in 'varied efforts', including trying to arrange a debate in the House of Lords: was Lord Horder being approached, asked Stella, and was Viscount Stansgate, 'one of our friendly peers?' It seemed to her '*absolutely necessary* ... to get the utmost support, not only from young people, but from all the active and interested individuals likely to be in sympathy'. She had approached several personal friends, including 'another much younger and quite well-to-do woman, a relative of my own'. She also suggested that Janet Chance's daughter, Rachel Conrad, should be asked to become a vice-president.[95]

She received a rather discouraging response from Dorothy Thurtle, who declared:

> My opinion is that it is a waste of time and effort to [not of] carry on along these lines. Our need is not for names – we have a glittering list of these on our note heading – but for active workers.

She therefore hoped 'that you will do your best to refrain from making demands which will involve additional correspondence'. She apologised 'if I appear blunt or rude, but it is too easy to lay down the law for other people to carry out, from a distance of several miles'.[96] No response survives.

Sending Stella a receipt for a shilling postal order – retaining the latter until she had some others 'so as not to give the bank the trouble and expense of acknowledging such a small sum', Alice Jenkins wrote (and this may be as much an expression of guilt as anything, given Stella's perennial state of penury):

> There is really no need for you to send money in this way, as at present our funds are more than sufficient for our needs; and everyone in this Association owes gratitude to you for your unique pioneering, and does not expect you to contribute money at all.[97]

Stella bounced back from the setback of the failure of Lord Amulree's Bill,[98] since at least they could be 'proud and glad to have secured definite promise of support from the Eugenics Society – a very suitable memorial of Janet and her work'. 'As regards future plans' and speaking for herself only:

> I have for years, urged vigorous and planned action in Parl[iamen]t and elsewhere, and only accepted the minimum terms of the Bill, because it was repeatedly declared from many quarters that anything wider would have NO HOPE ... It seems to me that for adequate support, we need a much wider membership and a larger proportion of active propagandists, to supplement your work – especially since the lamentable loss of Janet. It would be a good thing if some mass demonstration or manifesto in favour of reform could be organised.

However, she added, on a note of realism, 'there again, who will do the work that anything of that kind entails?', and concluded by asking 'Please let me know when the date of any meeting of supporters is fixed and if there is to be any formal Agenda.'[99]

Jenkins took a week before sending Stella a considered and detailed reply, in which she suggested that 'such a Bill if continually rejected, might worsen the position'. In addition, she thought that Stella did not 'realise the steady progress which is being made *without* statutory change', among doctors prepared to provide abortions within the National Health Service, so that 'the good work is going on ...' Failing entirely to avoid a tone of exasperation at Stella's calls for action, she wrote 'We can only seize opportunities which present themselves'. Jenkins's own health was not robust: her husband was taking her to South and Central Africa the following winter for that reason.[100]

There was cheering news that the Women's Cooperative Guild had passed another resolution in favour of abortion law reform – 'How pleased

Janet wd. have been!', Stella wrote to Alice Jenkins. She congratulated the latter 'most heartily, on this success of your efforts, indeed I realize the energy, tact, and oh god! *patience*, it has entailed'. Moreover, it would 'be a good jumping-off ground for press letters', and she also continued to agitate for a reprint of the 'In Desperation' leaflet, since this contained 'raw facts, and ... individual cases of the practical human costs of the present law', and it provided 'umpteen pegs to hang Press letters on'.[101]

Conceding, in a response to Jenkins, that she 'well knew from friends' accounts that life in London, as regards both transport and domestic help, is very difficult', she pointed out that 'the same is true of provincial places'. Possibly this was 'the price that modern towns pay *for existing at all*'.[102]

It seems as though Stella was increasingly irrelevant to the active members of ALRA, however much she was still regarded as a 'veteran pioneer of the movement'.[103] During 1954, she had 'a letter' published in *The Individualist*:[104] no actual letter can be found, but a paragraph on 'The sensible Swiss' in August 1954 strikes a familiar note:

> Under our antiquated laws 200 women risk their lives every day with drugs and back-street abortion treatment because we will not allow them access to skilled treatment. The wealthy among them will go to Switzerland. Cannot the Labour Party be induced to do something for the others?[105]

But if Stella was using current events as pegs to hang letters to the Press on, these were not getting published. In October 1954, the Executive 'decided unanimously but with reluctance to ask Miss Browne to tender her resignation as Vice-Chairman on ground of long absenteeism'.[106] Stella's response is not recorded.

A rare glimpse of Stella in her domestic and familial context comes in a letter from Sylvia (signing herself 'S.B. II' – presumably, in the family Stella was 'S.B. I') to 'Dora' – Dorothea, the wife of their cousin Howard Branson Dodwell. She commented, 'It was curious when your letter came Stella's library book from Boots was Arthur Mee's "Northumberland"' which had 'a good deal about Hexham' (where the Dodwells were moving). It is nice to think that Stella was at least able to afford a subscription to Boots' Library. According to Sylvia, 'Stella sends her love to you & is much interested in your move.'[107]

Stella remained in touch with ALRA: early in January 1955, she sent Alice Jenkins the 'facts of a recent Liverpool event'. A seventeen-year-old fishcake cutter, with a mental age of seven, had appeared in the local magistrates' court,

> charged with throwing her baby son, *immediately after birth*, out of the bedroom window, thereby injuring his head and face ... she had been too ignorant & terrified to tell anyone, & her mother will not take her back. She is now under special medical supervision – beneficient, but rather late!

Stella hoped that 'this instance of the secondary effects of the present law', to which she was endeavouring to draw public attention, would be kept on record.[108]

But there were still bright sides for Stella to look on. As a 'worker for reform since 1915', she congratulated the *Eugenics Review* for 'material of special interest to me in recent issues': in particular, 'reviews and comments on Kinsey's memorable study' (*The Sexual Life of the American Woman*, which bore out her own views on the extreme variability of women's sexual needs).[109] It was also 'an encouragement and further inspiration' that the Society was 'co-ordinating its work with that of more specialized societies' for reform in the abortion laws.[110]

In March, with a general election pending, she assumed that ALRA would be questioning candidates on their attitude towards the draft Bill.[111] Very good news came from Alice Jenkins of official support from the Family Planning Association, and confirmation of what Stella had heard, 'that strictly medical terminations are now much more frequent'. However, 'what a lot there is still to do!', but she congratulated Jenkins on her 'unremitting and statesmanlike work'.[112]

In spite of this upbeat tone, Stella was facing a 'sad outlook'. Although she was 'just able to read with a magnifying glass', a sight examination in April 'showed her gradually increasing blindness', on top of her arthritis. Nonetheless, she was 'marvellously plucky, kept her depression to herself', and her 'interest and pride' in what ALRA was doing 'kept her mind clear and courage bright'. About the beginning of May, she had a severe heart attack and, although she improved slightly, 'on the eve of her 75th birthday she died in the night between the 8th and 9th of May'. Sylvia found her in the morning. In her final days, she received 'much pleasure' from a letter from Alice Jenkins and satisfaction at the latter's opinion about the two paragraphs she had had published in *The Eugenics Review*.

The cremation took place very soon after Stella's death – too soon for ALRA to send a representative – at Llandican cemetery 'across the river beyond Birkenhead, a pretty spot'. However, although Sylvia acknowledged that 'Stella had courage to fight for anything she thought needed protecting',[113] her death certificate, under 'Occupation', records her in incongruously patriarchal terms as 'Spinster, no occupation; daughter of Daniel Marshall Browne, Lieutenant-Commander, Royal Navy' – Sylvia rather exaggerated her father's rank.[114]

In the ALRA Annual Report for 1954–5, the 'valued supporters' lost during the year included 'Stella Browne, our Vice-Chairman and a gallant fighter, [who] will some day be acclaimed for her outspokenness at a time when the words "abortion problem" were hardly articulated above a shocked whisper'.[115] The doctor Dorothy Kerslake wrote that she 'was so sorry that Miss Browne died, and I never had the chance of meeting her. I had two most kind letters from her.'[116]

Alice Jenkins contributed the *Eugenics Review* obituary of this 'humanitarian and uncompromising feminist ... the first advocate in the country of abortion law reform', touching on Stella's internationalist perspective. She recalled Stella's 'indomitable courage' at stating the case for abortion law reform 'whenever occasion furnished opportunity' and, in particular, the first time that she raised the topic at a Eugenics Society meeting in the early 1930s, to be greeted by 'a silence that could be felt'. Even when 'hampered by badly failing sight and enforced absence from London', she 'actively supported the cause by her vigorous pen'.[117]

Old colleagues from the FPSI recalled her in the pages of *Plan*. Ashton Burall praised his 'tough, humourous, forthright, affectionate, courageous and sincere' friend and comrade. He had never known anyone more congenial, she had been 'one of the most civilised and mature minded people' he had ever known, 'a remarkable blend of moral earnestness, crusading fervour, and a lighthearted determination to get the best out of life', 'interesting and amusing ... a wonderful companion and friend'. Although it was 'impossible to imagine anyone less like a blue stocking', she had had 'a wide range of academic knowledge, was a first rate speaker and a brilliant linguist'. She had kept him in touch with contemporary French literature, including enthusiastically recommending Malraux' *La Condition Humaine* on its first publication. Although 'first and foremost a feminist ... her primary motive as a sex reformer', it was not possible to disentangle her feminism and her humanitarianism. In her later years, she had continued to write to him every few months 'letters full of fun, high spirits and wisdom'.[118]

Beryl Henderson, in a letter to *Plan*, thought that although few present members of the Progressive League would have known Stella, they probably did know of her work. Henderson thought that it was 'almost impossible for young women today to realise the courage Stella Browne showed as a young woman in voicing the plea that a woman should be mistress of her own body'. To put her belief in women's right to decide whether or not to continue a pregnancy 'in print was more than the religious and respectable – or even ordinary "decent people" – could stomach'. But Stella had 'stuck to it'.[119]

Alec Craig provided a few paragraphs on Stella's writing: while her 'literary work was ancilliary to her activities as a sex reformer', what she had written was 'of abiding interest'. Her translations 'were no mere hack work, but were inspired with a sympathetic understanding of their originals and motivated by a keen desire that the best of continental sexological thought should be available in English'. Of her original works, *Sexual Variety and Variability among Women* was 'written with so much insight and vision that it hardly dates at all'. Her most important contribution, her essay in *Abortion*, was epoch-making in freeing 'the subject of abortion from the odium of squalid criminality in the mind of the general reading public', and she had never 'favoured compromise over… a vital factor in the emancipation of woman' or the 'social worker approach' towards 'deserving' cases. While, Craig commented, they mourned Stella's passing, they should also 'regret the flagging of the reform movement of which she was so brilliant a leader', given the lack of 'enthusiasm for completing sexual reform in those parts of the world where it has been most successful'.[120]

Notes

1. 'Report 1939–1945', Abortion Law Reform Association Archives, Wellcome Library, SA/ALR/A.1/3.
2. F.W. Stella Browne, 'Report of activities 1939–1945, for the Chairman and Executive Committee of the Abortion Law Reform Association', SA/ALR/B.5.
3. F.W. Stella Browne, 'The fifth freedom', *Tribune*, 9 October 1942, p. 12.
4. Browne, 'Report of activities 1939–1945', SA/ALR/B.5.
5. F.W. Stella Browne, 'Other freedoms', *The News Chronicle*, 19 October 1942, p. 2.
6. Browne, 'The fifth freedom', 'Other freedoms'.
7. Entry for 23 February 1941, 'Notes and Various Writings', Volume 106, George Ives papers in the Harry Ransom Humanities Research Centre, University of Texas at Austin.
8. Entry for 27 February 1941, 'Notes and Various Writings', Volume 106, Ives papers.

9. Entry for 9 March 1941, 'Notes and Various Writings', Volume 106, Ives papers.
10. South Place Ethical Society to George Ives, 25 March 1941, Ives papers.
11. Stella Browne to Alice Jenkins, 25 July 1954, SA/ALR/B.5.
12. Letter from John Dodwell, 12 August 1997 (personal communication).
13. Liverpool electoral rolls.
14. F.W. Stella Browne to Julian Huxley, 7 May 1942, Julian Huxley papers at Rice University, Houston, Texas, file 16.2.
15. F.W. Stella Browne, 'Instructions for women', *Tribune*, 12 March 1943, p. 14.
16. F.W. Stella Browne to Olaf Stapledon, 7 February 1949, Stapledon papers in the Sydney Jones Library, University of Liverpool, STAP H VIII B 9/21.
17. 'Society for Sex Education and Guidance, 1945–1952', Family Planning Association Archives Wellcome Library, SA/FPA/A.13/86; additional material among the Vera Brittain papers, Archives and Research Collections, McMaster University Library, Hamilton, Ontario.
18. See entry in *Oxford Dictionary of National Biography*. Chesser's own papers are not known to survive.
19. Bertram Lloyd to George Ives, 6 May 1944, Ives papers.
20. 'Report of activities 1939–1945', SA/ALR/B.5.
21. 'Report 1939–1945', SA/ALR/A.1/3.
22. Minutes of Informal Meeting at Brown's Hotel, 13 July 1944, SA/ALR/A.1/2/1.
23. F.W. Stella Browne, 'Statement of Case for Evidence from A.L.R.A. to the Royal Commission', SA/ALR/A.2/3.
24. 'Report of activities 1939–1945', SA/ALR/B.5.
25. Browne to Jenkins, 27 August 1945, SA/ALR/A.17/1.
26. Minutes of Members' Meeting, 10 October 1945, SA/ALR/A.1/2/1.
27. 'Editor's notes', *Plan*, vol. 13, no. 4, April 1946.
28. F.W. Stella Browne, to the Editor, Leslie Minchin, *Plan*, vol. 13, no. 4, April 1946, pp. 10, 11.
29. F.W. Stella Browne, to the Editor, *Plan*, vol. 13, no. 4, April 1946, p. 10.
30. F.W. Stella Browne to Max Hodann, 28 June 1946, Hodann papers in the Swedish Labour Movement Archives and Library, Stockholm.
31. Browne to Stapledon, 7 February 1949, STAP H VIII B 9/21.
32. Browne to Hodann, 25 July 1946, Hodann papers. I am indebted to Ralf Dose for translating the German passages for me.
33. Browne to Hodann, 7 August 1946, Hodann papers.
34. Report of meeting, Janet Chance's scrapbook, SA/ALR/B.1, report in *The New Generation*, November 1946, SA/ALR/A.2/1.
35. Browne to Hodann, 28 October 1946, Hodann papers.
36. Max Hodann to F.W. Stella Browne, 22 November 1946, Hodann papers. I am indebted to Ralf Dose for translating this letter for me.
37. Browne to Hodann, 28 November 1946, Hodann papers.

38. Minutes, London School of Economics, LSE/Fabian Society/C20, membership records and records of local societies.
39. Article by Alice Jenkins, *John Bull*, 20 August 1947, SA/ALR/B.1
40. 'Vega', 'Seven children in seven years', *News Chronicle*, 31 July 1947, p. 2; Minutes of Executive Committee meeting of 17 October 1947, SA/ALR/1/2/1.
41. Minutes of Executive Committee meeting of 5 November 1947, SA/ALR/1/2/1.
42. Margaret Sanger to Vincent Brome, 23 January 1953, Sanger papers in the Library of Congress, Washington, DC, 'Personal', Volume 2.
43. Browne to Stapledon, 7 February 1949, STAP H VIII B 9/21.
44. Robert Crossley, *Olaf Stapledon: Speaking for the Future* (Liverpool: Liverpool University Press, 1994), pp. 358–63.
45. Browne to Stapledon, 7 February 1949, STAP H VIII B 9/21.
46. Browne to Stapledon, 7 February 1949, STAP H VIII B 9/21.
47. 'Note of the ALRA Private Conference March 23 1949', SA/ALR/A.3/1.
48. Minutes of Annual General Meeting, 28 September 1949, SA/ALR/A.1/2/1.
49. Minutes of Executive Committee meeting, 4 June 1951, SA/ALR/A.1/2/1.
50. Minutes of Executive Committee meeting, 4 June 1951, SA/ALR/A.1/2/1.
51. Doris H. Linder, *Crusader for Sex Education: Elise Ottesen-Jensen (1886–1973) in Scandinavia and on the International Scene* (Lanham, NY and London: University Press of America, 1996).
52. Stella Browne to Janet Chance, 15 August 1951, 'Arrangements for Mrs Ottesen-Jensen's visit Aug 1951', SA/ALR/A/17/4.
53. Janet Chance to Stella Browne, 15 September 1951, SA/ALR/B.5.
54. Professor Bruno Wanrooij suggests that this alludes to the speech of Pope Pius XII to the congress of the Italian National Union of Catholic Obstetricians, 29 October 1951. This speech underlined the legitimacy of sexual pleasure for married couples, but condemned the 'anti-christian hedonism' of those who ignored the primary purpose of the sexual act, i.e. reproduction (Personal communication).
55. Browne to Chance, 12 December 1951, SA/ALR/B.5.
56. Minutes of ALRA Executive Committee meeting, 16 January 1952, SA/ALR/A.1/2/1.
57. Barbara Brookes, *Abortion in England, 1900–1967* (London: Croom Helm, 1988), pp. 144–9.
58. Browne to Chance, 12 December 1951, SA/ALR/B.5.
59. Browne to Chance, 29 December 1951, SA/ALR/B.5.
60. Browne to Chance, 1 January 1952, SA/ALR/B.5.
61. Browne to Chance, 15 January 1952, SA/ALR/B.5.
62. Gerald Thesiger to Janet Chance, 24 January 1952, SA/ALR/A.17/2.
63. Chance to Browne, 27 January 1952, SA/ALR/B.5.

64. Browne to Chance, 25 January 1952, SA/ALR/B.5.
65. Browne to Chance, 27 January 1952, SA/ALR/B.5.
66. Chance to Browne, 30 January 1952, SA/ALR/B.5.
67. Browne to Chance, 2 February 1952, SA/ALR/B.5.
68. Browne to Chance, 2 February 1952, SA/ALR/B.5.
69. Annual Reports, SA/ALR/A.1/3.
70. Browne to Chance, 4 May 1952, SA/ALR/B.5.
71. Browne to Jenkins, 5 July 1952, SA/ALR/B.5.
72. Rachel Conrad (Janet Chance's daughter) to Margaret Sanger, 22 December 1953, Sanger LC, Volume 2.
73. Minutes of Executive Committee meeting, 29 May 1952, SA/ALRA/A.1/2/2.
74. Browne to Jenkins, 5 July 1952, SA/ALR/B.5.
75. Janet Chance, 'The Abortion Law Reform Association', *Plan*, vol, 22, no. 2, February 1953, pp. 4–5.
76. Minutes of the Executive Committee meeting, 7 July 1953, SA/ALR/A.1/2/2.
77. Browne to Huxley, 20 May 1953, Huxley papers, file 21.3.
78. Browne to Jenkins, 21 July 1953, SA/ALR/B.5.
79. Browne to Jenkins, 27 July 1953, SA/ALR/B.5.
80. Browne to Jenkins, 3 August 1953, SA/ALR/B.5.
81. Browne to Jenkins, 5 August 1953, SA/ALR/B.5.
82. Browne to Jenkins, 25 August 1953, SA/ALR/B.5.
83. Alice Jenkins to Stella Browne, 26 August 1953, SA/ALR/B.5.
84. Browne to Jenkins, 31 August 1953, SA/ALR/B.5.
85. Jenkins to Browne, 25 May 1954, SA/ALR/B.5.
86. Browne to Jenkins, 2 October 1953, SA/ALR/B.5.
87. Browne to Jenkins, 19 October 1953, SA/ALR/B.5.
88. Report of Annual General Meeting, 21 October 1953, SA/ALR/A.1/2/2.
89. Browne to Jenkins, 1 November 1953, SA/ALR/B.5.
90. Browne to Jenkins, 17 November 1953, SA/ALR/B.5.
91. Browne to Jenkins, 28 November 1953, SA/ALR/B.5.
92. Conrad to Sanger, 22 December 1953, LC, Volume 2.
93. Browne to Jenkins, 23 December 1953, SA/ALR/B.5.
94. Extract from *The Eugenics Review*, SA/ALR/A.3/3.
95. Stella Browne to Dorothy Thurtle, 24 January 1954, SA/ALR/B.5.
96. Dorothy Thurtle to Stella Browne, 23 January 1954, SA/ALR/B.5.
97. Jenkins to Browne, 25 March 1954, SA/ALR/B.5.
98. Browne to Jenkins, 9 April 1954, SA/ALR/B.5.
99. Browne to Jenkins, 21 April 1954, SA/ALR/B.5.
100. Jenkins to Browne, 28 April 1954, SA/ALR/B.5.
101. Browne to Jenkins, 27 May 1954, SA/ALR/B.5.
102. Browne to Jenkins, 25 July 1954, SA/ALR/B.5.

103. Report of Annual General Meeting, 29 September 1954, SA/ALR/A.1/2/2.
104. Annual Report for 1953/54, SA/ALR/A.1/3.
105. 'The sensible Swiss', *The Individualist*, August 1954, p. 43.
106. Minutes of Executive Committee meeting, 27 October 1954, SA/ALR/A.1/2/2.
107. Sylvia Browne to Dora, 26 December 1954. I am indebted to John Dodwell for providing me with a copy of this letter.
108. Browne to Jenkins, 6 January 1955, SA/ALR/B.5.
109. Approaches were made, without success, to the Kinsey Institute to see if there were any letters from Stella to Kinsey or his associates.
110. F.W. Stella Browne, 'The Eugenics Society', *The Eugenics Review*, vol. 47, April 1955, p. 67.
111. Browne to Jenkins, 23 March 1955, SA/ALR/B.5.
112. Browne to Jenkins, 30 March 1955, SA/ALR/B.5.
113. Sylvia Browne to Alice Jenkins, 11 May 1955, SA/ALR/A.3/4.
114. Death certificate of Frances Worsley Stella Browne.
115. ALRA Annual Report, 1954/55, SA/ALR/A.1/3.
116. D. Kerslake to the Executive, 13 July 1955, SA/ALR/A.3/4.
117. Alice Jenkins, 'Miss F.W. Stella Browne', *The Eugenics Review*, vol. 47, July 1955, pp. 78–9.
118. A.A. Burall. 'Obituary: Stella Browne (1880–1955)', *Plan*, vol. 25, no. 7, July 1955, p. 81.
119. Beryl Henderson, 'Letter to the editor', *Plan*, vol. 25, no. 8, August 1955, p. 94.
120. Alec Craig, 'Stella Browne's writings', *Plan*, vol. 25, no. 9, September 1955, p. 101.

Coda: Stella's Afterlife

The obituaries and reminiscences following Stella's death tended to position her as a relic of an earlier generation, whose 'courage was impossible for young women today to realise',[1] a symbol of a reform movement which was flagging. But, although Stella herself might look back for inspiration to the suffrage movement, the fights for divorce law reform and birth control, she had not lived in the past but looked to the future. The 1950s may not have been the most congenial era for her. While she would surely have welcomed the recommendations of the Wolfenden Report, 1957, on the decriminalisation of homosexuality, she would have been a good deal less taken by its views on prostitution, which led to the Street Offences Act of 1959, a measure of which she would almost certainly not have approved.

Historians of the abortion law reform movement have described the influx of new blood in the 1960s, as a younger generation of women – proving for themselves the unreliability of existing contraceptives and appalled by the handling of the thalidomide scandal (the drug, given for morning sickness of pregnancy, that caused severe deformity, and was finally withdrawn in 1961) – joined the Association and began to fight for reform. But, if ALRA gained from this new generation, it also focused their struggle, as an established society with experience in campaigning and Parliamentary connections already in place. Leslie Reagan, in her study of abortion in the USA, has remarked on the politicised nature of British women's quest for abortion provision, and the much broader sympathy for legalisation in the UK, contrasting with the continued stigma, furtiveness and exploitation associated with abortion in the USA.[2] In spite of the new fervour and increasing political viability of abortion law reform in the 1960s, a strong case can be made that the foundations laid in the previous thirty years played an important part. And those foundations themselves owed a good deal to 'Stella campaign[ing] alone' during a period when even birth control was discussed, if at all, in hushed undertones.

But at least the effect of Stella's struggle for abortion law reform can be measured by its result in the 1967 Abortion Act, even if this, which gave the force of statutory law to the requirement for two doctors to concur on the need and left the final decision in medical hands, did not go as far as she would have desired. The effects of her wider concerns for women and their sexual lives are much harder to assess. How far they insidiously permeated the various bodies she spoke to and had an impact on individuals' lives is impossible to guess.

She certainly made a considerable impression on women influenced by the 'second wave' of feminism from the late 1960s (although her whole life leads us to query the idea that feminism simply vanished between 1918 and 1968). As woman historians started to explore their feminist past, they rediscovered this fascinating and radical woman. Where other early proponents of birth control were speaking from agendas inflected by eugenics or notions of innate maternality, Stella was speaking out for the primacy of female sexual fulfilment.

Stella, thus, achieved a certain kind of afterlife in mentions in histories of the birth control and abortion law reform movements, and in studies of the debates around sexuality in 'first-wave' feminism. Because her own writings were very scattered, these accounts were often based on very partial evidence and, in some cases, assumed that a debating position was a fixed stance, without making any allowance for change and development. In 1977, Sheila Rowbotham produced the first detailed study, *A New World for Women: Stella Browne – Socialist Feminist.*[3] This put Stella firmly on the map, although she continued to be a somewhat controversial figure. Sheila Jeffreys, in *The Spinster and Her Enemies: Feminism and Sexuality, 1880–1930*, made the remarkable claim that sex reformers such as Stella and Dora Russell 'did not seek to transform men or agitate against the sexual abuse of women and girls ... They did not seek to question the form of heterosexuality but only to relieve its symptoms.' This claim can be refuted in exhaustive detail, as can the positively hilarious charge that Stella 'might have suffered from constraint and the need for men's approval when writing about sex.'[4] But even otherwise sympathetic accounts – such as that of Jeffrey Weeks in *Sex, Politics and Society: The Regulation of Sexuality since 1800* (London: Longman, 2nd edition 1989) – have placed Stella as a eugenist of the kind she would surely have repudiated,[5] while Jane Lewis charges her (without citing any supporting evidence) with being an 'active eugenicist' and a proponent of compulsory sterilisation for the mentally defective,[6] quite the reverse of Stella's expressed views on the subject. These misinterpretations continue to inflect descriptions of her position: the brief mention in Morgan *et al.*'s *Communists and British Society* (2007) aligns her with a eugenicist 'aseptic elitism' much more characteristic of the Pauls' position than her own.[7]

Stella's writings are not easy to locate, and the development of her ideas over time has to be tentatively and painstakingly reconstructed from a range of materials, often responding to very immediate local events. It is only by a detailed delving into Stella's writings over a period of time that it is possible to refute claims, such as those of Margaret Jackson, that Stella believed "sexology was based on pure "fact"' and to contradict her assertion that only in the 1960s did feminist critiques of science develop.[8] Stella clearly saw sexology as a body of knowledge in the process of development, and manifested an understanding of the patriarchal basis of knowledge claims more generally, as evinced in her critiques of psychoanalysis. However, even from the basis of the somewhat more readily accessible and cited texts such as *The Freewoman* correspondence and *Sexual Variety and Variability Among Women*, it seems a misreading of the nuances of Stella's viewpoint to claim that she made 'a simplistic categorization of women as either "cold" or "ardent"'.[9] Even the outlines of her life were vague, and R.A. Soloway's misrepresentation of her as a 'working-class communist'[10] is understandable (especially given the complex nature of Stella's downwardly mobile, chosen outsider, class position).

Fortunately, a number of relevant archival collections became available for research during the 1980s and 1990s, and these provided leads towards other sources to build up a fuller and more nuanced picture of Stella Browne and her significance. My own interest in Stella began as I came across her in cataloguing the archives of the Abortion Law Reform Association after they were transferred to what was then the Wellcome Institute for the History of Medicine. During research for my PhD, I came across a copy of Stella's *Sexual Variety and Variability among Women* among Marie Stopes's pamphlet collection in the British Library.

In 1992, I was awarded a fellowship to spend a month at the Harry Ransom Humanities Research Center in Texas, undertaking research on the archives of the BSSSP which they held, in the course of which I encountered not only the dry minuting of Stella's involvement with this organisation, but also her correspondence with her colleagues, theirs about her, and various mentions in George Ives's 'Notes and Writings'. The picture was already coming to seem much more complex, more nuanced, with more shadings. Around the same time, Havelock Ellis's papers were acquired by the British Library, including letters from Stella covering more than twenty years. Shortly after my return from Texas, during conversation at an after-symposium dinner, the late Roy Porter asked me the question which sowed the seed of this biography: 'Who *was* Stella Browne?'

I began to investigate the availability of materials on Stella Browne and the possibility of writing a biography. It took several years to accumulate material, and even very recently I was finding new clues and new leads. Archival collections of relevance were scattered over Britain, North America, and Europe. Her writings were traced in obscure periodicals of which few copies could be located. While still unsure that the materials were sufficient to sustain a full biography, I was able to show in several articles and conference papers the ways in which Stella Browne illuminated a number of issues about women, feminism and sexuality in the first part of the twentieth century, including the persistence of feminism into the interwar years, continuities between the 'New Woman' of the 1890s and the *Freewoman* generation, and what the relationship between feminist thinkers such as herself and sexology really was.[11]

I became convinced that, in spite of the gaps and the questions which remained unanswerable, a full-length biography of Stella was feasible. There is much that I have been unable to discover about Stella Browne: her inner life remains a matter of intriguing flashes and hints, sources of speculation. A good deal even about the outer and more public details of her life remains obscure. This account, therefore, is a tentative mapping of the territory with large tracts of terra incognita. Other narratives are possible. More materials may emerge (I sometimes have dreams about this). Nonetheless, in spite of all we do not and possibly cannot know, Stella Browne was a remarkable and intriguing woman. She had an impact on other lives which resonates onwards. Her life illuminates the possibilities for, and the constraints upon, the daring and experimental woman of the earlier twentieth century. Her career as an outspoken activist reveals the complex interweaving of campaigns, networks, and trends of thought over five decades. I have enjoyed spending so many years of my life on Stella and hope to remain on visiting terms.

Notes

1. Beryl Henderson, Letter to the Editor, *Plan*, vol. 25, no. 8, August 1955, p. 94.
2. Leslie Reagan, *When Abortion was a Crime: Women, Medicine and the Law in the United States, 1867–1973* (Berkeley, CA: University of California Press, 1997), pp. 140–1, 220.
3. Sheila Rowbotham, *A New World for Women: Stella Browne – Socialist Feminist* (London: Pluto Press, 1977).
4. Sheila Jeffreys, *The Spinster and Her Enemies: Feminism and Sexuality, 1880–1930* (London: Pandora Press, 1985), p. 159.

5. Jeffrey Weeks, *Sex, Politics and Society: The Regulation of Sexuality since 1800*, 2nd edn (London: Longman, 1989), pp. 136, 187.
6. Jane Lewis, *Women in England 1870–1950* (Brighton: Wheatsheaf Books, 1984), p. 105.
7. Kevin Morgan, Gidon Cohen, and Andrew Flinn, *Communists and British Society 1920–1991* (London: Rivers Oram, 2007), p. 154.
8. Margaret Jackson, *The Real Facts of Life: Feminism and the Politics of Sexuality c. 1850–1940* (London: Taylor & Francis, 1994), p. 126.
9. Jackson, *The Real Facts of Life*, p. 94.
10. R.A. Soloway, *Birth Control and the Population Question in England, 1877–1930* (Chapel Hill, NC: University of North Carolina Press, 1982), p. 178.
11. Lesley A. Hall, '"I have never met the normal woman": Stella Browne and the politics of womanhood' *Women's History Review*, vol. 6, no. 2, 1997, pp. 157–82; 'Feminist reconfigurations of heterosexuality in the 1920s', in Lucy Bland and Laura Doan (eds), *Sexology and Culture: Labelling Bodies and Desires* (Oxford: Polity Press, 1998), pp. 135–49; '"What a lot there is still to do": Stella Browne (1880–1955) carrying the struggle ever onward', in Claire Eustance, Joan Ryan, and Laura Ugolini (eds), *A Suffrage Reader: Charting Directions in British Suffrage History, 1850–1950* (Leicester: Leicester University Press, 2000), pp. 190–295; '"Not a domestic utensil, but a woman and a citizen": Stella Browne on women, health and society', in Chris Lawrence and Anna Mayer (eds), *Regenerating England: Science, Medicine and Culture in Inter-War Britain* (Amsterdam: Rodopi, 2000), pp. 275–302; 'The next generation: Stella Browne, the New Woman as Freewoman', in Angelique Richardson and Chris Willis (eds), *The New Woman in Fiction and in Fact: Fin-de-Siècle Feminisms* (London: Palgrave, 2001), pp. 224–38; '"In great haste": the personal and the political in the letters of F.W. Stella Browne (1880–1955), feminist socialist sex radical', in Caroline Bland and Maire Cross (eds), *Gender and Politics in the Age of Letter-Writing: 1750–2000* (Farnham: Ashgate, 2004), pp. 213–23; 'Stella Browne and the German radical sex reform tradition', in Willem de Blécourt (ed.), *Sisters of Subversion: Histories of Women, Tales of Gender: A Festschrift* (Amsterdam: AMB, 2008), pp. 152–61.

Bibliography

Archives

Arthur and Elizabeth Schlesinger Library on the History of Women in America, Cambridge, MA: Mary Ware Dennett papers, Ethel Sturges Dummer papers
Beinecke Library, Yale University: Bryher papers
Bodleian Library, Oxford: Archives of the Society for the Protection of Science and Learning
Boston Medical Library in the Francis A. Countway Library of Medicine, Boston, MA: Robert Latou Dickinson papers, Norman Himes papers
British Library Department of Manuscripts: Havelock Ellis papers, Marie Stopes papers, Harriet Shaw Weaver papers, Peter Wells papers
Chelsea Local Studies Library: electoral registers
Fisher Library, University of Sydney: Norman Haire papers
Fondren Library, Rice University, Houston: Sir Julian Huxley papers
Harry Ransom Humanities Research Center, University of Texas at Austin: British Sexology Society archives, George Ives papers, correspondence between Havelock Ellis and Edward Carpenter
Howard Gotlieb Archival Research Center, Boston University: correspondence between Havelock Ellis and Françoise Lafitte-Cyon
Hull City Archives: Winifred Holtby papers
Hull University Library: Women's Cooperative League archives
International Institute for Social History, Amsterdam: Dora Russell papers
Labour Archive Stockholm: Max Hodann papers
Labour Movement Archives, Manchester: Labour Party National Executive Committee Minutes
Library of Congress, Washington, DC: Margaret Sanger papers
Liverpool Record Office: electoral registers
Liverpool University Manuscript Collections: Olaf Stapledon papers

London School of Economics: Fabian Society archives, Progressive League archives
Maritime Command Museum, Halifax, Nova Scotia
McMaster University Archives and Research Collections, Hamilton, Ontario: Vera Brittain papers, C.K. Ogden papers, Bertrand Russell archives
Sheffield City Archives: Edward Carpenter papers
Princeton University Library: Dora Marsden papers
Public Archives of Nova Scotia and the Probate District of the County of Halifax, Nova Scotia
Somerville College Archives, Oxford
Sophia Smith Collection, Smith College, Northampton, MA: Jane Burr papers, Stella Bloch Hanau papers, Margaret Sanger papers
South Wales Miners' Library, University of Swansea, oral history collections
The National Archives, Kew: records of the Interdepartmental Committee on Induced Abortion (Birkett Committee), MH 71, Admiralty records
University of Illinois at Urbana-Champaign Rare Books and Manuscripts Library: H.G. Wells papers
University of Reading Archives of British Publishing and Printing: George Allen & Unwin archives
Wellcome Library London: Abortion Law Reform Association archives, Family Planning Association archives, National Birthday Trust Fund archives, Carlos Paton Blacker papers, Marie Stopes papers
The Women's Library, London Metropolitan University: autograph letters collection

Journals and periodicals

Beauty and Health
Birth Control Review
The Call
The Clarion
The Communist
The Egoist
The English Review
Ethical Societies Chronicle
The Eugenics Review
The Freeman
The Freewoman
Fritillary
The Humanitarian
Humanity
The Individualist
International Journal of Ethics
Labour Leader

Lansbury's Labour Weekly
The Malthusian (renamed *The New Generation* in 1922)
Marriage Hygiene
Medical Critic and Guide
Modern Astrology
Morley College Magazine
Die Neue Generation
The New Age
The New Generation (formerly *The Malthusian*)
New Leader
New Statesman
News Chronicle
Plan
The Spectator
The Socialist Review: A Quarterly Review of Modern Thought
Sunday Mercury and Sunday News (Birmingham)
Time and Tide
Tribune
The Week-end Review
Women's Social and Political Union, *Annual Reports*

Books and pamphlets: primary sources

Billington-Greig, Teresa. 'The Militant Suffrage Movement: Emancipation in a Hurry' (first published 1911), in C. McPhee and A. Fitzgerald (eds), *The Non-Violent Militant: Selected Writings of Teresa Billington-Greig*, London: Routledge & Kegan Paul, 1987, pp. 141–2.

The Diary of Otto Braun, with selections from his letters and poems. Edited by Julie Vogelstein. With an introduction by Havelock Ellis. (Translated by Ella Winter. Poetry translated by F.W. Stella Browne.), London: William Heinemann, 1924.

Browne, F.W. Stella, 'Edith Ellis: A Memory', in Joseph Ishill (ed.), *Stories and Essays by Mrs Havelock Ellis*, New Jersey: published privately by the Free Spirit Press, 1924, pp. ix–xi.

Browne, F.W. Stella, 'Studies in Feminine Inversion', *Journal of Sexology and Psychanalysis*, 1 (1923), pp. 51–8.

Browne, F.W. Stella, *The Sexual Variety and Variability among Women, and their Bearing on Social Reconstruction*, London: British Society for the Study of Sex Psychology, 1917.

Browne, F.W. Stella, 'Some Problems of Sex', *International Journal of Ethics*, 27, 1916/17, pp. 464–71.

Browne, F.W. Stella, 'Women and Birth-Control' in Eden and Cedar Paul (eds), *Population and Birth-Control: A Symposium*, New York: Critic and Guide Company, 1917, pp. 247–57.

Browne, F.W. Stella, 'Women and the Race', *The Socialist Review: A Quarterly Review of Modern Thought* (Edited by J. Bruce Glasier), vol. 14, no. 81, May–June 1917, pp. 151–7.

Browne, F.W. Stella, A.M. Ludovici, and Harry Roberts, *Abortion*, London: George Allen & Unwin Ltd, 1935.

Delisle, Françoise, *Françoise: In Love with Love*, London: Delisle, 1962.

Delisle, Françoise, *Friendship's Odyssey: In Love with Life*, London: Delisle, 1964.

Graham, John W. *Conscription and Conscience: A History 1916–1919*, London: George Allen & Unwin, 1922.

Haire, Norman (ed.). *Sexual Reform Congress, London 8–14: IX: 1929. World League for Sexual Reform: Proceedings of the Third Congress*, London: Kegan Paul, Trench and Trubner & Co. Ltd, 1930.

Himes, Norman E. *Practical Birth-Control Methods* (English edn revised by Margaret Hadley Jackson; introduction by Robert L. Dickinson; foreword by Havelock Ellis), London: G. Allen & Unwin, 1940.

Hodann, Max. *History of Modern Morals* (translated by Stella Browne), London: William Heinemann Medical, 1937.

Holtby, Winifred. *Women and a Changing Civilisation*, London: John Lane, The Bodley Head, 1934.

Lloyd, Bertram. *The Great Kinship: An Anthology of Humanitarian Poetry*, London: George Allen & Unwin, 1921.

Lloyd, Bertram (ed.). *The Paths of Glory: A Collection of Poems Written during the War, 1914–1919*, London: George Allen & Unwin Ltd, [1920].

Malleson, Constance. *After Ten Years: A Personal Record*, London: Jonathan Cape, 1931.

Müller-Lyer, F.C. *The Family* (translated by F.W. Stella Browne), London: Allen & Unwin, 1931.

Pierpoint, Raymond (ed.). *Report of the Fifth International Neo-Malthusian and Birth Control Conference*, Kingsway Hall, London July 11th to 14th, 1922, London: William Heinemann (Medical Books) Ltd, 1922.

Russell, Dora. *The Tamarisk Tree, Volume I*, London: Virago Press, 1975.

Sanger, Margaret. *An Autobiography*, London: Victor Gollancz Ltd, 1939.

Sanger, Margaret. *My Fight for Birth Control*, London: Faber & Faber Ltd, 1932.

Sanger, Margaret. *The Pivot of Civilisation*, New York: Brentano's, 1922.

Van de Velde, Theodor H. *Fertility and Sterility in Marriage: Their Voluntary Promotion and Limitation* (translated by F.W. Stella Browne), London: William Heinemann Ltd, 1931.

Van de Velde, Theodor H. *Ideal Marriage: Its Physiology and Technique* (translated by Stella Browne), London: William Heinemann Ltd, 1928.

West, Rebecca. '*The Freewoman*' first published 16 July 1926 in *Time and Tide*, reprinted in Dale Spender (ed.), *Time and Tide Wait for No Man*, London: Pandora, 1984, pp. 63–8.

Books, articles, and theses: secondary sources

Adams, Pauline. *Somerville for Women: An Oxford College 1879–1993*, Oxford: Oxford University Press, 1996.

Avery, Gillian. *The Best Type of Girl: A History of Girls' Independent Schools*, London: Andre Deutsch, 1991.

Birkenhead. Lord *Rudyard Kipling*, London: Weidenfeld & Nicholson Ltd, 1978.

Bland, Lucy. 'Trial by Sexology? Maud Allan, *Salome*, and the "Cult of the Clitoris" Case', in Lucy Bland and Laura Doan (eds), *Sexology in Culture: Labelling Bodies and Desires*, Oxford: Polity Press, 1998, pp. 183–98.

Brecher, Edward M. *The Sex Researchers*, London: André Deutsch, 1970.

Brittain, Vera. *The Women at Oxford: A Fragment of History*, London: George G. Harrap & Co Ltd, 1960.

Brookes, Barbara. *Abortion in England, 1900–1967*, London: Croom Helm, 1988.

Bruley, Sue. *Leninism, Stalinism and the Women's Movement in Britain, 1920–1939*, New York: Garland Publishing Inc., 1986.

Byrne, Muriel St Clare and Catherine Hope Mansfield. *Somerville College 1897–1921*, Oxford: Oxford University Press [1922].

Ceadel, Martin. *Semi-Detached Idealists: The British Peace Movement and International Relations, 1854–1945,* Oxford: Oxford University Press, 2000.

Chandos, John. *Norman Birkett: Uncommon Advocate*, London: Mayflower, 1963.

Chesler, Ellen. *Woman of Valor: Margaret Sanger and the American Birth Control Movement*, New York: Simon & Schuster, 1992.

Chewter, Emma. 'The League of National Life', BA History Dissertation, University of Reading, March 2002.

Crawford, Elizabeth. *The Women's Suffrage Movement: A Reference Guide 1866–1928*, London: UCL Press, 1999.

Crossley, Robert. *Olaf Stapledon: Speaking for the Future*, Liverpool: Liverpool University Press, 1994.

Curry, Patrick. *A Confusion of Prophets: Victorian and Edwardian Astrology*, London: Collins & Brown, A Juliet Gardiner Book, 1992.

D'Arch Smith, Timothy. 'Montague Summers', in *The Books of the Beast: Essays on Aleister Crowley, Montague Summers and others*, London: Mandrake, 1991, pp. 37–45.

D'Arch Smith, Timothy. *Montague Summers: A Bibliography*, Wellingborough: Aquarian Press, 1983.

Douglas, Emily Taft. *Margaret Sanger: Pioneer of the Future*, Garrett Park, MD: Garrett Park Press, 1975.

Fielding, Charles. *The Story of Dion Fortune. As told to Charles Fielding and Carr Collins*, Loughborough: Thoth Publications, 1998.

Garner, Les. *A Brave and Beautiful Spirit: Dora Marsden 1882–1960*, Aldershot: Avebury, 1991.

Gertzman, Jay A. *Bookleggers and Smuthounds: The Trade in Erotica, 1920–1940*, Philadelphia: University of Pennsylvania Press, 1999.

Gilbert, Mizpah. 'The Position of Women in Public Libraries', first published in *Library World*, vol. 18, October 1915, pp. 100–5, reprinted in Kathleen Webel and Kathleen M. Heim with assistance from Dianne J. Ellsworth (eds), *The Role of Women in Librarianship, 1876–1976: The Entry, Advancement and Struggle for Equalization in One Profession*, London: Oryx Press, 1979, pp. 67–71.

Glendinning, Victoria. *Rebecca West: A Life*. London: Weidenfeld & Nicolson, 1987.

Goldring, Douglas, *The Nineteen Twenties: A General Survey and Some Personal Memories*, London: Nicholson & Watson, 1945.

Gordon, W. Terrence. *C.K. Ogden: A Bio-Bibliographical Study*, Metuchen, NJ and London: Scarecrow Press, 1990.

Grosskurth, Phyllis. *Havelock Ellis: A Biography*, London: Allen Lane, 1980.

Grossman, Atina. *Reforming Sex: The German Movement for Birth Control and Abortion Reform, 1920–1950*, Oxford: Oxford University Press, 1995.

Hackett, Amy. 'Helene Stöcker: Left-Wing Intellectual and Sex Reformer', in Renate Bridenthal, Atina Grossman and Marion Kaplan (eds), *When Biology Became Destiny: Women in Weimar and Nazi Germany*, New York: Monthly Review Press, 1984, pp. 109–30.

Hall, Lesley A. '"Disinterested enthusiasm for sexual misconduct": the British Society for the Study of Sex Psychology, 1913–1947', *Journal of Contemporary History*, vol. 30, 1995, pp. 665–86.

Hall, Lesley A. 'Feminist Reconfigurations of Heterosexuality in the 1920s', in Lucy Bland and Laura Doan (eds), *Sexology and Culture: Labelling Bodies and Desires*, Oxford: Polity Press, 1998, pp. 135–49.

Hall, Lesley A. 'The Archives of the Pioneer Health Centre, Peckham, in the Wellcome Library', *Social History of Medicine*, vol. 14, 2001, pp. 525–38.

Hall, Lesley A. 'Hauling down the Double Standard: Feminism, Social Purity, and Sexual Science in Late Nineteenth Century Britain', *Gender and History*, vol. 16, no. 1, April 2004, pp. 36–56.

Hall, Lesley A. '"I Have Never Met the Normal Woman": Stella Browne and the Politics of Womanhood', *Women's History Review*, vol. 6, no. 2, 1997, pp. 157–82.

Hall, Lesley A. '"In great haste": the personal and the political in the letters of F.W. Stella Browne (1880–1955), feminist socialist sex radical', in Caroline Bland and Maire Cross (eds), *Gender and Politics in the Age of Letter-Writing: 1750–2000*, Farnham: Ashgate, 2004, pp. 213–23.

Hall, Lesley A. 'The Next Generation: Stella Browne, the New Woman as Freewoman', in Angelique Richardson and Chris Willis (eds), *The New Woman in Fiction and in Fact: Fin-de-Siècle Feminisms*, London: Palgrave, 2001, pp. 224–38.

Hall, Lesley A. 'Not a Domestic Utensil, but a Woman and a Citizen": Stella Browne on Women, Health and Society', in Chris Lawrence and Anna Mayer (eds), *Regenerating England: Science, Medicine and Culture in Inter-war Britain*, Amsterdam: Rodopi, 2000, pp. 275–302.

Hall, Lesley A. 'Stella Browne and the German Radical Sex Reform Tradition', in Willem de Blécourt (ed.), *Sisters of Subversion: Histories of Women, Tales of Gender: A Festschrift*, Amsterdam: AMB, 2008, pp. 152–61.

Hall, Lesley A. 'Venereal Disease in Britain from the Contagious Diseases Acts to the National Health Service', in Roger Davidson and Lesley A. Hall (eds), *Sex, Sin, and Suffering: Venereal Disease in European Social Context since 1870*, London: Routledge, 2001, pp. 120–36.

Hall, Lesley A. '"What a Lot There Is still to do': Stella Browne (1880–1955) Carrying the Struggle Ever Onward', in Claire Eustance, Joan Ryan, and Laura Ugolini (eds), *A Suffrage Reader: Charting Directions in British Suffrage History, 1850–1950*, Leicester: Leicester University Press, 2000, pp. 190–295.

Hindell, Keith and Madeleine Simms. *Abortion Law Reformed*, London: Peter Owen, 1971.

Hutton, Ronald. *The Triumph of the Moon: A History of Modern Pagan Witchcraft*, Oxford: Oxford University Press, 2000.

Hyde, H. Montgomery. *Norman Birkett: The Life of Lord Birkett of Ulverston*, London: Hamish Hamilton, 1964.

Jackson, Margaret. *The Real Facts of Life: Feminism and the Politics of Sexuality, c. 1850–1940*, London: Taylor & Francis, 1994.

Jeffreys, Sheila. *The Spinster and Her Enemies: Feminism and Sexuality, 1880–1950*, London: Pandora Press, 1985.

Jones, Greta. 'Women and Eugenics in Britain: The Case of Mary Scharlieb, Elizabeth Sloan Chesser, and Stella Browne', *Annals of Science*, vol. 52, 1995, pp. 481–502.

Keeling, Bernard, assisted by Nancie Pelling. *St Felix School Southwold and the Old Felicians: Pioneers in the Emancipation of Women since 1897*, Sevenoaks: Bernard Keeling, 1999.

Klugmann, James. *History of the Communist Party of Great Britain: Volume 1: Formation and Early Years, 1919–1924*, London: Laurence & Wishart, 1969.

Lachman, Gary. *Politics and the Occult: The Left, the Right, and the Radically Unseen*, London: Quest Books, 2008.

Laity, Paul. *The British Peace Movement 1870–1914*, Oxford: Oxford University Press, 2001.

Lanchester, Elsa. *Elsa Lanchester Herself*, New York: St Martin's Press, 1983.

Lewis, Jane. *Women in England 1870–1950*, Brighton: Wheatsheaf Books, 1984.

Lidderdale, Jane and Mary Nicholson. *Dear Miss Weaver: Harriet Shaw Weaver 1876–1961*, London: Faber & Faber, 1970.

Linder, Doris H. *Crusader for Sex Education: Elise Ottesen-Jensen (1886–1973) in Scandinavia and on the International Scene*, Lanham, NY and London: University Press of America, 1996.

McLaren, Angus. *The Trials of Masculinity: Policing Sexual Boundaries, 1870–1930*, Chicago: University of Chicago Press, 1997.

Martin, Lindsay. 'Virginia Woolf at Morley College', *The Charleston Magazine*, Winter/Spring 1991, pp. 20–5.

Mercer, John. 'Shopping for Suffrage: The Campaign Shops of the Women's Social and Political Union', *Women's History Review*, vol. 18, no. 2, Apr 2009, pp. 293–309.

Monk, Ray. *Bertrand Russell: The Spirit of Solitude*, London: Vintage, 1997.

Morgan, Kevin, Gidon Cohen and Andrew Flinn. *Communists and British Society 1920–1991*, London: Rivers Oram, 2007.

Oldfield, Sybil. *Spinsters of this Parish*, London: Virago, 1984.

Oram, Alison. *Women Teachers and Feminist Politics 1900–39*, Manchester: Manchester University Press, 1996.

Oxford Dictionary of National Biography.

Pugh, R.B. 'General Introduction', *The Victoria History of the Counties of England*, London: University of London Institute of Historical Research, 1970, pp. 1–27.

Rapp, Dean. 'The Early Discovery of Freud by the British General Public', *Social History of Medicine*, vol. 3, 1990, pp. 217–43.

Reagan, Leslie. *When Abortion was a Crime: Women, Medicine and the Law in the United States, 1867–1973*, Berkeley, CA: University of California Press, 1997.

Rollyson, Carl. *Rebecca West: A Saga of the Century*, London: Hodder & Stoughton, 1995.

Rowbotham, Sheila. *Edward Carpenter: A Life of Liberty and Love*, London: Verso, 2008.

Rowbotham, Sheila. *A New World for Women: Stella Browne, Socialist Feminist*, London: Pluto Press, 1977.

Seymour-Smith, Martin. *Rudyard Kipling*, London: Macdonald Queen Anne Press, 1989.

Soloway, R.A. *Birth Control and the Population Question in England, 1877–1930*, Chapel Hill, NC: University of North Carolina Press, 1982.

Thomas, James and A. Susan Williams. 'Women and Abortion in 1930s Britain: A Survey and Its Data', *Social History of Medicine*, 11, 1998, pp. 283–309.

Thorpe, Andrew. 'The Membership of the Communist Party of Great Britain, 1920–1945', *The Historical Journal*, vol. 43/3, 2000, pp. 777–800.

Usborne, Cornelie. *The Politics of the Body in Weimar Germany: Women's Reproductive Rights and Duties*, Ann Arbor, MI: University of Michigan Press, 1992.

Verter, Bradford. 'Dark Star Rising: The Emergence of Modern Occultism, 1800–1950', Dissertation, Princeton University, 1997 (Dept of Religion).

Weeks, Jeffrey. *Sex, Politics and Society: The Regulation of Sexuality since 1800*, 2nd edn, London: Longman, 1989.

Weinbren, Dan. '"Against all Cruelty". The Humanitarian League 1891–1919', *History Workshop Journal*, vol. 38, 1994, pp. 86–105.

Whitelaw, Lis. *The Life and Rebellious Times of Cicely Hamilton: Actress, Writer, Suffragist*, London: The Women's Press, 1990.

Index